June 17–19, 2015
Portland, Oregon, USA

**Association for
Computing Machinery**

Advancing Computing as a Science & Profession

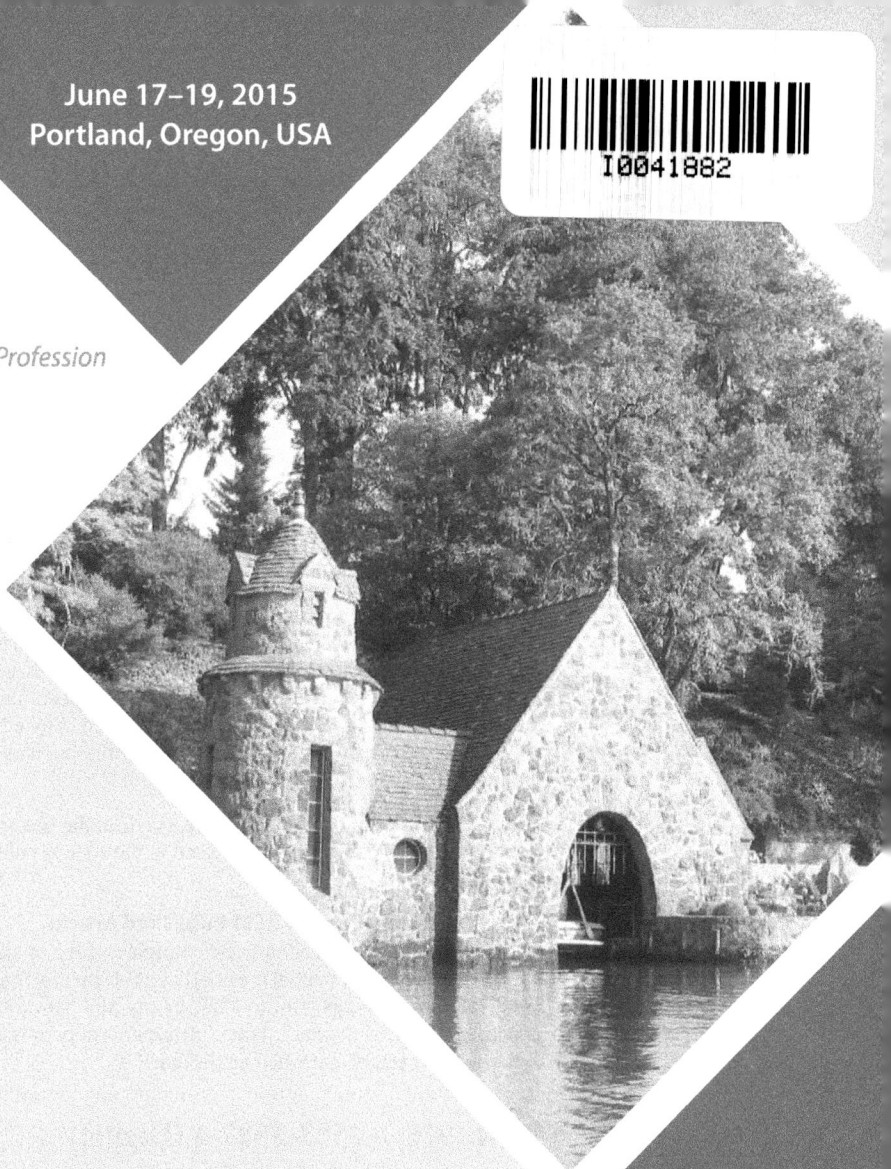

IH&MMSec'15

Proceedings of the 2015 ACM Workshop on
Information Hiding and Multimedia Security

Sponsored by:
ACM SIGMM

Supported by:
Digimarc, Technicolor, Nielsen, Aucsmith Consulting LLC, & Intel

**Association for
Computing Machinery**

Advancing Computing as a Science & Profession

The Association for Computing Machinery
2 Penn Plaza, Suite 701
New York, New York 10121-0701

ISBN: 978-1-4503-3587-4 (Digital)

ISBN: 978-1-4503-3871-4 (Print)

Additional copies may be ordered prepaid from:

ACM Order Department
PO Box 30777
New York, NY 10087-0777, USA

Phone: 1-800-342-6626 (USA and Canada)
+1-212-626-0500 (Global)
Fax: +1-212-944-1318
E-mail: acmhelp@acm.org
Hours of Operation: 8:30 am – 4:30 pm ET

Printed in the USA

Preface

It is our great pleasure to welcome you to the *3rd ACM Information Hiding and Multimedia Security Workshop – IH&MMSec'15* in Portland, Oregon. Portland is also where the 2nd Information Hiding Workshop (IHW) was held 17 years ago. Over these years, the field has developed tremendously by the relentless effort of many scientists and researchers all over the globe, and many of their research results have been implemented into useful products.

In response to our call for papers, 45 excellent papers were submitted from the United States, Canada, Europe, Asia, and Malaysia. The best 20 of these papers were accepted (44% acceptance rate) and assembled into a strong technical program. The accepted papers cover the fields of steganography and steganalysis in digital media, digital watermarking of 3D objects, covert channels, watermarking and fingerprinting codes, digital forensics, biometric and authentication, encryption, and privacy.

The technical program also features two invited keynote speakers. The first presentation is about the implications of cyber warfare, and it is given by Mr. David Aucsmith, from Aucsmith Consulting LLC. The second presentation is about the privacy of the Internet of Things, and it is given by Dr. Richard Chow, from Intel Corporation.

As usual, the workshop is structured into three days with the afternoon of the second day devoted to a social event. The social event is designed to promote discussions and to help establish relationships for future collaboration among participants. Also, at the end of the first day, an hour is reserved for a rump session during which the participants are encouraged to share their work in progress, discuss unpublished results, demo new products, and make relevant announcements.

A great team effort put together the technical program. The Program Committee assisted by 16 external reviewers provided timely and high-quality reviews. A double-blind review process was used to ensure fairness. Each paper was carefully read and appraised by at least three reviewers. To let the Program Chairs select the best quality and relevant work, papers with conflicting reviews were discussed at length. We expect the selected papers to be of wide interest to researchers working in the field and to participants from industry and from government institutions. We thank all participants for their help in putting together this great program.

We also thank Digimarc Corporation, Technicolor, Nielsen, Aucsmith Consulting LLC, and Intel for their financial support. Our appreciation goes to Digimarc for sponsoring hosting the website and to Tomas Filler from Digimarc for administering the website. We also thank Crystal Chandler from Digimarc for helping with the social event and for the local organization of the workshop.

Finally, we hope that you will find this program very interesting, that you will enjoy interacting with colleagues, and that you will enjoy your stay in Portland, the City of Roses.

Adnan Alattar
IH&MMSec'15 General Chair
Digimarc Corporation, USA

Jessica Fridrich[1]
Ned Smith[2]
Pedro Comesaña Alfaro[3]
IH&MMSec'15 Program Chairs
[1]*Binghamton University, USA*
[2]*Intel, USA*
[3]*University of Vigo, Spain*

Table of Contents

Keynote Address
Session Chair: Adnan Alattar *(Digimarc Corporation)*

Session: Media Steganography and Steganalysis
Session Chair: Jessica Fridrich *(Binghamton University)*

Session: Covert Channels
Session Chair: Gwenael Doerr *(Technicolor)*

Session: Media Forensics
Session Chair: Patrick Bas *(CNRS)*

Session: Watermarking and Fingerprinting

Session Chair: Pedro Comesana *(University of Vigo)*

Session: Encryption and Computer Security

Session Chair: Scott Craver *(Binghamton University)*

Session: Biometrics and Forensics

Session Chair: Ned Smith *(Intel Corporation)*

IH&MMSec 2015 Workshop Organization

General Chair: Adnan Alattar *(Digimarc Corporation, USA)*

Program Chairs: Jessica Fridrich *(Binghamton University, USA)*
Ned Smith *(Intel, USA)*
Pedro Comesaña Alfaro *(University of Vigo, Spain)*

ACM Liaison: Jana Dittmann *(University of Magdeburg, Germany)*

Industrial Liaison: Dave Aucsmith *(Aucsmith Consulting LLC, USA)*

Steering Committee: Patrizio Campisi *(University of Roma TRE, Italy)*
George Danezis *(Microsoft Research Cambridge, UK)*
Jana Dittmann *(Otto-von-Guericke University, Germany)*
Jessica Fridrich *(SUNY Binghamton, USA)*
Stefan Katzenbeisser *(TU Darmstadt, Germany)*
Balakrishnan Prabhakaran *(University of Dallas, USA)*

Program Committee: Boris Assanovich *(University of Grodno, Belarus)*
Morgan Barbier *(École polytechnique, France)*
Mauro Barni *(University of Siena, Italy)*
Patrick Bas *(LAGIS, France)*
Rainer Böhme *(University of Münster, Germany)*
Adrian Bors *(University of York, UK)*
Patrizio Campisi *(University of Rome, Italy)*
Marco Carli *(University of Rome (Italy)*
Ee-Chien Chang *(University of Singapore, Singapore)*
Christophe Charrier *(University of Caen, France)*
Marc Chaumont *(University of Montpellier, France)*
Rémi Cogranne *(University of Troyes, France)*
Christian Collberg *(University of Arizona, USA)*
Scott Craver *(University of Binghamton, UK)*
George Danezis *(University College London, UK)*
Jan De Cock *(University of Ghent, Belgium)*
Claude Delpha *(University of South Paris, France)*
Jana Dittmann *(Otto-von-Guericke University, Germany)*
Gwenaël Doërr *(Technicolor, France)*
Jean-Luc Dugelay *(EURECOM, France)*
Dominik Engel *(Salzburg University of Applied Sciences, Austria)*
Zekeriya Erkin *(Telft University of Technology, NL)*
Tomáš Filler *(Digimarc Corporation, USA)*

IH&MMSec 2015 Sponsor & Supporters

Sponsor:

Supporters:

FEEL THE WONDER

nielsen

Aucsmith Consulting LLC

Implications of Cyber Warfare

David Aucsmith
Aucsmith Consulting LLC
Bellevue, WA 98008
+1 425.985.8873
aucsmith@comcast.net

ABSTRACT

Freedom of operation in cyberspace has become an object of contestation between nation states. Cyber warfare is emerging as a realistic threat. This talk will explore the implications of the development of cyberspace as a domain of warfare and how military theory developed for the other domains of war may be applicable to cyberspace. Far from being a completely different domain, the talk will demonstrate that cyberspace is simply an obvious evolution in conflict theory.

Categories and Subject Descriptors

D.0 [General]

Keywords

Cyber Warfare; military theory; conflict theory.

BIO

David Aucsmith is the founder of Aucsmith Consulting LLC, which is a privately held management-consulting firm specializing in computer and communications security. It advises companies and governments around the world on a variety of matters including business development and the technology and processes to collect and utilize intelligence to manage risk. It also provides history and policy research in cybercrime, cyber espionage, and cyber warfare.

Prior to forming Aucsmith Consulting LLC, David Aucsmith was the Senior Director of Microsoft's Institute for Advanced Technology in Governments from 2002 until 2014 where he was responsible for technical relationships with agencies of the United States and other Governments, as well as on select special projects. Before joining Microsoft, Aucsmith was the chief security architect for Intel Corporation from 1994 to 2002.

He has worked in a variety of security technology areas including secure computer systems, secure communications systems, random number generation, cryptography, steganography and network intrusion detection. Aucsmith is a former officer in the U.S. Navy and has been heavily involved in computer security and cybercrime issues for more than 30 years. He has been an industry representative to numerous international, government and academic organizations including the technical advisory boards of the National Security Agency, the National Reconnaissance Office, the National Academy advisory board on Survivability and Lethality Analysis and the Directorate Advisory Council for the National Security Directorate of Pacific Northwest National Labs. He is co-chairman of the FBI's Information Technology Study Group, a member of the Secret Service Task Force on Computer Aided Counterfeiting, a member of the President's Task Force on National Defense and Computer Technology and a member of the Department of Defense's Global Information Grid Senior Industry Review Group. Aucsmith was also U.S. industry representative to the G8 Committee on Organized, Transnational, and Technological Crime where he participated directly in the G8 summits in Paris, Berlin and Tokyo.

Aucsmith holds 33 patents for digital security and is a member of the advisory board for the College of Computing at the Georgia Institute of Technology. Aucsmith holds a Bachelor of Science degree in biochemistry from the University of Georgia and Master of Science degrees in physics from the Naval Postgraduate School and information and computer sciences from the Georgia Institute of Technology respectively. Additionally, he has a Certificate in Fine Arts Photography from the University of Washington. He is the author of numerous papers and currently lectures at the Naval Postgraduate School, the Naval War College, and the Air Command and Staff College.

IH&MMSec'15, June 17–19, 2015, Salzburg, Austria.
ACM 978-1-4503-3587-4/15/06.
http://dx.doi.org/10.1145/2756601.2756622.

IoT Privacy: Can We Regain Control?

Richard Chow
Intel Corporation
Santa Clara, CA 95054
+1 408.653.7467
richard.chow@intel.com

ABSTRACT

Privacy is part of the Internet of Things (IoT) discussion because of the increased potential for sensitive data collection. In the vision for IoT, sensors penetrate ubiquitously into our physical lives and are funneled into big data systems for analysis. IoT data allows new benefits to end users - but also allows new inferences that erode privacy.

The usual privacy mechanisms employed by users no longer work in the context of IoT. Users can no longer turn off a service (e.g., GPS), nor can they even turn off a device and expect to be safe from tracking. IoT means the monitoring and data collection is continuing even in the physical world. On a computer, we have at least a semblance of control and can in principle determine what applications are running and what data they are collecting. For example, on a traditional computer, we do have malware defenses - even if imperfect. Such defenses are strikingly absent for IoT, and it is unclear how traditional defenses can be applied to IoT.

The issue of control is the main privacy problem in the context of IoT. Users generally don't know about all the sensors in the environment (with the potential exception of sensors in the user's own home). Present-day examples are WiFi MAC trackers and Google Glass, of course, but systems in the future will become even less discernible. In one sense, this is a security problem - detecting malicious devices or "environmental malware." But it is also a privacy problem - many sensor devices in fact want to be transparent to users (for instance, by adopting a traditional notice-and-consent model), but are blocked by the lack of a natural communication channel to the user.

Even assuming communication mechanisms, we have complex usability problems. For instance, we need to understand what sensors a person might be worried about and in what contexts. Audio capture at home is different from audio capture in a lecture hall. What processing is done on the sensor data may also be important. A camera capturing video for purposes of gesture recognition may be less worrisome than for purposes of facial recognition (and, of course, the user needs assurance on the proclaimed processing). Finally, given the large number of "things", the problem of notice fatigue must be dealt with, or notifications will become no more useful than browser security warnings. In this talk, we discuss all these problems in detail, together with potential solutions.

Categories and Subject Descriptors

K.4 [**Computers and Society**]: Privacy; C.2 [**Computer-Communication Networks**]: Distributed Systems

Keywords

Privacy; Internet of Things; Ubiquitous Computing

BIO

Richard Chow is a security and privacy researcher and architect at Intel Corporation. In the past he has held positions as Research Scientist at PARC, Research Scientist at Samsung Electronics R&D, and Security Architect at Yahoo and Motorola. His work concentrates on privacy, big data, mobile, and the cloud. He has over 20 US patents and patent applications and over 25 peer-reviewed journals, conference papers, and book chapters. He was awarded runner-up for the 2010 PET Award for Outstanding Research in Privacy Enhancing Technologies. He has given invited talks at academic conferences and venues such as the RSA Conference, Blackhat, and OWASP. He has been invited to serve on numerous Program Committees and has served as Guest Editor of IEEE Security and Privacy Magazine. He has a Ph.D. in mathematics from the University of California at Los Angeles.

Improving Steganographic Security by Synchronizing the Selection Channel

Tomáš Denemark
Binghamton University
Department of ECE
Binghamton, NY 13902-6000
tdenema1@binghamton.edu

Jessica Fridrich
Binghamton University
Department of ECE
Binghamton, NY 13902-6000
fridrich@binghamton.edu

ABSTRACT

This paper describes a general method for increasing the security of additive steganographic schemes for digital images represented in the spatial domain. Additive embedding schemes first assign costs to individual pixels and then embed the desired payload by minimizing the sum of costs of all changed pixels. The proposed framework can be applied to any such scheme – it starts with the cost assignment and forms a non-additive distortion function that forces adjacent embedding changes to synchronize. Since the distortion function is purposely designed as a sum of locally supported potentials, one can use the Gibbs construction to realize the embedding in practice. The beneficial impact of synchronizing the embedding changes is linked to the fact that modern steganalysis detectors use higher-order statistics of noise residuals obtained by filters with sign-changing kernels and to the fundamental difficulty of accurately estimating the selection channel of a non-additive embedding scheme implemented with several Gibbs sweeps. Both decrease the accuracy of detectors built using rich media models, including their selection-channel-aware versions.

Categories and Subject Descriptors

I.4.9 [**Computing Methodologies**]: Image Processing and Computer Vision—*Applications*

General Terms

Security, Algorithms, Theory

Keywords

Steganography, Gibbs construction, non-additive distortion, selection channel, synchronization, security

1. MOTIVATION

The prevalent paradigm for designing new steganographic schemes for digital images is based on the concept of minimizing an additive distortion function defined as the sum of costs of all changed pixels. This design has proved extremely successful in both the spatial and JPEG domain [16, 9, 7, 11, 15, 14]. Additive distortion functions, however, cannot capture the fact that executing the embedding changes in a group of adjacent pixels will likely have a smaller statistical impact than changing the same number of isolated pixels. Moreover, spatially synchronized adjacent embedding changes will also be less detectable than independent changes. Both claims can be understood on an intuitive level when one takes into account how steganography is being detected – with various statistical descriptors of noise residuals. Two adjacent pixels will disturb fewer residual values than two spatially separated pixels. Also, the detectability of changing an entire connected patch of pixels by +1 should depend only on the length of its boundary. In the extreme case, changing all pixels by +1 should not be detectable at least when ignoring the effects of pixels' limited dynamic range.

While the design of additive distortion functions is a well-researched subject, non-additive distortion is much less understood. Surprisingly, the first content-adaptive scheme, HUGO [16], already employed a non-additive element. First, a binary Syndrome-Trellis Code [3] (STC) was used to determine which least significant bits were to be changed. Then, the embedding proceeded in a pixel-by-pixel fashion, each time recomputing the cost of the pixel when changing it by +1 or −1 (based on adjacent and potentially already modified pixels) and selecting the option with the smaller cost. This approach, however, gave HUGO only a rather limited ability to consider adjacent embedding changes. A better founded version of this embedding algorithm called HUGO-BD (Bounding Distortion) starts with a distortion between the cover and stego image in the form of a difference between features in a selected feature space. As this distortion is not only non-additive but most importantly nonlocal, it is upper-bounded by another function that can be written as a sum of locally supported potentials and one that can be implemented using the Gibbs construction [2]. HUGO-BD's empirical security, however, is subpar when compared to current state-of-the-art additive schemes, such as S-UNIWARD [11], HILL [15], and the approach based on minimizing the detectability of an optimal detector within a chosen cover model [17].

The algorithm called S-UNIWARD uses an additive approximation of a distortion function that is natively non-additive. Because it is a sum of locally supported potentials, the Gibbs construction can be used for practical embedding. However, as the recent study reports [8], the Gibbs construction when applied to the distortion of S-UNIWARD does not

IH&MMSec'15, June 17–19, 2015, Portland, Oregon, USA.
Copyright © 2015 ACM 978-1-4503-3587-4/15/06 ...$15.00.
http://dx.doi.org/10.1145/2756601.2756620.

provide satisfactory performance in practice. The author attributed this to the suboptimality of the Gibbs construction when the individual sublattices are strongly dependent. The problem of designing non-additive distortion functions for steganography is generally not well understood because it is not clear how the interactions among neighboring embedding changes affect security and how to capture this using a distortion measure.

The approach taken in this paper starts with a cost assignment of an additive scheme and builds from it a simple non-additive distortion function purposely designed to discourage adjacent desynchronized embedding changes and to satisfy certain natural a priori requirements. Because the distortion is a sum of potential functions on two-pixel cliques, only two interleaved sublattices are needed for practical embedding using STCs in a Gibbs-like manner. Since the empirical detectability does not change with an increased number of sweeps, the proposed scheme utilizes merely a single Gibbs sweep. We prove the usefulness of the framework by applying it to the costs of the (ternary) scheme proposed in [17] with the multivariate Gaussian cover model (MVG) and HILL [15]. In both cases, the empirical security is markedly improved when testing with the spatial rich model [5] (SRM) as well as its selection-channel aware version [1] (maxSRMd2).

The entire framework is described in Section 2. In Section 3, we analyze the properties of the embedding and study the influence of the single parameter that controls the severity of penalizing desynchronized adjacent embedding changes. On a test image, we further study the properties of the selection channel with increased number of Gibbs sweeps. All experimental results on the BOSSbase 1.01 source appear in Section 4. In Section 5, we provide further arguments supporting our design and investigate possible avenues for attacks. The paper is closed in Section 6, where we summarize the contribution and list future research directions.

2. STEGANOGRAPHY WITH SYNCHRONIZED EMBEDDING CHANGES

This part of the paper introduces a general procedure how to form a non-additive distortion function from an additive scheme and then describes how to use it for steganography within a Gibbs-like construction.

Let $\mathbf{x}$ be an $M \times N$ grayscale cover image with pixel values $x_{ij} \in \{0, \ldots, 255\}$, $1 \leq i \leq M$, $1 \leq j \leq N$, and $\mathcal{A}$ be an additive steganographic scheme that modifies each pixel by at most ± 1. We will further assume that $\mathcal{A}$ is such that the cost of changing each cover pixel x_{ij} to $y_{ij} = x_{ij} + 1$ or $y_{ij} = x_{ij} - 1$ is the same and equal to ρ_{ij}.[1] Note that for each pixel, $x_{ij} - y_{ij} \in \{-1, 0, 1\}$. Let us further denote with $\mathcal{C}$ the index set of all two-pixel cliques formed by two vertically or horizontally adjacent pixels. For example, given a pixel index (i, j), there are four cliques that contain this pixel: $((i, j), (i+1, j))$, $((i, j), (i-1, j))$, $((i, j), (i, j+1))$, and $((i, j), (i, j-1))$. The non-additive distortion function has the following form:

$$D(\mathbf{x}, \mathbf{y}) = \sum_{((i,j),(k,l)) \in \mathcal{C}} S_{\mathcal{C}}(x_{ij} - y_{ij}, x_{kl} - y_{kl}), \quad (1)$$

---

[1]Virtually all state-of-the-art additive steganographic techniques have this cost symmetry to be able to utilize the more powerful ternary STCs.

where $S_{\mathcal{C}}(a, b)$, $-1 \leq a, b \leq 1$,

$$S_{\mathcal{C}} = \begin{array}{c|ccc} & -1 & 0 & 1 \\ \hline -1 & 0 & A_{\mathcal{C}} & \nu A_{\mathcal{C}} \\ 0 & A_{\mathcal{C}} & 0 & A_{\mathcal{C}} \\ 1 & \nu A_{\mathcal{C}} & A_{\mathcal{C}} & 0 \end{array} \quad (2)$$

is a 3×3 array that depends on the average clique cost $A_{\mathcal{C}} = (\rho_{ij} + \rho_{kl})/2$, and $\nu \geq 0$ is a parameter controlling the strength of penalizing *desynchronized* changes. Alternatively and equivalently, one can define the array as

$$S_{\mathcal{C}}(a, b) = \begin{cases} 0 & \text{when } a = b \\ A_{\mathcal{C}} & \text{when } |a| + |b| = 1 \\ \nu A_{\mathcal{C}} & \text{when } a \neq b \text{ and } |a| + |b| = 2. \end{cases} \quad (3)$$

The distortion function (1) has the form of a sum of locally supported potentials and the embedding can be implemented using a Gibbs-like construction on two interleaved sublattices

$$\mathcal{L}_1 = \{(i, j) | \mod (i + j, 2) = 0\}, \quad (4)$$
$$\mathcal{L}_2 = \{(i, j) | \mod (i + j, 2) = 1\}. \quad (5)$$

The support of each potential is the two-pixel clique. The zeros on the diagonal of $S_{\mathcal{C}}$ enforce the requirement we formulated in the introduction – changing all pixels by $+1$ (or -1) should not have any effect on detectability. Furthermore, when modifying a connected patch of pixels all by the same amount, only the boundary pixels will intuitively contribute to the distortion.

The parameter ν has a major effect on the properties of the selection channel and needs to be suitably chosen. From our experiments with rich image models (SRM and maxSRMd2), the empirical security is not very sensitive to ν as long as it stays within a certain range (see Figure 3 in Section 3).

The entire embedding algorithm is described using Algorithm 1. The inputs are the cover image $\mathbf{x}$, the cost assignment of the additive scheme $\mathcal{A}$ via an $M \times N$ array ρ_{ij}, and the payload $\mathbf{m}$, while its output is the stego image $\mathbf{y}$. In the pseudo-code, we used the following notation. The additive approximation of the distortion function (1) is defined as

$$D_A(\mathbf{x}, \mathbf{y}) = \sum_{x_{ij} \neq y_{ij}} D(\mathbf{x}, y_{ij} \mathbf{x}_{\sim ij}), \quad (6)$$

where $D(\mathbf{x}, y_{ij} \mathbf{x}_{\sim ij})$ is the distortion between image $\mathbf{x}$ and $y_{ij} \mathbf{x}_{\sim ij}$, which is a shorthand for $\mathbf{x}$ in which only the (i, j)th

---

Algorithm 1 Pseudo-code for the embedding algorithm. The initial image can be selected as the cover, $\mathbf{x}$, or the stego image $\mathbf{y}$ embedded with the additive scheme $\mathcal{A}$.

1: Divide message into two equal size parts $\mathbf{m} = \mathbf{m}_1 \cup \mathbf{m}_2$
2: Compute the costs ρ_{ij} from the cover image $\mathbf{x}$
3: Set $\mathbf{y} =$ Initial image
4: **for** $k = 1$ to Number of sweeps **do**
5:     **for** $l = 1$ to 2 **do**
6:         Execute for all $(i, j) \in \mathcal{L}_l$
7:         $\rho_{ij}^{(+)} = D_A(\mathbf{y}, x_{ij} + 1 \; \mathbf{y}_{\sim ij})$
8:         $\rho_{ij}^{(0)} = D_A(\mathbf{y}, x_{ij} \; \mathbf{y}_{\sim ij})$
9:         $\rho_{ij}^{(-)} = D_A(\mathbf{y}, x_{ij} - 1 \; \mathbf{y}_{\sim ij})$
10:         $\mathbf{y}_{\mathcal{L}_l} = \text{STC}(\mathbf{y}_{\mathcal{L}_l}, \rho^{(+)}, \rho^{(0)}, \rho^{(-)}, \mathbf{m}_l)$
11:     **end for**$\{l\}$
12: **end for**$\{k\}$

---

pixel x_{ij} was changed to y_{ij}. The symbol STC(.) stands for the actual embedding using STCs with the specified costs of changes by $+1$, 0, and -1.

In contrast to additive schemes where the cost of *not* making a change is always zero, in a non-additive scheme it may not be so because of the influence of surrounding pixels. A positive cost of no change will increase the payload (entropy) that one can embed at a given pixel but will also increase the number of embedding changes. Whether the increased payload outweighs the increased change rate depends on how well the non-additive distortion captures statistical detectability.

Embedding with different costs of all three possibilities $(+1, 0, -1)$ requires the use of the so-called multi-layered STCs [3]. We would also like to stress that the costs A_C are computed only once before the embedding starts and are kept the same throughout the embedding, i.e., they are not recomputed after every sweep. Finally, we note that the recipient reads the secret message using the same STCs applied to each sublattice and concatenating both parts. Also, for security as well as efficiency of the STCs, before applying the code for embedding or reading, the sublattice elements should be rearranged by a permutation that depends on the stego key.

When starting with the costs from an additive embedding scheme $\mathcal{A}$, we will call the embedding algorithm with the synchronized selection channel as Synch-$\mathcal{A}$.

3. SELECTION CHANNEL PROPERTIES

In this section we study the effect of the parameter ν on the selection channel and the overall performance of the proposed scheme, and then discuss some issues related to the Gibbs construction.

Figure 1 illustrates how the value of the parameter ν controls the strength of the separation between neighboring clusters with synchronized changes. The experiment was set up to amplify the effect of separation for easy viewing. The viewer is advised to magnify the figure in the PDF viewer to better see the properties of the selection channel. For larger values of ν the embedding forces areas with changes by $+1$ and by -1 to be separated by a small area with no changes. As we do not use any model of the cover source, the parameter ν has to be set experimentally. Figure 3 shows the detection error on the test set when steganalyzing Synch-HILL (and MVG) with the maxSRMd2 feature set and the FLD ensemble as a function of ν for two different relative payloads. For both embedding schemes and both payloads, the optimal value is near $\nu = 5$. Therefore, we will use this value in the rest of this paper.

The distortion function of Synch-$\mathcal{A}$ is fully defined after selecting the additive scheme $\mathcal{A}$ and the parameter ν. To embed a message in a given cover image while introducing minimal total distortion, one can use the Gibbs construction as introduced in [2]. For the payload limited sender, the task is to find a probability distribution over stego images $\pi(\mathbf{y})$ that carries the required payload expressed by the entropy $H(\pi)$ and has the minimal expected distortion $E_\pi[D(\mathbf{x}, \mathbf{y})]$. The optimal distribution has the Gibbs form $\pi_\lambda(\mathbf{y}) \propto \exp\left(-\lambda D(\mathbf{x}, \mathbf{y})\right)$, where λ is a scalar parameter determined from the payload constraint. For any given $\lambda \geq 0$, one can use the Gibbs sampler [20] to obtain a stego image $\mathbf{y}$ drawn with the correct probability $\pi(\mathbf{y})$. In practice, however, the Gibbs sampler cannot be used directly since

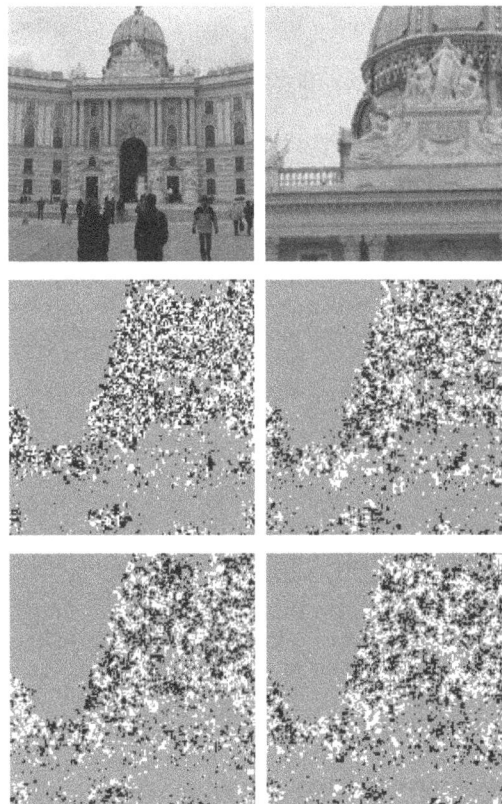

Figure 1: **Actual embedding changes executed by Synch-HILL at 0.4 bpp after 10 sweeps of the Gibbs construction for a crop of BOSSbase image '1013.pgm'. White corresponds to changes by $+1$, black to -1, and medium gray is used for pixels that did not change. Top-left: original image, top-right: crop, middle-left: $\nu = 2$, middle-right: $\nu = 10$, bottom-left: $\nu = 100$, bottom-right: $\nu = 1000$.**

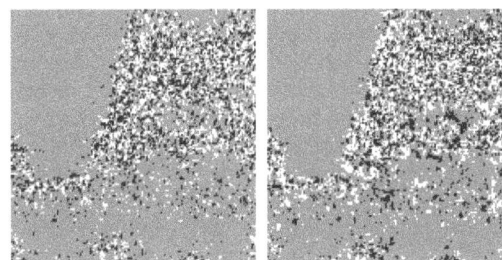

Figure 2: **Actual embedding changes executed by Synch-HILL at 0.4 bpp for a crop of BOSSbase image '1013.pgm', $\nu = 5$. White corresponds to changes by $+1$, black to -1, and medium gray is used for pixels that did not change. Left: after 1 sweep, right: after 10 sweeps.**

we need to communicate a specific message and we do not know the value of λ. The Gibbs construction can be thought of as an approximation of the Gibbs sampler that allows embedding the secret message.

Figure 4 (left) shows how the distortion (1) and the change rate evolve with consequent iterations (sweeps) of the Gibbs construction. The initial image was a stego image embedded with the additive scheme $\mathcal{A}$. During the first sweep, the distortion can dramatically decrease if $\mathcal{A}$ changes pixels adjacent to pixels with wet costs. After the first sweep, the distortion saturates (there is a small increase with sweeps) because the Gibbs construction does not exactly execute the Gibbs sampler, at least not for a small number of sweeps. The effect of the sweeps on the selection channel is shown in Figure 2.

There exists a transitional period when the Gibbs construction treats each sublattice slightly differently, which leads to different values of the parameter λ in each sublattice (see Figure 5). Another deviation of the Gibbs construction from the Gibbs sampler is that, asymptotically, it embeds the payload corresponding to the erasure entropy $H^{-}(\pi)$ [19] but introduces a larger distortion that corresponds to the larger entropy $H(\pi)$ [2]. This difference increases with stronger dependencies between the two sublattices, which makes the Gibbs construction suboptimal. Despite these limitations, the "Synched" algorithms still perform better than their additive versions.

Since in our experiments, we saw no advantage (or harm) when using more then one sweep, in Algorithm 1, we fixed the number of embedding sweeps to 1 when initializing the image with the stego image obtained by embedding the required payload with the additive scheme $\mathcal{A}$.

4. EXPERIMENTS AND COMPARISON TO PRIOR ART

In this section, we first describe the common core of all experiments. Then, we apply the proposed framework to two additive steganographic schemes that appear as the current state of the art, and we subject the proposed steganography to tests on a standard image database using two types of rich media models.

4.1 Cover source

All experiments were conducted on the BOSSbase database ver. 1.01 [4] containing 10,000 512×512 8-bit grayscale images coming from eight different cameras. The steganographic security was evaluated empirically using binary classifiers trained on the given cover source and its stego version embedded with a fixed payload. Even though this setup is artificial and does not correspond to real-life applications, it allows assessment of security w.r.t. the payload size, which is customarily done in academic investigations of this type.

4.2 Features and machine learning

All steganographic methods will be analyzed using what became a standard today, the Spatial Rich Model [5] consisting of 39 symmetrized sub-models quantized with three different quantization factors with a total dimension of $34,671$. We will also use the maxSRMd2 model [1], which has the same dimension and is a selection-channel aware version of the SRM and a generalization of the tSRM introduced in [18]. The maxSRMd2 uses the approximate knowledge of the embedding change probabilities extracted from the stego image. We conservatively assume the worst case scenario in which the Warden knows the payload size but, of course, not the cover image. Moreover, as the original study reports [1], the decrease of detection power of the maxSRMd2 when steganalyzing with a mismatched payload is rather small.

All classifiers were implemented using the ensemble [13] with Fisher linear discriminant as the base learner. The security is quantified using the ensemble's minimal total testing error under equal priors,

$$P_{\mathrm{E}} = \min_{P_{\mathrm{FA}}} \frac{1}{2}(P_{\mathrm{FA}} + P_{\mathrm{MD}}), \qquad (7)$$

when training on one randomly chosen half of the database and testing on the remaining half. Repeating ten times, we use the average of these ten testing errors, $\overline{P}_{\mathrm{E}}$, to quantify the algorithm's security.

To show how the statistical detectability increases with payload, we produce graphs showing $\overline{P}_{\mathrm{E}}$ as a function of the relative payload. With the feature dimensionality and the database size, the statistical scatter of $\overline{P}_{\mathrm{E}}$ over multiple ensemble runs with different seeds was typically so small that drawing error bars around the data points in the graphs would not show two visually discernible horizontal lines, which is why we omit this information in our graphs. As will be seen later, the differences in detectability between the proposed methods and prior art are so large that there should be no doubt about the statistical significance of the improvement. The code for extractors of all rich models as well as the ensemble is available at http://dde.binghamton.edu/download.

4.3 Tested steganographic schemes

We implemented the proposed Synch scheme for two adaptive steganographic algorithms that appear the current state of the art as of writing this paper (January 2015) and that work in entirely different fashion. They are the HIgh Low Low (HILL) algorithm [15] and the ternary version of the MVG [17], which is an abbreviation for an embedding scheme designed to minimize the power of optimal detector within the multivariate Gaussian cover model. HILL is a modification of the WOW algorithm [9] in which the three Daubechies directional kernels were replaced by one KB (Ker–Böhme) kernel [12] (this is the high-pass part of the algorithm). The KB residual is further low-pass filtered with a 3×3 averaging filter and used in the same manner as in WOW to compute the pixel costs. The resulting costs are again low-pass filtered with a quite large 15×15 kernel. The benefit of low-pass filtering the costs has also been demonstrated in [14]. A short explanation of why low-pass filtering the costs improves empirical security is because the costs are made more uniform, which increases the entropy of embedding changes in highly textured regions, which allows decreasing the distortion for the same payload. Additionally, the averaging spills large costs into the neighboring pixels, which makes the algorithm more conservative.

The MVG algorithm works in an entirely different manner. First, the cover is modeled as a sequence of independent but not identically distributed Gaussian random variables. The parameters of this model (the local pixel variances) are then estimated and the optimal embedding change rates are derived from the principle of minimizing the statistical detectability expressed in the form of the Kullback–Leibler divergence between the MVG cover distribution and the MVG stego mixture. Since the KL divergence can be analytically expressed using the estimated cover variances and the change rates, one can derive the change rates using the method of Lagrange multipliers. The main difference between the prior art [6] and the MVG algorithm as implemented in the current paper is the variance

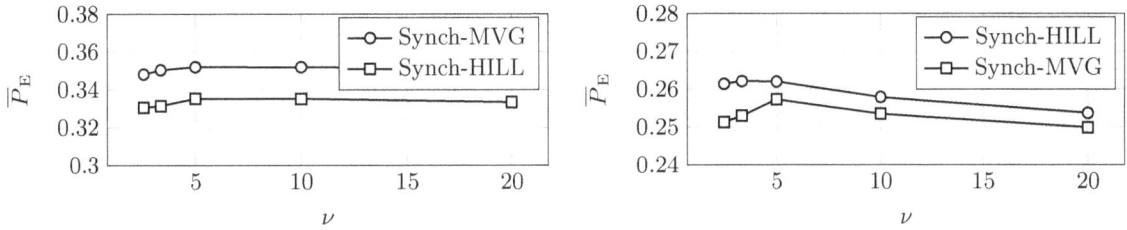

Figure 3: Search for the optimal value of ν with maxSRMd2 at 0.2 bpp (left) and 0.4 bpp (right).

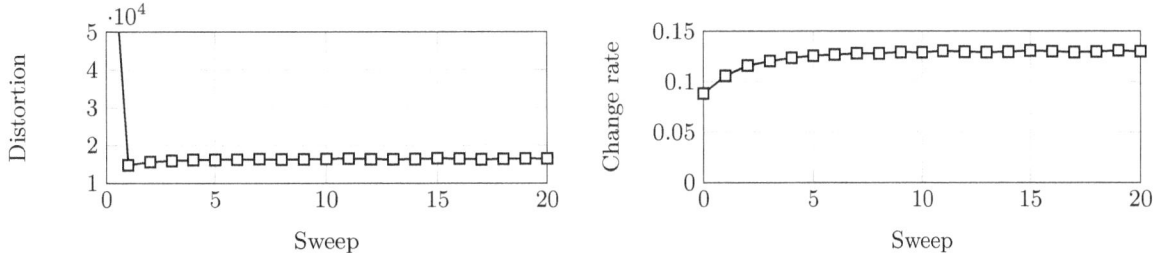

Figure 4: Distortion (1) (left) and the embedding change rate (right) as a function of sweeps for BOSSbase image 1013.pgm when embedding with Synch-HILL at 0.4 bpp, $\nu = 5$.

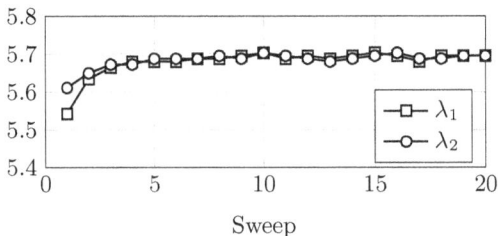

Figure 5: The parameters λ_1 and λ_2 in sublattices $\mathcal{L}_1$ and $\mathcal{L}_2$ as a function of the number of embedding sweeps when embedding with Synch-HILL at 0.4 bpp in BOSSbase image '1013.pgm', $\nu = 5$.

estimator. Instead of a very simple estimator used in [6], we estimate the local pixel variance as in [17]. First, the Wiener 2×2 denoising filter is used to extract a noise residual, which is subsequently locally fitted with DCT bases to reject more of the content. The variance estimator is described in detail in Section 5 in [17] available from http://ws2.binghamton.edu/fridrich/publications.html. Finally, the Fisher information estimated for each pixel is smoothed with a 7×7 averaging kernel. The reason for the smoothing is also explained in [17].

Before describing the experimental results, we elaborate on the important issue of how to attack non-additive steganographic schemes when using the selection-channel-aware maxSRMd2 features. These features require an estimation of the actual embedding change probabilities, which, however, strongly depend on the actual embedding changes in the pixel neighborhood and thus vary across the sweeps as well as different messages and steganographic keys. We study this in great detail in the next section, where we explain that the best the Warden can do is to use the embedding change probabilities computed from the additive scheme $\mathcal{A}$. For this, we grant the Warden the knowledge of the payload.

Figure 6 and Table 1 show that both algorithms, Synch-HILL and Synch-MVG achieve approximately the same level of security. Synch-HILL appears to be slightly more secure when steganalyzing with the SRM, while MVG is slightly more secure when the selection-channel-aware model, maxSRMd2, is used. The detection error of methods employing a synchronized selection channel is higher by approximately 2% (for payload 0.1 bpp) and 5% for the largest tested payload of 0.5 bpp.

The last two rows of the Table 1 show the detection errors when computing the maxSRMd2 features with the actual embedding change probabilities used during embedding within the Gibbs construction. Our intention is to show the lower bound on the security in the absolutely worst possible case for the sender. We stress that this case is completely unrealistic because in order to obtain these probabilities, the Warden would need to know the actual embedding changes in the first sublatice. This means that she would need to know the the corresponding portion of the secret message, the embedding costs obtained from the cover, and the permutation of the sublattice (the stego key).

5. FURTHER ANALYSIS

To better explain the increase in security, in this section we include further study of the impact of synchronizing the embedding changes on the distribution of noise residuals. Furthermore, we also study how feasible it is for the Warden to estimate the embedding change probabilities (and attack the proposed scheme using this knowledge of the selection channel) and explain that a good choice for the Warden is to use the probabilities of the additive embedding scheme $\mathcal{A}$.

5.1 Sign-changing kernels

The synchronizing of embedding changes in the proposed Synch-$\mathcal{A}$ algorithm is rather subtle, especially when embedding with a single sweep (see Figure 2). In this section, we

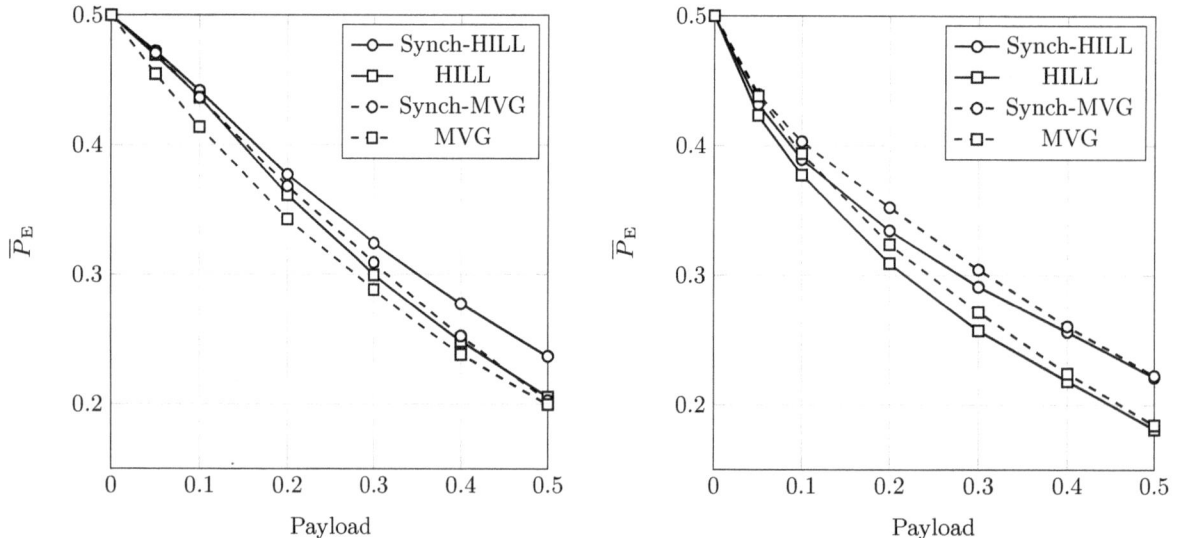

Figure 6: Average testing error $\overline{P}_\mathrm{E}$ versus payload for HILL and MVG and their synchronized version when steganalyzing with SRM (left) and maxSRMd2 (right).

Feature set	SRM						maxSRMd2					
Payload (bpp)	0.05	0.1	0.2	0.3	0.4	0.5	0.05	0.1	0.2	0.3	0.4	0.5
Synch-HILL	0.4720	0.4416	0.3768	0.3241	0.2773	0.2368	0.4317	0.3893	0.3343	0.2912	0.2563	0.2213
HILL	0.4691	0.4364	0.3611	0.2996	0.2482	0.2055	0.4232	0.3771	0.3091	0.2573	0.2184	0.1814
Synch-MVG	0.4705	0.4362	0.3680	0.3091	0.2523	0.2028	0.4394	0.4031	0.3522	0.3044	0.2606	0.2225
MVG	0.4543	0.4137	0.3425	0.2882	0.2382	0.1997	0.4380	0.3939	0.3237	0.2717	0.2243	0.1845
*Synch-HILL	x	x	x	x	x	x	0.4056	0.3640	0.3008	0.2553	0.2203	0.1855
*Synch-MVG	x	x	x	x	x	x	0.4189	0.3725	0.3289	0.2735	0.2236	0.1868

Table 1: Numerical values of testing error $\overline{P}_\mathrm{E}$ from Figure 6. The last two rows contain errors for the ideal case when the actual embedding probabilities are known to the Warden.

provide additional insight into why even subtle synchronization decreases the detectability using current steganalysis features.

Virtually all features for spatial domain steganalysis are constructed as higher-order statistical descriptors (either co-occurrences or histograms of projections in projection-type versions [10]) of noise residuals designed from local polynomial models of content. As such, all residuals used in the SRM model (and all other features based on SRM residuals) use kernels that *change signs*. For example, the first-, second-, and third-order residuals use kernels $[-1\ 1]$, $[1/2\ -1\ 1/2]$, and $[-1/3\ 1\ -1\ 1/3]$, respectively. This is true also for larger kernels, such as the 3×3 KB kernel and the 5×5 kernel used in the SRM for all 3×3 and 5×5 EDGE submodels as well as the SQUARE submodel [5]. Thus, a pair of adjacent synchronized embedding changes will disturb the residual less than a pair of desynchronized changes. This effect can be easily quantified.

Figure 7 (top) shows the relative change in the sample variance, v_i, $i = 1, \ldots, 100$, of the KB residual computed from 100 stego images randomly selected from BOSSbase and embedded with HILL and with Synch-HILL with one sweep with relative payload 0.4 bpp:

$$r_i = 100 \times \frac{v_i^{(\mathrm{HILL})} - v_i^{(\mathrm{SYNCH})}}{v_i^{(\mathrm{HILL})}}. \qquad (8)$$

The graph confirms that the variance of the KB residual of stego images produced with Synch-HILL is mostly lower than for HILL stego images. To further strengthen our interpretation of the results, we compute this ratio from the same 100 images but this time with a high-pass 3×3 kernel, which we denote KB^{++}, whose elements change the sign less frequently:

$$\mathrm{KB}^{++} = \begin{pmatrix} 0.25 & -0.2 & 0.25 \\ -0.2 & -0.2 & -0.2 \\ 0.25 & -0.2 & 0.25 \end{pmatrix}. \qquad (9)$$

The result is shown in the bottom graph of Figure 7. Note that the change between the KB^{++} residual variances between the stego images of both schemes is now much smaller and one can even observe a very small bias towards larger variance for Synch-HILL. The detection performance of the KB^{++} kernel is, however, much lower than that of the KB kernel. Moreover, the KB^{++} kernel still detects HILL slightly better than Synch-HILL (Table 2).

A natural choice for high-pass filters that do not frequently change signs is the discrete cosine basis. Table 3 shows the ratio r_i when all 64 DCT bases are used for computing the residuals. As expected, the higher the spatial frequency of the DCT mode is, the more it changes the sign, and the higher the variance of HILL stego images becomes when compared to Synch-HILL images. The DCT modes (k, l),

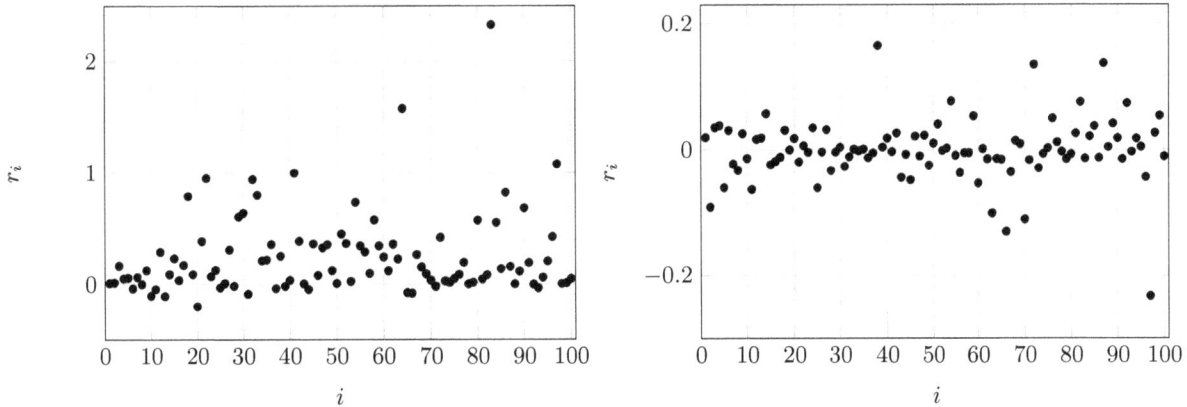

Figure 7: Relative change in the variance of the KB (left) and KB^{++} (right) residual across 100 randomly selected images from BOSSbase 1.01.

k/l	0	1	2	3	4	5	6	7
0	-0.0018	-0.0067	-0.0076	-0.0105	-0.0115	-0.0119	-0.0119	-0.0190
1	-0.0028	-0.0170	-0.0410	-0.0631	-0.0589	-0.0623	-0.0369	0.0015
2	-0.0064	-0.0313	-0.0739	-0.0926	-0.0815	-0.0779	-0.0176	0.1384
3	-0.0061	-0.0529	-0.1180	-0.1181	-0.0821	-0.0399	0.0599	0.2787
4	-0.0062	-0.0602	-0.1232	-0.0952	-0.0346	0.0497	0.1968	0.4314
5	-0.0044	-0.0470	-0.0747	-0.0065	0.0578	0.1660	0.3549	0.6533
6	0.0018	-0.0385	-0.0135	0.0866	0.2342	0.4214	0.6264	1.0071
7	0.0126	0.0086	0.0834	0.2008	0.4227	0.6242	0.8601	1.2453

Table 3: The ratio r_i averaged over all 100 images for DCT modes (k, l). Note the most promising DCT modes for attacking Synch-HILL are $(4, 2)$, $(3, 2)$, and $(3, 2)$. Predictably, with higher spatial frequency, the ratio becomes again positive – the kernels change the sign too frequently.

Stego algorithm	$\overline{P}_{\mathrm{E}}$
HILL	0.4410 ± 0.0036
Synch-HILL	0.4523 ± 0.0033

Table 2: Average testing detection error for the 6,084 DCT features on BOSSbase 1.01. The DCT features perform very poorly and still detect HILL better than Synch-HILL.

$0 \leq k, l \leq 7$, that exhibit a higher variance in Synch-HILL images are approximately those that satisfy $k + l \leq 7$. To investigate their power for detecting Synch-HILL, we selected all such 36 DCT kernels, normalized each to an L_2 norm 1, computed from them 36 noise residuals, and finally formed 36 co-occurrence matrices after quantizing them with quantization step $q = 1$ and truncating with $T = 2$ as in the SRM residuals. The resulting feature vector of dimension $36 \times 169 = 6084$ was used to steganalyze both HILL and Synch-HILL. The detection error for Synch-HILL is, however, still higher than for HILL. Moreover, the overall detection using these features is very poor considering its dimensionality. Although these experiments point out a possible attack on Synch-$\mathcal{A}$ schemes, it appears unlikely that a reliable detection can be obtained by enriching the existing rich models by co-occurrences computed from residuals obtained using smoother kernels.

5.2 Estimating embedding change probabilities

Recently, steganalysis features built as co-occurrences of noise residuals have been made more powerful for detection of content-adaptive steganography by incorporating estimated embedding change probabilities (the Bayesian priors) into the feature construction [18, 1]. In particular, when building, e.g., the horizontal co-occurrence in the maxSRMd2 model [1] from a quantized and truncated noise residual z_{ij}, instead of adding 1 to the co-occurrence bin $(z_{ij}, z_{i,j+1}, z_{i+1,j+2}, z_{i+1,j+3})$, one adds to the bin the value of $\max\{p_{ij}, p_{i,j+1}, p_{i+1,j+2}, p_{i+1,j+3}\}$, where $p_{ij} = p_{ij}^{(+)} + p_{ij}^{(-)}$ is the probability of modifying pixel x_{ij} by either $+1$ or -1:

$$p_{ij} = \frac{\exp(-\lambda \rho_{ij}^{(+)}) + \exp(-\lambda \rho_{ij}^{(-)})}{\exp(-\lambda \rho_{ij}^{(0)}) + \exp(-\lambda \rho_{ij}^{(+)}) + \exp(-\lambda \rho_{ij}^{(-)})}. \quad (10)$$

While it is possible to relatively accurately estimate these probabilities from the stego image for additive schemes, it is much harder to estimate them for non-additive schemes of the type investigated in this report. This is because the cost of changing x_{ij} depends on the embedding changes executed in the previous sweep at all four neighboring pixels. As the pixels in both sublatices (4) and (5) change during the sweeps, the value of p_{ij} may change quite rapidly and unpredictably. Figure 8 shows p_{ij} versus the sweeps for five selected pixels in the cover image '1013.pgm' when embedding 0.4 bpp using Synch-HILL. The p_{ij} also depends on the stego key and the specific message that is being embedded.

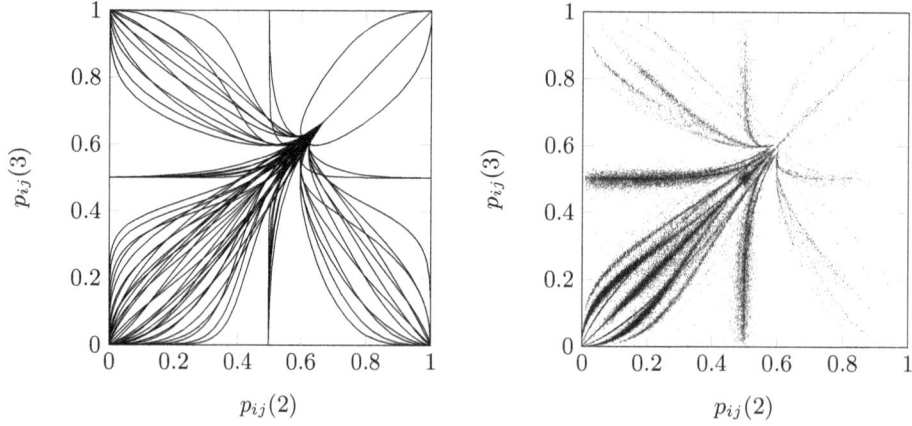

Figure 9: Theoretical (left) and real (right) total embedding change probabilities in Sweep 3 versus Sweep 2, $(p_{ij}(3), p_{ij}(2))$, for image '1013.pgm' when embedding 0.4 bpp with Synch-HILL ($\nu = 5$).

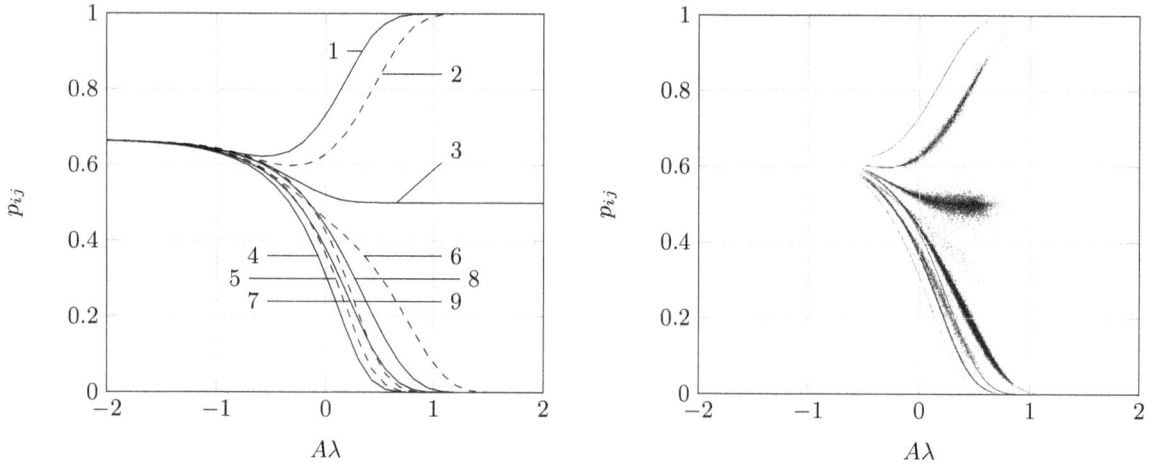

Figure 10: Theoretical (left) and real (right) total embedding change probabilities p_{ij} for image '1013.pgm' when embedding 0.4 bpp with Synch-HILL ($\nu = 5$).

To better understand what is happening during the sweeps, in Figure 9 (right) we plotted the points $(p_{ij}(3), p_{ij}(2))$ for all pixels (i, j) in the image '1013.pgm'. Here, $p_{ij}(k)$ stands for the total embedding change probability p_{ij} (10) at pixel (i, j) in kth sweep. The probabilities seem to approximately lie on a collection of well-defined smooth curves resembling an orchid. This can be explained by observing that the cost at pixel (i, j) depends on the actual embedding changes executed at its four neighboring pixels, namely those belonging to the four two-pixel cliques containing the pixel (i, j). For simplicity, let us assume that the costs ρ_{ij} of the additive scheme $\mathcal{A}$ are locally constant. Then, $A_{\mathcal{C}} \approx A$ for all four cliques, and there exist only nine types of neighborhood that lead to different costs of changing the pixel (i, j). The neighborhood types and the costs of changing the central pixel are all listed in Table 4. The last column is the frequency with which a given neighborhood type occurs if the embedding changes in the four neighboring pixels were executed equally likely. Only one representative example is listed for each neighborhood type. The rest is obtained by permutations. Also, some neighborhood types appear in two forms depending on the signs of the embedding changes.

The listed costs correspond to the neighborhood types in the first column.

Therefore, when plotting $p_{ij}(k+1)$ (10) versus $p_{ij}(k)$, the points have to lie on 81 curves parametrized by λ. In fact, because the parameter A can be factored from the costs in the table, it is only the product $\lambda A = \lambda'$ that determines the value of $p_{ij}(k)$ (10) for each neighborhood type. Thus, when plotting the points $(p_{ij}(3), p_{ij}(2))$, they can lie on 81 curves depending on which type of neighborhood pixel (i, j) has in sweep $k + 1$ and k. For example, one of the curves corresponding to the case when the pixel (i, j) has a neighborhood of type 1 in sweep $k+1$ and type 2 in sweep k (both taken from the first column), the pair $(p_{ij}(k+1), p_{ij}(k))$ will lie on a curve given in its parametric form ($0 \leq \lambda' < \infty$):

$$p_{ij}(k+1) = \frac{\exp(-4\nu\lambda')}{\exp(-4\lambda') + \exp(-4\nu\lambda')}, \quad (11)$$

$$p_{ij}(k) = \frac{\exp(-\lambda') + \exp(-\lambda'(1+3\nu))}{\exp(-3\lambda') + \exp(-\lambda') + \exp(-\lambda'(1+3\nu))}. \quad (12)$$

When drawing all 81 possible curves in one graph, we

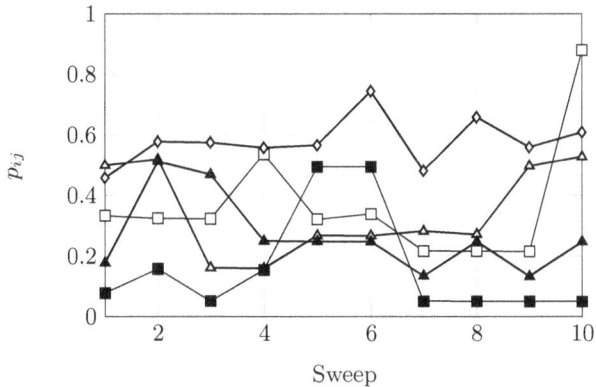

Figure 8: Embedding change probability p_{ij} for selected pixels as a function of sweeps. Note the rather unpredictable and rapid changes.

	Neighborhood type		$\rho^{(0)}$	$\rho^{(+)}$	$\rho^{(-)}$	Freq.
1	(1,1,1,1)	(-1,-1,-1,-1)	$4A$	0	$4\nu A$	2/81
2	(1,1,1,0)	(-1,-1,-1,0)	$3A$	A	$A + 3\nu A$	8/81
3	(1,1,0,0)	(-1,-1,0,0)	$2A$	$2A$	$2A + 2\nu A$	12/81
4	(1,1,-1,-1)		$4A$	$2\nu A$	$2\nu A$	6/81
5	(-1,1,0,0)		$2A$	$2A + \nu A$	$2A + \nu A$	12/81
6	(1,0,0,0)	(-1,0,0,0)	A	$3A$	$3A + \nu A$	8/81
7	(1,1,1,-1)	(-1,-1,-1,1)	$4A$	νA	$3\nu A$	8/81
8	(-1,1,1,0)	(1,-1,-1,0)	$3A$	$A + \nu A$	$A + 2\nu A$	24/81
9	(0,0,0,0)		0	$4A$	$4A$	1/81

Table 4: Pixel costs for nine different types of changes to four neighboring pixels.

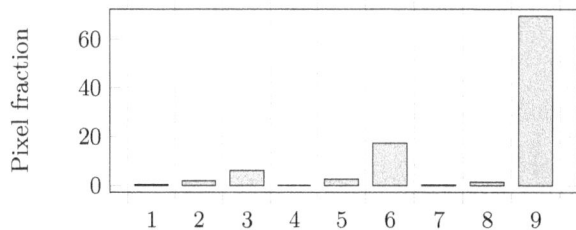

Figure 11: Percentage of pixels with embedding change probabilities lying on curves numbered 1–9 in Figure 10 (left). Curve no. 9 corresponds to the embedding change probabilities of the additive approximation to Synch-HILL.

obtain Figure 9 (left). The noise visible in Figure 9 (right) is due to the fact that the value of $A_{\mathcal{C}}$ depends on the clique and is in general not the same for all four two-pixel cliques surrounding the pixel (i, j).

An even better insight is obtained when plotting p_{ij} as a function of $\lambda' = \lambda A$ for all nine types of neighborhoods (Figure 10 left). Note that some pixels will be changed with an almost certainty since p_{ij} approaches 1 for neighborhood types 1 and 2. For type 3, the probability approaches 1/2 as $\lambda' \to \infty$. The probabilities of all types approach 2/3 when $\lambda' \to 0$, which is natural as this corresponds to a fully embedded image (maximal entropy at each pixel). Type 9 corresponds to the case when embedding with an additive approximation (6), whose pixel costs are just the slightly smoothed costs of the original additive scheme $\mathcal{A}$.

Figure 10 (right) shows the real embedding change probabilities computed from image '1013.pgm' for payload 0.4 bpp with Synch-HILL. Note that, with the exception of curves no. 1 and 9, there is some statistical spread of the values due to the fact that not all four values of $A_{\mathcal{C}}$ are the same (c.f. Table 4).

Figure 9 demonstrates the difficulty of estimating the embedding change probabilities for individual pixels. In fact, estimating on which curve the probability should lie is equivalent to estimating the *specific* embedding changes around each pixel! This indicates that attacking the Synch schemes using the selection channel will generally be much more difficult. The best choice of the embedding change probabilities for the Warden is thus to select the curve in Figure 10 (right) that has the majority of points (pixels), which is the curve corresponding to neighborhood type 9, namely its lower portion close to the x axis (for payload 0.4 bpp). This can be seen in Figure 11 where we plotted the percentage of pixels with neighborhood of type 1–9. Thus, considering the difficulty of estimating the pixel neighborhood type, the best the attacker can do is to use the embedding change probabilities of the additive scheme $\mathcal{A}$. Using the probabilities of the additive approximation (6) produced basically the same detection errors. This justifies the steganalysis carried out in Section 4.

6. CONCLUSION

This paper shows that the empirical security of additive spatial-domain steganographic schemes can be significantly improved when synchronizing adjacent embedding changes. The beneficial impact of the synchronization was linked to the fact that pixel prediction kernels frequently change sign as well as the fact that clustered changes disturb fewer noise residuals than scattered changes. Moreover, attacks that use an approximate knowledge of the selection channel are also less effective because it is significantly harder to estimate the embedding change probabilities of individual pixels as they strongly depend on the embedding changes in adjacent pixels.

The proposed approach is general and can be applied to any additive scheme. It uses the pixel costs of the additive scheme to construct a non-additive distortion function in which non-synchronized embedding changes made to adjacent pixels are penalized. The actual embedding is implemented with a single sweep of the Gibbs construction.

We subject the proposed scheme to steganalysis with rich models including their selection-aware versions. Detailed analysis of the embedding change probabilities in the synchronized schemes revealed that the embedding probabilities of individual pixels are of nine possible types depending on the actual embedding changes executed at the four neighboring pixels. Barring an accurate technique capable of estimating the individual embedding changes, the best option for the Warden is to steganalyze with the selection channel of the original additive scheme, which is how the steganalysis was executed in this paper.

There are a number of possible extensions of this work that may bring further improvement. First, one could consider larger neighborhoods than the four-pixel cross neighborhood to allow the embedding to "see" modifications along the diagonal direction. Second, it may be possible to extend the model-based approach to designing steganography (called MVG in this paper) to dependent pixels. The central problem we foresee with this direction is the estimation of the local model parameters.

7. ACKNOWLEDGMENTS

The work on this paper was supported by Air Force Office of Scientific Research under the research grant number FA9950-12-1-0124. The U.S. Government is authorized to reproduce and distribute reprints for Governmental purposes notwithstanding any copyright notation there on. The views and conclusions contained herein are those of the authors and should not be interpreted as necessarily representing the official policies, either expressed or implied of AFOSR or the U.S. Government. The authors would like to thank Vahid Sedighi for useful discussions.

8. REFERENCES

[1] T. Denemark, V. Sedighi, V. Holub, R. Cogranne, and J. Fridrich. Selection-channel-aware rich model for steganalysis of digital images. In *IEEE International Workshop on Information Forensics and Security*, Atlanta, GA, December 3–5, 2014.

[2] T. Filler and J. Fridrich. Gibbs construction in steganography. *IEEE Transactions on Information Forensics and Security*, 5(4):705–720, 2010.

[3] T. Filler, J. Judas, and J. Fridrich. Minimizing additive distortion in steganography using syndrome-trellis codes. *IEEE Transactions on Information Forensics and Security*, 6(3):920–935, September 2011.

[4] T. Filler, T. Pevný, and P. Bas. BOSS (Break Our Steganography System). http://www.agents.cz/boss, July 2010.

[5] J. Fridrich and J. Kodovský. Rich models for steganalysis of digital images. *IEEE Transactions on Information Forensics and Security*, 7(3):868–882, June 2011.

[6] J. Fridrich and J. Kodovský. Multivariate Gaussian model for designing additive distortion for steganography. In *Proc. IEEE ICASSP*, Vancouver, BC, May 26–31, 2013.

[7] L. Guo, J. Ni, and Y.-Q. Shi. An efficient JPEG steganographic scheme using uniform embedding. In *Fourth IEEE International Workshop on Information Forensics and Security*, Tenerife, Spain, December 2–5, 2012.

[8] V. Holub. *Content Adaptive Steganography – Design and Detection*. PhD thesis, Binghamton University, May 2014.

[9] V. Holub and J. Fridrich. Designing steganographic distortion using directional filters. In *Fourth IEEE International Workshop on Information Forensics and Security*, Tenerife, Spain, December 2–5, 2012.

[10] V. Holub and J. Fridrich. Random projections of residuals for digital image steganalysis. *IEEE Transactions on Information Forensics and Security*, 8(12):1996–2006, December 2013.

[11] V. Holub, J. Fridrich, and T. Denemark. Universal distortion design for steganography in an arbitrary domain. *EURASIP Journal on Information Security, Special Issue on Revised Selected Papers of the 1st ACM IH and MMS Workshop*, 2014:1, 2014.

[12] A. D. Ker and R. Böhme. Revisiting weighted stego-image steganalysis. In E. J. Delp, P. W. Wong, J. Dittmann, and N. D. Memon, editors, *Proceedings SPIE, Electronic Imaging, Security, Forensics, Steganography, and Watermarking of Multimedia Contents X*, volume 6819, pages 5 1–17, San Jose, CA, January 27–31, 2008.

[13] J. Kodovský, J. Fridrich, and V. Holub. Ensemble classifiers for steganalysis of digital media. *IEEE Transactions on Information Forensics and Security*, 7(2):432–444, 2012.

[14] B. Li, S. Tan, M. Wang, and J. Huang. Investigation on cost assignment in spatial image steganography. *IEEE Transactions on Information Forensics and Security*, 9(8):1264–1277, August 2014.

[15] B. Li, M. Wang, and J. Huang. A new cost function for spatial image steganography. In *Proceedings IEEE, International Conference on Image Processing, ICIP*, Paris, France, October 27–30, 2014.

[16] T. Pevný, T. Filler, and P. Bas. Using high-dimensional image models to perform highly undetectable steganography. In R. Böhme and R. Safavi-Naini, editors, *Information Hiding, 12th International Conference*, volume 6387 of *Lecture Notes in Computer Science*, pages 161–177, Calgary, Canada, June 28–30, 2010. Springer-Verlag, New York.

[17] V. Sedighi, J. Fridrich, and R. Cogranne. Content-adaptive pentary steganography using the multivariate generalized Gaussian cover model. In A. Alattar, N. D. Memon, and C. Heitzenrater, editors, *Proceedings SPIE, Electronic Imaging, Media Watermarking, Security, and Forensics 2015*, volume 9409, San Francisco, CA, February 8–12, 2015.

[18] W. Tang, H. Li, W. Luo, and J. Huang. Adaptive steganalysis against WOW embedding algorithm. In A. Uhl, S. Katzenbeisser, R. Kwitt, and A. Piva, editors, *2nd ACM IH&MMSec. Workshop*, Salzburg, Austria, June 11–13, 2014.

[19] S. Verdú and T. Weissman. Erasure entropy. In *Proc. of ISIT*, Seattle, WA, July 9–14, 2006.

[20] G. Winkler. *Image Analysis, Random Fields and Markov Chain Monte Carlo Methods: A Mathematical Introduction (Stochastic Modelling and Applied Probability)*. Springer-Verlag, Berlin Heidelberg, 2nd edition, 2003.

Steganalysis of Adaptive JPEG Steganography Using 2D Gabor Filters

Xiaofeng Song[*]
State Key Laboratory of
Mathematical Engineering and
Advanced Computing
Zhengzhou 450001, China
xiaofengsong@sina.com

Fenlin Liu
Zhengzhou Information
Science and Technology
Institute
Zhengzhou 450001, China
liufenlin@sina.vip.com

Chunfang Yang[†]
Zhengzhou Information
Science and Technology
Institute
Zhengzhou 450001, China
chunfangyang@126.com

Xiangyang Luo[‡]
Zhengzhou Information
Science and Technology
Institute
Zhengzhou 450001, China
xiangyangluo@126.com

Yi Zhang
Zhengzhou Information
Science and Technology
Institute
Zhengzhou 450001, China
yizhang0125@163.com

ABSTRACT

Adaptive JPEG steganographic schemes are difficult to p-
reserve the image texture features in all scales and orientations when the embedding changes are constrained to the
complicated texture regions, then a steganalysis feature extraction method is proposed based on 2 dimensional (2D)
Gabor filters. The 2D Gabor filters have certain optimal
joint localization properties in the spatial domain and in
the spatial frequency domain. They can describe the image
texture features from different scales and orientations, therefore the changes of image statistical characteristics caused
by steganography embedding can be captured more effectively. For the proposed feature extraction method, the decompressed JPEG image is filtered by 2D Gabor filters with
different scales and orientations firstly. Then, the histogram
features are extracted from all the filtered images.Lastly, the
ensemble classifier is used to assemble the proposed steganalysis feature as well as the final steganalyzer. The experimental results show that the proposed steganalysis feature can
achieve a competitive performance by comparing with the
other steganalysis features when they are used for the detection performance of adaptive JPEG steganography such
as UED, JUNIWARD and SI-UNIWARD.

[*]Xiaofeng Song is also a PhD candidates at Zhengzhou Information Science and Technology Institute .

[†]The corresponding author

[‡]Xiangyang Luo is also a researcher at State Key Laboratory
of Information Assurance,Beijing 100072,China.

Categories and Subject Descriptors

I.4.9 [**Computing Methodologies**]: Image Processing and
Computer Vision—*Applications*

General Terms

Algorithms, Design, Security

Keywords

Adaptive steganography; JPEG; steganalysis; feature extraction; 2D Gabor filters

1. INTRODUCTION

JPEG is one of the most popular image formats on the
internet, so the steganography and steganalysis techniques
about JPEG image attract more attentions. For now, the
steganography algorithms for JPEG image can be divided
into two parts: non-adaptive steganography and adaptive
steganography. The former include Jsteg, MB1 [22], M-
B2, Outguess [21], F5 [25], nsF5 [9], MME (modified matrix encoding) [16], PQ (perturbed quantization) [7], etc.
The latter include PQt (texture-adaptive PQ), PQe (energy-
adaptive PQ) [9], MOD (Model Optimized Distortion) [4],
EBS (Entropy Block Steganography) [24], UED (Uniform
Embedding Distortion) [11], JUNIWARD (JPEG Universal Wavelet Relative Distortion) [12], SI-UNIWARD (Side-
informed Universal Wavelet Relative Distortion) [12] and so
on. The main difference between non-adaptive and adaptive
steganography algorithms is that the former do not consider
the image content characteristics when the changed cover
elements are selected while the latter constrain the embedding changes to the complicated image texture and edge
regions which are difficult to model. For the above adaptive JPEG steganography algorithms, the frameworks of the
steganographic schemes are similar. They all define a distortion function firstly and then the messages are embedded
by encoding method. For example, as to PQt and PQe,
the distortion functions are defined according to the texture and energy measure respectively, and then the given

messages are embedded by wet paper code [6]; as to MOD, UED, EBS, JUNIWARD and SI-UNIWARD, the different distortion functions are defined respectively and the messages are embedded while minimizing the distortion function by Syndrome-Trellis Codes (STCs) [5]. Compared with the non-adaptive JPEG steganography, the adaptive JPEG steganography can achieve better anti-detection abilities because the embedding changes are constrained to complicated image texture and edge regions.

For the detection of the adaptive JPEG steganography, some steganalysis methods have been proposed in recent years. In literature [18], for MOD steganography, the distortion function optimized to maximize security has been overtrained to an incomplete cover model, therefore the inter-block co-occurrences features beyond the optimized model are proposed for the detection performance. In literature [23], the principle of PQ steganography is analyzed and the enhanced histogram features are proposed to improve the detection performance for PQ, PQt and PQe. In literature [17], in order to capture embedding changes more comprehensively, a rich model of DCT coefficients in a JPEG files is proposed. In literature [12], the CC-JRM (Cartesian calibration JPEG rich model) features are combined with SR-MQ1 (Spatial Rich Model with the single quantization $q = 1$) [8] to detect adaptive JPEG steganography. In literature [13], by projecting neighboring residual samples onto a set of random vectors, the PSRM (projection spatial rich model) features are proposed. PSRM take the first-order statistic (histogram) of the projections as the feature instead of forming the co-occurrence matrix. In literature [14], the DCTR (Discrete Cosine Transform Residual) features which utilize 64 kernels of the discrete cosine transform are proposed. For DCTR, the decompressed JPEG image is convoluted with each DCT kernel firstly and then the first-order statistics of quantized noise residuals are obtained by subsampling residual images. The DCTR features can achieve better detection performance while preserve relative low feature dimensions. In addition, in literature [23, 17, 8, 13, 14], the final detection accuracy are all obtained by ensemble classifier [19] after features extraction.

From all above, it can be seen that the current steganalysis methods mainly depend on more effective features to improve the detection performance for adaptive JPEG steganography. However, the existing steganalysis features are not extracted from different scales and more orientations to capture the embedding changes. In fact, as we all know, adaptive JPEG steganography constrains the embedding changes to image texture and edge regions. Moreover, these steganography algorithms often define the embedding distortion in single scale, such as JUNIWARD steganography utilizes the wavelet decomposition coefficients in one scale and three different orientations to define distortion. Therefore, for the steganalyzer, if the image texture and edge features can be described accurately from different scales and orientations, then the statistical features extracted from the rich image representation can reflect the image changes more effectively and the detection performance can also be improved. Base on this idea, a steganalysis feature extraction method is proposed based on 2D Gabor filters. For the proposed method, the decompressed JPEG image is decomposed by the 2D Gabor filters [2] with different scales and orientations, and then the steganalysis features are extracted from the image filtering coefficients. The 2D Gabor filter acts as a local band-pass filter with certain optimal joint localization properties in the spatial domain and in the spatial frequency domain. It can describe the image texture and edge features effectively. In contrast to DCTR features which utilize 64 DCT kernels for image filtering, the 2D Gabor filters can capture the embedding changes from more scales and orientations, so the steganalysis feature extracted from image filtering coefficients got by 2D Gabor filters might be more effective for the detection performances of adaptive JPEG steganography. The usage of 2D Gabor filters is the main differences between DCTR features and the proposed steganalysis feature in this paper.

The rest of this paper is organized as follows. In section 2, the image representation using 2D Gabor filters is introduced; in section 3, the changes of image filtering coefficients are analyzed after steganography embedding; in section 4, the proposed steganalysis feature extraction method is given and analyzed in details, and then the parameters setting are also discussed; in section 5, the proposed steganalysis feature are compared with the other steganalysis features for adaptive JPEG steganography, in section 6, the conclusion is drawn.

2. IMAGE REPRESENTATION USING 2D GABOR FILTERS

The Gabor transform belongs to a short time Fourier transform, and it adds the Gaussian window to Fourier transform in order to realize the local analysis in spatial domain and spatial frequency domain. In literature [2], Daugman proposes the 2D Gabor filter theory based on Gabor transform and points out an important property of the family of 2D Gabor filters is their achievement of the theoretical lower bound of joint uncertainty in the two conjoint domains of visual space and spatial frequency variables. In other words, 2D Gabor filter can achieve optimal joint localization properties in the spatial domain and in the spatial frequency domain. In literature [3], the 2D Gabor filter has been used for the distortion definition of adaptive JPEG steganography, and the better anti-detection ability is achieved than db8 wavelet. In the following, the 2D Gabor filter is introduced.

When the 2D Gabor filters are used for image processing and analysis, the image should be filtered by 2D Gabor filters firstly, and then the feature extraction, edge detection, denoising and so on processing or analysis can be performed. The 2D Gabor filtering for image is that an input image $I(x, y)$ is convolved with a 2-D Gabor function $g(x, y)$ to obtain a Gabor feature image $u(x, y)$ as follows:

$$u(x, y) = \iint\limits_{\Omega} I(\xi, \eta) g(x - \xi, y - \eta) d\xi d\eta \qquad (1)$$

where, $(x, y) \in \Omega$, Ω denotes the set of image points.

In this paper, the 2D Gabor function $g(x, y)$ in equation (1) use the following family of Gabor functions [10], it is a product of a Gaussian and a cosine function.

$$g_{\lambda, \theta, \phi}(x, y) = e^{-((x'^2 + \gamma^2 y'^2)/2\sigma^2)} \cos\left(2\pi \frac{x'}{\lambda} + \phi\right) \qquad (2)$$

where, $x' = x \cos\theta + y \sin\theta$, $y' = -x \sin\theta + y \cos\theta$, $\sigma = 0.56\lambda$, $\gamma = 0.5$. In equation (2), σ represents the scale parameter, the small σ means high spatial resolution, the image filtering coefficients reflect local properties in fine scale, while the large σ means low spatial resolution, the coefficients reflect local properties in coarse scale. The other parameters in equation (2) can be explained as follows: θ specifies the orientations of 2D Gabor filters, λ denotes the wavelength of the cosine factor, γ is the spatial aspect ratio and specifies the ellipticity of Gaussian factor, ϕ specifies the phase offset of the cosine factor ($\phi = 0, \pi$ correspond to symmetric "centre-on" functions, while $\phi = -\pi/2, \pi/2$ correspond to anti-symmetric functions). In addition, in order to capture the embedding changes, all the 2D Gabor filters are made zero mean by subtracting the kernel mean from all its elements to form high-pass filter.

In Figure 1, the filtered images generated by convolving Lena image[1] with 2D Gabor filters are given. For the top filtered images,the corresponding parameters are set as $\sigma = 0.5$, $\phi = \pi/2$, $\theta = \{0, \pi/4, \pi/2, 3\pi/4\}$; as to the bottom filtered images, only the scale parameter σ is different. From the filtered image shown in Figure 1, it can be seen that the image local properties in different scales and orientations can be captured effectively. For real applications, the image should be filtered by 2D Gabor filters with more scales and orientations to capture rich texture and edge information. From Figure 1, it also can be found that the image local properties such as texture, edge are more obvious when the scale parameter σ is relative small and the spatial resolution is relative high, for example, as to the top filtered images, the texture and edge is highlighted. As to the bottom filtered images, the scale parameter σ is relative large, the filtered image reflect the image local properties in relative low resolution, so the texture and edge are relative obscure.

Adaptive JPEG steganography constrains the embedding changes to complex image texture and edge regions. The image filtering by 2D Gabor filters with different scales and orientations can capture the image texture and edge features accurately. So, the steganalysis feature extracted from image 2D Gabor filtering coefficients would be more effective.

3. EMBEDDING CHNAGES OF IMAGE FILTERING COEFFICIENTS

Adaptive JPEG steganography embeds the messages by modifying the DCT coefficients. The modifications will cause the changes of image filtering coefficients in different scales and orientations. In this section, we will take a look how the image filtering coefficients are affected by modifying one DCT coefficient of JPEG image.

Before the JPEG image is filtered by 2D Gabor filters, the JPEG file should be decompressed to the spatial domain. In order to avoid any loss of information, the JPEG image should be decompressed without quantizing the pixel values to $\{0,1,\ldots,255\}$. Let us suppose the decompressed JPEG image is denoted as $\mathbf{I}'$, then the filtered image $\mathbf{U}^{s,l}=\mathbf{I}'*\mathbf{G}^{s,l}$, $\mathbf{G}^{s,l}$ specifies the 8×8 2D Gabor filter in s scale and l orientation, '*' denotes a convolution without padding. Furthermore, suppose $\mathbf{B}^{(i,j)}$ denotes a 8×8 DCT basis pattern, $\mathbf{B}^{(i,j)} = \left(B_{mn}^{(i,j)}\right), 0 \leq m, n \leq 7, 0 \leq i, j \leq 7,$

$$B_{mn}^{(i,j)} = \frac{w_i w_j}{4} \cos \frac{\pi i(2m+1)}{16} \cos \frac{\pi j(2n+1)}{16} \quad (3)$$

where, $w_0 = 1/\sqrt{2}$, $w_i = 1$ ($i > 0$).

[1]Lena image [EB/OL]. http://en.wikipedia.org/wiki/lenna.

Figure 2: The absolute difference values between image filtering coefficients of Lena image and the corresponding stego image, from left to right, top to bottom, $\theta = 0, \pi/4, \pi/2, 3\pi/4$ respectively

Then , the modification of DCT coefficient in mode (i, j) of 8×8 DCT block will affect all 8×8 pixels in the corresponding block, and an entire 15×15 neighborhood of values in $\mathbf{U}^{s,l}$. The values will be modified by "unit response" [14] expressed in equation (4).

$$\mathbf{R}^{(i,j)\,(s,l)} = \mathbf{B}^{(i,j)} \otimes \mathbf{G}^{s,l} \quad (4)$$

where, $\otimes$ denotes the full cross-correlation.

In Figure 2, the absolute difference values between image filtering coefficients of Lena and the corresponding stego image are shown. The parameters of 2D Gabor filters are set as $\sigma = 1$, $\phi = \pi/2$, $\theta = \{0, \pi/4, \pi/2, 3\pi/4\}$. The payload of stego image is 0.4 bit per non-zero AC DCT coefficient (b-pac). From Figure 2, it can be seen that the image filtering coefficients are changed after steganography embedding.

4. STEGANALYSIS FEATURE EXTRACTION BASED ON 2D GABOR FILTERS

In this section, the steganalysis feature extraction method based on 2D Gabor filters is described in details firstly, and then the parameters setting are discussed for feature extraction.

4.1 Feature extraction method

When the steganalysis feature is extracted, the decompressed JPEG image is convolved with 2D Gabor filters to get the filtered images firstly. However, the statistical feature is not extracted directly from the filtered images in different scales and orientations. As we known, the JPEG image can be divided into 8×8 DCT blocks. According to the 64 DCT modes in 8×8DCT block, the each filtered image can be subsampled by step 8 to form 64 subimages. The

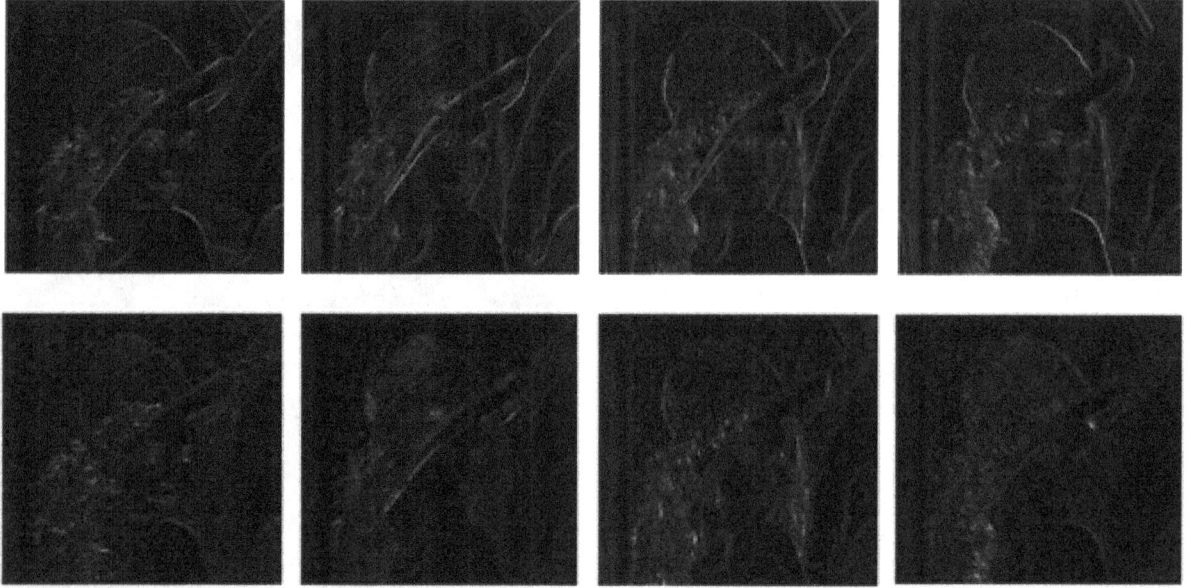

Figure 1: The filtered image obtained by convolving Lena image with different 2D Gabor filters (orientations are $0^0, 45^0$, 90^0, 135^0), the Scale parameter σ equals 0.5 for the top filtered images and it equals 1 for the bottom.

feature of each filtered image is formed by combing the features of 64 corresponding subimages. Lastly, the features of all filtered image are joined to obtain the steganalysis feature.

The flaw diagram of the proposed feature extraction method is shown in Figure 3 and the detailed extraction procedures are described as follows:

Step1: The JPEG image is decompressed to spatial domain without quantizing the pixel values to $\{0,1,\ldots,255\}$ to avoid any loss of information.

Step2: The 2D Gabor filter bank is generated and the filter bank includes 2D Gabor filters with different scales and orientations.

Step3: The decompressed JPEG image is convolved with each 8×8 2D Gabor filter $\mathbf{G}^{s,l}$, the filtered image $\mathbf{U}^{s,l}$ is operated as the following:

(1) According to the 64 DCT modes $(a,b)(0 \leq a \leq 7, 0 \leq b \leq 7)$ in 8×8 DCT block, the filtered image $\mathbf{U}^{s,l}$ is subsampled by step 8 to get 64 subimages $\mathbf{U}^{s,l}_{a,b}$ (as shown in Figure 4);

(2) For each subimage $\mathbf{U}^{s,l}_{a,b}$, the histogram feature is extracted by equation (5),

$$\mathbf{h}^{s,l}_{a,b}(x) = \frac{1}{\left|\mathbf{U}^{s,l}_{a,b}\right|} \sum_{u \in \mathbf{U}^{s,l}_{a,b}} [Q_T(|u|/q) = x] \qquad (5)$$

where, Q_T is a quantizer with integer centroids $\{0, 1, \cdots, T\}$, q denotes the quantization step, and $[P]$ is the Iverson bracket equal to 0 when the statement P is false and 1 when P is true.

(3) According to the method in literature [14], all the histogram features of 64 subimages $\mathbf{U}^{s,l}_{a,b}$ is merged and combined to obtain the histogram features $\mathbf{h}^{s,l}$ of the filtered image $\mathbf{U}^{s,l}$.

Step4: For the filtered image generated by 2D Gabor filters with the same scale parameter σ, the corresponding

histogram features are merged according to the symmetrical orientations. For example, suppose the orientation parameter $\theta = \{0, \pi/8, 2\pi/8, \cdots, 6\pi/8, 7\pi/8\}$, then the histogram features of the filtered image with $\theta = \pi/8, 7\pi/8$, $\theta = 2\pi/8, 6\pi/8$ and so on should be merged by averaging.

Step5: All the merged histogram features are combined to form the final steganglysis feature.

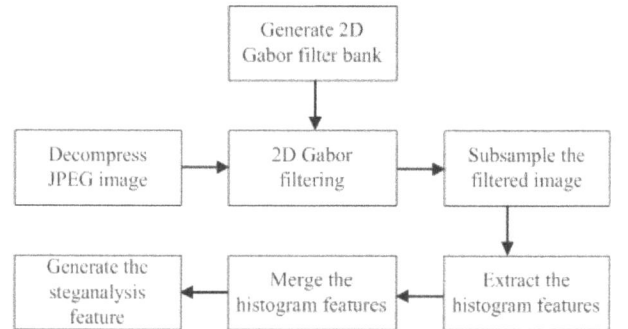

Figure 3: The flaw diagram of the proposed feature extraction method

From the above descriptions, it can be seen that the proposed feature extraction method mainly includes three parts: the generation of 2D Gabor filter bank, the histogram features extraction, the merging of histogram features. In the following, the further descriptions are given for these three parts.

(1) Generation of 2D Gabor filter bank

For the generation of 2D Gabor filter bank with different scales and orientations, suppose the number of scales equals L (the scale parameter σ has L different values), the number of orientations equals S, the parameter ϕ is set to 0 and $\pi/2$, so the number of the 2D Gabor filters is $2 \cdot L \cdot S$. For example, if $L=4$ and $S = 32$, then the number of the 2D Gabor filters

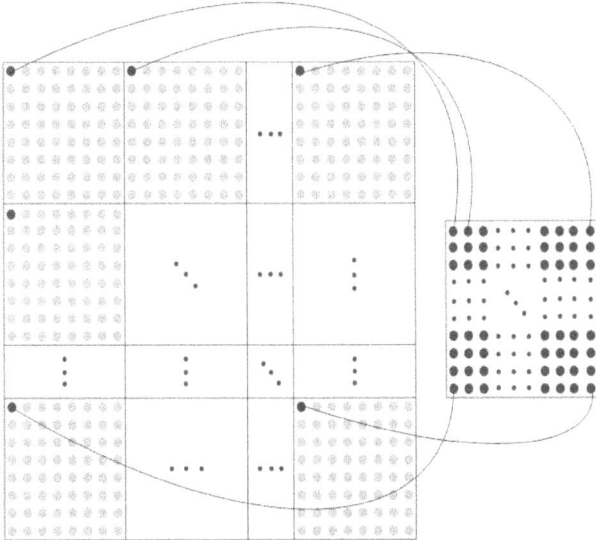

Figure 4: The procedure of the filtered image subsampling

is 256. The scale parameter L and orientation parameter S are both important for the extraction of steganalysis feature. In this paper, the two parameters are set according to the experiences.

(2) Histogram features extraction

For the histogram features extraction, the decompressed JPEG image is convolved with each 2D Gabor filter, and then the filtered image is subsampled and the histogram features are extracted. The features extraction by subsampling the filtered image into 64 subimages according to the 64 DCT modes in 8×8 DCT block can enhance the diversity and effectiveness of the steganalysis features, the similar idea has been used for the local histogram features extraction in literature [20, 14]. In addition, the histogram features extracted from the 64 subimages can be merged [14] to reduce the feature dimensionality according to the affects for filtered image which are caused by modifying the DCT coefficients in different DCT modes. For each filtered image, the 64 histogram features with $T + 1$ dimensions can be got when the cut threshold is set to T, then these histogram features can be merged to one histogram feature with $25 \times (T+1)$ dimensions. Furthermore, the histogram feature with $2 \cdot L \cdot S \cdot 25 \cdot (T+1)$ dimension can be obtained by all the $2 \cdot L \cdot S$ 2D Gabor filters.

(3) Merging of histogram features

When the histogram feature of the decompressed JPEG image is obtained, the dimensions of the histogram feature can be reduced further by merging the features extracted by 2D Gabor filters with symmetrical direction and same scale. For example, the histogram features of the filtered image with $\theta = \pi/8, 7\pi/8$, $\theta = 2\pi/8, 6\pi/8$ and so on should be merged by averaging. This merging operation has been used in many feature extraction method [17, 8, 13] because images have similar statistical characteristics in symmetrical orientations and same scale. After the histogram features are merged by symmetrical orientations, the dimensions of the final feature are $2 \cdot L \cdot (S/2 + 1) \cdot 25 \cdot (T + 1)$. In the experiments, it can be found that the detection performance of the merging features will be better.

4.2 Parameters setting

For the feature extraction method proposed in this paper, all the parameters θ, σ, q, T should be set before feature extraction. In the following, the detection performances of different parameter settings are discussed. In the experiments of this section, 10000 grayscale images from BossBase1.01 [1] are converted into JPEG image with quality factor 75, and then stego images are generated by JUNIWARD steganography which is a state-of-the-art hiding method in JPEG domain. The detectors are trained as binary classifiers implemented using ensemble classifier proposed in literature [19].The E_{OOB}(out-of-bag estimate of the testing error) is used to evaluate the detection performance of the proposed steganalysis feature.

(1) Direction parameter θ

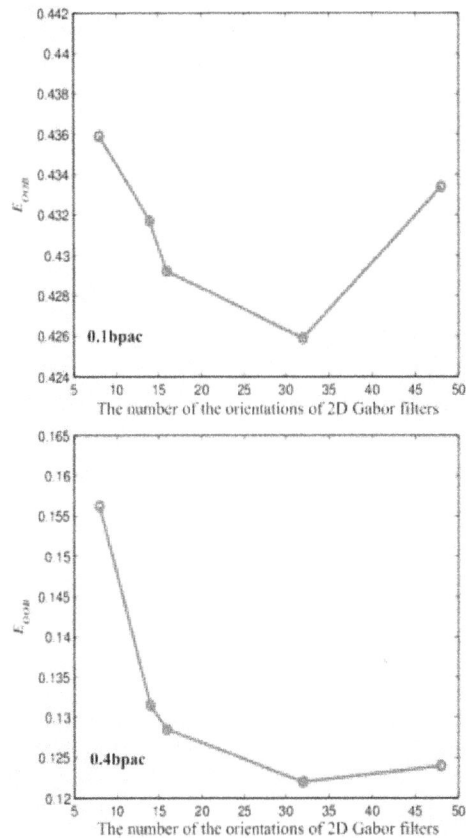

Figure 5: The effect of the number of orientations of 2D Gabor filters on detection accuracy(quality factor (QF) is 75).

By the 2D Gabor filters with different orientations, the changes of the statistical features of JPEG image can be captured more effectively for steganography embedding. In Figure 5, for JUNIWARD with paylaod 0.1bpac and 0.4bpac,the detection performance are presented when the orientations of 2D Gabor filters equal 8, 14, 16, 32, 48 respectively. The other parameters for the detection performance are set as $\sigma = 1$, $q = 6$, and $T = 4$. In addition, in Figure 5, from top to bottom, the payloads of JUNIWARD steganography are 0.1bpac and 0.4bpac respectively.

From Figure 5, it can be seen that the detection accuracy of the proposed steganalysis feature will be better when more 2D Gabor filters with different orientations are utilized. At the same time, it should be noticed that the feature dimension will be increased with more orientations. The increase in feature dimension will lead to more time and space consumptions; on the other hand, more training samples are need for classifier and this will affect the detection accuracy when the training samples are limited.

(2) Scale parameter σ

With the 2D Gabor filters with different scales, the changes of JPEG image statistical features can be captured from more scales. In Table 1, the detection performances are given for JUNIWARD with quality factor 75 when the scale parameter σ of 2D Gabor filters is set as 0.5, 0.75, 1, and 1.25 respectively. The orientations of 2D Gabor filters equal 32 for each scale and the threshold T equals 4. The Quantization step q is set to 2, 4, 6, 8 respectively for different scales. The detection performances of combinatorial feature which is formed by combining the histogram features got in different scales are also given in Table 1.

Table 1: Detection error E_{OOB} for JUNIWARD by 2D Gabor filters with different scales.

Payload	Scale parameter σ				
	0.5	0.75	1	1.25	combine
0.1bpac	0.4300	0.4277	0.4273	0.4350	**0.4158**
0.2bpac	0.3373	0.3233	0.3259	0.3438	**0.2974**
0.3bpac	0.2376	0.2202	0.2233	0.2504	**0.1847**
0.4bpac	0.1626	0.1326	0.1237	0.1553	**0.0956**

From Table 1, it can be seen that the detection error of the features extracted in different scales are also different and the combinatorial feature can achieve better detection accuracy. This is because that the features extracted from different scales reflect the changes of JPEG image statistical characteristics in different scales after steganography embedding. The combination of these features enhances the diversity and effectiveness of the steganalysis feature, thus the detection accuracy is improved.

(3) Quantization step q

For the steganalysis feature extraction, the quantization for the image filtering coefficients can make the feature more sensitive to embedding changes at spatial discontinuities in the image [8]. Therefore, the image filtering coefficients are quantized to improve the detection accuracy in the proposed feature extraction method. In Figure 6, the effects of the quantization step q on detection accuracy are shown for JUNIWARD steganography at 0.4bpac payload with quality factor 75 and 95. The other parameters of 2D Gabor filters are set as $\sigma = 1$, the orientations equal 32, the threshold $T = 4$.

From Figure 6, it can be seen that the detection accuracy will be changeable with different quantization step q and appropriate value of q can improve the detection accuracy. In addition, for the same quality factor, we notice that the quantization step q for optimal detection accuracy is larger when the scale parameters σ is relative large.

(4) Threshold T

The threshold T is also a parameter for feature extraction. For the histogram feature, the feature dimension will be increased when the larger threshold T is set. In Table 2, the effects of the threshold T on detection accuracy are given for

quality factor 75. The scale parameter σ is set as 0.5, 0.75, 1, 1.25 respectively, the corresponding quantization steps q are 2, 4, 6, 8, and the orientations equal 32 for all scales.

Table 2: The effect of the threshold T on detection accuracy.

T	3	4	5	6
E_{OOB}	0.0999	0.0956	0.0996	0.1004

From Table 2, it can be seen that the detection performances are insensitive to threshold T, so the threshold T is set to 4 in this paper.

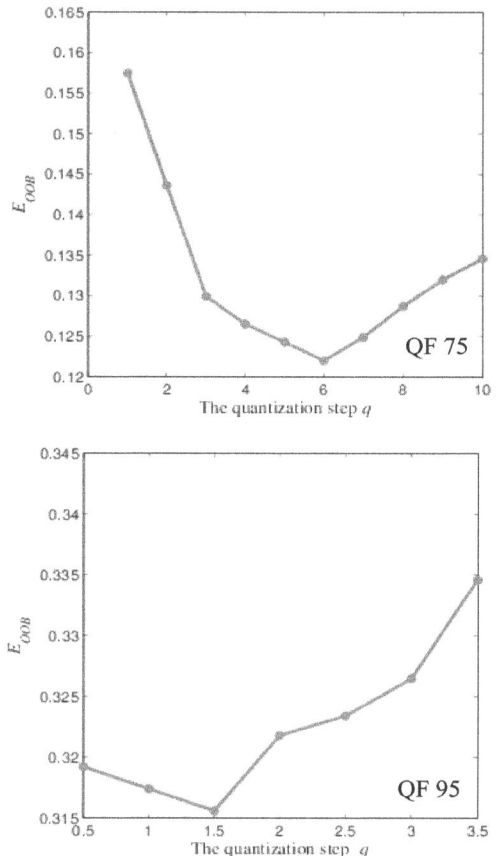

Figure 6: The effect of the quantization step q on detection accuracy.

5. EXPERIMENTAL RESULTS AND ANALYSIS

This section is organized as the following. In section 5.1, the image database and experiment setup are introduced; in section 5.2, by comparing to CC-JRM and DCTR, the proposed feature are evaluated according to the detection performance for adaptive JPEG steganography such as UED, JUNIWARD and SI-UNIWARD; in section 5.3, the detection performances of the combinatorial feature steganalysis are presented and the complement among different features are analyzed.

5.1 Image Database and Experiment setup

In the experiments, the image database is BossBase-1.01 containing 10000 grayscale 512×512 images with PGM format. For UED and JUNIWARD steganography, all these grayscale images are converted into JPEG image with quality factor 75 and 95 respectively, and then the corresponding stego images are generated with payload 0.05, 0.1, 0.2, 0.3, 0.4, 0.5bpac. For SI-UNIWARD steganography, the original grayscale images are used as precover images, and then the corresponding stego images are generated with payload from 0.05bpac to 0.5bpac when the grayscale images are compressed to JPEG image with quality factor 75 and 95. So, for each steganography algorithm and quality factor, we have one group cover images and six group stego images, one group cover images and one group corresponding stego images are used as image samples for one payload.

For the steganalysis feature extraction, the parameters are set as: scales parameter $\sigma = 0.5$, 0.75, 1, 1.25 respectively, the number of the orientations of 2D Gabor filters equal 32 for each scale, the threshold T is set to 4, the quantization step q is set to 2, 4, 6, 8 for different scales with σ in ascending order when quality factor is 75, the q is set to 0.5, 1, 1.5, 2 for quality factor is 95. Lastly, the steganalysis feature is obtained with 17000 dimensions. In all experiments, ensemble classifier [19] is used for the training and testing. The proportion of training set to test set is set to 5:5 and the E_{OOB} is used to evaluate the detection performance of the steganalysis feature. The detection accuracy is the average value of ten duplicate experiments.

5.2 Comparison to prior art

In this section, the proposed steganalysis feature is compared with CC-JRM and DCTR, the detection errors E_{OOB} are given for UED, JUNIWARD and SI-UNIWARD with different payloads.

In Figure 7, the detection errors E_{OOB} of the three different steganalysis features are presented for UED with seven payloads and two quality factors. From Figure 7, it can be seen that the proposed steganalysis feature based on 2D Gabor filters can achieve competitive detection performance by comparing with the other steganalysis features. For example, in contrast to DCTR, the testing error E_{OOB} can be improved by 5.27% when payload is 0.2bpac and quality factor is 75, the improvement is 12.47% by comparison with CC-JRM. When quality factor is 95, the improvement is 3.16% and 6.88% respectively for payload 0.2bpac. This is because that the 2D Gabor filters with different scales and orientations can capture the embedding changes more effectively.

In Figure 8, the detection errors E_{OOB} of the three steganalysis features are given for JUNIWARD with different payloads. From Figure 8, it can be seen that the proposed steganalysis feature can achieve the best detection performance for JUNIWARD with different payloads and quality factors. For example, when quality factor is 75, in contrast to DCTR, the testing error E_{OOB} can be improved by 4.05% when payload is 0.2bpac, the improvement is 12.07% by comparison with CC-JRM; when quality factor is 95, the improvements are 2.44% and 4.78% respectively for payload 0.2bpac.

In Figure9, the detection errors E_{OOB} of the three steganalysis features are given for SI-UNIWARD with different payloads. From Figure 9, it can be seen that the proposed

steganalysis feature can achieve the best detection performance when quality factor is 75. For example, when payload is 0.2bpac and quality factor is 75, in contrast to DCTR, the testing error E_{OOB} can be improved by 1.1%, the improvement is 2.1% by comparison with CC-JRM. However, the detection performance of DCTR is more accurate when quality factor is 95.

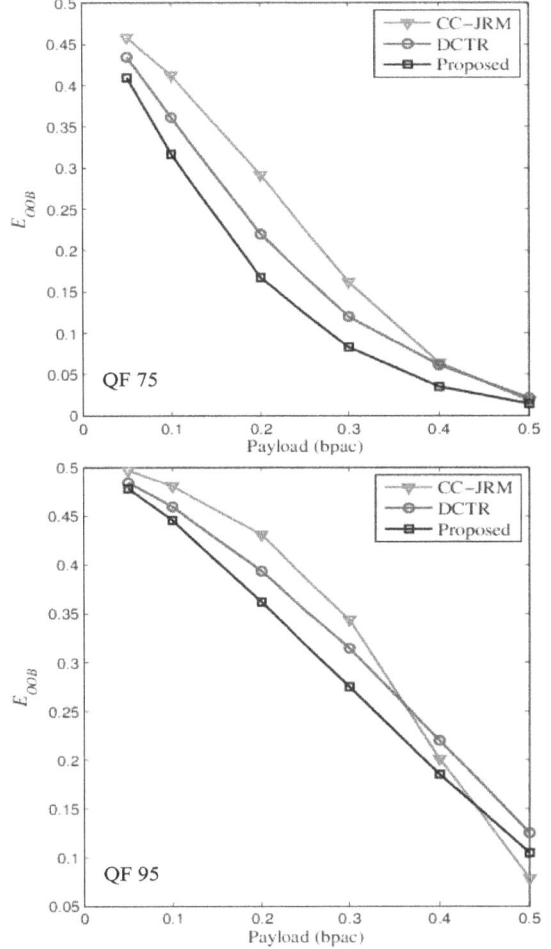

Figure 7: The detection error E_{OOB} for UED for quality factor 75 and 95 when steganalyzed with different features.

Furthermore, it should be noticed that the dimensions of the proposed steganalysis feature can be reduced 8000 when scale parameter σ is still set to four different values and orientations equal 14 for each scale. In this case, the feature dimension of the proposed steganalysis feature is same to DCTR feature. In the experiments, the detection performances of the proposed steganalysis feature with 8000 dimensions are also evaluated. The experimental results show the proposed steganalysis feature with 8000 dimensions can also achieve competitive detection accuracy by comparison with other steganalysis features. For example, for UED and JUNIWARD with payload 0.2bpac, the improvements are 4.2% and 2.14% respectively for JPEG image with quality factor 75 in contrast to DCTR; when quality factor is 95, the improvements are 2.15% and 1.91%. For SI-UNIWARD, the detection performances of the proposed steganalysis feature with 8000 dimensions are comparative to DCTR when quality factor is 75; however, it is still inferior to DCTR when quality factor is 95.

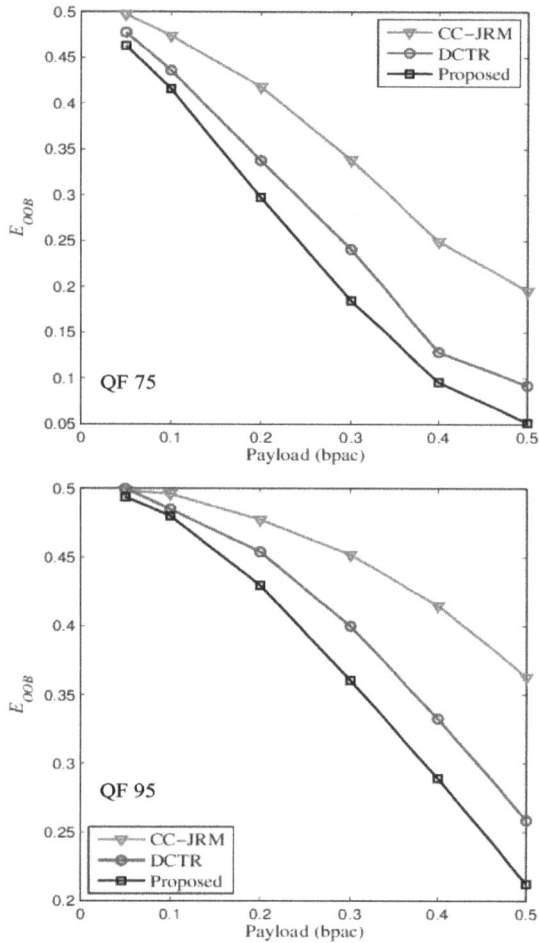

Figure 8: The detection error E_{OOB} for JUNIWARD for quality factor 75 and 95 when steganalyzed with different features.

5.3 Detection accuracy of the combinatorial features

In this section, the detection performances of the combinatorial features which are formed by combining different steganalysis features are compared for JUNIWARD with payload 0.4bpac. In Table 3 and Table 4, the detection error E_{OOB} is given for quality factors 75 and 95.

From Table 3 and Table 4, it can be seen that the combination of different steganalysis features only can improve the detection performance slightly. It is possible that the complements among these steganalysis features are not strong.

6. CONCLUSION

In this paper, a steganalysis feature extraction method based on 2D Gabor filters is proposed for adaptive JPEG steganography which often constrains the embedding changes to complicated texture and edge regions. Firstly, the definition and advantages of 2D Gabor filters are introduced. Secondly, the proposed feature extraction method based on 2D

Table 3: The detection error E_{OOB} of the combinatorial features for QF 75.

Proposed	DCTR	CC-JRM	E_{OOB}	Dim.
●			0.0956	17000
	●		0.1284	8000
		●	0.2494	22510
●	●		0.0860	25000
●		●	0.0929	39510
●	●	●	0.0872	47510

Table 4: The detection error E_{OOB} of the combinatorial features for QF 95

Proposed	DCTR	CC-JRM	E_{OOB}	Dim.
●			0.2893	17000
	●		0.3328	8000
		●	0.4151	22510
●	●		0.2739	25000
●		●	0.2846	39510
●	●	●	0.2759	47510

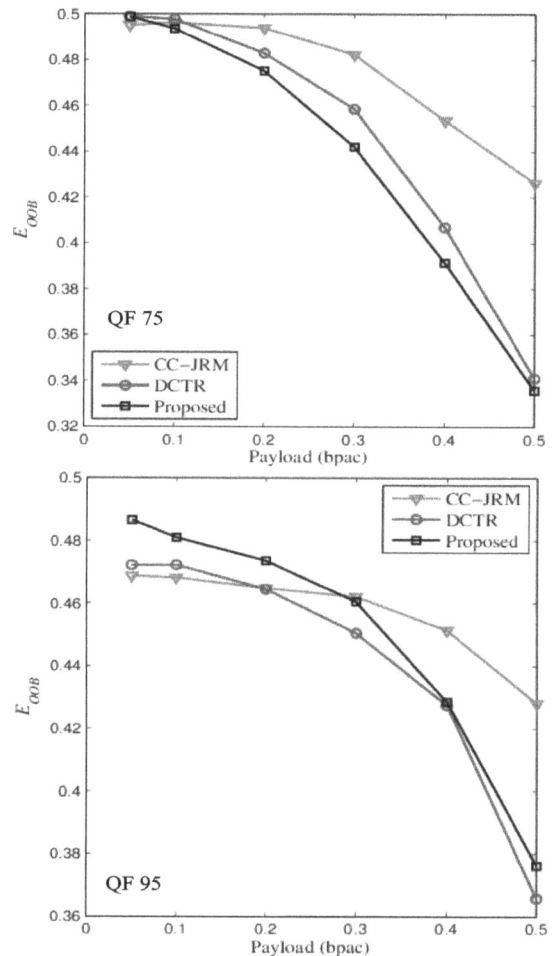

Figure 9: The detection error E_{OOB} for SI-UNIWARD for quality factor 75 and 95 when steganalyzed with different features.

Gabor filters is given in details, and then the parameters setting are also discussed. Lastly, the detection performance of the proposed steganalysis feature is evaluated by comparing with CC-JRM and DCTR features. From the experimental results, it can be seen that the detection performance can be improved effectively. For the proposed steganalysis feature extraction method, the generation of 2D Gabor filters is very important, in the future, the effect of 2D Gabor filter construction for steganalysis of adaptive JPEG steganography will be studied to improve the detection accuracy further. In addition, in literature [15], PHARM feature has been proposed for steganalysis of JPEG steganography and can achieve competitive detection performance. So, we will compare the proposed feature with PHARM feature in the future research.

7. ACKNOWLEDGMENTS

This work was supported by the National Natural Science Foundation of China (No. 61379151, 61272489, 61302159, and 61401512), the Excellent Youth Foundation of Henan Province of China (No.144100510001), the National Cryptography Development Fund of China (No.MMJJ201301005) and the Foundation of Science and Technology on Information Assurance Laboratory (No.KJ-14-108).

8. REFERENCES

[1] P. Bas, T. Filler, and T. Pevnỳ. ąś break our steganographic systemąś: The ins and outs of organizing boss. In *Information Hiding*, pages 59–70. Springer, 2011.

[2] J. G. Daugman. Uncertainty relation for resolution in space, spatial frequency, and orientation optimized by two-dimensional visual cortical filters. *JOSA A*, 2(7):1160–1169, 1985.

[3] T. Denemark, V. Sedighi, V. Holub, R. Cogranne, and J. Fridrich. Selection-channel-aware rich model for steganalysis of digital images. In *IEEE Workshop on Information Forensic and Security, Atlanta, GA*, 2014.

[4] T. Filler and J. Fridrich. Design of adaptive steganographic schemes for digital images. In *IS&T/SPIE Electronic Imaging*, pages 78800F–78800F. International Society for Optics and Photonics, 2011.

[5] T. Filler, J. Judas, and J. Fridrich. Minimizing additive distortion in steganography using syndrome-trellis codes. *Information Forensics and Security, IEEE Transactions on*, 6(3):920–935, 2011.

[6] J. Fridrich, M. Goljan, P. Lisonek, and D. Soukal. Writing on wet paper. *Signal Processing, IEEE Transactions on*, 53(10):3923–3935, 2005.

[7] J. Fridrich, M. Goljan, and D. Soukal. Perturbed quantization steganography. *Multimedia Systems*, 11(2):98–107, 2005.

[8] J. Fridrich and J. Kodovsky. Rich models for steganalysis of digital images. *Information Forensics and Security, IEEE Transactions on*, 7(3):868–882, 2012.

[9] J. Fridrich, T. Pevnỳ, and J. Kodovskỳ. Statistically undetectable jpeg steganography: dead ends challenges, and opportunities. In *Proceedings of the 9th workshop on Multimedia & security*, pages 3–14. ACM, 2007.

[10] S. E. Grigorescu, N. Petkov, and P. Kruizinga. Comparison of texture features based on gabor filters. *Image Processing, IEEE Transactions on*, 11(10):1160–1167, 2002.

[11] L. Guo, J. Ni, and Y.-Q. Shi. An efficient jpeg steganographic scheme using uniform embedding. In *WIFS*, pages 169–174, 2012.

[12] V. Holub and J. Fridrich. Digital image steganography using universal distortion. In *Proceedings of the first ACM workshop on Information hiding and multimedia security*, pages 59–68. ACM, 2013.

[13] V. Holub and J. Fridrich. Random projections of residuals for digital image steganalysis. *Information Forensics and Security, IEEE Transactions on*, 8(12):1996–2006, 2013.

[14] V. Holub and J. Fridrich. Low complexity features for jpeg steganalysis using undecimated dct. *Information Forensics and Security, IEEE Transactions on*, 10(2):219–228, 2015.

[15] V. Holub and J. Fridrich. Phase-aware projection model for steganalysis of jpeg images. *Proc. SPIE, Electronic Imaging, Media Watermarking, Security, and Forensics XVII, to appear, San Francisco, CA*, 2015.

[16] Y. Kim, Z. Duric, and D. Richards. Modified matrix encoding technique for minimal distortion steganography. In *Information hiding*, pages 314–327. Springer, 2007.

[17] J. Kodovskỳ and J. Fridrich. Steganalysis of jpeg images using rich models. In *IS&T/SPIE Electronic Imaging*, pages 83030A–83030A. International Society for Optics and Photonics, 2012.

[18] J. Kodovsky, J. Fridrich, and V. Holub. On dangers of overtraining steganography to incomplete cover model. In *Proceedings of the thirteenth ACM multimedia workshop on Multimedia and security*, pages 69–76. ACM, 2011.

[19] J. Kodovsky, J. Fridrich, and V. Holub. Ensemble classifiers for steganalysis of digital media. *Information Forensics and Security, IEEE Transactions on*, 7(2):432–444, 2012.

[20] T. Pevny and J. Fridrich. Merging markov and dct features for multi-class jpeg steganalysis. In *Electronic Imaging 2007*, pages 650503–650503. International Society for Optics and Photonics, 2007.

[21] N. Provos. Defending against statistical steganalysis. In *Usenix Security Symposium*, volume 10, pages 323–336, 2001.

[22] P. Sallee. Model-based steganography. In *Digital watermarking*, pages 154–167. Springer, 2004.

[23] X. Song, F. Liu, X. Luo, J. Lu, and Y. Zhang. Steganalysis of perturbed quantization steganography based on the enhanced histogram features. *Multimedia Tools and Applications*, pages 1–27, 2014.

[24] C. Wang and J. Ni. An efficient jpeg steganographic scheme based on the block entropy of dct coefficients. In *Acoustics, Speech and Signal Processing (ICASSP), 2012 IEEE International Conference on*, pages 1785–1788. IEEE, 2012.

[25] A. Westfeld. F5ąła steganographic algorithm. In *Information hiding*, pages 289–302. Springer, 2001.

Video Steganography Based on Optimized Motion Estimation Perturbation

Yun Cao
State Key Laboratory of
Information Security,
Institute of Information
Engineering, Chinese
Academy of Sciences,
Beijing 100093, China
caoyun@iie.ac.cn

Hong Zhang
State Key Laboratory of
Information Security,
Institute of Information
Engineering, Chinese
Academy of Sciences,
Beijing 100093, China
zhanghong@iie.ac.cn

Xianfeng Zhao
State Key Laboratory of
Information Security,
Institute of Information
Engineering, Chinese
Academy of Sciences,
Beijing 100093, China
zhaoxianfeng@iie.ac.cn

Haibo Yu
State Key Laboratory of
Information Security,
Institute of Information
Engineering, Chinese
Academy of Sciences,
Beijing 100093, China
yuhaibo@iie.ac.cn

ABSTRACT

In this paper, a novel motion vector-based video stegano-graphic scheme is proposed, which is capable of withstanding the current best statistical detection method. With this scheme, secret message bits are embedded into motion vector (MV) values by slightly perturbing their motion estimation (ME) processes. In general, two measures are taken for steganographic security (statistical undetectability) enhancement. First, the ME perturbations are optimized ensuring the modified MVs are still local optimal, which essentially makes targeted detectors ineffective. Secondly, to minimize the overall embedding impact under a given relative payload, a double-layered coding structure is used to control the ME perturbations. Experimental results demonstrate that the proposed scheme achieves a much higher level of security compared with other existing MV-based approaches. Meanwhile, the reconstructed visual quality and the coding efficiency are slightly affected as well.

Categories and Subject Descriptors

D.2.11 [**SOFTWARE ENGINEERING**]: Software Architectures—*Information hiding*; H.5.1 [**INFORMATION INTERFACES AND PRESENTATION**]: Multimedia Information Systems—*Video*

IH&MMSec'15, June 17–19, 2015, Portland, Oregon, USA.
Copyright © 2015 ACM 978-1-4503-3587-4/15/06 ...$15.00.
http://dx.doi.org/10.1145/2756601.2756609.

Keywords

Information hiding; video; steganography; H.264/AVC; motion estimation

1. INTRODUCTION

Steganography is the science and art of covert communication, a steganographic system thus embeds secret messages in innocent-looking cover media so as not to arouse any eavesdropper's suspicion. As video streaming has become one of the most popular networked applications, transmission of compressed video can be used as an ideal cloak of secret message delivery. What's more, as a hotspot in both industry and academia [1], Cloud Computing has greatly facilitated covert communication via videos by enabling ondemand provisioning of computational and storage resources. As illustrated in Figure 1, normally the steganographer (embedder/sender) can either capture or download video clips as the cover media, embed the secret messages in an innocent-looking way and deliver the stego media via internet. However, with the help of Cloud Computing, the computation intensive works, e.g., video downloading or uploading, data embedding and video transcoding, can be moved from lightweight end users onto trusted heavy-weight data centers.

Three different aspects in information-hiding systems contend with each other: capacity, security, and robustness [2]. As an important subdiscipline, steganography's primary goal is to achieve a high level of security–that is, it should be impossible for an eavesdropper to detect the existence of hidden information. This raises two basic requirements of a steganographic system: first, the used cover media should be regularly seen on internet, which implies the storages and the transmissions are of frequent occurrence; secondly, the entity for data representation, i.e., the elements actually modified to represent hidden messages, should help preserving perceptual and statistical properties. Nowadays, since compressed videos contribute a considerable fraction of internet storage

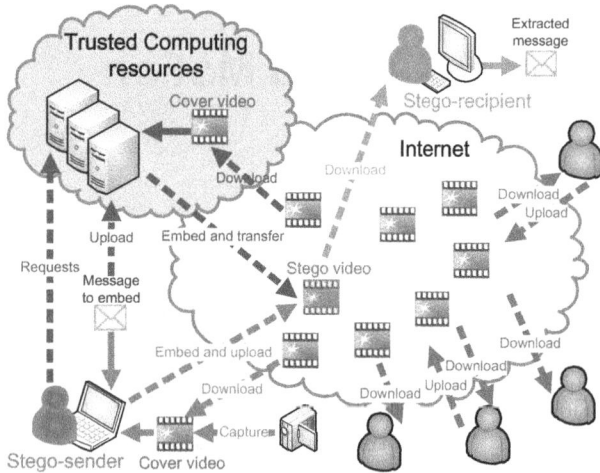

Figure 1: Regular and Cloud-aided covert communication using video steganography.

and traffic, it has received by far the most attention from the stego community. State-of-art video steganographic systems usually combine data hiding and compression together to guarantee the coding performance. In general, the embedding elements of compressed video include discrete cosine transform (DCT) coefficients, MV values, prediction modes, partition modes etc.

It is noticed that, MV has been utilized as the covert information carrier in a major type of video steganographic approaches. It is believed that MV has at least three good steganographic properties. First, MV has a relatively large value range, so that it is convenient to design embedding schemes preserving the statistical characteristics. Secondly, the modification applied to MV will not affect the coding performance much. Because the mechanisms of motion estimation and compensation ensure that once a MV is modified, the caused error will be handled automatically (i.e., absorbed into the residual signal). Finally, compressed video streams usually contain rich motion information, which ensures sufficient embedding capacity [3].

On the other hand, the state-of-art steganalytic approaches [3, 4, 5] have posed new challenges to the MV-based steganography. In their views, nearly all the current MV-based schemes modify MV values in unsecured ways that their local optimalities are likely to be destroyed. Consequently, based on the MV's probability of been locally optimal, a variety of statistical features are designed for trainings and classifications. Among these features, Wang *et al*'s AoSO (Add-or-Subtract-One) feature [5] achieves the best detection accuracy. This paper is devoted to enhancing the steganographic security of MV-based schemes. We suggest making improvements in two directions. First, to modify MVs in such a manner that their local optimalities can be well preserved. Secondly, to control the ME perturbations utilizing a double-layered coding structure, which achieves low embedding impacts as well as a high embedding efficiency (average number of bits embedded by per change). Based on these, a novel video steganographic scheme capable of withstanding the attack by AoSO is proposed.

The rest of the paper is structured as follows. Section 2 outlines the related work. Section 3 discusses the oppor-

tunities to embed with preserved local optimality. Section 4 describes the proposed steganographic scheme in details. Section 5 presents the experimental results. Finally, Section 5 draws conclusions and addresses possible future work.

2. RELATED WORK

The design philosophy of the early MV-based steganographic approaches is quite simple, that is to minimize the embedding impact on coding performance (reconstructed visual quality and achieved bit-rate). Xu *et al*. and Fang *et al*. proposed their methods which choose candidate MVs according to magnitudes. They believe modification applied to MV with a larger magnitude introduces less distortion. The former method embeds message bits in MV's horizontal or vertical components using LSB (Least Significant Bit) replacement [6] whereas the other modifies adjacent two MVs until the difference between phase angles satisfies the embedding condition [7]. Later, Aly suggested choosing candidate MVs associated with large prediction errors, and both the MV's horizontal and vertical components are used for embedding with LSB replacement.

In recent years, to cope with the evolving statistical detection methods, mainstream MV-based approaches are designed with the purpose of minimizing the overall embedding impact under a given payload [8]. Pan *et al*. and Hao *et al*. suggested that the modification rate of the MVs phase angles can be reduced by using linear block codes [9, 10]. Cao *et al*. presented a new selection rule directly associated with the prediction error differences [11], and suggested confining modifications only to the selected MVs by the use of wet paper code (WPC) [12]. Recently, Yao *et al*. elaborated a reasonable distortion function for MV modification and adopted a flexible stego-coding technique named syndrome-trellis code (STC) to minimize the overall distortion. Then MV values are modified using $\pm$ embedding.

3. MOTION VECTOR MODIFICATION WITH PRESERVED LOCAL OPTIMALITY

3.1 Motion Vector's Local Optimality

The local optimality is one of MV's intrinsic qualities ensured by the block based ME. According to [5], in an attacker's view, a MV V directly obtained from the compressed video is recognized as local optimal if it can pass the following test. First, calculate V's surrounding SAD (sum of absolute differences) matrix $\mathbf{M}_V$ as

$$\mathbf{M}_V = \begin{pmatrix} S_{(h-1,v-1)} & S_{(h,v-1)} & S_{(h+1,v-1)} \\ S_{(h-1,v)} & S_{(h,v)} & S_{(h+1,v)} \\ S_{(h-1,v+1)} & S_{(h,v+1)} & S_{(h+1,v+1)} \end{pmatrix} \quad (1)$$

where h and v are V's horizontal and vertical components, $S_{(h,v)}$ denotes the SAD corresponding to the MV $V = (h,v)$. Secondly, compare $S_{(h,v)}$ with the others in $\mathbf{M}_V$, and if it is found the minimum, V is identified as local optimal.

It has to be noticed that because video compression is an information-reducing process, many fine detailed information (side-information), e.g., the pixel values before transformation and quantization, get lost after compression. In consequence, to the same MV V, the embedder (at the encoder) and the attacker (at the decoder) will calculate different matrices. For distinction, we denote by $\mathbf{M}_V^E$ and $\mathbf{M}_V^D$ the two matrices respectively. As illustrated in Figure 2,

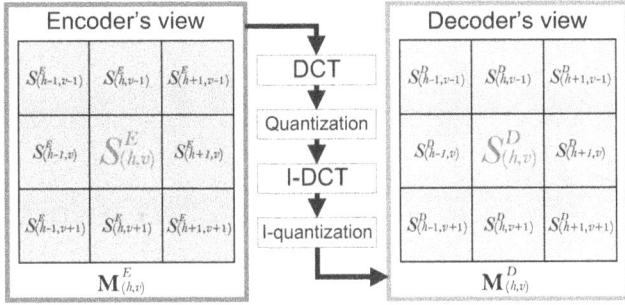

Figure 2: MV's surrounding SAD matrices at the encoder and at the decoder.

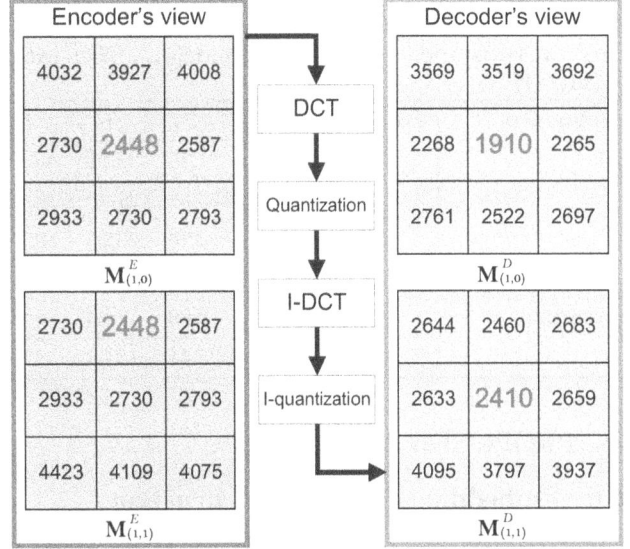

Figure 3: An example of adjacent local optimal MVs.

at the encoder, $\mathbf{M}_V^E$ is calculated based on the original MB $\mathbf{B}$ associated to V, but at the decoder, $\mathbf{M}_V^D$ can only be calculated based on $\mathbf{B}$'s reconstruction denoted as $\mathbf{B}_V^r$.

Anyway, related analysis in [5] has shown that although $\mathbf{M}_V^D$ is usually different from $\mathbf{M}_V^E$, provided that V is not modified during compression, it will still pass the local optimal test at the decoder with a great opportunity.

3.2 Opportunity to Preserve Local Optimality

The current best steganalytic feature, i.e., AoSO, is designed based on the assumption that "MV values directly obtained from the compressed video are locally optimal, which means data hiding on MVs will shift the local optimal MVs to non-optimal". As discussed in 3.1, the first part of this assumption is true. However, our study has revealed the fact that the modified MVs also have their chances to be local optimal, which contradicts with the second part. Hence, provided that the MVs can be modified in such a way that their local optimalities can be well preserved, the embedding changes may be made undetectable.

First, an example is given in Figure 3. With a customized H.264 codec [13], we compress and decompress a test sequence "Coastguard.yuv" (CIF, 352×288) at the bit-rate of 1 Mbit/s, and investigate into the encoding and decoding processes of a specific inter-MB $\mathbf{B}$. At the encoder, $\mathbf{B}$ is subjected to quarter-pixel ME and the searched MV turns out to be $(1,0)$. Then its surrounding SAD matrix is calculated as $\mathbf{M}_{(1,0)}^E$. At the decoder, $\mathbf{B}$ is reconstructed as $\mathbf{B}_{(1,0)}^r$, and the corresponding SAD matrix is calculated as $\mathbf{M}_{(1,0)}^D$. Again, at the encoder, to the same MB $\mathbf{B}$, its MV is modified into $(1,1)$, then $(1,1)$'s surrounding SAD matrix is calculated as $\mathbf{M}_{(1,1)}^E$. At the decoder, $\mathbf{B}$ is reconstructed as $\mathbf{B}_{(1,1)}^r$, and the corresponding SAD matrix is calculated as $\mathbf{M}_{(1,1)}^D$. It can be seen from Figure 3 that both $(1,0)$ and $(1,1)$ can pass the local optimal test. In this sense, $(1,1)$ is called one of $(1,0)$'s 1-distance optimal neighbor(s) defined as Definition 1.

Definition 1. i-distance optimal neighbor. Let $V = (h,v)$ be the MV of an inter-MB, $V' = (h',v')$ is called one of V's i-distance optimal neighbor(s) if

1. $S_{V'}^D$ is the minimum element in $\mathbf{M}_{V'}^D$.

2. $\| (h-h') + (v-v') \| = i$.

Although the fact that some MV has optimal neighbor(s) appears to be surprising, it is explicable. At the encoder, $\mathbf{B}$ is allowed to be matched with those from its reference frame(s), and the block associated with the minimal SAD is chosen as $\mathbf{B}$'s prediction denoted as $\mathbf{P}_V^r$. Then, the residual block $\mathbf{D}_V = \mathbf{B} - \mathbf{P}_V^r$ is subjected to DCT transformation and quantization. Finally, the MV V and the quantized residual block $\mathbf{Q}_V$ are losslessly coded into bit stream. At the decoder, V is decoded and used to locate the predicted block $\mathbf{P}_V^r$, and $\mathbf{Q}_V$ is subjected to the inverse quantization and inverse DCT transformation to get $\mathbf{D}_V^r$. Then $\mathbf{B}$ can be reconstructed as $\mathbf{B}_V^r = \mathbf{P}_V^r + \mathbf{D}_V^r$. Assuming at the encoder V is modified into V' for data hiding. In consequence the block $\mathbf{P}_{V'}^r$ corresponding to V' should be chosen as $\mathbf{B}$'s prediction, and the residual block will be calculated as $\mathbf{D}_{V'} = \mathbf{B} - \mathbf{P}_{V'}^r$. Accordingly, at the decoder, $\mathbf{B}$ will be reconstructed as $\mathbf{B}_{V'}^r = \mathbf{P}_{V'}^r + \mathbf{D}_{V'}^r$. Note that, $\mathbf{M}_V^D$ is calculated based on $\mathbf{B}_V^r$ whereas $\mathbf{M}_{V'}^D$ based on $\mathbf{B}_{V'}^r$. Although, V' is not likely to pass the local optimal test at the encoder ($S_{V'}^E$ is almost always larger than S_V^E), the quantization error still make it possible for V' to pass the local optimal test at the decoder.

In our study, it is found that the compressed videos usually contain a considerable portion of MVs with optimal neighbor(s). To demonstrate this, we use a customized H.264 encoder [13] to compress CIF video sequences at common internet bit-rates (0.5 Mbit/s and 1 Mbit/s). For every inter-MB $\mathbf{B}$, after searching its MV $V = (h,v)$, the number of V's 1-distance optimal neighbor(s) is calculated. To achieve this, first, for every MV $(h'v') \in \{(h-1,v),(h+1,v),(h,v-1),(h,v+1)\}$, reconstruct the corresponding $\mathbf{B}_{(h'v')}^r$, then calculate $\mathbf{M}_{(h'v')}^D$ to see whether $S_{(h'v')}^D$ is the minimum. After compression, the proportions of MVs with different numbers of 1-distance optimal neighbor(s) are calculated and recorded in Table 1. It can be seen that regular internet videos usually contain large portions of MVs that can be modified with preserved local optimality, which is sufficient to support practical steganographic designing.

27

Table 1: Proportions of MVs with different numbers of 1-distance optimal neighbor(s). (Bit-rate (Mbit/s))

Sequence	Bit-rate	1	2	3	4
Bus.yuv	0.5	2.76	11.75	24.21	60.46
	1	12.89	23.52	21.46	38.15
Coastguard.yuv	0.5	3.26	12.18	23.25	60.93
	1	10.79	19.56	26.49	40.58
Foreman.yuv	0.5	6.49	19.89	19.20	52.06
	1	18.55	25.41	15.93	32.07

4. PROPOSED APPROACH

4.1 Embedding Channel Construction

Inspired by the ± 1 embedding applied to gray-scale pixel values [14], with N MVs, i.e., $\mathbf{V} = (V_1, \ldots, V_N)$, as the cover, a double-layered coding structure is used to control MV modifications. In the first layer, with every MV assigned an impact factor reflecting its ability in local optimality preservation, STC is used to minimize the overall embedding impact. In the second layer, by using WPC, additional message bits can be embedded without modifying any more MVs. The corresponding two embedding channels are constructed as follows.

4.1.1 The First Channel

The first channel $\mathbf{p} = (p_1, \ldots, p_N)$ is formed utilizing the binary parity check function

$$\mathcal{P}_1(V) = LSB(h + v), \qquad (2)$$

where $LSB(\cdot)$ is used to get the least significant bit of the given binary integer and $p_i = \mathcal{P}_1(V_i)$. With a given related payload α, $\mathbf{p}$ is used to embed an αN-bit message $\mathbf{m}_1$.

Assume the MV modifications are mutually independent and let each element $p_i \in \mathbf{p}$ be assigned a scalar γ_i expressing the contribution of making an embedding change to overall detectability, STC is used to minimize the overall embedding impact $D(\mathbf{p}, \mathbf{p}') = \sum_{i=1}^{N} \gamma_i [p_i \neq p_i']^1$, and its embedding and extraction can be formulated as

$$\text{Emb}_{stc}(\mathbf{p}, \Gamma, \mathbf{m}_1) = \arg \min_{\mathbf{p}' \in \mathcal{C}(\mathbf{m}_1)} D(\mathbf{p}, \mathbf{p}') = \tilde{\mathbf{p}}, \qquad (3)$$

$$\text{Ext}_{stc}(\tilde{\mathbf{p}}) = \tilde{\mathbf{p}} \mathbf{H}_{stc}^T = \mathbf{m}_1. \qquad (4)$$

Here, Γ denotes the distortion scalar vector, $\mathcal{C}(\mathbf{m}_1)$ is the coset corresponding to syndrome $\mathbf{m}_1$ and $\mathbf{H}_{stc} \in \{0,1\}^{\alpha N \times N}$ is the parity-check matrix of the used STC shared between the sender and the recipient. For more details of the STC, please refer to [8].

Note that, the core problem of distortion minimization lies in the definition of the distortion scale. In this paper, the distortion scale is assigned according to MV's ability to preserve its local optimality. Intuitively, to a specific MV, the more optimal neighbors it has, the more suitable it can be modified for embedding, hence the smaller distortion scale should be assigned to. Let V has k 1-distance optimal

---

¹The Iverson bracket $[I]$ is defined to be 1 if the logical expression I is true and 0 otherwise.

neighbor(s), i.e., $\{V^j\}_{j=1}^k$, its associated distortion scale is calculated as

$$\gamma = \begin{cases} (\frac{1}{k} \sum_{j=1}^{k} (S_{V^j}^D - S_V^D)^2)^{\frac{1}{2k}} & k > 0 \\ S_V^D & k = 0. \end{cases} \qquad (5)$$

4.1.2 The Second Channel

The second channel $\mathbf{q} = (q_1, \ldots, q_N)$ is formed utilizing the binary parity check function

$$\mathcal{P}_2(V) = LSB(\lfloor (h + v)/2 \rfloor), \qquad (6)$$

where $q_i = \mathcal{P}_2(V_i)$. Assuming after the first-layer embedding, r bits in $\mathbf{p}$ have to be flipped, $\mathbf{q}$ is used to embed an additional r-bit message $\mathbf{m}_2$ without modifying any more MVs.

This is achieved by the usage of the WPC which is designed for embedding using the cover with some defective cells that cannot be changed [12]. According to the parity check function (2), if p_i has to be flipped, either h_i or v_i is free to be added or subtracted by one, and the choice of addition or subtraction makes q_i a "dry" spot to which modification is forbidden. In this sense, $\mathbf{q}$ is treated as a wet paper channel with r "dry" spots, and the embedding and extraction upon it can be formulated as

$$\text{Emb}_{wpc}(\mathbf{q}, \mathbf{I}, \mathbf{m}_2) = \tilde{\mathbf{q}}, \qquad (7)$$

$$\text{Ext}_{wpc}(\tilde{\mathbf{q}}) = \tilde{\mathbf{q}} \mathbf{H}_{wpc}^T = \mathbf{m}_2. \qquad (8)$$

Here, $\mathbf{I}$ denotes the indices of dry spots, $\mathbf{H}_{wpc} \in \{0,1\}^{r \times N}$ is a pseudo-random binary matrix shared between the sender and the recipient. For more details of the WPC, please refer to [12].

4.2 Practical Implementation

In practice, almost all available video codecs can be customized to implement the proposed approach. Typically, the secret message bits are embedded in a frame-by-frame manner. Without loss of generality, the processes of embedding and extraction with one single frame are described as follows.

4.2.1 Data Embedding

The entire embedding procedure combined with inter-frame coding is illustrated as in Figure 4. First, partition the raw frame into MBs and fed them into the customized encoder for the first round ME. For each inter-MB, search its MV, and calculate its associated distortion scale according to (5). After that, the MV vector $\mathbf{V} = (V_1, \ldots, V_N)$, and the associated distortion scale vector $\Gamma = (\gamma_1, \ldots, \gamma_N)$ are obtained. Based on $\mathbf{V}$, construct the first and second binary channels as $\mathbf{p} = (p_1, \ldots, p_N)$ and $\mathbf{q} = (q_1, \ldots, q_N)$ according to (2) and (6).

Secondly, carry out a two-step coding process. In the first step, use a constructed STC to embed an αN-bit message $\mathbf{m}_1$ by turning $\mathbf{p}$ into $\tilde{\mathbf{p}}$ as $\text{Emb}_{stc}(\mathbf{p}, \Gamma, \mathbf{m}_1) = \tilde{\mathbf{p}}$. In the second step, compare $\tilde{\mathbf{p}}$ and $\mathbf{p}$, record the indices of different bits as $\mathbf{I} = (I_1, \ldots, I_r)$, and use a constructed WPC to embed an additional r-bit message $\mathbf{m}_2$ by turning $\mathbf{q}$ into $\tilde{\mathbf{q}}$ as $\text{Emb}_{wpc}(\mathbf{q}, \mathbf{I}, \mathbf{m}_2) = \tilde{\mathbf{q}}$.

Thirdly, fed the raw frame into the encoder again. For $i = 1$ to N, subject the ith inter-MB to a perturbed ME process controlled by $\tilde{p}_i$ and $\tilde{q}_i$. Specifically, if $\tilde{p}_i = p_i$, its

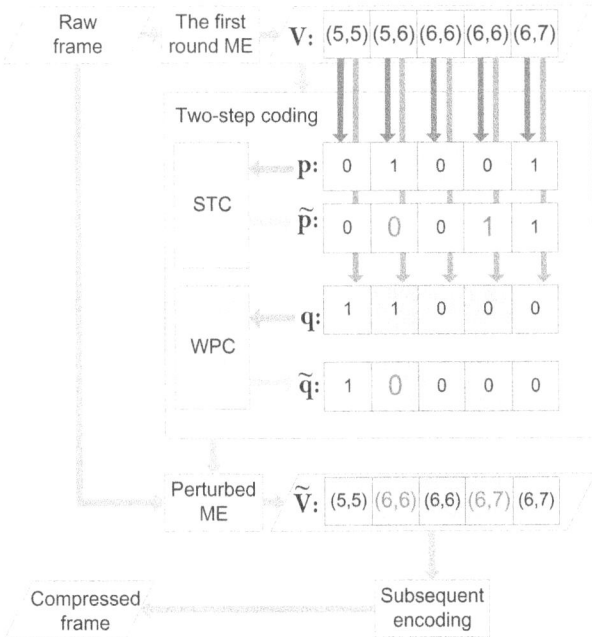

Figure 4: Embedding with one single frame.

MV $\tilde{V}_i$ is left unchanged; otherwise, a new MV $\tilde{V}_i$ is searched for replacement as

$$\tilde{V}_i = \begin{cases} \arg \min\limits_{V' \in (\Omega_i \cap \Psi_i)} S_{V'}^D & \Omega_i \cap \Psi_i \neq \varnothing \\ \arg \min\limits_{V' \in \Psi_i} S_{V'}^D & \Omega_i \cap \Psi_i = \varnothing. \end{cases} \quad (9)$$

Here, Ω_i denotes the set of all V_i's 1-distance optimal neighbor(s) and Ψ_i denotes the set of all MVs satisfying $\mathcal{P}_1(V) = \tilde{p}_i$ and $\mathcal{P}_2(V) = \tilde{q}_i$. It must be explained that, in the case that $\Omega_i \cap \Psi_i = \varnothing$, the modified MV $\tilde{V}_i$ is not likely to be local optimal. But fortunately this rarely occurs in practice so that the impact on steganographic security is ignored for now.

Finally, the compressed frame is obtained with N MVs carrying $\alpha N + r$ secret message bits.

4.2.2 Data Extraction

Compared to the embedding process, the message extraction is much easier. With the received frame, the recipient uses a common decoder to obtain all the N MV values, and reconstructs the binary channel $\tilde{p}$ and $\tilde{q}$, then extracts the secret message as $\mathbf{m}_1 = \tilde{p}\mathbf{H}_{stc}^T$ and $\mathbf{m}_2 = \tilde{q}\mathbf{H}_{wpc}^T$.

5. EVALUATION

5.1 Experimental Setup

In our experiments, a well-known H.264/AVC codec named x264 [13] is customized to implement our proposed embedding scheme, and the basic profile is used. Besides, Aly's [15] and Yao's methods [16] are also implemented for performance comparisons.

The test database is comprised of 30 standard 4:2:0 YUV sequences in the CIF, and the frame numbers vary from 90 to 376 at a frame rate of 30 frame/second. Two regular bit-rates of the compressed CIF videos, i.e., 0.5 Mbit/s and 1

Table 2: Coding performance. (AP(Average Payload (kbit/s), BR(achieved Bit-Rate(kbit/s))), PSNR (dB))

Sequence	Method	AP	BR	PSNR
Bus.yuv	STD	N/A	488.50	29.53
	Ours	4.67	486.19	29.21
	Aly's	4.43	491.14	28.98
	Yao's	4.50	489.67	29.06
	STD	N/A	983.55	33.00
	Ours	2.71	983.74	32.98
	Aly's	2.44	985.19	32.74
	Yao's	2.52	984.85	32.81
Coastguard.yuv	STD	N/A	482.30	31.17
	Ours	4.59	481.29	31.04
	Aly's	4.32	484.14	30.83
	Yao's	4.41	483.56	30.91
	STD	N/A	955.94	33.87
	Ours	2.96	956.66	33.83
	Aly's	2.68	959.13	33.66
	Yao's	2.74	958.24	33.72
Foreman.yuv	STD	N/A	517.37	35.94
	Ours	4.55	515.27	35.77
	Aly's	4.23	523.47	35.45
	Yao's	4.34	519.41	36.59
	STD	N/A	1070.38	38.87
	Ours	2.84	1071.98	38.86
	Aly's	2.56	1080.70	38.65
	Yao's	2.71	1077.59	38.74

Mbit/s are considered with the achieved relative payloads around 0.5 and 0.25 respectively.

5.2 Coding Efficiency

As a major advantage, MV-based steganographic methods do not affect the coding efficiency (PSNR and bit-rate) much. The mechanism of motion estimation and compensation ensures that once a MV is modified, the caused error will be handled automatically. Example coding results of three sequences, i.e., "Bus.yuv", "Coastguard.yuv" and "Foreman.yuv", are recorded in Table 2 where STD refers to standard compression without embedding. It is observed that for all embedding methods, both the video quality and the compression ratio are affected very slightly, and generally our proposed scheme outperforms its competitors for smaller embedding impacts.

5.3 Steganalysis

The steganalytic work consists of tests against our proposed, Aly's and Yao's steganographic schemes. For security evaluation, the recently proposed AoSO feature [5] is leveraged, which shows the best effectiveness in detecting MV-based schemes. The LibSVM toolbox [17] is employed for classification, and 2 kernels, i.e., the polynomial kernel and the Gaussian kernel, are used to mitigate the effect of randomness.

To compare with the results in [5], we use CMVR (corrupted MV ratio) to denote the embedding ratio, which represents the ratio of modified MVs, and all the steganographic encoders are tuned to achieve CMVRs around 0.2 at the bit-

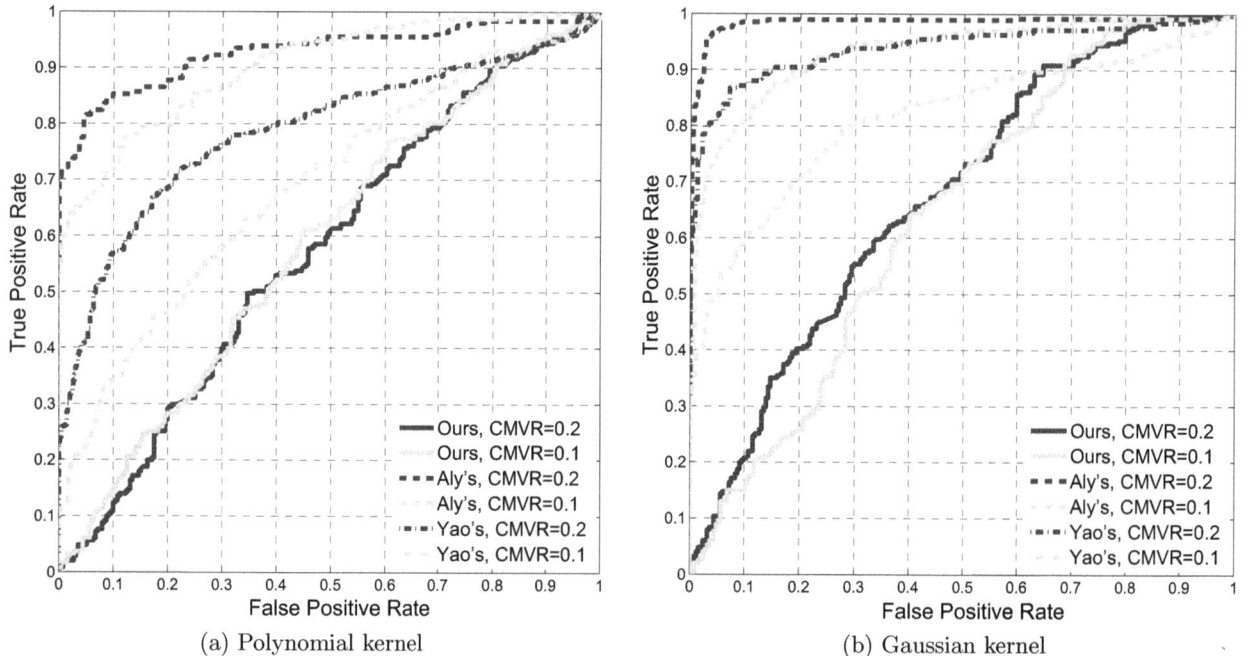

(a) Polynomial kernel   (b) Gaussian kernel

Figure 5: ROC curves of different tests.

Table 3: Anti-steganalysis Performance (%)

CMVR	Method	Pol. kernel		Gau. kernel	
		TN	TP	TN	TP
0.2	Ours	57.4	53.9	64.2	63.8
	Aly's	90.0	85.2	96.9	95.4
	Yao's	74.8	73.2	90.6	87.5
0.1	Ours	56.3	54.1	62.1	60.3
	Aly's	84.6	79.8	85.3	86.9
	Yao's	64.1	63.2	76.9	73.8

rate of 0.5 Mbit/s, and 0.1 at 1 Mbit/s. For example, to test our scheme with a CMVR of 0.2, first, all 30 sequences are compressed at 0.5 Mbit/s with and without embedding to generate the classes of stego videos and clean videos. Then 18 pairs of the compressed videos (stego and clean) are randomly selected for the training purpose, and the remaining 12 pairs are left for testing. As suggested by [5], the AoSO features are extracted out of every 12 frames. After that, the true negative (TN) rates, true positive (TP) rates are computed by counting the number of detections in the test sets, and corresponding results are recorded in Table 3. Besides, the receiver operating characteristic (ROC) curves using steganalyzers with the two kernels are depicted in Figure 5.

In comparisons with Aly's and Yao's schemes, the detection rates and the ROC curves indicate that our proposed method reduces the probability of detection significantly, which implies a higher level of steganographic security.

6. CONCLUSION AND FUTURE WORK

In this paper, a novel MV-based steganographic scheme is proposed. With respect to the current best steganalytic method, the probability of being detected is significantly re-duced by modifying MVs without destroying their local opti-malities. For the sake of low embedding impacts and a high embedding efficiency, optimized ME perturbations are con-trolled by a double-layered coding structure. Experimental results show that, satisfactory levels of steganographic se-curity and coding performance are achieved with adequate payloads.

As part of our future work, the genesis of the MV's local optimal neighbor(s) is to be further studied. Besides, the mechanism of ME perturbation makes our proposed scheme a very computationally intensive one. Therefore, measures to reduce the computational overhead are also to be ex-plored. What's more, more coding schemes, e.g., the multi-layer STC, are to be tested for performance enhancement.

7. ACKNOWLEDGMENTS

This work was supported by the NSFC under 61303259 and 61170281, the Strategic Priority Research Program of CAS under XDA06030600, and the Project of IIE, CAS, under Y4Z0031102 and Y3Z0071502.

8. REFERENCES

[1] Z. Xiao and Y. Xiao. Security and privacy in cloud computing. *IEEE Communications Surveys and Tutorials*, 15(2):843–859, 2013.

[2] B. Chen and G.W. Wornell. Quantization index modulation: A class of provably good methods for digital watermarking and information embedding. *IEEE Trans. Information Theory*, 47(4):1423–1443, 2001.

[3] Y. Cao, X. Zhao, and D. Feng. Video steganalysis exploiting motion vector reversion-based features. *IEEE Sig. Proc. Lett.*, 19(1):35–38, 2012.

[4] Y. Ren, L. Zhai, L. Wang, and T. Zhu. Video steganalysis based on subtractive probability of

optimal matching feature. In *Proc. ACM IH and MMSec'14*, pages 83–90, 2014.

[5] K. Wang, H. Zhao, and H. Wang. Video steganalysis against motion vector-based steganography by adding or subtracting one motion vector value. *IEEE Trans. Inf. Foren. Sec.*, 9(5):741–751, 2014.

[6] C. Xu, X. Ping, and T. Zhang. Steganography in compressed video stream. In *Proc. ICICIC'06*, pages 269–272, 2006.

[7] D. Fang and L. Chang. Data hiding for digital video with phase of motion vector. In *Proc. ISCAS'06*, pages 1422–1425, 2006.

[8] T. Filler, J. Judas, and J. Fridrich. Minimizing additive distortion in steganography using syndrome-trellis codes. *IEEE Trans. Inf. Foren. Sec.*, 6(3):920–935, 2011.

[9] F. Pan, L. Xiang, X. Yang, and Y. Guo. Video steganography using motion vector and linear block codes. In *Proc. ICSESS'10*, pages 592–595, 2010.

[10] B. Hao, L. Zhao, and W. Zhong. A novel steganography algorithm based on motion vector and matrix encoding. In *Proc. ICCSN'11*, pages 406–409, 2011.

[11] Y. Cao, X. Zhao, D. Feng, and R. Sheng. Video steganography with perturbed motion estimation. In *Proc. IH'11*, volume 6958 of LNCS, pages 193–207, 2011.

[12] J. Fridrich, M. Goljan, P. Lisoněk, and D. Soukal. Writing on wet paper. *IEEE Trans. Sig. Proc.*, 53(10):3923–3935, 2005.

[13] VideoLAN. x264.

[14] X. Zhang, W. Zhang, and S. Wang. Efficient double-layered steganographic embedding. *Electron. Lett.*, 43(8):482–483, 2007.

[15] H. Aly. Data hiding in motion vectors of compressed video based on their associated prediction error. *IEEE Trans. Inf. Foren. Sec.*, 6(1):14–18, 2011.

[16] Y. Yao, W. Zhang, N. Yu, and X. Zhao. Defining embedding distortion for motion vector-based video steganography. *Multimedia Tools and Applications*, Article in Press, 2014.

[17] C. Chang and C. Lin. Libsvm – a library for support vector machines.

Effect of Imprecise Knowledge of the Selection Channel on Steganalysis

Vahid Sedighi
Binghamton University
Department of ECE
Binghamton, NY 13902-6000
vsedighi1@binghamton.edu

Jessica Fridrich
Binghamton University
Department of ECE
Binghamton, NY 13902-6000
fridrich@binghamton.edu

ABSTRACT

It has recently been shown that steganalysis of content-adaptive steganography can be improved when the Warden incorporates in her detector the knowledge of the selection channel – the probabilities with which the individual cover elements were modified during embedding. Such attacks implicitly assume that the Warden knows at least approximately the payload size. In this paper, we study the loss of detection accuracy when the Warden uses a selection channel that was imprecisely determined either due to lack of information or the stego changes themselves. The loss is investigated for two types of qualitatively different detectors – binary classifiers equipped with selection-channel-aware rich models and optimal detectors derived using the theory of hypothesis testing from a cover model. Two different embedding paradigms are addressed – steganography based on minimizing distortion and embedding that minimizes the detectability of an optimal detector within a chosen cover model. Remarkably, the experimental and theoretical evidence are qualitatively in agreement across different embedding methods, and both point out that inaccuracies in the selection channel do not have a strong effect on steganalysis detection errors. It pays off to use imprecise selection channel rather than none. Our findings validate the use of selection-channel-aware detectors in practice.

Categories and Subject Descriptors

I.4.9 [**Computing Methodologies**]: Image Processing and Computer Vision—*Applications*

General Terms

Security, Algorithms, Theory

Keywords

Steganography, steganalysis, adaptive, selection channel

IH&MMSec'15, June 17–19, 2015, Portland, Oregon, USA.
Copyright ⓒ 2015 ACM 978-1-4503-3587-4/15/06 ...$15.00.
http://dx.doi.org/10.1145/2756601.2756621.

1. INTRODUCTION

Steganography in digital images has seen great advances in the recent years. The main paradigm shift occurred in 2010 with the introduction of near-optimal codes [12] that allowed the sender to assign "costs" of changing individual image elements (e.g., pixels) and then embed the secret message while minimizing the sum of costs of all modified pixels. By assigning large costs to pixels in smooth regions and low costs in highly textured content, the embedding is forced to execute the modifications where they would be presumably harder to detect. The first method based on this framework was HUGO [36]. Soon, many other content-adaptive schemes with increasingly improved security operating in both the spatial [22, 25, 33, 32] and JPEG domain [25, 19] appeared. Recently, steganalysts began investigating the possibility of using an approximate knowledge of the embedding change probabilities to better detect adaptive embedding. Indeed, since the pixel costs are driven by content, they can be usually accurately estimated from the stego image because the embedding changes themselves are rather subtle.

The first fundamental insight was given by Schöttle et al. [39] who showed on a simple example that it is advantageous for the sender to deviate from her optimal embedding strategy in exchange for a mismatched detector of the Warden. Framing the interaction between the sender and the Warden within the game theory, the authors showed that the Nash equilibrium, attained in mixed strategies, was an overall better choice for the sender than minimizing the KL divergence between cover and stego objects. The same authors showed in [40] that it is possible to use the knowledge of the embedding change probabilities in naive LSB replacement to improve the weighted-stego detector [27]. Experimental evidence was also presented that embedding schemes whose selection channel is more sensitive to the embedding changes themselves are harder to attack than schemes with a more robust selection channel.

In [8], it was shown that the security of S-UNIWARD [23] was compromised due to a faulty selection channel in which pixels with high and low embedding change probabilities were tightly interleaved. The problem was tied to an improperly selected parameter whose role was to merely stabilize the numerical computation, and it disappeared after adjusting this parameter to produce a selection channel free of artifacts [25].

The first general-purpose attack on content-adaptive steganography appeared in [43] but was, for some reason, presented as an attack specific to WOW [22]. The authors proposed to form the 4D co-occurrences of quantized noise residuals in the Spatial Rich Model [15] (SRM) only from a fraction of pixels with the lowest costs. This attack, which was later nicknamed "thresholded SRM" (tSRM) in [9] was further improved by forming the co-occurrences from all pixels but letting each pixel contribute to a specific co-occurrence bin only with the maximum of the four probabilities corresponding to pixels whose residuals point to the specific co-occurrence bin (the so-called maxSRM [9]).

All steganalysis attacks that use the selection channel inherently assume that the Warden is able to estimate the embedding change probabilities, which usually strongly depend on the payload size. Estimating the payload size, however, is rather difficult especially for modern embedding schemes whose detection requires high-dimensional rich media models, which substantially complicates the payload estimator construction in practice (e.g., the search for support vector regressor hyperparameters [37]). In fact, it seems hard to substantially improve upon the trivial estimator that always outputs the mean payload [28].

It is thus important to study the effect of payload mismatch on the accuracy of detection when selection-channel-aware detectors are used. The above cited prior art [43, 9] already contains a limited experimental investigation of this issue. In particular, classifiers equipped with the maxSRM feature set appear to lose less detection power due to payload mismatch than the tSRM features.

In this paper, we work with two qualitatively different steganography detectors – classifiers built using machine learning and tests designed in an optimal manner from a cover model. We do so for the widely popular embedding by minimizing distortion and the newly emerged model-based steganography minimizing the power of the most powerful detector within a chosen cover model [41]. Interestingly, both detectors seem to point to the same evidence. First, the loss of detection power due to imprecise knowledge of the selection channel is rather small – it still pays off to use selection-channel-aware detector even with an incorrect payload. Second, the misjudged payload is much less of an issue for detection of the model-based steganography than for minimal-distortion steganography. Finally, the inaccuracy due to estimating the embedding change probabilities from the stego image rather than the cover has a negligible effect for the tested stego schemes.

In the next section, two different steganography detectors that utilize the selection channel are reviewed. Then, in Section 3 we introduce four types of Warden to better show the effect of imprecision in the selection channel on detection accuracy. The paper continues in Section 4, where we describe four steganographic schemes used in our experiments. In Section 5, we explain the setup of our experiments and how the loss (gain) of the detection power will be measured and the results reported. All experiments and their interpretation appear in Section 6. A summary of the paper is given in Section 7.

2. STEGANALYSIS WITH THE KNOWLEDGE OF SELECTION CHANNEL

Currently, there exist two major trends in steganalysis of digital images – detectors derived in some sense as optimal using the theory of statistical hypothesis testing based on a cover model [11, 6, 7, 46, 4, 3, 44] and detectors constructed as classifiers trained on examples of cover and stego images represented in a feature space [10, 34, 42, 48, 1, 18, 15, 2, 29, 24, 21, 17]. The former approach is usually rather successful when the embedding disturbs some statistics of images that can be well described using a model. This is the case of Jsteg, OutGuess [38], and F5 [45], as these algorithms introduce strong artifacts into the first-order statistics of DCT coefficients, and basically all algorithms that use LSB replacement [6, 47, 11, 44, 5]. The latter approach to detection based on trained classifiers is more successful in detecting modern steganographic algorithms that seem to better preserve the cover statistics. To detect such algorithms, one currently needs to form features as higher-order statistics of noise residuals extracted using a diverse bank of pixel predictors, the so-called rich media models [18, 15, 29, 2, 24, 21, 17].

Both types of detectors have been previously adapted for detection of content-adaptive embedding to utilize the prior knowledge of the embedding change probabilities. Since these detection paradigms will be used in this paper, below we explain how this is done. The exposition is kept short while referring the reader to the corresponding publications for more details.

2.1 Empirical detectors

While incorporating priors in the form of the probabilistic selection channel within statistical hypothesis testing is usually straightforward (see Section 2.2), it is much less clear how to utilize this information for empirical detectors. The first general-purpose feature set proposed to improve the detection of content-adaptive steganography was the thresholded SRM [43]. The authors discovered that the embedding algorithm WOW is so "overly adaptive" that it paid off to compute the co-occurrence matrices of the SRM only from a fraction $t \leq 1$ of pixels with the smallest embedding cost. This way, the authors avoided using the embedding change probabilities but, in return, had to adjust the threshold t based on the payload size for each embedding method separately. A mismatch between the estimated (assumed) and the true payload size caused a non-negligible detection loss.

In [9], the authors described an idea similar to the tSRM called the maxSRM. Due to space limitations, we only provide a very brief outline of the main idea. Let us assume that z_{ij}, $i = 1, \ldots, N_1$, $j = 1, \ldots, N_2$, is a noise residual computed from a grayscale image $\mathbf{x} = (x_{ij})$, $x_{ij} \in \{0, \ldots, 255\}^{N_1 \times N_2}$, using one of the pixel predictors employed in the SRM, $\mathbf{z} = \mathbf{x} - \text{Pred}(\mathbf{x})$. For example, $\text{Pred}(x_{ij}) = (x_{i,j-1} + x_{i,j+1})/2$ estimates the pixel value from its two closest horizontal neighbors. The residual is subsequently quantized with a quantizer $Q_{T,q} : \mathbb{R} \to \mathcal{Q}_{T,q}$ with centroids $\mathcal{Q}_{T,q} = \{-Tq, -(T-1)q, \ldots, (T-1)q, Tq\}$, $r_{ij} = Q_{T,q}(z_{ij})$. In SRM, the features are formed as 4D co-occurrences

$$C_{d_0 d_1 d_2 d_3} = \sum_{i=1}^{N_1} \sum_{j=1}^{N_2} [r_{i,j+k} = d_k, \forall k \in \{0,1,2,3\}], \quad (1)$$

where $[P]$ is the Iverson bracket equal to 1 when the statement P is true and 0 when P is false. In maxSRM, the Iverson bracket in (1) is simply replaced with $\max\{\beta_{ij}, \beta_{i,j+1}, \beta_{i,j+2}, \beta_{i,j+3}\}$, where β_{ij} is the probability of changing pixel x_{ij} during embedding computed from $\mathbf{x}$. Note that in order to compute β_{ij}, one needs to know the size of the embedded payload. On the other hand, in maxSRM there is no need to search for any parameters (e.g., the threshold t) for each payload and embedding scheme. As long as the payload size is given, one can readily form the feature vector. In contrast to tSRM, the maxSRM's detection accuracy degrades more gracefully with a mismatch between the true embedded payload and the assumed payload. (This is apparent from the studies that appeared in [43, 9, 41].)

2.2 Model-based optimal detectors

The second type of detector is derived using the theory of statistical hypothesis testing based on a cover model. The detectors described in this section are derived for content-adaptive LSB matching, which is the prevailing paradigm for spatial-domain steganography today. We start by describing the cover model, the embedding operation, and the ensuing stego image model, and finish with a closed-form expression for the deflection coefficient that describes the performance of the asymptotic likelihood ratio test.

During acquisition using an imaging sensor, pixel values become corrupted by noise, which is well modeled as a field of independent Gaussians with spatially-varying variance [26, 14, 20]. Even though the subsequent processing typically applied to images inside a digital camera, such as demosaicking, filtering, color correction, and anti-aliasing, make the noise component quite complicated by introducing dependencies among adjacent pixels, in order to derive the detector in a closed form, we adopt the following simplified multiparametric statistical model. Since the pixels' expectation can be estimated, e.g., using local pixel predictors or denoising, after subtracting the estimated expectation from the pixel value, the resulting noise residual will be modeled as a sequence of independent quantized realizations of Gaussian random variables with zero mean $X_n \sim \mathcal{N}(0, \sigma_n^2)$, $n = 1, \dots, N$, where $N = N_1 \times N_2$ is the total number of pixels. We note that, besides the acquisition noise, the variance σ_n^2 also contains the modeling error and will in general strongly depend on the local image content. Note that here we index the image pixels with a one-dimensional index n instead of ij as in the previous section since one can imagine the two-dimensional array (x_{ij}) to be unfolded, e.g., by columns. Due to the independence assumption, the exact ordering is unimportant in our study, and we will be switching between the representations back and forth hopefully without causing any misunderstanding on the reader's side.

Without loss of generality, we will assume that the quantization step is $\triangle = 1$. Assuming the fine quantization limit, $1 \ll \sigma_n$ for all n, the probability mass function (pmf) of X_n is given by $\mathcal{P}_{\sigma_n} = (p_{\sigma_n}(k))_{k \in \mathbb{Z}}$ with

$$p_{\sigma_n}(k) = \mathbb{P}(x_n = k) \propto (2\pi\sigma_n^2)^{-1/2} \exp\left(-k^2/(2\sigma_n^2)\right). \quad (2)$$

For simplicity, note that we assume that the pixel levels are unbounded. Also, the fine quantization assumption may cease to hold in (nearly) saturated image regions, such as overexposed light sources.

Virtually all steganographic algorithms in spatial domain use LSB matching to execute the actual embedding. Formally, given the cover $\mathbf{x} = (x_1, \dots, x_N)$, the stego object $\mathbf{y} = (y_1, \dots, y_N)$ is obtained from $\mathbf{x}$ using the following random process:

$$\mathbb{P}(y_n = x_n + 1) = \mathbb{P}(y_n = x_n - 1) = \beta_n, \quad (3)$$
$$\mathbb{P}(y_n = x_n) = 1 - 2\beta_n,$$

with $0 \leq \beta_n \leq 1/3$ being the so-called change rates. The stego object is thus a sequence of independent mixtures of quantized Gaussians $(Y_1, \dots, Y_N)$,

$$Y_n \sim \mathcal{Q}_{\sigma_n, \beta_n} = (q_{\sigma_n, \beta_n}(k))_{k \in \mathbb{Z}} \quad (4)$$

with

$$q_{\sigma_n, \beta_n}(k) = \mathbb{P}(Y_n = k) = (1 - 2\beta_n)p_{\sigma_n}(k) \\ + \beta_n p_{\sigma_n}(k+1) + \beta_n p_{\sigma_n}(k-1), \quad (5)$$

Assuming Alice uses optimal codes for embedding, she can communicate up to R nats per pixel

$$R(\boldsymbol{\beta}) = \frac{1}{N}\sum_{n=1}^{N} H(\beta_n), \quad (6)$$

where $H(x) = -2x \ln x - (1 - 2x)\ln(1 - 2x)$ is the ternary entropy function expressed in nats. To obtain the payload in bits per pixel (bpp), one needs to multiply R by $(\ln 2)^{-1}$.

2.2.1 The most powerful detector

Since the Warden will never have a perfect knowledge of the change rates β_n used by the sender, when building her detector she will use change rates $\boldsymbol{\gamma} = (\gamma_1, \dots, \gamma_N)$ that might not coincide with $\boldsymbol{\beta} = (\beta_1, \dots, \beta_N)$. Assuming that both Alice and the Warden use the same cover model and know the noise variances σ_n^2, for example by estimating them from the given image (see Section 5.2 for more details), the Warden faces the following simple hypothesis test for all n:

$$\begin{aligned} \mathcal{H}_0: \quad & x_n \sim \mathcal{P}_{\sigma_n} \\ \mathcal{H}_1: \quad & x_n \sim \mathcal{Q}_{\sigma_n, \gamma_n}. \end{aligned} \quad (7)$$

From the Neyman–Pearson Lemma [31], the most powerful test $\delta : \mathbb{Z}^N \to \{\mathcal{H}_0, \mathcal{H}_1\}$ that maximizes the detection power $\pi = \mathbb{P}(\delta(\mathbf{x}) = \mathcal{H}_1 | \mathcal{H}_1)$ for a prescribed false-alarm probability $\alpha = \mathbb{P}(\delta(\mathbf{x}) = \mathcal{H}_1 | \mathcal{H}_0)$ is the Likelihood Ratio Test (LRT), which can be expressed using the statistical independence of pixels as

$$\Lambda(\mathbf{x}, \boldsymbol{\sigma}) = \sum_{n=1}^{N} \Lambda_n = \sum_{n=1}^{N} \log\left(\frac{q_{\sigma_n, \gamma_n}(x_n)}{p_{\sigma_n}(x_n)}\right) \underset{\mathcal{H}_0}{\overset{\mathcal{H}_1}{\gtrless}} \tau. \quad (8)$$

Under the additional assumptions of a large number of pixels ($N \to \infty$), the Lindeberg's version of the Central Limit Theorem implies that[1]

$$\begin{aligned} \Lambda^\star(\mathbf{x}, \boldsymbol{\sigma}) &= \frac{\sum_{n=1}^{N} \Lambda_n - E_{\mathcal{H}_0}[\Lambda_n]}{\sqrt{\sum_{n=1}^{N} Var_{\mathcal{H}_0}[\Lambda_n]}} \\ &\rightsquigarrow \begin{cases} \mathcal{N}(0, 1) & \text{under } \mathcal{H}_0 \\ \mathcal{N}(\varrho, 1) & \text{under } \mathcal{H}_1 \end{cases}, \end{aligned} \quad (9)$$

where $\rightsquigarrow$ denotes the convergence in distribution and

$$\varrho = \frac{\sum_{n=1}^{N} I_n \beta_n \gamma_n}{\sqrt{\sum_{n=1}^{N} I_n \gamma_n^2}} \quad (10)$$

---

[1]See, e.g., the ternary case in [41] for the derivation, which uses the additional assumption of small payload, $\beta_n \ll 1$, which is not necessary to obtain the result but simplifies the derivation.

is the deflection coefficient, which completely characterizes the statistical detectability. In (10), we used $I_n = 2 \cdot \sigma_n^{-4}$ for the Fisher information of LSBM in $\mathcal{N}(0, \sigma_n^2)$ w.r.t. the change rate β_n (see [41] for more details).

Because the distribution of $\Lambda^\star(\mathbf{x}, \boldsymbol{\sigma})$ under $\mathcal{H}_0$ does not depend on any unknown parameters, one can set the threshold τ in (8) to maximize the detection power for any prescribed false-alarm probability α even when the true values of β_n are not known to the Warden.

3. FOUR TYPES OF WARDEN

In this work, we consider four different types of Warden to investigate how the detection power decreases with increased ignorance of the Warden regarding the selection channel. Below, the Warden types are ordered by the amount of available information.

Empirical detectors will be constructed as binary classifiers trained on a set of cover-stego image pairs represented with the maxSRM feature vector [9] with the embedding change probabilities β_n determined based on the Warden type as described below. Besides explaining how the maxSRM feature vector is computed, the construction of the actual empirical detectors (classifiers) also requires specifying the training database. We postpone discussing the training to Section 6, where we describe the experiments and their results. Note that LR detectors do not need any training phase and the Warden makes a decision on each individual image.

The *omniscient Warden* knows exactly the actions of the sender executed during embedding. The empirical detector will be constructed by computing the features for the pair of training cover (stego) images, $\mathbf{x}$ ($\mathbf{y}$), using the probabilities β_{ij} computed from the cover image $\mathbf{x}$ assuming the true embedded payload size R. (To prevent any misunderstanding, we note that we need to assume that the payload is R even when computing the cover feature.) For detectors implemented as a LRT, we simply use the change rates $\gamma_n = \beta_n$. Note that the deflection coefficient for the omniscient Warden (10) simplifies to:

$$\varrho^\star = \frac{\sum_{n=1}^N I_n \beta_n^2}{\sqrt{\sum_{n=1}^N I_n \beta_n^2}} = \sqrt{\sum_{n=1}^N I_n \beta_n^2}. \quad (11)$$

This Warden is unrealistic because one cannot assume that the detector has access to the cover image. We include this Warden in our study because it has the highest detection power and serves as a useful upper bound on detection.

The *payload-informed Warden* knows the size of the embedded payload, R (6), but has no access to the cover image. The Warden thus computes the change rates $\hat{\beta}_{ij}$ from the available image whether it is a cover or stego image. For the cover image, the maxSRM feature vector will be the same as for the omniscient Warden (and $\gamma_n = \beta_n$ for the LRT) while for the stego image, the change rates will be slightly different due to the embedding changes themselves (γ_n will generally be different from but close to β_n for the LRT).

The *fixed-payload Warden* does not know the embedded payload and computes the change rates (β_{ij} or γ_n) from the available image assuming some fixed value of the embedded payload size $\tilde{R}$, which can generally be different from R.

Although the Warden could in principle estimate R using a quantitative detector, as already mentioned in the introduction, for modern steganographic schemes whose detection requires high-dimensional rich models, it is fairly difficult to substantially improve upon the trivial estimator that always guesses the medium payload [28].

The *indifferent Warden* assumes non-adaptive embedding. For the empirical detector, this means that the Warden uses the SRM features while the LRT uses $\gamma_n = \gamma$ for all n. Note that, indeed, the maxSRM features match (up to a multiplicative constant) those of the original SRM when we set $\beta_{ij} = \beta > 0$ for all i, j.

By comparing the omniscient and payload-informed Wardens, we can study the effect of the embedding changes themselves on the estimated selection channel. The fixed-payload Warden is a realistic detector when the detector does not have any information about the embedded payload. By comparing the first three Wardens with the indifferent Warden, we will be able to assess the gain in detection when the Warden uses a selection-channel-aware detector.

4. TESTED STEGO SCHEMES

We selected four content-adaptive steganographic techniques that appear to be the current state of the art – WOW [22], S-UNIWARD implemented with the stabilizing constant $\sigma = 1$ as described in [25], HILL [33], and the ternary Multivariate Gaussian (MVG) method originally described in [16] and further improved by replacing the variance estimator as described in Section 5 of [41]. For HILL, we used the KB high-pass filter and the 3×3 and 15×15 averaging filters for the two low-pass filters because this setting provided the best security as reported in [33]. In contrast to [41], for simplicity, in MVG we skipped the smoothing of the Fisher information field.

Notice that WOW, S-UNIWARD, and HILL are cost-based schemes in the sense that the sender first identifies the cost of changing each (nth) pixel, ρ_n, and embeds the payload while minimizing the distortion

$$D(\mathbf{x}, \mathbf{y}) = \sum_{n=1}^N \rho_n [x_n \neq y_n], \quad (12)$$

which leads to the following embedding change probabilities:

$$\beta_n = e^{-\lambda \rho_n} / (1 + 2 e^{-\lambda \rho_n}), \quad (13)$$

with $\lambda > 0$ determined to satisfy the payload constraint (6). The costs are typically obtained by changing a single pixel by ± 1 and quantifying the impact of this change on selected noise residuals.

In contrast, the MVG scheme first estimates the cover model, the variances σ_n^2, and then computes the change rates β_n that minimize the deflection coefficient under the omniscient Warden (11) and satisfy the payload constraint (6). This constrained optimization problem is easily solved using the method of Lagrange multipliers [16, 41]. In particular, the change rates β_n and the Lagrange multiplier $\lambda > 0$ must satisfy $N + 1$ non-linear equations:

$$\beta_n = \frac{1}{\lambda I_n} \ln \frac{1 - 2\beta_n}{\beta_n}, \; n = 1, \ldots, N, \quad (14)$$

$$R = \frac{1}{N} \sum_{n=1}^N H(\beta_n). \quad (15)$$

To embed the message, e.g., using syndrome-trellis codes, the sender converts the change rates to costs by inverting (13): $\rho_n = \ln(1/\beta_n - 2)$.

5. SETUP OF EXPERIMENTS

Our experiments will be conducted on the BOSSbase database ver. 1.01 [13] containing 10,000 512×512 8-bit grayscale images coming from eight different cameras. We will consider two types of sender – the Payload Limited Sender (PLS) and the Random Payload Sender (RPS). The PLS always embeds a message of a fixed relative length R while the payload size embedded by a RPS is chosen uniformly randomly from $[0.05, 0.5]$ bpp. Three payloads will be used for the true embedded payload R for the PLS and the payload assumed by the fixed-payload Warden, $\tilde{R}$: small (0.05 bpp), medium (0.2 bpp), and large (0.5 bpp).

5.1 Executing experiments with empirical detectors

All empirical detectors will be built as FLD ensemble classifiers [30] with maxSRM (or SRM) features computed as described in Section 3. The BOSSbase database embedded with a PLS with payload R or with a random payload uniformly randomly distributed on $[0.05, 0.5]$ will be denoted with $\mathcal{B}_R$ and $\mathcal{B}_U$, respectively. The classifiers will be trained either on $\mathcal{B}_R$ or on $\mathcal{B}_U$ as described in the text. To assess the detection performance, the set of cover–stego image pairs from $\mathcal{B}_R$ ($\mathcal{B}_U$) will be randomly split into two parts of the same size – one used for training the ensemble while the other for its testing. We note that the hyperparameters d_{sub} and the number of base learners L are determined only once by minimizing the out-of-bag error estimate of the testing error using bootstrapping on the entire database as described in [30]. This is repeated for ten random 5000/5000 database splits to obtain the statistical spread and assess the statistical significance of the results.

5.2 Executing experiments with the LRT

The asymptotic LRT does not need a training phase as it is capable of detecting steganography in each individual image once the variances σ_n^2 are known. In all our experiments, we estimate the variances σ_n^2 from the given image using the variance estimator described in Section 5 of [41]. We note that the specific choice of the variance estimator seems to play a negligible role. We repeated the experiments reported in Section 6 with six other variance estimators and obtained almost identical results.

For the jth image, $j = 1, \ldots, 10,000$, the detection performance is completely described by the deflection coefficient (10) or the ROC curve

$$\pi^{(j)}(\alpha) = Q(Q^{-1}(\alpha) - \varrho^{(j)}), \qquad (16)$$

where $Q(x)$ is the complementary cumulative distribution function (the tail probability) of the standard normal random variable $\mathcal{N}(0, 1)$. The deflection coefficient $\varrho^{(j)}$ is obtained from (10), with the Fisher information I_n computed from the jth image and γ_n computed based on the type of the Warden. To obtain the overall performance of this detector on the chosen image source and assess the statistical significance of the results, we compute the average power for

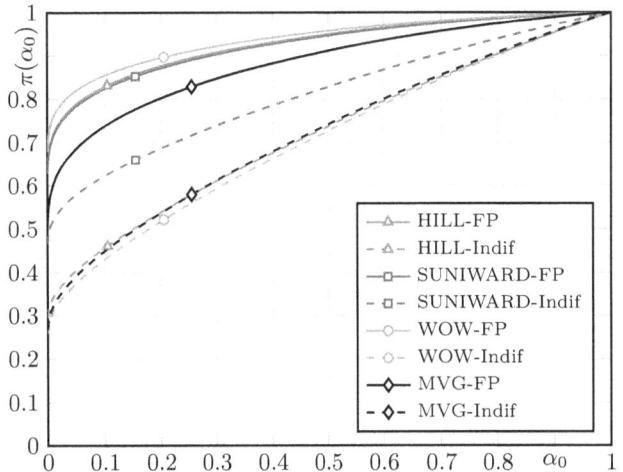

Figure 1: Examples of ROC curves for the LR detector for the fixed-payload Warden ($\alpha = 0.2$ bpp) and the indifferent Warden for different embedding schemes and the RPS.

each value[2] of the false alarm α for ten randomly selected subsets of 5000 images:

$$\overline{\pi}(\alpha) = \frac{1}{5000} \sum_{j=1}^{5000} \pi^{(j)}(\alpha). \qquad (17)$$

This quantity indeed correctly describes the expected value of the detector power for a fixed false alarm if the LRT was applied to images from the cover and stego sources. Examples of ROC curves for two types of warden and across four stego schemes for the RPS are shown in Figure 1. The asymmetrical shape is due to the large number of "easy to steganalyze" images in BOSSbase with very large deflection coefficients, such as images that are out of focus or have little content.

5.3 Evaluating detection loss/gain

In order to assess the change in the detection accuracy using a single scalar rather than an entire ROC curve, we will use the minimal total detection error under equal priors, which can be expressed as $P_{\mathrm{E}} = \min_\alpha \frac{1}{2}(1 - \overline{\pi}(\alpha) + \alpha)$ for the LR detector. For the empirical detectors, we obtain the value of P_{E} on the testing set from the ensemble. As explained above, the performance of both the empirical and LR detectors will be reported using the mean value and standard deviation of P_{E} over ten random database splits.

6. RESULTS

In practice, the Warden either knows the size of the embedded payload or she does not. The detection can obviously be more accurate when the payload size is available as the empirical Warden can form the training stego images and extract the maxSRM features with the true payload size. Likewise, the LRT can use the change rates extracted from the cover / stego image. In this case, it only makes sense to

---

[2]The false alarm α was sampled with a fixed step size of 5×10^{-4} on $[0, 1]$.

investigate the impact of computing the change rates from the stego image instead of the cover image.

6.1 Experiments with the PLS

In our first batch of experiments with the PLS, we thus only inspect the detection loss of the omniscient Warden vs. the payload-informed Warden. We will also study the gain of the payload-informed Warden vs. the indifferent Warden to see the advantage of using the selection-channel-aware detector.

The empirical Warden always trains her classifier on the set of cover/stego images $(\mathcal{B}_0, \mathcal{B}_R)$ with the maxSRM features computed based on the type of the Warden as described in Section 3. In Figure 2, we contrast the detection accuracy loss for the empirical detectors and the LRTs for the PLS with small, medium, and large payloads. The figure clearly shows that the impact of computing the change rates from the stego image rather than the cover image is negligible. For the empirical detector (left), the loss of the detection accuracy between the payload-informed and omniscient wardens is not statistically significant for either tested stego method. Figure 3 depicts the gain of the payload-informed Warden over the indifferent Warden for both types of detector. The gain is quite substantial and almost three times larger for the LR detector than for the empirical one. Given how differently both detectors are built, one can hardly expect even an approximate quantitative match between them. However, notice that the *relative* comparison of embedding schemes w.r.t. each other is approximately preserved in both figures.

6.2 Experiments with the RPS

We now turn our attention to the more interesting case of a Warden who does not know the payload size. Here, we will only consider the RPS. The problem of building a detector when the embedded payload is unknown has been investigated in [35], where the author provided experimental evidence that for the best robustness w.r.t. the payload size, the steganalyst should train on a uniform mixture of payloads.

Empirical detectors will be built as binary classifiers trained on $(\mathcal{B}_0, \mathcal{B}_U)$ with maxSRM features computed based on the Warden type. Since we already know that the difference between the omniscient and payload-informed Wardens is negligible, we focus on comparing the payload-informed, fixed-payload, and indifferent Wardens. In the considered case of the RPS, the payload-informed Warden is fictional and can hardly occur in real life. It is included merely as an upper performance bound.

In Figure 4, we show the loss of detection accuracy between the payload-informed Warden and the Warden with payload fixed at the small, medium, and large payload. In accordance with [9], both types of detectors indicate that using the medium fixed payload (0.2 bpp) for estimating the selection channel causes the smallest overall loss of detection performance. Figure 5 shows the gain in detection power between the Warden that uses the knowledge of the selection channel and the indifferent Warden. In both graphs, the bars marked with 0.05, 0.2, and 0.5 correspond to the difference $\overline{P}_{\mathrm{E}}^{(\mathrm{Indif})} - \overline{P}_{\mathrm{E}}^{(\mathrm{FP})}$ for the Warden who estimates the selection channel with payload size fixed to small, medium, and large, while the column marked with TRUE shows $\overline{P}_{\mathrm{E}}^{(\mathrm{Indif})} - \overline{P}_{\mathrm{E}}^{(\mathrm{PI})}$, which is maximal gain one could ob-

tain if the Warden always correctly guessed the true payload size. By comparing the loss in Figure 4 with the gain in Figure 5 for the fixed-payload Warden, it is clear that it is better to use an imprecise selection channel rather than none.

Comparing the detection loss in Figures 2 and 4 across stego methods, we can conclude that the loss of detection power due to mismatched payload is far smaller for the MVG steganography than for the three cost-based schemes, and this is true for both the empirical and LR detectors. We explain this observation for the LRT in the appendix by analyzing the sensitivity of the deflection coefficient w.r.t. the payload size (parameter λ) for the MVG.

Surprisingly, despite the fact that the empirical and LR detectors are built very differently, the results are qualitatively consistent in terms of relative comparison of losses and gains across the stego methods. Finally, and with a great caution, we note that if it is at all meaningful to relate these two detectors, it seems that the way the knowledge of the selection channel is incorporated in the empirical detector is highly suboptimal as the LR seems to benefit from the awareness of the selection channel much more.

7. CONCLUSION

Recently, it has been shown that the detection of content-adaptive steganography can be improved by incorporating in the detector the knowledge of the actions of the sender, which are in turn determined by the content itself. Because steganographic changes themselves are almost always subtle, the Warden can estimate the embedding change probabilities rather accurately as long as the size of the embedded payload is approximately known. Any difference between the assumed and embedded payload size will inevitably lead to a loss of detection power. As discovered in this paper, this loss appears to be rather small and it is advantageous for the Warden to use even imprecisely determined embedding change probabilities than not use them at all.

We establish this for four modern spatial-domain steganographic schemes for classifiers built using machine learning and for likelihood ratio detectors designed in an optimal manner from a cover model. Since both detectors are built from entirely different principles, one cannot expect a quantitative match between them. Nevertheless, both detectors exhibit qualitatively the same behavior and point to the same evidence: 1) the loss of detector power due to imprecise knowledge of the selection channel is rather small, 2) the misjudged payload size is much less of an issue for detection of model-based steganography than for minimal-distortion steganography, 3) the inaccuracy due to estimating the embedding change probabilities from the stego image rather than the cover has a completely negligible effect.

8. ACKNOWLEDGMENTS

The work on this paper was supported by Air Force Office of Scientific Research under the research grant number FA9950-12-1-0124. The U.S. Government is authorized to reproduce and distribute reprints for Governmental purposes notwithstanding any copyright notation there on. The views and conclusions contained herein are those of the authors and should not be interpreted as necessarily representing the official policies, either expressed or implied of AFOSR or the U.S. Government.

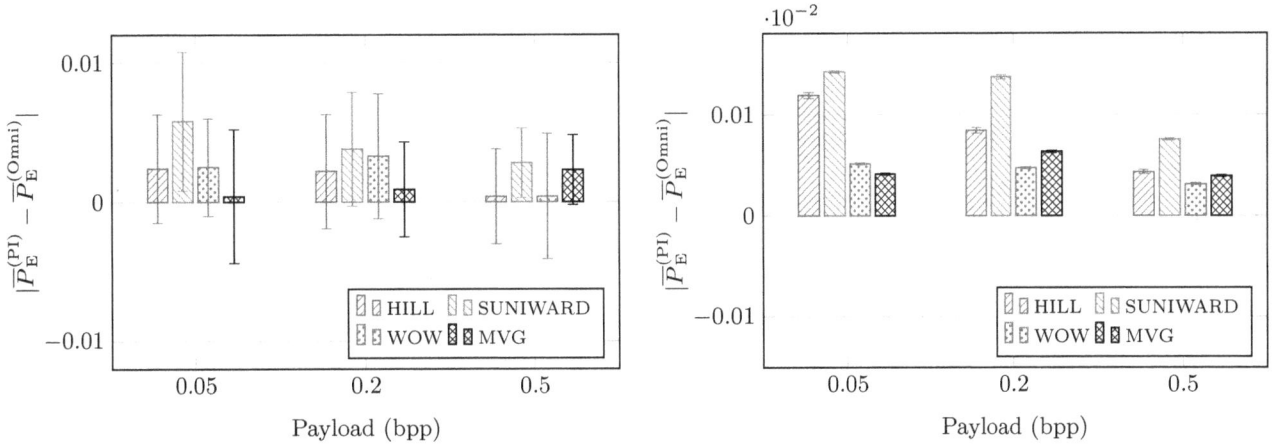

Figure 2: Difference in $\overline{P}_E$ when computing the change rates from the stego image (payload-informed Warden, PI) rather than the cover image (omniscient Warden) for four embedding methods and three payloads of the PLS. Left: empirical, Right: LR detector.

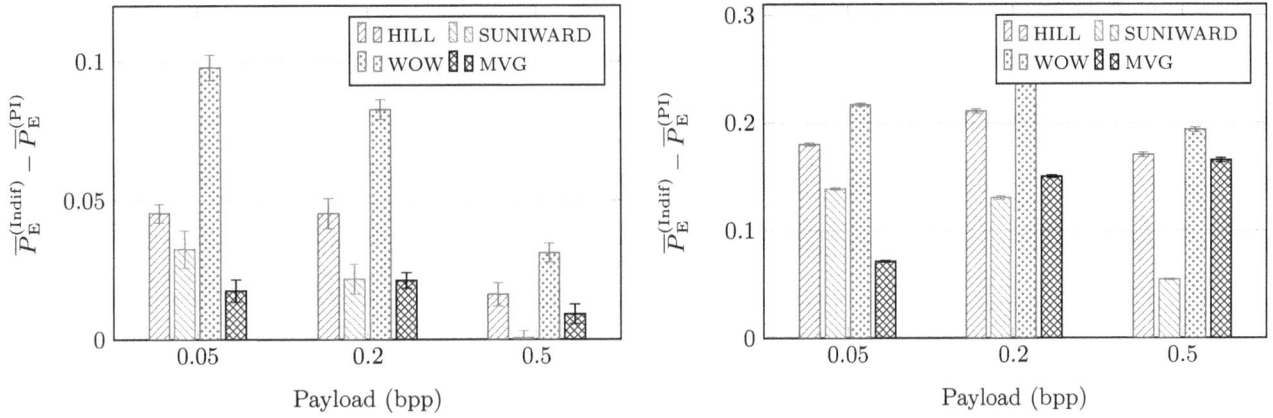

Figure 3: The gain in detection accuracy when using the knowledge of the selection channel (payload-informed Warden) vs. not using it (indifferent Warden) for three payloads of the PLS.

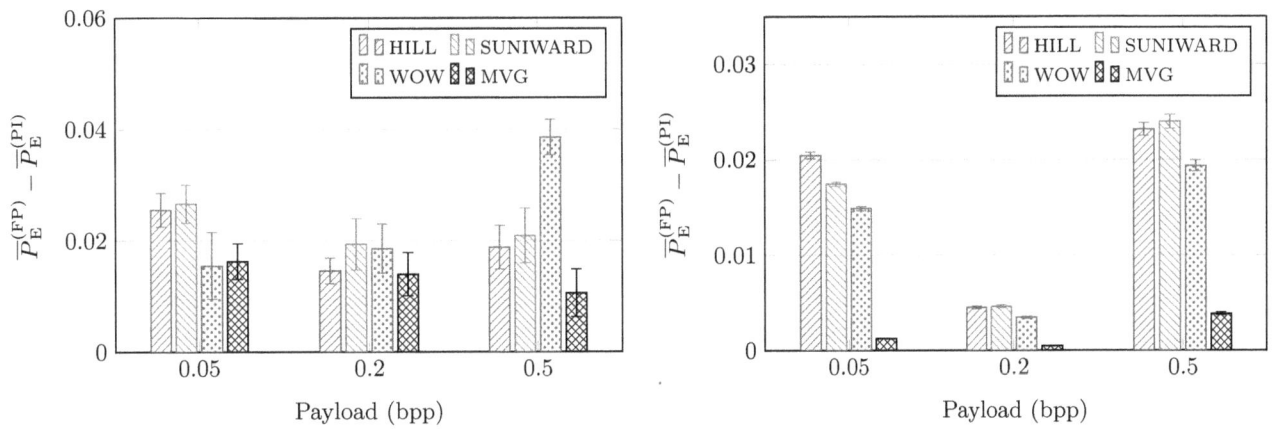

Figure 4: Loss of detection due to not knowing the payload size. Both graphs show the difference in $\overline{P}_E$ for the fixed-payload and payload-informed Wardens for the RPS. Left: empirical, Right: LR detector.

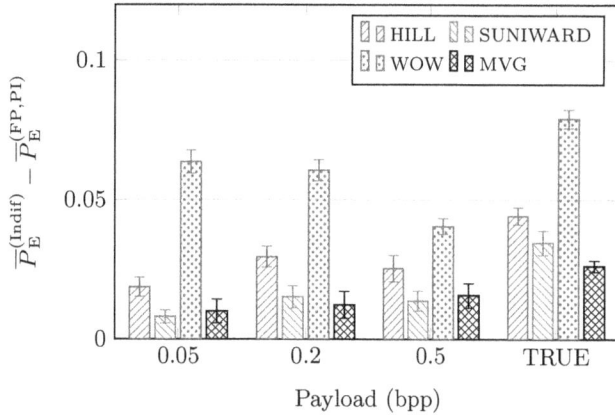

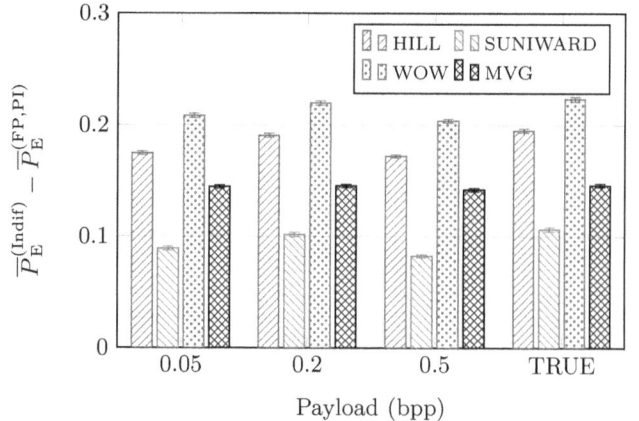

Figure 5: Gain in detection accuracy when using the knowledge of the selection channel w.r.t. the detector that does not. The three leftmost groups of bars show $\overline{P}_{\mathrm{E}}^{(\mathrm{Indif})} - \overline{P}_{\mathrm{E}}^{(\mathrm{FP})}$ when the FP Warden estimates the selection channel with a fixed small, medium, and large payload. The bars marked **TRUE** corresponds to $\overline{P}_{\mathrm{E}}^{(\mathrm{Indif})} - \overline{P}_{\mathrm{E}}^{(\mathrm{PI})}$ when the Warden always estimates the selection channel with the correct payload.

APPENDIX

Deflection coefficient as a function of payload for MVG stego

In MVG, the payload size is controlled by the Lagrange multiplier λ (see Eqs. (14)–(15)). In this appendix, we show that the deflection coefficient $\varrho^{\star}(\lambda)$ (10) for the MVG does not strongly depend on the payload size (on λ). In particular, we show that the ratio $r(\lambda, \lambda') = \varrho(\lambda')/\varrho^{\star}(\lambda)$ when the Warden uses change rates $\beta_n(\lambda')$ computed by solving (14) using the Lagrange multiplier λ' and for the omniscient Warden, $\varrho^{\star}$ (11), who uses $\beta_n(\lambda)$, $\lambda \neq \lambda'$:

$$r(\lambda, \lambda') = \frac{\sum_{n=1}^{N} I_n \beta_n(\lambda) \beta_n(\lambda')}{\sqrt{\sum_{n=1}^{N} I_n \beta_n^2(\lambda)} \sqrt{\sum_{n=1}^{N} I_n \beta_n^2(\lambda')}}, \quad (18)$$

is close to 1 for majority of images from BOSSbase. To this end, we first prove a useful lemma regarding the properties of the solution to the non-linear equation (14) for the change rate β_n. By e in the lemma we understand the Euler constant.

LEMMA 1. *Let $a > 0$ be such that $a/\ln(a-2) > 2+e$, which is equivalent with $a \gtrsim 9.52$. Then, the non-linear equation (14)*

$$\beta = \frac{1}{a} \ln(1/\beta - 2). \quad (19)$$

has a unique solution $\beta = \lim_{k \to \infty} \beta^{(k)}$, where $\beta^{(k)}$ is given by the following recursive formula:

$$\beta^{(0)} = \frac{1}{a},$$
$$\beta^{(k+1)} = \frac{1}{a} \ln(1/\beta^{(k)} - 2), \; k \geq 0. \quad (20)$$

Moreover, the subsequences $\beta^{(2l)}$ and $\beta^{(2l+1)}$ are monotone increasing and decreasing, respectively, and

$$\beta = \frac{\ln a}{a} + \delta, \; |\delta| \leq (4+c)\frac{\ln a}{a^2}, \quad (21)$$

where $c = 2(1 - \frac{1}{5} \ln 10)^{-1} \approx 3.71$.

PROOF. The convergence and the monotonicity of the subsequences can be established easily using induction. Note that $\beta^{(0)} < \beta^{(1)}$ and $\beta^{(2)} - \beta^{(0)} = \frac{1}{a} \ln \left[\left(\frac{a}{\ln(a-2)} - 2 \right)/e \right] > 0$ when $a/\ln(a-2) > 2+e$. Assuming $\beta^{(k)} \gtrless \beta^{(k-2)}$, we have using (20)

$$\beta^{(k+1)} - \beta^{(k-1)} = \frac{1}{a} \ln \frac{1/\beta^{(k)} - 2}{1/\beta^{(k-2)} - 2} \lessgtr 0, \quad (22)$$

which establishes the monotonicity of both sequences from the Lemma. Similarly, it can be shown that $\beta^{(k)} \gtrless \beta^{(k+1)} \Rightarrow \beta^{(k+1)} \lessgtr \beta^{(k+2)}$. Due to the monotonicity and boundedness of both sequences, both $\beta^{(2l)}$ and $\beta^{(2l+1)}$, $l = 0, 1, \ldots$, have finite limits, $\beta^{(\mathrm{even})}$ and $\beta^{(\mathrm{odd})}$, which must coincide because

$$0 \leq \beta^{(\mathrm{odd})} - \beta^{(\mathrm{even})} = \frac{1}{a} \ln \frac{1/\beta^{(\mathrm{odd})} - 2}{1/\beta^{(\mathrm{even})} - 2} \leq 0. \quad (23)$$

Due to space limitations, only an outline of the proof of (21) is given. By repeatedly applying the inequality

$$\frac{-x}{1-x} \leq \ln(1-x) \leq -x, \text{ for any } x > 0. \quad (24)$$

routine manipulations can be used to show that

$$0 < \beta - \beta^{(2)} < \beta^{(1)} - \beta^{(2)} = \ln \ln a + \delta_2, \quad (25)$$

$$\beta^{(2)} = \frac{\ln a}{a} - \frac{\ln \ln a}{a} + \delta_1, \quad (26)$$

with $|\delta_2| \leq 4 \ln a/a^2$ and $|\delta_1| \leq c \ln a/a^2$, which establishes (21). $\square$

We now express the ratio $r(\lambda, \lambda')$ (18) using (21). The value of r obviously depends on the profile of the Fisher information I_n, $n = 1, \ldots, N$, which strongly depends on content. Without loss on generality, let us assume that I_n are sorted from the smallest to the largest and that $\lambda < \lambda'$. For a given image and λ, let $\underline{n}(\lambda)$ be the smallest integer such that for all $n \geq \underline{n}$, $\lambda I_n / \ln(\lambda I_n - 2) > 2+e$, the assumption of the above Lemma. Note that with $\lambda < \lambda'$, we automatically have $\lambda' I_n / \ln(\lambda' I_n - 2) > 2+e$ as well. Among the images from BOSSbase 1.01, this condition is satisfied for payload 0.05 bpp, 0.2 bpp, and 0.5 bpp, on average for 99.99%, 99.1%, and 89.2% of all pixels. We can thus split each of the three sums in (18) into two terms – one over pixels for which $\lambda I_n < 9.52$ ($n = 1, \ldots, \underline{n} - 1$) and for which $\lambda I_n \geq 9.52$ ($n = \underline{n}, \ldots, N$). Since all change rates are at most $\beta_n(\lambda) \leq 1/3$, we have for any λ, λ'

$$\sum_{n=1}^{n-1} I_n \beta_n(\lambda) \beta_n(\lambda') \leq \frac{1}{9} \sum_{n=1}^{n-1} I_n = \omega. \quad (27)$$

Thus, (18) can be written as

$$r(\lambda, \lambda') = \frac{\omega + \mathbf{u} \cdot \mathbf{v}}{\sqrt{\omega + \|\mathbf{u}\|} \sqrt{\omega + \|\mathbf{v}\|}}, \quad (28)$$

where $\mathbf{u}, \mathbf{v} \in \mathbb{R}^{N-\underline{n}}$ are defined by ($n = 1, \ldots, N - \underline{n}$):

$$u_n = \frac{\ln(\lambda I_{n+\underline{n}}) + \epsilon_{n+\underline{n}}}{\lambda \sqrt{I_{n+\underline{n}}}}, \quad (29)$$

$$v_n = \frac{\ln(\lambda I_{n+\underline{n}}) + \epsilon'_{n+\underline{n}}}{\lambda' \sqrt{I_{n+\underline{n}}}} \quad (30)$$

with ϵ_n, ϵ'_n bounded from the Lemma

$$|\epsilon_n| \leq (4 + c) \frac{\ln(\lambda I_n)}{\lambda I_n} \quad (31)$$

$$|\epsilon'_n| \leq (4 + c) \frac{\ln(\lambda I_n)}{\lambda I_n} + \ln(\lambda'/\lambda). \quad (32)$$

Using Taylor expansion w.r.t. ω in (28):

$$\frac{\mathbf{u} \cdot \mathbf{v}}{\|\mathbf{u}\| \|\mathbf{v}\|} \left(1 + \mathcal{O}(\omega(\|\mathbf{u}\|^{-2} + \|\mathbf{v}\|^{-2})) \right)$$
$$\leq r(\lambda, \lambda') \leq \frac{\mathbf{u} \cdot \mathbf{v}}{\|\mathbf{u}\| \|\mathbf{v}\|} + \omega/(\|\mathbf{u}\| \|\mathbf{v}\|). \quad (33)$$

The vectors $\mathbf{u}$ and $\mathbf{v}$ are "almost" collinear because the dominant term in u_n and v_n is $\ln(\lambda I_{n+\underline{n}})$ as both $|\epsilon_n|$ and $|\epsilon'_n|$ are small by (31)-(32). Here, we need to know that for λ, λ' corresponding to payloads 0.05 bpp, and 0.2 bpp (and for 0.2 bpp and 0.5 bpp), $\lambda'/\lambda \approx 5 - 20$ with a median around 10, while the maximal values of λI_n reach $10^5 - 10^6$ in the vast majority of BOSSbase images.

A. REFERENCES

[1] C. Chen and Y. Q. Shi. JPEG image steganalysis utilizing both intrablock and interblock correlations. In *Circuits and Systems, ISCAS 2008. IEEE International Symposium on*, pages 3029–3032, Seattle, WA, May, 18–21, 2008.

[2] L. Chen, Y.Q. Shi, P. Sutthiwan, and X. Niu. A novel mapping scheme for steganalysis. In *Proc. IWDW*, volume 7809 of *LNCS*, pages 19–33. Springer Berlin Heidelberg, 2013.

[3] R. Cogranne and F. Retraint. Application of hypothesis testing theory for optimal detection of LSB matching data hiding. *Signal Processing*, 93(7):1724–1737, July, 2013.

[4] R. Cogranne and F. Retraint. An asymptotically uniformly most powerful test for LSB Matching detection. *IEEE TIFS*, 8(3):464–476, 2013.

[5] R. Cogranne and T. H. Thai. Optimal detection of OutGuess using an accurate model of DCT coefficients. In *Sixth IEEE International Workshop on Information Forensics and Security*, Atlanta, GA, December 3–5, 2014.

[6] R. Cogranne, C. Zitzmann, L. Fillatre, F. Retraint, I. Nikiforov, and P. Cornu. A cover image model for reliable steganalysis. In *Information Hiding, 13th International Conference*, volume 7692 of *LNCS*, pages 178–192, Prague, Czech Republic, May 18–20, 2011.

[7] R. Cogranne, C. Zitzmann, F. Retraint, I. Nikiforov, L. Fillatre, and P. Cornu. Statistical detection of LSB Matching using hypothesis testing theory. In *Information Hiding, 14th International Conference*, volume 7692 of *LNCS*, pages 46–62, Berkeley, California, May 15–18, 2012.

[8] T. Denemark, J. Fridrich, and V. Holub. Further study on the security of S-UNIWARD. In *Proceedings SPIE, Electronic Imaging, Media Watermarking, Security, and Forensics 2014*, volume 9028, pages 05 1–13, San Francisco, CA, February 3–5, 2014.

[9] T. Denemark, V. Sedighi, V. Holub, R. Cogranne, and J. Fridrich. Selection-channel-aware rich model for steganalysis of digital images. In *Proc. IEEE WIFS*, Atlanta, GA, December 3–5, 2014.

[10] H. Farid and L. Siwei. Detecting hidden messages using higher-order statistics and support vector machines. In *Information Hiding, 5th International Workshop*, volume 2578 of *LNCS*, pages 340–354, Noordwijkerhout, The Netherlands, October 7–9, 2002. Springer-Verlag, New York.

[11] L. Fillatre. Adaptive steganalysis of least significant bit replacement in grayscale images. *IEEE Transactions on Signal Processing*, 60(2):556–569, 2011.

[12] T. Filler, J. Judas, and J. Fridrich. Minimizing additive distortion in steganography using syndrome-trellis codes. *IEEE TIFS*, 6(3):920–935, September 2011.

[13] T. Filler, T. Pevný, and P. Bas. BOSS (Break Our Steganography System). http://www.agents.cz/boss, July 2010.

[14] A. Foi, M. Trimeche, V. Katkovnik, and K. Egiazarian. Practical Poissonian-Gaussian noise modeling and fitting for single-image raw-data. *IEEE TIP*, 17(10):1737–1754, Oct. 2008.

[15] J. Fridrich and J. Kodovský. Rich models for steganalysis of digital images. *IEEE TIFS*, 7(3):868–882, June 2011.

[16] J. Fridrich and J. Kodovský. Multivariate Gaussian model for designing additive distortion for steganography. In *Proc. IEEE ICASSP*, Vancouver, BC, May 26–31, 2013.

[17] M. Goljan, R. Cogranne, and J. Fridrich. Rich model for steganalysis of color images. In *Proc. IEEE WIFS*, Atlanta, GA, December 3–5, 2014.

[18] G. Gül and F. Kurugollu. A new methodology in steganalysis : Breaking highly undetactable steganograpy (HUGO). In *Information Hiding, 13th International Conference*, volume 7692 of *LNCS*, pages 71–84, Prague, Czech Republic, May 18–20, 2011.

[19] L. Guo, J. Ni, and Y.-Q. Shi. An efficient JPEG steganographic scheme using uniform embedding. In *Proc. IEEE WIFS*, Tenerife, Spain, December 2–5, 2012.

[20] G. E. Healey and R. Kondepudy. Radiometric CCD camera calibration and noise estimation. *IEEE TPAMI*, 16(3):267–276, March 1994.

[21] V. Holub and J. Fridrich. Low complexity features for JPEG steganalysis using undecimated DCT. *IEEE TIFS*, 10(2):219–228.

[22] V. Holub and J. Fridrich. Designing steganographic distortion using directional filters. In *Proc. IEEE WIFS*, Tenerife, Spain, December 2–5, 2012.

[23] V. Holub and J. Fridrich. Digital image steganography using universal distortion. In *1st ACM IH&MMSec. Workshop*, Montpellier, France, June 17–19, 2013.

[24] V. Holub and J. Fridrich. Random projections of residuals for digital image steganalysis. *IEEE TIFS*, 8(12):1996–2006, December 2013.

[25] V. Holub, J. Fridrich, and T. Denemark. Universal distortion design for steganography in an arbitrary domain. *EURASIP Journal on Information Security, Special Issue on Revised Selected Papers of the 1st ACM IH and MMS Workshop*, 2014:1, 2014.

[26] J. R. Janesick. *Scientific Charge-Coupled Devices*, volume Monograph PM83. Washington, DC: SPIE Press - The International Society for Optical Engineering, January 2001.

[27] A. D. Ker and R. Böhme. Revisiting weighted stego-image steganalysis. In *Proceedings SPIE, Electronic Imaging, Security, Forensics, Steganography, and Watermarking of Multimedia Contents X*, volume 6819, pages 5 1–17, San Jose, CA, January 27–31, 2008.

[28] J. Kodovký and J. Fridrich. Quantitative steganalysis using rich models. In *Proceedings SPIE, Electronic Imaging, Media Watermarking, Security, and Forensics 2013*, volume 8665, San Francisco, CA, February 5–7, 2013.

[29] J. Kodovský and J. Fridrich. Steganalysis of JPEG images using rich models. In *Proceedings SPIE, Electronic Imaging, Media Watermarking, Security, and Forensics 2012*, volume 8303, pages 0A 1–13, San Francisco, CA, January 23–26, 2012.

[30] J. Kodovský, J. Fridrich, and V. Holub. Ensemble classifiers for steganalysis of digital media. *IEEE TIFS*, 7(2):432–444, 2012.

[31] E.L. Lehmann and J.P. Romano. *Testing Statistical Hypotheses, 2nd edition*. Springer, 2005.

[32] B. Li, S. Tan, M. Wang, and J. Huang. Investigation on cost assignment in spatial image steganography. *IEEE TIFS*, 9(8):1264–1277, August 2014.

[33] B. Li, M. Wang, and J. Huang. A new cost function for spatial image steganography. In *Proceedings IEEE ICIP*, Paris, France, October 27–30, 2014.

[34] S. Lyu and H. Farid. Steganalysis using higher-order image statistics. *IEEE TIFS*, 1(1):111–119, 2006.

[35] T. Pevný. Detecting messages of unknown length. In A. Alattar, N. D. Memon, E. J. Delp, and J. Dittmann, editors, *Proceedings SPIE, Electronic Imaging, Media Watermarking, Security and Forensics III*, volume 7880, pages OT 1–12, San Francisco, CA, January 23–26, 2011.

[36] T. Pevný, T. Filler, and P. Bas. Using high-dimensional image models to perform highly undetectable steganography. In *Information Hiding, 12th International Conference*, volume 6387 of *LNCS*, pages 161–177, Calgary, Canada, June 28–30, 2010. Springer-Verlag, New York.

[37] T. Pevný, J. Fridrich, and A. D. Ker. From blind to quantitative steganalysis. *IEEE TIFS*, 7(2):445–454, 2011.

[38] N. Provos. Defending against statistical steganalysis. In *10th USENIX Security Symposium*, pages 323–335, Washington, DC, August 13–17, 2001.

[39] P. Schöttle and R. Böhme. A game-theoretic approach to content-adaptive steganography. In *Information Hiding, 14th International Conference*, volume 7692 of *LNCS*, pages 125–141, Berkeley, California, May 15–18, 2012.

[40] P. Schöttle, S. Korff, and R. Böhme. Weighted stego-image steganalysis for naive content-adaptive embedding. In *Proc. IEEE WIFS*, Tenerife, Spain, December 2–5, 2012.

[41] V. Sedighi, J. Fridrich, and R. Cogranne. Content-adaptive pentary steganography using the multivariate generalized Gaussian cover model. In *Proceedings SPIE, Electronic Imaging, Media Watermarking, Security, and Forensics 2015*, San Francisco, CA, February 9–11, 2015.

[42] Y. Q. Shi, C. Chen, and W. Chen. A Markov process based approach to effective attacking JPEG steganography. In *Information Hiding, 8th International Workshop*, volume 4437 of *LNCS*, pages 249–264, Alexandria, VA, July 10–12, 2006. Springer-Verlag, New York.

[43] W. Tang, H. Li, W. Luo, and J. Huang. Adaptive steganalysis against WOW embedding algorithm. In *2nd ACM IH&MMSec. Workshop*, Salzburg, Austria, June 11–13, 2014.

[44] T. Thai, R. Cogranne, and F. Retraint. Statistical model of quantized DCT coefficients: Application in the steganalysis of Jsteg algorithm. *IEEE TIP*, 23(5):1–14, May 2014.

[45] A. Westfeld. High capacity despite better steganalysis (F5 – a steganographic algorithm). In *Information Hiding, 4th International Workshop*, volume 2137 of *LNCS*, pages 289–302, Pittsburgh, PA, April 25–27, 2001. Springer-Verlag, New York.

[46] C. Zitzmann, R. Cogranne, L. Fillatre, I. Nikiforov, F. Retraint, and P. Cornu. Hidden information detection based on quantized Laplacian distribution. In *Proc. IEEE ICASSP*, Kyoto, Japan, March 25–30, 2012.

[47] C. Zitzmann, R. Cogranne, F. Retraint, I. Nikiforov, L. Fillatre, and P. Cornu. Statistical decision methods in hidden information detection. In *Information Hiding, 13th International Conference*, volume 7692 of *LNCS*, pages 163–177, Prague, Czech Republic, May 18–20, 2011.

[48] D. Zou, Y. Q. Shi, W. Su, and G. Xuan. Steganalysis based on Markov model of thresholded prediction-error image. In *Proceedings IEEE ICME*, pages 1365–1368, Toronto, Canada, July 9–12, 2006.

On Characterizing and Measuring
Out-of-Band Covert Channels

Brent Carrara and Carlisle Adams
School of Electrical Engineering and Computer Science
University of Ottawa
Ottawa, Ontario, Canada
bcarr092@uottawa.ca, cadams@uottawa.ca

ABSTRACT

A methodology for characterizing and measuring out-of-band covert channels (OOB-CCs) is proposed and used to evaluate covert-acoustic channels (i.e., covert channels established using speakers and microphones). OOB-CCs are low-probability of detection/low-probability of interception channels established using commodity devices that are not traditionally used for communication (e.g., speaker and microphone, display and FM radio, etc.). To date, OOB-CCs have been declared "covert" if the signals used to establish these channels could not be perceived by a human adversary. This work examines OOB-CCs from the perspective of a passive adversary and argues that a different methodology is required in order to effectively assess OOB-CCs.

Traditional communication systems are measured by their capacity and bit error rate; while important parameters, they do not capture the key measures of OOB-CCs: namely, the probability of an adversary detecting the channel and the amount of data that two covertly communicating parties can exchange without being detected. As a result, the adoption of the measure *steganographic capacity* is proposed and used to measure the amount of data (in bits) that can be transferred through an OOB-CC before a passive adversary's probability of detecting the channel reaches a given threshold. The theoretical steganographic capacity for discrete memoryless channels as well as additive white Gaussian noise channels is calculated in this paper and a case study is performed to measure the steganographic capacity of OOB covert-acoustic channels, when a passive adversary uses an energy detector to detect the covert communication. The case study reveals the conditions under which the covertly communicating parties can achieve *perfect steganography* (i.e., conditions under which data can be communicated without risk of detection).

Categories and Subject Descriptors

C.2.0 [**General**]: Security and Protection; D.4.6 [**Security and Protection**]: Invasive Software

IH&MMSec'15 June 17 - 19, 2015, Portland, OR, USA
ACM ISBN 978-1-4503-3587-4/15/06$15.00
DOI: http://dx.doi.org/10.1145/2756601.2756604

General Terms

Security, design

Keywords

Information hiding; covert channels; out-of-band covert channels; covert-acoustic channels; steganographic capacity; malware communication

1. INTRODUCTION

Formally, we define out-of-band covert channels (OOB-CCs) as a low-probability of intercept (LPI) / low-probability of detection (LPD) communication channel established between isolated processes (i.e., processes not able to communicate through traditional links) using existing commodity devices that are traditionally not used for communication. A literature review of the work on covert channels shows that OOB-CCs exist between a number of commodity device pairs: microphone and speaker [9, 17, 24, 25, 44], CPU and speaker [40, 50, 51], light source and ambient light sensor or camera [3, 4, 26, 36], speaker and accelerometer [26], vibration device and accelerometer [1, 17, 49], electromagnet and magnetometer [26], CPUs [43], as well as display and AM/FM radio [2, 23, 37]. OOB-CCs can be categorized as a separate class of covert channels as they differ from traditional network covert channels and steganographic channels because they do not require a cover protocol or object, respectively, to hide their communication within, i.e., where there is direct or indirect communication between the covertly communicating parties of network covert channels and steganographic channels, OOB-CCs establish a communication channel between parties that are not overtly communicating.

Additionally, OOB-CCs are relevant to a number of different contexts. Firstly, they could be used for malware communication between systems that are physically separated or isolated from one another, i.e., air-gapped systems [9,23,24,37]. Similarly, they could be used for malware communication between processes of secure operating systems that employ domain separation, i.e., "security by isolation" [17]. We also assume that OOB-CCs could be used for communication between entities not willing or allowed to use traditional communication links. These are common problems in applications supporting the expression of free speech in oppressive environments and during times of protest when traditional communication links are taken down, in whistleblower scenarios where sensitive information needs to be exfiltrated, and, in general, when the fact that communication is taking place needs to be kept hidden from detection by a third-party (e.g., governments, criminals, etc.). More generally, covert channels have also been discussed in the context of authentication [54]. Two parties that agree on both a medium and modulation scheme can use knowledge of the covert channel to authenticate each other. This type of authentication, however, is based on "security through obscurity" and is generally not recommended in direct application without some reliance on secret information [34]. Lastly, covert channels can be used to augment traditional communication links [54]. In general, we postulate that OOB-CCs provide a more deniable covert communication alternative to dedicated LPI/LPD communication systems since no additional hardware is required to establish communication.

OOB-CCs differ from both traditional and LPI/LPD communication systems in a number of different ways. Primarily, OOB-CCs are not necessarily concerned with general purpose communication. Often the main requirement of an OOB-CC, is to share a limited amount of high-value data (e.g., a password, an encryption key, or keystrokes in the case of malware, or a sensitive document in the whistle-blower scenario) and therefore their designers are concerned with the amount of data that can be transmitted before the channel is detectable by a passive adversary. Furthermore, OOB-CCs are constrained by the devices that are used for communication. Often the requirements for general-purpose communication in LPD systems call for communication at low signal-to-noise ratio (SNR) (e.g., below 0 dB), which might not be possible given that the commodity devices used in OOB-CCs were not designed for LPD communication and thus lack the necessary sensitivity to detect low SNR signals. Additionally, while the metrics used to measure traditional communication systems (e.g., data rate and bit error rate) and LPI/LPD communication systems (e.g., probability of detection) are useful measures for their respective systems, a more comprehensive metric is required for OOB-CCs that combines both their effectiveness (i.e., data rate) and efficiency (i.e., covertness) in order to characterize the covert channel. We point out, however, that despite the differences between OOB-CCs and general LPD communications systems, our analysis in this work from a passive adversary's perspective is similar to that of the analysis of LPD systems. We thus lean on the analysis of LPD communication systems in order to establish a framework for characterizing OOB-CCs.

The requirement for a measure to characterize OOB-CCs has led us to the *steganographic capacity* metric, which, in the context of steganography, is the largest payload which can be safely embedded in a cover object using a particular embedding method [33]. Previous researchers have measured the capacity of a number of steganographic systems and have empirically demonstrated or mathematically proven that their capacity is governed by a "square root law" (i.e., the maximum size of the embedded payload is proportional to the square root of the size of the cover) [20, 29, 30, 33]. Moreover, results in the low-probability of detection research community have also demonstrated a similar "square root law" governing their systems' capacity [5–7, 11–14, 27]. In both of these information hiding applications, the "square root law" demonstrates that the maximum amount of data that can be transmitted without detection is proportional to

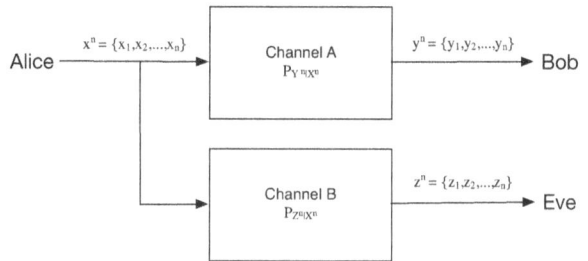

Figure 1: Our system model. Alice transmits a sequence of codewords $x^n = \{x_1, x_2, \ldots, x_n\} \in X^n$, $X^n \sim P_{X^n}$ through *Channel A* to Bob. Bob receives a sequence of codewords $y^n = \{y_1, y_2, \ldots, y_n\} \in Y^n$, $Y^n \sim P_{Y^n}$ where the sequence y^n is a possibly corrupted version of x^n and the distribution of Y^n is dependent on the channel transition probability distribution $P_{Y^n|X^n}$. Eve also receives a sequence of codewords $z^n = \{z_1, z_2, \ldots, z_n\} \in Z^n$, $Z^n \sim P_{Z^n}$ through *Channel B* where again the sequence z^n is a possibly corrupted version of x^n and Eve's distribution of codewords is dependent on $P_{Z^n|X^n}$. Once Eve observes z^n, she makes a decision and concludes whether or not Alice is communicating.

the square root of the size of the cover object or the number of channel uses, in the case of steganographic channels and low-probability of detection radar systems, respectively. Furthermore, the traditional rate used to measure communication systems is ineffective as the "rate" for information hiding systems tends to zero. Given these previous results, we measure the performance of the OOB-CCs studied in this work by calculating their *steganographic capacity*.

We measure the steganographic capacity of OOB-CCs, which we informally define as the maximum amount of data that can be communicated covertly before an adversary's probability of detection reaches a given threshold. We calculate the capacity by combining the communication rate achieved by two covertly communicating parties, Alice and Bob, and the probability of detection by an eavesdropper, Eve. Our analysis focusses on the passive adversary model shown in **Figure 1**. In our analysis, we assume that Eve is a passive adversary who is capable of monitoring the shared medium between Alice and Bob and is interested in answering the question: *is Alice communicating?* Previous research into OOB-CCs ([9, 17, 24, 25, 44]) has assumed that Eve is an unaware and unassuming adversary and an OOB-CC was deemed "covert" if the channel established between Alice and Bob was imperceptible to Eve's natural senses (e.g., sight, hearing). To evaluate the effectiveness of OOB-CCs in the presence of a passive adversary we make the reasonable assumption that Eve is able to deploy technical solutions to detect if Alice and Bob are communicating. We emphasize that this work deals with **detection** by a passive adversary and leaves the discussion of interception of Alice's codewords to later work. In this work, Alice is concerned with concealing the presence of her communication and not necessarily the confidentiality of the messages that she is sending. While confidentiality is an important requirement for secure communication systems, it is not the focus of this work.

As a result of our research, we make the following contributions to the covert channel literature. Using information theory and statistical hypothesis testing we determine the steganographic capacity of OOB-CCs when the channels between Alice and Bob as well as Alice and Eve are discrete memoryless channels (DMCs) (i.e., the input and output of the channel are modelled as discrete random variables and the output of the channel only depends on the current input). Moreover, we determine the steganographic capacity when both channels are corrupted by additive white Gaussian noise (AWGN) (i.e., the noise and information bearing signal are additive, the noise has constant power and the noise samples follow a Gaussian distribution), as well. Additionally, we perform a case study to measure the steganographic capacity of covert-acoustic channels (i.e., covert channels established using a speaker and microphone) when Eve deploys an energy detector to detect Alice's communications. Our case study allows us to determine the conditions under which Alice and Bob can communicate using *perfect steganography* (i.e., conditions under which data can be communicated without risk of detection) [8]. Lastly, we empirically determine the lowest SNR that commodity speakers and microphones can communicate at reliably in an effort to quantify the steganographic capacity of state-of-the-art covert-acoustic channels.

Our work impacts the evaluation of secure systems and has implications for the privacy-enhancing technologies community. Previously, the security risk associated with covert channels was measured by the bandwidth or channel capacity of the covert channel [38]. Both of these metrics on their own, however, do not adequately model the risk posed by covert channels that are only used to leak a fixed amount of data. In order to evaluate the security risk of these types of channels, a more comprehensive measure, i.e., steganographic capacity, is required. Furthermore, for the privacy-enhancing technologies community we show the conditions under which covert-acoustic OOB-CCs can be undetectable or require a passive adversary to capture a large number of samples in order to detect the channel.

This paper is organized as follows. In **Section 2**, we outline the background research in measuring steganographic channels, low probability of detection channels, and covert channels. In **Section 3**, we frame Eve's probability of detection problem in the context of statistical hypothesis testing to show that, on their own, probability of detect and channel capacity are not adequate measurements for OOB-CCs. We also examine how to measure the steganographic capacity and in **Section 4** we perform a case study to evaluate the steganographic capacity when Eve uses an energy detector to detect Alice's covert-acoustic communications. Lastly, in **Section 5** and **Section 6** we provide future work and conclude, respectively.

2. BACKGROUND
In [48], Shannon described a general mathematical theory for "secrecy systems" and broadly classified systems into *concealment systems*, *privacy systems*, and *"true" secrecy systems*. Shannon defined *concealment systems* as systems that ensured communication was hidden from the enemy and *"true" secrecy systems* as systems that ensured messages were unreadable by the enemy. Although Shannon's work

defined the concept of *concealment systems*, it was Wyner in [53] that looked at the ability for two communicating parties to reliably communicate over a DMC while limiting the ability of a passive adversary to decode the originally transmitted message after observing it through a second DMC, i.e., the *wire-tap channel*. In Wyner's analysis, the goal of the authentic transmitter was to not only maximize channel throughput but also to maximize the equivocation rate of the eavesdropper, i.e., the entropy of the original message conditioned on the message output from the wire-tap channel. Both Shannon and Wyner's works were groundbreaking and paved the way for the analysis that led to the development of LPI communication systems.

LPI/LPD systems have been the focus of military researchers for a number of years. Much of this focus has been on time and frequency spread spectrum modulation schemes, i.e., direct-sequence spread spectrum (DSSS) and frequency-hopping spread spectrum (FHSS) [45,46], respectively. Spread spectrum systems are difficult to detect because their transmitted signal's average power is lowered by spreading the signal's energy out over a much larger bandwidth than is required by the original signal. General detection of spread spectrum signals is performed using a radiometer [52], which is an energy detection device that filters, squares and sums a received signal before comparing it to a pre-determined threshold. If the signal's energy is above the threshold then the detector deems that communication has taken place; if it is below the threshold, the detector deems no communication occurred. The detection threshold is tuned by the detector to limit the probability of false alarm (false positive), α, and the probability of missed detection (false negative), β. In [52], Urkowitz showed that an energy detector is optimal when detecting a signal and only the signal's bandwidth, W, is known.

Recently, there have been a number of works outlining the theoretical limits of low-probability of detection communication for various channel models: the AWGN channel [5–7], the wire-tap channel [27], and the binary symmetric channel (BSC) (i.e., communication model where a bit is transmitted and received correctly with probability $1 - p$ and received incorrectly with probability p) [11–14]. In [5] and [6], Bash, et al., proved the "square root law" for LPD signals transmitted over an AWGN channel, which demonstrated that at most $O(\sqrt{n})$ and $o(\sqrt{n})$ bits can be communicated between Alice and Bob in n channel uses while lower bounding the sum of error probabilities $\alpha + \beta \geq 1 - \epsilon$ for some arbitrary $\epsilon > 0$ observed by Eve, when Eve's noise power is known by Alice and when it is not, respectively. The proof of their theorem showed that Alice's average transmit power is inversely proportional to the number of channel uses, n, and thus as $n \to \infty$ Alice's required transmit power $\to 0$. For practical systems, however, Bob must receive a signal from Alice with non-zero signal power in order to reliably communicate. Furthermore, their proof required that Alice and Bob had a shared secret that was at least equal in length to that of the messages transmitted by Alice to ensure confidentiality. In [7], Bash, et al., extended their result and showed that if Alice only transmitted in a single n-symbol slot out of a possible $T(n)$ slots, Alice could increase the amount of information she can transmit to Bob by a factor of $\sqrt{T(n)}$ at the cost of an extra $\log T(n)$ bits of shared secret between them.

In [11,13] and [14], Che, et al., examined the ability for Alice and Bob to communicate over a BSC while ensuring their communication is undetectable, which the authors referred to as being *deniable*. In their analysis, Eve observed Alice's transmissions through a noisier communication channel than Bob, i.e., the wire-tap channel, and were able to prove a similar "square root law" under this assumption. The difference between Che, et al.'s result and Bash, et al.'s result (other than the channel model) is that no secret information is required to be shared between Alice and Bob prior to communication under the authors' assumptions. In [12], Che, et al., extended their result to the situation where the noise observed by Bob and Eve was not deterministically known, but rather probabilistically distributed over a range. Their research showed that a "square root law" could still be observed under these conditions with the caveat that Eve's channel noise was still larger than Bob's. In [27], Hou and Kramer defined an information-theoretic measure "effective secrecy", which combined a measure for confidentiality and undetectability (or *confusion* and *stealth*, respectively, as defined by the authors). Their model relied again on the wire-tap channel to obtain confidentiality and to prove that an achievable rate does exist that satisfies constraints on both the confusion and stealth components of "effective security." While an important theoretical result, the work of Che, et al. and Hou and Kramer assume the wire-tap model, which is not a practical general assumption.

Prior to the works of Bash, et al., and Che, et al., a "square root law" was observed in information hiding systems by Ker while analyzing the capacity of batch steganography [30]. Since this seminal work was first published, other steganographic systems have also been found to respect this same law, namely Markov chain covers [20] and covers composed of i.i.d. elements [31]. In [33], a number of other covers were also empirically shown to follow the same law as well, but required the sender and receiver to share a secret "embedding key" at least linear in length to the payload in order to communicate without being detected. Additionally, under slightly different assumptions (i.e., the sender was able to combine more than one embedding location to convey one bit of information), Ker was able to show that no "embedding key" was required [32]. While no universal theory proving the "square root law" exists in general, the law is composed of a "collection of theories for different mathematical models" [33]. Given this collection of theories, more recent work has focussed on finding the "root rate", which is the proportionality constant in the calculation of steganographic capacity (i.e., capacity $\approx r\sqrt{n}$, where r is the "root rate"). The proportionality constant, r, is equivalent to the Kullback-Leibler (KL) divergence between stego object and cover object, however, estimating the KL divergence is difficult and instead the *Fisher information* of a stego-system is used to measure the system's performance given its relationship to the KL divergence (i.e., the Fisher information is the first term in the Taylor expansion of the KL divergence) [18, 19, 28]. Moreover, in [18], Filler and Fridrich show that under certain conditions (i.e., mutually independent embedding operations) Fisher information is equivalent to KL divergence. In this work, the mathematical models we analyze (e.g., DMC and AWGN) allow us to calculate the KL divergence directly.

Historically, covert channels, in general, have been measured by estimates on the channel's bandwidth. The Trusted Computer System Evaluation Criteria (TCSEC) [38], developed by the United States Department of Defense (DoD) to certify secure systems, classified covert channels in this way and laid out certification requirements for handling covert channels based on bandwidth limits [22]. It was Moskowitz and Kang in [42] who pointed out that both bandwidth and channel capacity alone were not appropriate measures to use when evaluating covert channels because of the fact that for short messages the capacity of the channel goes to zero while data is still effectively communicated through the covert channel. This conclusion is further supported by the square root laws presented in this section. Under the "square root law," a non-zero amount of data can be communicated through the channel undetected, but the capacity of the channel tends to zero as n gets large. Based on the observations of Moskowitz and Kang and the collection of "square root laws," it is clear that a more effective methodology is required to evaluate OOB-CCs.

3. MEASURING AN OOB-CC

For the remainder of this work, we use uppercase letters, X, to denote random variables and lowercase letters, x, $x \in X$, to denote a realization of a random variable. A random variable has a probability mass function, P_X, and we use the notation $X \sim P_X$ to indicate that X is distributed according to the distribution P_X. We denote sequences of random variables with the notation $X^n = X_1, X_2, \ldots, X_n$ and if each X is independent and identically distributed (i.i.d.) we write $P_{X^n} = P_X^n$.

In this section, we present the steganographic capacity for OOB-CCs when the channel between Alice and Bob as well as Alice and Eve is modelled by a DMC and we calculate the capacity by modelling Eve's problem of detecting Alice's communications as a statistical hypothesis test. Furthermore, we present the steganographic capacity under assumptions that are consistent with a large number of communication systems (e.g., the channels are DMCs as well as the channel noise model is AWGN and Alice is under an average power constraint). We present these results before studying the steganographic capacity of covert-acoustic signals in **Section 4**, where we assume that a passive adversary employs an energy detector to detect the covert signals.

3.1 Information-Theoretic Capacity

In this section, we quote generously from the discussion on statistical hypothesis testing in [39] and the discussion on information theory and statistical hypothesis testing in [15]. Using statistical hypothesis testing, Eve, upon making a sequence of observations, $\{z^n | z^n \in Z^n\}$ (where z^n is shown in **Figure 1**), decides whether to either accept the null hypothesis, H_0 (i.e., conclude "Alice is not communicating"), or reject the null hypothesis (i.e., conclude "Alice is communicating"). Eve constructs the distributions P_{H_0} and P_{H_1} in such a way that when H_0 is true the sequence $z^n \sim P_{H_0}$ and when H_1 is true the sequence $z^n \sim P_{H_1}$. In order to make a decision, Eve performs a *log-likelihood ratio test* (LLRT) and decides whether to accept or reject the null hypothesis.

As a result of performing the LLRT, Eve can make one of two types of errors: rejecting the null hypothesis when it is true (*Type I* error) or accepting the null hypothesis when it is false (*Type II* error). These two classes of errors are commonly referred to as false positive, whose probability is denoted by α, and false negative, whose probability is denoted by β, respectively. By the Neyman-Pearson Theorem, the LLRT is optimal in the sense that for a given false positive, α^*, β is minimized.

A common performance measure for statistical hypothesis tests is the *sum of probability errors*, $\alpha + \beta$, which we use throughout this discussion to evaluate Eve's performance when attempting to detect Alice's communications. Given that falsely accepting the alternate hypothesis represents falsely accusing Alice of covert communication, Eve would like to fix the level of significance to an arbitrarily low value and therefore minimize β for a set value of α. Using **Theorem 13.1.1** from [39], the sum of probability errors can be expressed as

$$\alpha + \beta = 1 - TV(P_{H_0}, P_{H_1}), \qquad (1)$$

where $TV(P_{H_0}, P_{H_1})$ is the *total variational distance* between P_{H_0} and P_{H_1} and is expressed as

$$TV(P_{H_0}, P_{H_1}) = \sum_{x \in \mathcal{X}} |P_{H_0}(x) - P_{H_1}(x)|, \qquad (2)$$

where $\mathcal{X}$ is the set of all possible n-length sequences of observations that Eve can observe. Using **Lemma 11.6.1** in [15], we can bound $TV(P_{H_0}, P_{H_1})$ using the following inequality

$$\sqrt{2 \ln 2 D(P_{H_0} \| P_{H_1})} \geq TV(P_{H_0}, P_{H_1}), \qquad (3)$$

where $D(P_{H_0}, P_{H_1})$ is the KL divergence and is defined as $D(P \| Q) = \sum_x P(x) \log \frac{P(x)}{Q(x)}$ for two probability distributions P and Q. Given **Equation 3**, Eve's sum of probability errors is lower bounded by $1 - \epsilon_1$, where

$$\epsilon_1 = \sqrt{2 \ln 2 D(P_{H_0} \| P_{H_1})}. \qquad (4)$$

Based on these preliminaries, we present **Theorem 1**:

THEOREM 1. *If the channel between Alice and Bob as well as Alice and Eve are DMCs and Alice generates sequences of codewords $\{x^n | x^n \in X^n\}$ such that each $X_i \sim P_X$ in $X^n = \{X_1, X_2, \ldots, X_n\}$, $1 \leq i \leq n$, is i.i.d.. then Alice can transmit L bits of information to Bob while ensuring the upper bound on Eve's probability of detection is $1 - \epsilon_2$, for some arbitrary $\epsilon_2 \in (0, 1 - \alpha)$, where L is*

$$L = \begin{cases} \infty & if \ D(Q_Z \| P_Z) = 0, C > 0 \\ n^* TC & if \ D(Q_Z \| P_Z) > 0, C > 0 \ , \\ 0 & if \ C = 0 \end{cases} \qquad (5)$$

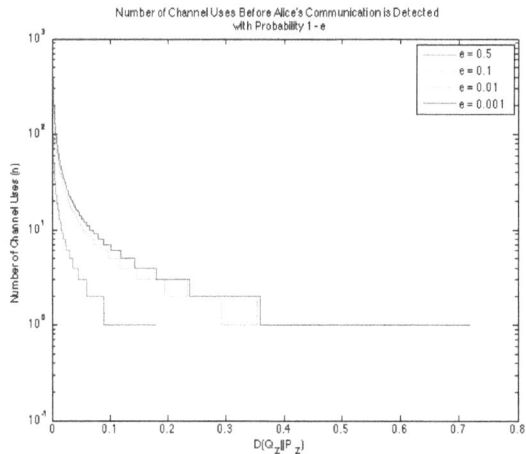

Figure 2: Plot of n versus $D(Q_Z \| P_Z)$ for various values of ϵ, where n is the number of channel uses that Alice can use to transmit data to Bob, while ensuring Eve's probability of detection, $P_D < 1 - \epsilon$ (*Note: $n = 0$ is not shown because the ordinate is plotted on a log scale*).

T is the duration of an observation, in seconds, C is the capacity of the channel between Alice and Bob, Q_Z is the probability distribution when Alice is not communicating, P_Z is the probability distribution when Alice is communicating and n^* is

$$n^* = \left\lfloor \frac{(1 - \alpha - \epsilon_2)^2}{2 \ln 2 D(Q_Z \| P_Z)} \right\rfloor \qquad (6)$$

For a complete proof of **Theorem 1** see **Section 1** in [10].

Given **Theorem 1**, we take L to be the steganographic capacity and plot n^* versus $D(Q_Z \| P_Z)$ in **Figure 2**. From the plot in **Figure 2** and **Equation 6** it is clear that Alice's best strategy is to construct P_X such that P_Z matches Eve's model when Alice is not communicating, Q_Z, as closely as possible. Or, more formally,

$$\max_{P_X} C \qquad (7)$$

$$\min_{P_X} D(Q_Z \| P_Z) \qquad (8)$$

Conversely, Eve's strategy is to model the distributions when Alice is communicating and when she is not as closely as possible in order to maximize the distance, in the KL divergence sense, between P_Z and Q_Z.

3.2 Capacity for AWGN Channels
We now study the steganographic capacity assuming AWGN channel corruption for both *Channel A* and *Channel B* (shown in **Figure 1**) with noise variances, σ_B^2 and σ_E^2, respectively. Under the AWGN noise assumption, Eve's channel model when Alice is not transmitting can be expressed as $Z_1 =$

W_E, where $W_E \sim \mathcal{N}(0, \sigma_E^2)$. From [15], we know that when Alice's average transmit power is subject to an average power constraint (shown in **Equation 9**), Alice and Bob's channel capacity is maximized by distributing $X \sim \mathcal{N}(0, P_t)$, which can be achieved by Alice using random coding (e.g., encrypting the data stream, compressing the data stream).

$$\frac{1}{m} \sum_{i=1}^{m} x_i^2 = P_t \qquad (9)$$

Assuming Alice generates symbols with a normal distribution and variance P_t, Eve's observation of the channel is $Z_2 = X + W_E$, $Z_2 \sim (0, \alpha_E^2 P_t + \sigma_E^2)$, where α_E is Eve's attenuation factor. Similarly, Bob's observation of the channel is $Y = X + W_B$, where $W_B \sim \mathcal{N}(0, \sigma_B^2)$ and $Y \sim \mathcal{N}(0, \alpha_B^2 P_t + \sigma_B^2)$, where α_B is Bob's attenuation factor. Eve's expected distributions, Q_Z and P_Z, are, therefore $\mathcal{N}(0, \sigma_E^2)$ and $\mathcal{N}(0, \alpha_E^2 P_t + \sigma_E^2)$ to model when Alice is communicating and when she is not, respectively.

Given these preliminaries, we present **Theorem 2**:

THEOREM 2. *If*

1. *the channel between Alice and Bob as well as Alice and Ever are DMCs,*

2. *both channels are corrupted by AWGN with distributions $\mathcal{N}(0, \sigma_B^2)$ and $\mathcal{N}(0, \sigma_E^2)$, respectively,*

3. *Alice transmits symbols i.i.d. with distribution $\mathcal{N}(0, P_t)$,*

4. *and Alice is subject to the average power constraint shown in **Equation 9**, then*

Alice can transmit L bits of information to Bob while ensuring the upper bound on Eve's probability of detection is $1 - \epsilon_2$, for some arbitrary $\epsilon_2 \in (0, 1 - \alpha)$, where L is

$$L = \begin{cases} \infty & \text{if } D(Q_Z \| P_Z) = 0, C > 0 \\ n^* T C & \text{if } D(Q_Z \| P_Z) > 0, C > 0 \\ 0 & \text{if } C = 0 \end{cases},$$

T is the duration of an observation, in seconds, C is the capacity of the channel between Alice and Bob, Q_Z is the probability distribution when Alice is not communicating, P_Z is the probability distribution when Alice is communicating, n^* is

$$n^* = \left\lfloor \frac{(1 - \alpha - \epsilon_2)^2}{2 \ln 2 D(Q_Z \| P_Z)} \right\rfloor,$$

and $D(Q_Z \| P_Z)$ is

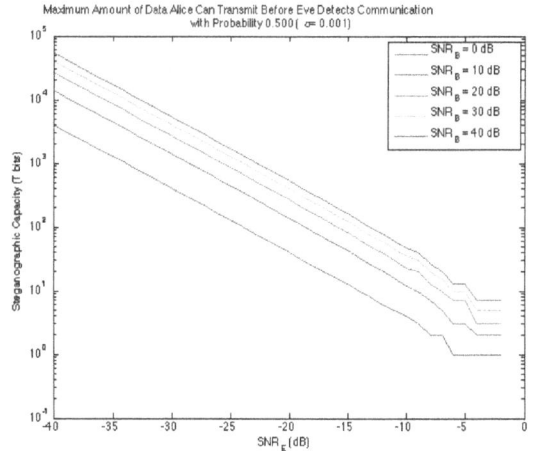

Figure 3: **The steganographic capacity for the AWGN channel model is shown for a fixed false alarm rate, $\alpha = 0.001$ and threshold value, ϵ_2, of 0.5.**

$$\frac{1}{2} \log \left(1 + \frac{\alpha_E^2 P_t}{\sigma_E^2}\right) + \frac{1}{2} \left(\frac{1}{1 + \frac{\alpha_E^2 P_t}{\sigma_E^2}} - 1\right).$$

For a complete proof of **Theorem 2** see **Section 2** in [10].

Denoting $\text{SNR}_E = \frac{\alpha_E^2 P_t}{\sigma_E^2}$ and $\text{SNR}_B = \frac{\alpha_B^2 P_t}{\sigma_B^2}$ for Eve and Bob's power signal-to-noise ratio, respectively, we plot the steganographic capacity versus SNR_E for various values of SNR_B in **Figure 3**. In the figure, the channel capacity between Alice and Bob is $C = \frac{1}{2} \log (1 + \text{SNR}_B)$ [15]. We show steganographic capacity curves for the case where $\epsilon_2 = 0.5$ to show the amount of data that Alice can transmit to Bob before Eve has a better than guessing chance of detecting her communication. The steganographic capacity plotted in **Figure 3** represents the absolute best case scenario for Eve since she knows the exact distribution of Alice's symbols and performs an optimal Neyman-Pearson test to detect Alice's communications for a fixed probability of false alarm. Conversely, this plot shows the worst case scenario for Alice; however, it is clear that Alice's strategy is to ensure that as little signal power, P_t, as possible gets to Eve in order to minimize her level of detection. Although this plot does paint a bleak picture for Alice (her capacity is at most 1 kilobyte at $\text{SNR}_E = -20$ dB) it makes generous assumptions about Eve's capabilities. As we will see in **Section 4**, Alice is able to communicate more data covertly when a simple energy detector is used for detection.

4. CASE STUDY

In [9, 17, 24, 25], and [44], various researchers showed covert-acoustic signals could be sent in the near ultrasonic, i.e., 17-20 kHz, and ultrasonic, i.e., > 20 kHz, ranges using commodity hardware from various vendors. In their respective works, the researchers used various modulation schemes (e.g., frequency-shift keying (FSK), orthogonal frequency-division multiplexing (OFDM)) to show that bit rates of over 100 bits per second (bps) could be achieved with low bit error rates (BERs). In all of these referenced works, the researchers assumed their adversary was unaware and unassuming and used only their natural ability to hear in order to detect the covert-audio communication. In this section, we evaluate the covertness of the scheme that was proposed in [9], which demonstrated that by using the OFDM modulation scheme, acoustic signals in the ultrasonic frequency range between 20 kHz and 20.5 kHz could be covertly communicated at data rates over 200 bps with a BER below 10%. Specifically, we calculate the steganographic capacity for covert-acoustic channels when Eve employs a radiometer, i.e., an energy detector. We build on the work in [9] because the researchers achieved the best results from a data throughput perspective when using truly ultrasonic (> 20 kHz) signals, and by determining the steganographic capacity of their scheme we can set limits on how much data can be covertly communicated using ultrasonic audio signals when OFDM is used.

4.1 Acoustic Channel Model

Before proceeding with our analysis, we justify the application of the results from **Section 3** to the acoustic channel. In general, acoustic signals are corrupted by pink noise (i.e., the interfering noise power is inversely proportional to frequency) as opposed to white noise (i.e., the interfering noise power is spectrally flat for all frequencies) over the bandwidth supported by commodity microphones (i.e., 0 Hz to 22.050 kHz) [9,21]. Furthermore, the source of noise in the acoustic spectrum is a combination of environmental noise (e.g., background conversations, electronic equipment) and imperfections in the receiver's audio equipment (i.e., microphone). The noise power, however, over the 20 kHz to 20.5 kHz bandwidth can be characterized as white noise, which we confirmed by performing a Kolmogorov-Smirnov test at a significance level of 0.001 [41].

Moreover, acoustic signals can suffer significant multi-path delay spreads (i.e., the receiver can continue to receive copies of a transmitted signal long after the signal is initially received) due to reflections of the transmitted signal off of objects in the environment. Carrara and Adams measured the multi-path delay spread for a common single desk closed-door office environment at upwards of 250 ms [9]. Therefore, if a transmitter sends signals with an inter-symbol time less than the multi-path delay spread of the channel, the channel cannot be considered a DMC as the receiver would receive a copy of the previously transmitted signal plus the currently transmitted symbol. However, if the multi-path delay spread is respected by the transmitter (often referred to as the transmitter inserting a "guard interval") the receiver would receive a copy of the transmitted symbol independent of the previously transmitted symbol. Under these circumstances the acoustic channel can be considered a DMC.

Lastly, one major factor to account for when dealing with acoustic signals is the attenuation of audio signals in air, especially if they contain high frequency components. The attenuation factor for acoustic signals depends on a number of elements: frequency of the transmitted signal, temperature of the air, relative humidity in the air, obstacles in the environment and distance between the sender and receiver [16,35]. As an example, the attenuation rate of audio

signals is roughly $0.5 \frac{\mathrm{dB}}{\mathrm{m}}$, when the relative humidity in the air is 50 % and the ambient temperature is 20 ° C. The environmental factors and the distance between both Bob and Alice as well as Alice and Eve could have significant impact on SNR_E and SNR_B. We thus study the effect of distance on attenuation and the steganographic capacity at the end of this section.

Given our measurement of the noise in the 500 Hz bandwidth between 20 kHz and 20.5 kHz, the effect of attenuation on acoustic signals, and the characterization of the acoustic channel being modelled by a DMC, we proceed with applying the results of the previous section to covert-acoustic signals in our case study.

4.2 Analysis

In **Section 3.2**, we showed that for the AWGN channel model, the steganographic capacity of the channel is zero when $\mathrm{SNR}_E \geq 0$ dB. As previously noted, this represents the best-case scenario for Eve and thus a lower bound on the steganographic capacity as Eve knows the exact statistical distribution both when Alice is communicating and when she is not and constructs an optimal test based on this information. In this section, we complement our previous result and evaluate the steganographic capacity in the best-case scenario for Alice when Alice is band-limited and Eve is attempting to passively detect her communications. In our analysis, we assume that Eve only knows the bandwidth of Alice's signal, W, and thus builds an optimal device based on simply knowledge of W and the fact that the channel model is AWGN.

Previous researchers, [52], have shown that the optimal device to detect signals in AWGN when only the signal's bandwidth is known is an energy detector. An energy detector is designed to distinguish between a received signal, $r(t)$, composed of either simply noise, i.e., $r(t) = n(t)$, or a signal plus noise, i.e., $r(t) = s(t) + n(t)$, and works as follows. First, the received signal, $r(t)$, is passed through a bandpass filter whose bandwidth matches the bandwidth of the signal being detected, $s(t)$. Once filtered, the signal is squared and integrated and the output is compared to a threshold, K. If the output of the integrator is above the detector's threshold it is concluded that the received signal contains $s(t)$, otherwise it is concluded that the received signal just contains noise, $n(t)$. The distribution at the output of the integrator when only $n(t)$ is received can be modelled by a central chi-squared distribution with $\eta = 2TW$ degrees of freedom, where T is the integrator's evaluation time, in seconds [45]. Moreover, when $s(t) + n(t)$ is received, the output from the integrator can be modelled by a non-central chi-squared distribution with $\eta = 2TW$ degrees of freedom and a non-centrality parameter, $\lambda = \frac{\eta \mathrm{SNR}_E}{W}$, where $\mathrm{SNR}_E = \frac{\alpha_E^2 P_t}{\sigma_E^2}$ represents the power SNR of the signal received by Eve [45].

When using a radiometer, a false alarm is raised if the output of the integrator, k, is above the threshold K, but the signal $s(t)$ was not present. Similarly, a missed detection error occurs when the output of the integrator, k, is below the threshold, K, but the signal $s(t)$ was present. The false alarm probability, α, is shown in **Equation 11** and the missed detection probability, β, is shown in **Equation**

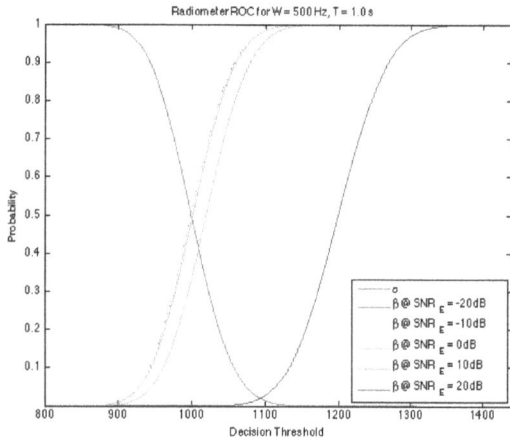

Figure 4: The receiver operating characteristics (ROC) for Eve's energy detector. We plot the probability of missed detection, β, for various values of SNR_E.

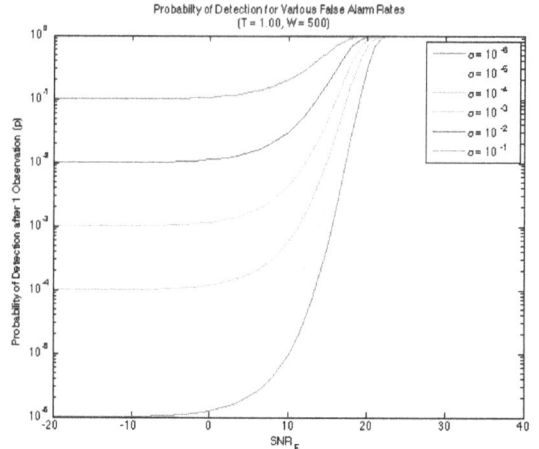

Figure 5: Plot of the single channel use probability of detection, p, versus SNR_E for various false alarm rates α.

13, where $P_{\chi^2_\eta}$ represents a central chi-squared distribution with η degrees of freedom and $P_{\chi^2_{\eta,\lambda}}$ represents a non-central chi-squared distribution with η degrees of freedom and a non-centrality parameter, λ.

$$\alpha = Pr[k > K | s(t) \text{ not present}] \qquad (10)$$

$$= \int_K^\infty P_{\chi^2_\eta}(x)dx \qquad (11)$$

$$\beta = Pr[k < K | s(t) \text{ present }] \qquad (12)$$

$$= \int_{-\infty}^K P_{\chi^2_{\eta,\lambda}}(x)dx \qquad (13)$$

We plot the receiver operating characteristics (ROC) for various values of SNR_E in **Figure 4** and note that the equal error rate (EER) for the various β curves are 0.50, 0.50, 0.49, 0.41, and 0.02 for $\text{SNR}_E = -20$ dB, -10 dB, 0 dB, 10 dB and 20 dB, respectively; thus as $\text{SNR}_E \to -\infty$, $\alpha + \beta \to 1$, and, therefore, Alice can communicate without being reliably detected, i.e., Alice has achieved *perfect steganography*. (*Note that we use the term perfect steganography when $\alpha + \beta = 1$ even though the original definition of perfect steganography was related to the condition that the KL divergence between stego object and covert object is zero [8]. A proof showing that if $\alpha + \beta = 1$, then perfect steganography is achieved is in* **Section 3** *of [10], which justifies our use of the term in this fashion*).

Given the energy detector's construction, in each observation Eve detects if Alice is communicating with probability $p = 1 - \beta$. The tradeoff between α and p is shown in **Figure 5**. This plot empirically confirms that as $\text{SNR}_E \to -\infty$, $p \to \alpha$ and thus $\alpha + \beta \to 1$. Similar to the analysis in the previous section, we assume that Eve performs multiple observations to increase her overall probability of detecting Alice's communications. From Alice's perspective, we assume she transmits data in intervals with a duration of T seconds

and that she wants to maximize the amount of data she can transmit to Bob. Furthermore, we point out that the value, T, is completely within Alice's control and we assume that Alice separates the intervals she transmits in with intervals of silence. Otherwise, Eve could use an integrator observation time greater than T (we analyze the effect of varying T at the end of this section). Given that Eve detects Alice's communications with probability p in each observation, we model the number of trials that Eve must perform before detecting Alice's communications for the first time using the geometric random variable, M, with parameter p and probability mass function $Pr[M = m] = (1-p)^{m-1}p$. The probability that Eve detects Alice's communications at least once after m observations is then $1-(1-p)^m$, i.e., one minus the probability of the event that Eve doesn't detect Alice's communications in any of the m observations. If we again define n^* to be the maximum number of observations such that Eve's upper bound on P_D is $1 - \epsilon$ for some arbitrary $\epsilon \in (0, 1-\alpha)$ we get

$$1 - (1 - p)^{n^*} = 1 - \epsilon \qquad (14)$$

$$(1 - p)^{n^*} = \epsilon \qquad (15)$$

$$n^* = \left\lfloor \frac{\log \epsilon}{\log (1 - p)} \right\rfloor \qquad (16)$$

where we take the floor because we want to upper bound Eve's P_D. The steganographic capacity is then $L = n^*CT$, where T is the integrator's evaluation time, n^* is shown in **Equation 16** and C is the channel capacity of the channel between Alice and Bob and can be expressed as

$$C = W \log \left(1 + \frac{\alpha_B^2 P_t}{\sigma_B^2 W} \right) \frac{\text{bits}}{\text{second}}. \qquad (17)$$

In order to determine Eve's threshold, K, she first chooses an acceptable level for the false alarm rate, α^*, then solves

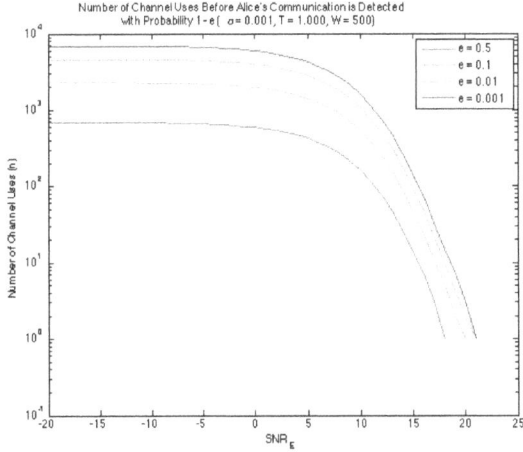

Figure 6: Plot of n versus SNR_E for various values of ϵ. Eve determines her threshold value, K, based on the level of false alarm, $\alpha = 0.001$.

Equation 11 for K. Once the value for K is obtained, Eve's per-observation probability of detection, p, is calculated by applying Equation 13 and subtracting the result from one. This procedure is the application of the Neyman Pearson criterion for detection [45]. We plot various curves for different values of ϵ to determine the maximum number of channel uses, n^*, that Alice can transmit on while upper bounding Eve's probability of detection in Figure 6. We remark that below approximately $\text{SNR}_E = -10$ dB, the number of channel uses that Alice can use to transmit data plateaus. This again reflects the situation where $\alpha + \beta \to 1$.

The steganographic capacity when Eve uses a radiometer to detect Alice's communications is shown in Figure 7. Comparing this plot to the plot shown in Figure 3, we note that Alice has the potential to send much more data when Eve employs an energy detector than she does when Eve employs an optimal detector even though Alice is bandlimited to $W = 500$ Hz. We show independent SNR values for SNR_E and SNR_B to model the different attenuation factors, α_B and α_E, for Bob and Eve, respectively. We also show the effects of modifying the integrator evaluation time T in Figure 8. In Figure 8, the probability that Eve detects Alice's communication after one observation, p, and the effects of Alice varying her transmit time T when Bob's SNR is held constant at $\text{SNR}_B = 10$ dB is shown. We see that as Eve increases her observation time, she is able to detect Alice's communication in just one observation (hence Alice can send no data covertly) at lower and lower values for SNR_E. It is clearly in Alice's best interest, therefore, to restrict how long she transmits for in order to limit Eve's observation time. This can be seen by examining the effect of lowering T in Figure 8. For fixed SNR, as $T \to 0$, the sum of probability errors, $\alpha + \beta \to 1$.

We end our case study with an analysis of the attenuation factors α_E and α_B as well as the BER at Bob at low received SNR, SNR_B. The effect of lowering Bob's received SNR on the BER is shown in Figure 9. From the plot it is clear that for Bob to communicate at a SNR of 10 dB and below, a sig-

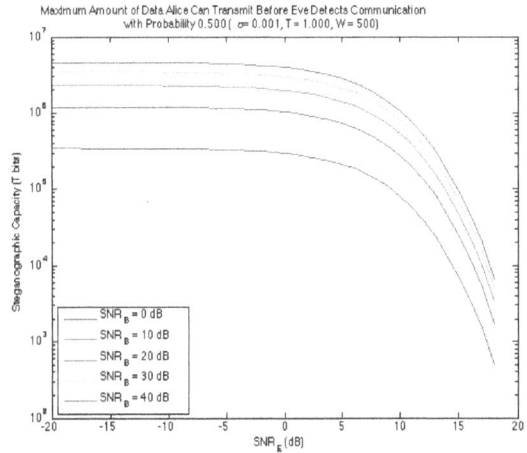

Figure 7: The steganographic capacity when Eve uses an energy detector to detect Alice's communication is shown for a fixed false alarm rate of 0.001 and a threshold value, ϵ, of 0.5.

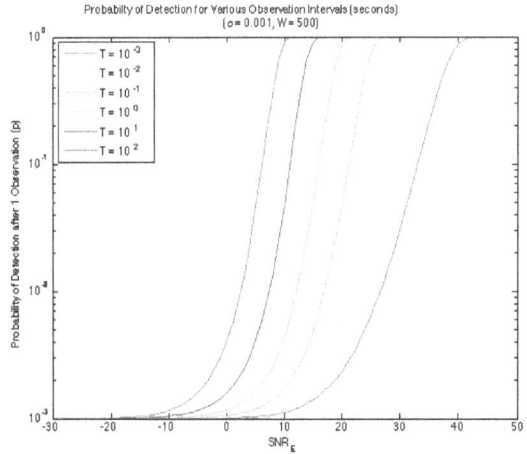

Figure 8: The tradeoff between the probability of detection, p, and the observation interval, T, is shown for a fixed probability of false alarm, $\alpha = 0.001$. As T increases, p increases for a given SNR_E, however, as T decreases, the point where $\alpha = p$, i.e., $\alpha + \beta = 1$, for a given SNR_E, increases.

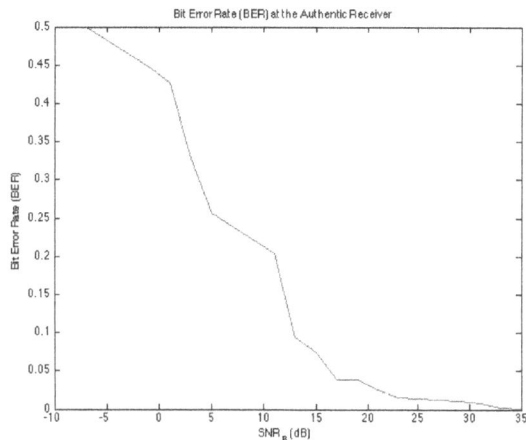

Figure 9: The effect of varying Bob's received SNR on the bit error rate is shown. Clearly, as Bob's received SNR drops below the noise threshold (i.e., ≤ 0 dB) Bob cannot reliably decode Alice's transmissions when commodity hardware is used and symbols are transmitted using OFDM.

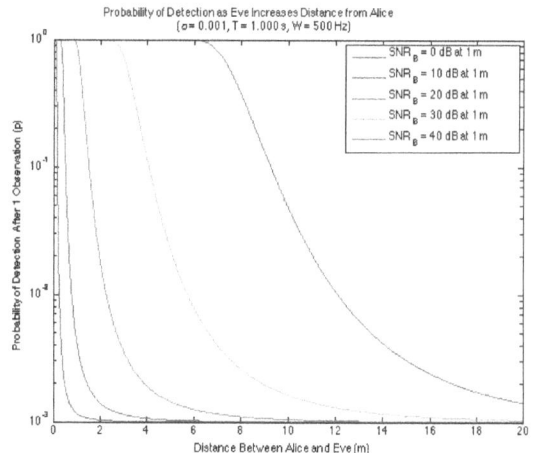

Figure 10: The relationship between Eve's probability of detection after one observation, p, is shown with respect to her distance from Alice. Multiple curves are shown, each of which correspond to a received SNR at Bob, SNR_B, at a distance of 1 m.

nificant number of errors need to be corrected. A plot of the probability of detection, p, versus distance is also shown in **Figure 10**. In the plot we show multiple curves corresponding to different received SNR values at Bob, SNR_B. For each curve, you can see the deleterious effect that distance has on Eve's probability of detection as her distance from Alice increases. This plot shows that if Alice can make assumptions about Eve's location and Alice knows Bob's location, then Alice has a better chance of approaching *perfect steganography*. Furthermore, given the physical properties of acoustic signals, it is clearly within Eve and Bob's best interest to be as close to Alice as possible when she is transmitting and within Alice's best interest to transmit signals to Bob at the lowest possible SNR value.

5. FUTURE WORK

To move this research forward, appropriate low SNR modulation and coding schemes need to be evaluated and the most error tolerant, high rate scheme needs to be implemented to increase the steganographic capacity between Alice and Bob while decreasing Bob's BER. The results presented in this work show that at an $\text{SNR}_B = 5$ dB, an average BER of 0.25 can be expected when using commodity hardware and OFDM modulation. In order to reduce these error rates to acceptable levels, an $[n, k, d]$ forward error correcting code (where n is the block length, k is the message length, and d is the distance), capable of correcting $\lfloor \frac{d-1}{2} \rfloor$ random errors, such as $[n, k, n - k + 1]$ Reed-Solomon Codes [47], would need to be used. To correct up to 25% bit errors using Reed-Solomon codes, an overheard of approximately 50% is required, thus reducing the effective bit rate by half.

From a detection perspective, more analysis is required to study the effects on the steganographic capacity when a detector is employed that takes more information into account than just the signal's bandwidth, W. While the energy detector we studied is optimal when only the signal's band-

width is known, a motivated detector would try to employ a detection scheme that takes into account as much of the signal's information as possible to achieve the theoretical results we presented. A study where the detector, Eve, has knowledge of all the signal's properties except for some secret information that is shared between Alice and Bob, like we did in the analysis of AWGN, would be appropriate as a next step.

Furthermore, a study on the effects of the steganographic capacity when Eve is active is required to determine the effect of an active adversary. Certainly, if Eve has knowledge of the modulation scheme (e.g., OFDM) being used by Alice and Eve knows the bandwidth of Alice's signals, Eve can transmit noise on the same frequencies that Alice is using and jam Alice's signal, causing Bob's BER to increase. Lastly, now that the theoretical steganographic capacity has been calculated for DMCs when Alice transmits symbols i.i.d., as well as when the channel noise model is AWGN, research is required to study the steganographic capacity in other typical channel models (e.g., fading channel) that characterize OOB-CCs.

6. CONCLUSION

Previous researchers and certification bodies have relied on bandwidth and channel capacity to determine the security threat of covert channels. Our research shows that while these measures are useful, they do not evaluate how effective the channel is at communicating fixed amounts of data without being detected, nor do they capture the effect of the channel being monitored by a passive detector. We thus propose the adoption of the metric *steganographic capacity* to measure and characterize OOB-CCs. The steganographic capacity takes into account a passive detector and measures the maximum amount of data that can be transmitted through the covert channel while limiting a passive detector's ability to conclusively detect the channel by upper bounding its probability of detection.

By studying the theoretical steganographic capacity when the communication channel is a DMC, we showed that Alice, the transmitter, must maximize the channel capacity between her and her intended receiver, Bob, while minimizing Eve, the eavesdropper's, ability to calculate a difference between the probability distribution of symbols she detects when Alice is transmitting and when she is not. Furthermore, when the channel noise model is additive white Gaussian noise, we showed that the most important parameter in the system is Alice's transmit power, P_t. Lastly, we evaluated the ability for Eve to detect a covert-acoustic channel between Alice and Bob and determined that for Alice and Bob to maximize the data they can transmit between each other, Alice must send transmissions in short bursts and send signals to Bob at the lowest allowable SNR, while minimizing the SNR of the signal that Eve receives.

7. ACKNOWLEDGMENTS

Thanks are due to Dr. Rainer Böhme for advice and discussions as well as the anonymous reviewers of an earlier version of this paper for their suggestions.

8. REFERENCES

[1] A. Al-Haiqi, M. Ismail, and R. Nordin. A new sensors-based covert channel on Android. *The Scientific World Journal*, 2014, 2014.

[2] R. J. Anderson and M. G. Kuhn. Soft tempest–an opportunity for NATO. *Protecting NATO Information Systems in the 21st Century*, 1999.

[3] M. Backes, T. Chen, M. Duermuth, H. Lensch, and M. Welk. Tempest in a teapot: Compromising reflections revisited. In *Security and Privacy, 2009 30th IEEE Symposium on*, pages 315–327, May 2009.

[4] M. Backes, M. Durmuth, and D. Unruh. Compromising reflections-or-how to read LCD monitors around the corner. In *Security and Privacy, 2008. SP 2008. IEEE Symposium on*, pages 158–169, May 2008.

[5] B. Bash, D. Goeckel, and D. Towsley. Square root law for communication with low probability of detection on AWGN channels. In *Information Theory Proceedings (ISIT), 2012 IEEE International Symposium on*, pages 448–452, July 2012.

[6] B. Bash, D. Goeckel, and D. Towsley. Limits of reliable communication with low probability of detection on AWGN channels. *Selected Areas in Communications, IEEE Journal on*, 31(9):1921–1930, September 2013.

[7] B. A. Bash, D. Goeckel, and D. Towsley. LPD communication when the warden does not know when. *CoRR*, abs/1403.1013, 2014.

[8] C. Cachin. An information-theoretic model for steganography. In *Information Hiding*, volume 1525 of *Lecture Notes in Computer Science*, pages 306–318. Springer Berlin Heidelberg, 1998.

[9] B. Carrara and C. Adams. On acoustic covert channels between air-gapped systems. In *Foundations and Practice of Security*, volume 8930 of *Lecture Notes in Computer Science*, pages 3–16. Springer, 2015.

[10] B. Carrara and C. Adams. Proofs for "On characterizing and measuring out-of-band covert channels". http://www.site.uottawa.ca/~cadams/papers/Appendix.pdf, 2015. Accessed: 2015-04-15.

[11] P. H. Che, M. Bakshi, C. Chan, and S. Jaggi. Reliable, deniable and hidable communication. In *Information Theory and Applications Workshop (ITA), 2014*, pages 1–10, Feb 2014.

[12] P. H. Che, M. Bakshi, C. Chan, and S. Jaggi. Reliable deniable communication with channel uncertainty. In *Information Theory Workshop (ITW), 2014 IEEE*, pages 30–34, Nov 2014.

[13] P. H. Che, M. Bakshi, and S. Jaggi. Reliable deniable communication: Hiding messages in noise. In *Information Theory Proceedings (ISIT), 2013 IEEE International Symposium on*, pages 2945–2949, July 2013.

[14] P. H. Che, M. Bakshi, and S. Jaggi. Reliable Deniable Communication: Hiding Messages in Noise. *ArXiv e-prints*, Apr. 2013.

[15] T. M. Cover and J. A. Thomas. *Elements of information theory*. John Wiley & Sons, 2012.

[16] M. J. Crocker. *Handbook of acoustics*. John Wiley & Sons, 1998.

[17] L. Deshotels. Inaudible sound as a covert channel in mobile devices. In *8th USENIX Workshop on Offensive Technologies (WOOT 14)*, 2014.

[18] T. Filler and J. Fridrich. Complete characterization of perfectly secure stego-systems with mutually independent embedding operation. In *Acoustics, Speech and Signal Processing, 2009. ICASSP 2009. IEEE International Conference on*, pages 1429–1432, April 2009.

[19] T. Filler and J. Fridrich. Fisher information determines capacity of ε-secure steganography. In *Information Hiding*, Lecture Notes in Computer Science, pages 31–47. Springer Berlin Heidelberg, 2009.

[20] T. Filler, A. D. Ker, and J. Fridrich. The square root law of steganographic capacity for markov covers. In *Proc. SPIE*, volume 7254, pages 725408–725408–11, 2009.

[21] V. Gerasimov and W. Bender. Things that talk: using sound for device-to-device and device-to-human communication. *IBM Systems Journal*, 39(3.4):530–546, 2000.

[22] V. D. Gligor. *A guide to understanding covert channel analysis of trusted systems*. National Computer Security Center, 1994.

[23] M. Guri, G. Kedma, A. Kachlon, and Y. Elovici. Airhopper: Bridging the air-gap between isolated networks and mobile phones using radio frequencies. In *Malicious and Unwanted Software: The Americas (MALWARE), 2014 9th International Conference on*, pages 58–67, Oct 2014.

[24] M. Hanspach and M. Goetz. On covert acoustical mesh networks in air. *CoRR*, abs/1406.1213, 2014.

[25] M. Hanspach and M. Goetz. Recent developments in covert acoustical communications. In *Sicherheit*, pages 243–254, 2014.

[26] R. Hasan, N. Saxena, T. Haleviz, S. Zawoad, and D. Rinehart. Sensing-enabled channels for hard-to-detect command and control of mobile devices. In *Proceedings of the 8th ACM SIGSAC Symposium on Information, Computer and Communications Security*, ASIA CCS '13, pages 469–480, 2013.

[27] J. Hou and G. Kramer. Effective secrecy: Reliability, confusion and stealth. *CoRR*, abs/1311.1411, 2013.

[28] A. Ker. Estimating steganographic fisher information in real images. In *Information Hiding*, volume 5806 of *Lecture Notes in Computer Science*, pages 73–88. Springer Berlin Heidelberg, 2009.

[29] A. Ker. The square root law in stegosystems with imperfect information. In *Information Hiding*, volume 6387 of *Lecture Notes in Computer Science*, pages 145–160. Springer Berlin Heidelberg, 2010.

[30] A. D. Ker. A capacity result for batch steganography. *Signal Processing Letters, IEEE*, 14(8):525–528, 2007.

[31] A. D. Ker. The square root law requires a linear key. In *Proceedings of the 11th ACM Workshop on Multimedia and Security*, MM&Sec '09, pages 85–92. ACM, 2009.

[32] A. D. Ker. The square root law does not require a linear key. In *Proceedings of the 12th ACM Workshop on Multimedia and Security*, MM&Sec '10, pages 213–224. ACM, 2010.

[33] A. D. Ker, T. Pevný, J. Kodovský, and J. Fridrich. The square root law of steganographic capacity. In *Proceedings of the 10th ACM Workshop on Multimedia and Security*, pages 107–116, 2008.

[34] A. Kerckhoffs. *La cryptographie militaire*, volume 9. 1 1883.

[35] L. E. Kinsler, A. R. Frey, A. B. Coppens, and J. V. Sanders. Fundamentals of acoustics. *Fundamentals of Acoustics, 4th Edition, by Lawrence E. Kinsler, Austin R. Frey, Alan B. Coppens, James V. Sanders, pp. 560. ISBN 0-471-84789-5. Wiley-VCH, December 1999.*, 1, 1999.

[36] M. Kuhn. Optical time-domain eavesdropping risks of CRT displays. In *Security and Privacy, 2002. Proceedings. 2002 IEEE Symposium on*, pages 3–18, 2002.

[37] M. Kuhn and R. Anderson. Soft tempest: Hidden data transmission using electromagnetic emanations. In *Information Hiding*, volume 1525 of *Lecture Notes in Computer Science*, pages 124–142, 1998.

[38] D. C. Latham. Department of Defense trusted computer system evaluation criteria. *Department of Defense*, 1986.

[39] E. L. Lehmann and J. P. Romano. *Testing statistical hypotheses*. Springer, 2006.

[40] M. LeMay and J. Tan. Acoustic surveillance of physically unmodified PCs. In *Security and Management*, pages 328–334, 2006.

[41] F. J. Massey. The Kolmogorov-Smirnov test for goodness of fit. *Journal of the American Statistical Association*, 46(253):68–78, 1951.

[42] I. S. Moskowitz and M. H. Kang. Covert channels-here to stay? In *Computer Assurance, 1994. COMPASS'94 Safety, Reliability, Fault Tolerance, Concurrency and Real Time, Security. Proceedings of the Ninth Annual Conference on*, pages 235–243. IEEE, 1994.

[43] S. J. Murdoch. Hot or not: Revealing hidden services by their clock skew. In *Proceedings of the 13th ACM Conference on Computer and Communications Security*, CCS '06, pages 27–36, 2006.

[44] S. J. O'Malley and K.-K. R. Choo. Bridging the air gap: Inaudible data exfiltration by insiders. In *20th Americas Conference on Information Systems (AMCIS 2014)*, 2014.

[45] R. L. Peterson, R. E. Ziemer, and D. E. Borth. *Introduction to spread-spectrum communications*, volume 995. Prentice Hall New Jersey, 1995.

[46] J. G. Proakis. *Digital communications*. McGraw-Hill, New York, 2008.

[47] I. S. Reed and G. Solomon. Polynomial codes over certain finite fields. *Journal of the Society for Industrial & Applied Mathematics*, 8(2):300–304, 1960.

[48] C. E. Shannon. Communication theory of secrecy systems. *Bell System Technical Journal*, 28(4):656–715, 1949.

[49] V. Subramanian, S. Uluagac, H. Cam, and R. Beyah. Examining the characteristics and implications of sensor side channels. In *Communications (ICC), 2013 IEEE International Conference on*, pages 2205–2210, June 2013.

[50] E. Tromer. Acoustic cryptanalysis: on nosy people and noisy machines. *Eurocrypt2004 Rump Session, May*, 2004.

[51] E. Tromer. Hardware-based cryptanalysis. *Weizmann Institute of Science, Tese de Doutorado*, 2007.

[52] H. Urkowitz. Energy detection of unknown deterministic signals. *Proceedings of the IEEE*, 55(4):523–531, April 1967.

[53] A. Wyner. The wire-tap channel. *Bell System Technical Journal, The*, 54(8):1355–1387, Oct 1975.

[54] S. Zander, G. J. Armitage, and P. Branch. A survey of covert channels and countermeasures in computer network protocols. *IEEE Communications Surveys and Tutorials*, 9(1-4):44–57, 2007.

LiHB: Lost in HTTP Behaviors

A Behavior-Based Covert Channel in HTTP

Yao Shen[*]
Suzhou Institute for
Advanced Study
School of CS & Tech.
University of Science and
Technology of China
Hefei, 230026, China
shenyao@mail.ustc.edu.cn

Liusheng Huang
Suzhou Institute for
Advanced Study
School of CS & Tech.
University of Science and
Technology of China
Hefei, 230026, China
lshuang@ustc.edu.cn

Fei Wang
Department of
Computer Science
Purdue University
West Lafayette
Indiana, USA
feiwang@purdue.edu

Xiaorong Lu
Suzhou Institute for
Advanced Study
School of CS & Tech.
University of Science and
Technology of China
Hefei, 230026, China
ldayy@mail.ustc.edu.cn

Wei Yang
Suzhou Institute for
Advanced Study
School of CS & Tech.
University of Science and
Technology of China
Hefei, 230026, China
qubit@ustc.edu.cn

Lu Li
Suzhou Institute for
Advanced Study
School of CS & Tech.
University of Science and
Technology of China
Hefei, 230026, China
liluzq@mail.ustc.edu.cn

ABSTRACT

The application-layer covert channels have been extensively studied in recent years. Information-hiding in ubiquitous application packets can significantly improve the capacity of covert channels. However, the undetectability is still a knotty problem, because the existing covert channels are all frustrated by proper detection schemes. In this paper, we propose LiHB, a behavior-based covert channel in HTTP. When a client is browsing a website and downloading web-page objects, we can reveal some fluctuation behaviors that the distribution relationship between the ports opening and HTTP requests are flexible. Based on combinatorial nature of distributing N HTTP requests over M HTTP flows, such fluctuation can be exploited by LiHB channel to encode covert messages, which can obtain high stealthiness. Besides, LiHB achieves a considerable and controllable capacity by setting the number of webpage objects and HTTP flows. Compared with existing techniques, LiHB is the first covert channel implemented based on the unsuspicious behavior of browsers, the most important application-layer software. Because most HTTP proxies are using NAPT techniques, LiHB can also operate well even when a proxy is equipped, which poses a serious threat to individual privacy. Experimental results show that LiHB covert channel achieves a good capacity, reliability and high undetectability.

[*]The corresponding author.

IH&MMSec'15, June 17–19, 2015, Portland, Oregon, USA.
Copyright © 2015 ACM 978-1-4503-3587-4/15/06 ...$15.00.
http://dx.doi.org/10.1145/2756601.2756605.

Categories and Subject Descriptors

D.2.11 [**Software Engineering**]: Software Architectures-Information hiding

Keywords

Covert Channels; HTTP Behaviors; Combinatorics; Application Layer; Proxy; Browser

1. INTRODUCTION

Covert channel is a malicious conversation disguised in legitimate network communication allowing information leak to unauthorized receiver, which is a prevalent attack technique in the Internet today. Inchoate covert channels are implemented as steganographic methods in some static media, such as texts, audio files and images [23, 28]. However, with the accelerating development of internet, the ubiquity of network packets motivates the demand for covert channels in diverse network protocols. In recent years, the protocol-based covert channel has gained more attention in covert transmission and information hiding.

There are two kinds of protocol-based covert channels: covert timing channels and covert storage channels [4]. Covert timing channels encode messages by modulating the inter-packet delays (IPD). In general, covert timing channels are more undetectable but less reliable than the covert storage ones [12]. As previous research shows, the reliability, meaning that the covert message in the covert traffic should be rightly decoded, is always a difficult and inevitable problem for covert timing channels, because embedded signals in the IPDs can be easily distorted by unpredictable network jitters in the transmission route [4, 18]. Consequently, covert timing channels cannot be widely applied to practical use.

Previous protocol-based storage covert channels were mainly carried out in the header of TCP/IP packets, modifying the packet contents. But these channels can be easily ruined by the firewalls which just reset all the unused bits to zero or detected by simple test methods [29]. Considering the relatively rigorous formats of the header in lower-layer-protocol packets (like TCP, UDP, IP, etc), researchers focus on building covert channels in application-layer protocols. Since the variety of practical applications causes the flexibility of application-layer packets, which brings capacious room to covert attackers, application-layer protocols are more promising covert carriers than those lower-layer protocols.

Nowadays web-based network applications, including webpage browsing, e-mail and online shopping have become indispensable elements in people's jobs and daily lives. Thus the omnipresent HTTP packets now are regarded as suitable carriers for covert channels. Furthermore, information-hiding in ubiquitous HTTP packets greatly increases the capacity of covert channels. In the past decade, lots of HTTP-based storage channels were worked out. Brown et al. [3] proposed using URL strings and cookie strings to embed covert messages. Dyatlov et al. [8] adopted modification of the headers order and the case of a header name, or adding a custom field to hide information. Nevertheless, most of these channels are merely confined to the modification of packet contents and they can be frustrated by some advanced firewalls or statistical detection schemes. The undetectability of covert channels is still a knotty problem. As a result, to devise a new undetectable covert channel in HTTP is really an attractive and challenging task.

In this paper, we propose LiHB (Lost in HTTP Behaviors), a novel behavior-based covert channel in HTTP. According to lots of investigation and researches, we reveal the normal behavior fluctuations that distribution relationships between the ports opening and HTTP requests are flexible, when client is browsing a website and downloading webpage objects. Based on this, we design a reliable covert channel in HTTP. The main contributions can be summarized as follows.

1. We design LiHB based on the unsuspicious application-layer behaviors, without changing anything of HTTP envelope. The normal browser behavior gives an ideal shield for LiHB channel and no special client software is required. To the best of our knowledge, LiHB is the first covert channel that is implemented based on the natural behaviors of browsers, the most important application-layer software.

2. We apply the Enumerative Combinatorics to LiHB covert channel. LiHB uses a unique distribution relationship between N HTTP requests and M HTTP flows to encode a covert message. The hiding capacity of LiHB covert channel increases with encoding mechanism (N, M). By setting the number of webpage objects and flows, LiHB channel achieves a considerable and controllable hiding capacity.

3. Another important innovation is that, LiHB channel is capable of passing through HTTP proxy and covertly transfer covert messages to outside, which poses a serious threat to individual privacy.

4. We analyze capacity, reliability and undetectability of LiHB channel, evaluate its performance with corresponding experiments, and conclude that the capacity and undetectability of LiHB channel are pretty well.

Furthermore, the LiHB channel keeps a high reliability under poor network environment.

The remainder of this paper is organized as follows. In Section 2, a brief review of steganography methods in HTTP is given. Then we describe the preliminaries including the behaviors of browsers and the adversary detection methods in Section 3. In Section 4, we present the LiHB covert channel, and describe the detailed refinements. Next, we provide the proxy-based LiHB covert scheme in Section 5. In Section 6, we implement LiHB covert channel and evaluate its capacity, reliability and undetectability with experiments. Finally, we conclude our work in Section 7.

2. RELATED WORK

A typical covert channel in HTTP is called *HTTP tunnel*. In the majority of protected networks, many protocols are inhibited while as the commonest application-layer protocol, HTTP communications are barely intercepted. For this reason, the tunnel just disguises the prohibited protocols as legitimate-looking HTTP traffic by encapsulating the covert transmission inside the payload of HTTP, bypassing configured scrutiny. As Fig. 1 shows, a TCP packet of HTTP tunnel has a transport-layer shell and an unsuspicious HTTP header. Such tunnels were successfully defeated by

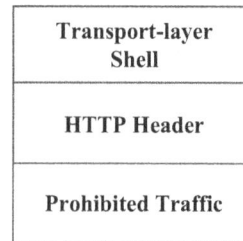

| Transport-layer Shell |
| HTTP Header |
| Prohibited Traffic |

Figure 1: Packet structure of HTTP tunnels

the fingerprint-based detection (FBD) mechanism proposed by Dusi et al. [7]. The FBD method believes that if there are other protocols encapsulated in HTTP, the behavior characteristics of the communication will be much different from that of a legitimate one. The mechanism concentrates on some statistical characteristics deriving from two elements of TCP packets, inter-packet delays and packet sizes in normal HTTP interactions and composes them as a protocol fingerprint in order to differentiate the covert tunnels, achieving a detection accuracy of 98%.

Another covert channel in HTTP utilizes URL strings and cookie strings to embed cover messages [3]. However, the inexistent URLs, the illegal tampering in cookies and the traffic anomalies caused by such techniques cannot evade application-layer gateways and deep payload inspections [7]. The latest study of HTTP covert channel indicates that the format of header in the HTTP envelope can be exploited to generate covert traffic. In the HTTP envelope, there are abundant keys and optional parameters, some of which have default values and can be omitted. If we need their default values in packets, the presence and absence of them can encode bits [3], as illustrated in Fig. 2.

According to RFC2616 [10], HTTP is insensitive to the order, the word space and the letter case of those keys and parameters, which provides sufficient format redundancy for

```
GET / HTTP/1.1
Accept: */*
Accept-Language: en-gb
Accept-Encoding: gzip, deflate
User-Agent: Mozilla/4.0(compatible; MSIE 6.0)
Host: www.google.com
Connection: Keep-Alive

GET / HTTP /1.1
Accept: */*
Accept-Language: en-gb
Accept-Encoding: gzip, deflate
User-Agent: Mozilla/4.0(compatible; MSIE 6.0)
Host: www.google.com
```

Figure 2: Presence and absence of the "Connection" Key

covert channels by reordering keys or parameters, adjusting spaces and modulating letter cases. Additionally, in practice, most HTTP applications are designed to neglect any unrecognized keys or parameters and only treat the problematic packets with the surplus recognized keys. Hence, to insert custom strings into appropriate location is also a useful technique [8]. Figure 3 and 4 illustrate examples of the two HTTP covert channels, respectively.

```
GET / HTTP/1.1
Accept: */*
Accept-Language: en-gb
Accept-Encoding: gzip, deflate
User-Agent: Mozilla/4.0 (compatible; MSIE 6.0)
Host: www.google.com
Connection: Keep-Alive

GET / HTTP /1.1
Accept: */*
Accept-Language: en-gb
Accept-Encoding: gzip, deflate
Host: www.google.com
User-Agent: Mozilla/4.0 (compatible; MSIE 6.0)
Connection: Keep-Alive
```

Figure 3: Reordering the "Host" and "User-Agent" key

```
GET / HTTP/1.1
Accept: Hello, */*
Accept-Language: en-gb
Accept-Encoding: gzip, deflate
User-Agent: Mozilla/4.0 (compatible; MSIE 6.0)
Host: www.google.com
Connection: Keep-Alive
```

Figure 4: Use of a custom string "Hello"

These artful channels [1] were revealed by the signature-based detection (SBD) method. The SBD mechanism was first proposed by Castro [5], then improved by Borders et al. [2] and Kwecka [17]. The SBD method can collect signatures of common HTTP applications so as to discover abnormal communications in an efficient way by signature searching and comparing. So far, various covert channels in HTTP

have been proposed while they were all routed by proper detection schemes or haunted by high bit error rate [11]. They failed because they can't get away from fixed mind-sets that we can only encode messages by altering something of HTTP envelope. Thus the undetectability of the covert channels in HTTP is still a burning question.

In the transport-layer, some researches have made use of Enumerative Combinatorics [26] to convey hidden messages, one of main techniques in our work. Especially, Luo et al. [20–22] designed a combinatorics-based scheme, called Cloak, to transmit information in the ordering of packets within different flows. Based on the 12-fold way in [26], Cloak offers ten different encoding and decoding methods, each of which has a unique tradeoff between undetectability and capacity. While it was carefully crafted, the encoding method for Cloak was rooted in transport layer, in which the traffic was more strictly censored by security applications than that of application layer. Moreover, manipulating the TCP packet-flow distribution artificially is prone to rousing suspicion of adversaries. In [13,20], the authors proposed a detection method that targeted the Cloak channel by measuring the intervals between acknowledgment and data packets. Therefore, it is more desirable to have a more stealthy covert channel with combinatorial algorithms.

Differences from This Work: Our work distinguishes itself from others by designing an application-layer covert channel, LiHB, based on the unsuspicious HTTP behaviors of browsers. Unlike previous work [20] that exploited Enumerative Combinatorics in transport layer, this work utilizes combinatorial nature of distributing HTTP requests into HTTP flows to convey covert messages under the shield of the application-layer behavior, without changing any content of HTTP packets. Especially, the LiHB channel rooted in application layer can circumvent censorship by many security applications. Furthermore, this work features that the LiHB is capable of transferring secret messages stealthily through the proxy server, and no additional application is required for the LiHB channel.

3. PRELIMINARY

3.1 HTTP Behaviors

All the existing HTTP covert channels are concerned about how to slightly modify the packet contents to embed covert messages without overt anomalies. As the saying goes, as vice rises one foot, virtues rises ten; virtue dwarfs vice. No matter how subtle the content variation is, it can always be caught by an intended monitor. Completely different from those steganography techniques, LiHB doesn't change any solid elements which may cause communication anomalies in the packets, but it only utilizes the unsuspicious fluctuations of protocol behaviors in practical HTTP applications. In the following of this section, we'll discuss what the behavior of fluctuation should be.

Among numerous HTTP applications, the web browser is the commonest. So, we focus on the communication behaviors of those browsers. When a browser downloads a webpage, it will first ask for the HTML document and then receive other associated network objects, e.g. images and scripts. The scenario in Fig. 5 illustrates the amounts of HTTP requests at different times when a client is browsing a website. It can be seen in this figure that the request distribution has crests and troughs. Every crest is a busy time

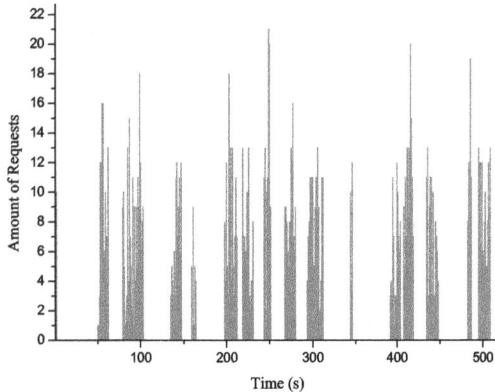

Figure 5: Distribution of requests in web-browsing

denote the requests for them by r_1, r_2, r_3, r_4, r_5. Assuming that we always build two HTTP flows (F_1, F_2) for this page, when we first visit this page, the correspondence is r_1, r_2 sent in F_1 and r_3, r_4, r_5 sent in F_2, while it may be r_1, r_3, r_4 sent in F_1 and r_2, r_5 sent in F_2 at the second time.

With the above observation, we define this natural behavior as behavior fluctuation of browsers. In practice, it is almost always overlooked due to irrelevance or its university in browsers. Actually, the fluctuation is mainly caused by the scheduling algorithm used by browsers. Since one HTTP flow corresponds to a opening port, the behavior fluctuation in web-browsing is the uncertainty of distribution relationships between the ports opening and the HTTP requests. Designed based on this characteristic, the LiHB channel can transmit information imperceptibly from the client to the receiver outside.

3.2 Adversary Detection Model

The adversary of our covert channel is an HTTP detection system, which is armed with two most effective detection methods, the FBD (fingerprint-based detection) [6,7], the SBD (signature-based detection) [5,17] and the state-of-the-art detection methods [4,12,14] for covert timing channels. The adversary detection system is deployed on the gateway or proxy server of the private network, monitoring the incoming and outgoing traffic flows.

The FBD is a statistical method analyzing behaviors of protocols [27]. HTTP has its own behavior characteristics, named HTTP fingerprint, which is clearly different from that of other protocols. The fingerprint is measured by the IPD sequence and the packet size sequence in a flow. The fingerprint is trained by massive legitimate flows of this protocol. Each tested flow will be given an anomaly score computed from its fingerprint, and the flow will be identified as a covert one if its anomaly score is much higher than that of legitimate flows.

The SBD is a useful logical method to alert textual anomaly in protocols [17]. The technique treats the format features in the envelope as a signature of an HTTP application and is sure that the signature is a constant. As a result, if an HTTP application is observed changing its signature in its packets during a communication, it will be identified as covert [17]. So when an HTTP flow starts, the textual features will be recorded as a signature denoted by a regular expression. If the signature is changed during the flow, which means that the the signature cannot match the original regular expression, the flow will be considered as a covert one.

interval with the outburst in requests while every trough is a silent period containing no requests. In terms of the HTTP behaviors, a crest represents the requests for an integrated HTML file including the text webpage and its associated objects, while a trough between two consecutive crests is the time for visitors to handle the documents, such as reading news, thinking over a problem and saving elements. Based on researches in [19,27], the trough period should be longer than 10s, otherwise two request crests would belong to one period.

In each crest, the HTTP requests are not sent in a single port and a port can also send more than one request. In practice, to open how many ports for requests and to dispatch how many requests in a single HTTP session are not invariable behaviors and differ from implementation to implementation. We use two different PCs, including a Lenovo desktop and ThinkPad laptop, to visit the homepage of the SINA website [24] by three popular browsers (i.e. Google Chrome, Firefox and Microsoft Internet Explorer) twice in half an hour. The page has 240 associated objects in total and the amounts of ports opened for downloading the whole page are listed in Table 1.

Table 1: The Variety of Port Amounts

Browser	PC1	PC2
Chrome	46	42
	43	44
Firefox	37	39
	40	43
Microsoft IE	49	45
	42	48

As shown in Table 1, in order to open a web page quickly for users, the browser generally adopts to establish several HTTP flows simultaneously to download webpage objects. More specially, the statistical results adequately demonstrate that the amounts of ports for opening a webpage are flexible, even in the same HTTP application and the same machine. Besides, we also track all the HTTP requests and their corresponding ports simultaneously, disclosing that congruent relationships between the HTTP requests and the HTTP flows are not constant either. For instance, a webpage consisting of a HTML document and 4 associated network objects is stored in a single HTTP server and we

4. LIHB COVERT CHANNEL

HTTP [10] is an application-level protocol used for information transfer on the internet, and the Internet browser is the commonest HTTP application. This is the foundation of our LiHB covert channel. In this section, we describe the covert scheme of the LiHB channel.

In Fig. 6, we depict a common scenario during internet surfing: the client browser sends HTTP requests for downloading the webpage objects when browsing webpages. The communication channel in HTTP consists of a encoder, which is usually an HTTP client, and a decoder, which usually eavesdrops and decodes the secret information in the transmission path or on the gateway. The true receiver (i.e. the decoder) decodes covert messages whereas the seeming

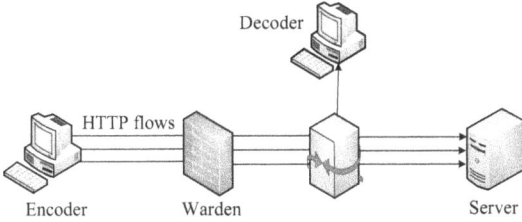

Figure 6: Communication scenario of LiHB in web-browsing

receiver (i.e. the web server) responds to the client browser. The detailed scheme is described below.

4.1 The Encoding and Decoding Scheme

The covert messages in LiHB are encoded based on the request-flow combination, that is, each covert message is encoded with a unique request distribution over HTTP flows. The sender adopts normal distribution of HTTP requests over flows in browsing webpages to encode covert messages, without changing any packet contents. Thus the whole encoding and sending processes are legitimate looking.

Inherent characteristics of LiHB channel guarantee its synchronicity and reliability. In principle, LiHB exploits a fixed number of requests for webpage objects to convey a covert message. More Specially, the encoder transmits the $i + 1$th segment only after receiving all the N ACKs for ith segment. The decoder, on the other hand, starts decoding as soon as collecting N requests from encoder, which ensures the synchronicity of transmission. Besides, the HTTP behaviors of browser that LiHB adopts is based on TCP at the transport layer, which is a connection-oriented reliable protocol via flow control, error control and congestion control. Therefore, without additional mechanism, LiHB channel can achieve nearly 100% decoding accuracy, even in presence of packet losses, delay jitters and packet reordering.

The encoder and decoder agree on the values of N and M beforehand. The N network objects are chose from a webpage. The requests for webpage objects are identified as same, whereas the M HTTP flows are distinguished and ordered based on the sequence of TCP three-way handshaking between the encoder and server. The encoder distributes the N HTTP requests over M HTTP flows, and sends the requests to the receiver. This distribution relationship constitutes the encoding mechanism (N, M). In this round, the total number of possible arrangements is $C(N + M - 1, M - 1)$. Hence LiHB can transmit L-bit messages one time, where $L = \lfloor \log_2 C(N + M - 1, M - 1) \rfloor$.

Table 2: Encoding 4-bit Messages into Request-Flow Distribution when $(N, M) = (6, 3)$

Messages	F_1	F_2	F_3	Messages	F_1	F_2	F_3
0	6	0	0	8	3	1	2
1	5	1	0	9	3	0	3
2	5	0	1	10	2	4	0
3	4	2	0	11	2	3	1
4	4	1	1	12	2	2	2
5	4	0	2	13	2	1	3
6	3	3	0	14	2	0	4
7	3	2	1	15	1	5	0

Consider a simple example of mechanism $(6, 3)$. There are a total of $C_2^8 = 28$ possible ways of distributing the 6 requests over the 3 HTTP flows. Given that $\lfloor \log_2(28) \rfloor = 4$ bits, we use 16 of the 28 combinations to encode 4-bit secret information. Table 2 shows the specific correspondence between 4-bit messages and request distributions, where F_i is number of HTTP requests dispatched to ith HTTP flow. As we can see, if the sender encodes secret messages "1010", its corresponding decimal value is '10', and its request distribution is $F_1 = 2$, $F_2 = 4$, $F_3 = 0$.

Since the request-flow encoding space is potentially huge, a table-lookup approach does not work effectively. Moreover, exchanging explicit codebook between encoder and decoder is not absolutely safe. Therefore based on combinatorial algorithms 2.7 and 2.8 in [16], two functions $Rank()$ and $Unrank()$ are used for coding and decoding, respectively. The $Rank()$ function takes a request-flow distribution, denoted by $\boldsymbol{F}$, and returns the index (i.e. the $rank$), denoted by R, of the array in all distributions that are arranged in a lexicographic ordering. The $Unrank()$ function performs the opposite.

Algorithm 1: LiHB Channel Encoding Algorithm

Input: The encoder holds the covert messages, Meg;
Output: A sequence of request-flow distributions, $\boldsymbol{F}$;
1: agree on the values of N and M beforehand
2: establish M HTTP flows with three-way handshake
3: split covert messages Meg into L-bit segments, Seg_1, Seg_2, $\cdots$
4: convert the binary Seg_i to decimal $rank$ R_i
5: call $Unrank(R_i)$, return its distribution $\boldsymbol{F}$
6: $\boldsymbol{F} = \langle F_1, F_2, \cdots, F_M \rangle$
7: distribute F_i HTTP requests to the ith flow
8: send HTTP requests to server according to normal behavior patterns
9: count the number of ACKs in each flow
10: partially retransmit unacknowledged requests
11: return to step 4 until transmission is terminated

Covert traffic in the sender is generated in the following four steps, as shown in Algorithm 1.

1. First of all, the encoder and decoder determine the number of selected webpage objects N and agree on the values of HTTP flows M beforehand. Encoder and decoder use three-way handshake to establish M flows successively (lines 1-2), so that both the encoder and decoder can distinguish the flows according to handshake sequence.

2. The encoder splits the binary covert messages Meg into L-bit segments, Seg_1, Seg_2, $\cdots$. The message Seg_i is converted into its decimal $rank$, R_i. Then the encoder translates the R_i into the request-distribution $\boldsymbol{F} = \langle F_1, F_2, \cdots, F_M \rangle$ by calling the $Unrank()$ function (lines 3-6).

3. The encoder distributes F_i requests to the ith flow and sends the HTTP requests successively according to normal sending patterns (lines 7-8), which we discuss in Section 4.4.

4. Encoder counts the number of ACKs for the requests in each HTTP flow. If some HTTP requests are

not responded or a timeout occurs, encoder partially retransmits the HTTP requests in the corresponding flows (lines 9-10). Encoder cannot send the next segment Seg_{i+1} until all the ACKs for Seg_i are received. Subsequently, encoding process returns to Step 4, and sends the next segment until the whole transmission is completed.

The four-step process in encoding scheme above is reversed for decoding covert messages. In the first step, the decoder obtains the request-flow distribution $\boldsymbol{F}$ from the M flows and the requests received from the encoder. It is noteworthy that the decoder can distinguish the flows and count the number of requests in each flow, based on the order of three-way handshake. As soon as the decoder receives the N requests for the ith message, it invokes the function $Rank(\boldsymbol{F})$ to generate the corresponding $rank$. At the same time, the web server normally acknowledges the HTTP requests immediately after they arrive. In the end, the decimal information (i.e., the $rank$s) are converted to the original secret messages.

4.2 Multi-website Visiting Mechanism

During internet surfing, it is suspicious to access to the same webpage continuously, which may induce anomalies and be detected by security applications. Therefore, it is more desirable to have a usual access behavior of normal user for LiHB covert channel. In this section, we consider an important refinement to LiHB.

To mimic the normal visiting behavior and eliminate such anomalies, we propose a *multi-website visiting* mechanism. The basic idea of this method is that, the encoder and decoder agree on a group of web pages denoted by $\mathbb{W}$, each of which consists of at least N associated objects. Note that the selected web pages $W_1, \cdots, W_g$ in $\mathbb{W}$ is chosen from usual visited web pages of normal user. In this way, the visiting behavior utilized in LiHB channel will not raise any suspicion.

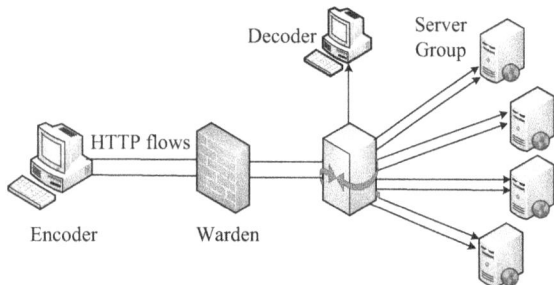

Figure 7: Multi-website visiting mode

After using one webpage for encoding, the encoder will ask for a new page to embed covert messages. To avoid using a fixed sequence of webpages, we let the index of $(i+1)$th webpage be computed as follows:

$$W_{i+1} = H(W_i, Seg_i) \tag{1}$$

where $H(\cdot)$ is a hash function that generates the pseudo-random value of in the range of $[1, g]$, g is the number of selected webpages, W_i is the index of the ith page and Seg_i is the message to be sent in page W_i.

The encoder and decoder can update and enlarge the group of web sites after a period of time. Moreover, they agree on the method to select web pages. The hash chain employed by encoder and decoder generates the random index of next visited webpage, which to some content mimic the normal visiting behavior.

4.3 Head-of-Line Blocking Problem

Head-of-line blocking (HOL blocking) in computer networking is a performance-limiting phenomenon that occurs when a line of packets is held-up by the first packet. We consider this problem in the design, otherwise it would decrease the data rate of transmission.

To tackle this problem, we adopt the D-limited transmission scheme following [21]. The basic idea of D-limited transmission scheme admits limiting the maximum number of requests assigned to a HTTP flow to D considering TCP $cwnd$. That is, it enforces $max\{F_1, \cdots, F_m\} \leq D$, where all the packet size of the D requests should be less than the encoder's TCP $cwnd$. Therefore, in the encoding scheme, LiHB channel should choose more reasonable request-flow distributions to embed covert messages, ignoring the combinations in which $F_i > D$.

At the same time, the encoder will dispatch the HTTP requests belonging to the kth message after receiving all ACKs that acknowledge the requests for $(k-1)$th message or a timer with period T_E expires. If the encoder does not receive all the expected ACKs before T_E, it will retransmit the unacknowledged requests and reset the timer based on the estimated RTT.

4.4 Evading Detection

No additional client software is required for LiHB. The design is based on the unsuspicious behavior of browsers in terms of the request distribution over HTTP flows. Therefore the LiHB traffic is identified as legitimate-looking when passing wardens or firewalls. Furthermore, LiHB channel does not modify any content of packets, thus evading those content-based detection methods [2] against the HTTP-based covert channels.

The timing-based detection tests can be divided into two classes: shape test and regularity test [12]. The shape of traffic for LiHB channel is related to the request distribution, which depends on the inter-request delay (IRD) between HTTP requests. To evade the shape test, the sending pattern of requests in LiHB is carefully crafted to imitate the request distribution illustrated in Fig. 5 with the IRDs extracted from normal web sessions.

The regularity of traffic is determined by the inter-packet delays (IPD). To evade such detection, LiHB can mimic the normal timing behaviors of browsers by dispatching HTTP requests according to the IPD distribution extracted from traces of normal web sessions. According to the actual statistical results and researches in [19, 27], in this paper we assume the normal time delays between HTTP requests follow the Poisson distribution. Furthermore, the IPDs between packets depend on the algorithm of IPD generator. Thus in our channel, we exploit a Poisson generator to generate the discrete time sequence. The generator is denoted by the formula:

$$\mathbf{T}_{len} = PoissonDist(\lambda, len) \tag{2}$$

where $\mathbf{T}_{len}$ is the time series patterns $(\Delta_1, \Delta_2, \cdots, \Delta_{len})$, λ is the expectation of the Poisson distribution, and len is the amount of intervals needed for sending requests.

On the timeline, HTTP requests are sent on basis of the generated Poisson timeline, which commendably simulates the time series model of normal communication.

5. LIHB THROUGH PROXY SERVER

In our work, LiHB channel is capable of transferring secret messages stealthily through the proxy server, which incorporated with intrusions would pose a serious threat to individual privacy.

5.1 NAPT in HTTP Proxy

Nowadays, the ways of accessing to the Internet can be classified into three groups: direct routing, NAT based, and proxy based.

The covert scheme above is under condition of accessing internet by direct routing. NAT (Network Address Translation) [9] service uses a gateway connected to the Internet, translating between local and global addresses. Compared to direct routing, LiHB channel is also equally applicable to the NAT based. Only one difference is that it has a process of address translation between internal IP and public IP.

The proxy server is a software service based on HTTP and serves as a agent between the browser and Web server [15]. The client doesn't need external routable address because it isn't directly connected to the Internet. Using proxy server, it is quick to obtain internet resources by its caching functionality. Besides, it can also regularize behaviors of users by controlling access to internet resources and enhance security of private network by protecting their IP addresses from attacks. Thus accessing internet via a HTTP proxy service is more common. Specially, middle and small scale network generally use proxy servers for accessing internet.

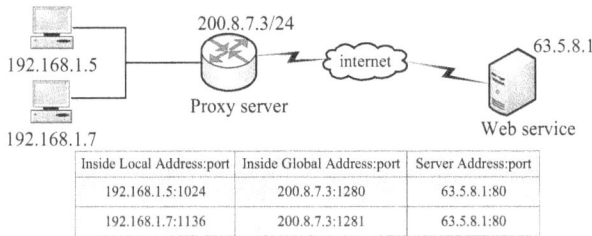

Inside Local Address:port	Inside Global Address:port	Server Address:port
192.168.1.5:1024	200.8.7.3:1280	63.5.8.1:80
192.168.1.7:1136	200.8.7.3:1281	63.5.8.1:80

Figure 8: Working principle of HTTP proxy

Based on lots of investigation, the working principle of HTTP proxy is based on NAPT (Network Address Port Translation) [25]. NAPT can be considered as a extension of NAT. Given the potential snag of NAT that global addresses may be insufficient for LAN users, NAPT service adopts to map multiple internal addresses to a legitimate public IP address using different port numbers, which is address translation between tuples $\langle internal\ IP : internal\ port \rangle$ and tuples $\langle external\ IP : external\ port \rangle$. In practice, the common proxy ISA 2006 and Wingate are in this way.

As illustrated in Fig. 8, for example, there are two machines, 192.168.1.5 and 192.168.1.7, connected to the server in the internet, 63.5.8.1. When the requests of two machines are passing through the HTTP proxy, the proxy server not only converts the source address of the IP packet to the public IP, 200.8.7.3, but also converts the source port to an external port. At the same time, the proxy server puts the mapping relationship into its cache. We can see that the

two machines are assigned to same external IP but different external ports. The combination of an IP address and port uniquely identifies a HTTP flow. The proxy server forwards the modified requests to the internet, receives the response, and then sends it back to the machine in the internal network according to the mapping table.

5.2 LiHB Through HTTP Proxy

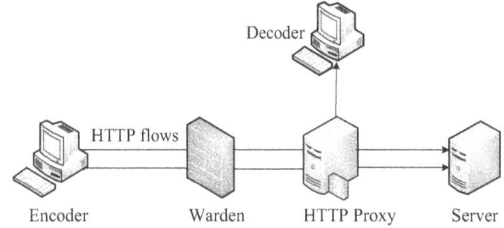

Figure 9: Communication scenario of LiHB covert channel through HTTP proxy

The proxy-based service is one of main methods to access the Internet. LiHB channel is also applicable to this case to transmit secret messages "silently" through the HTTP proxy. As depicted in Fig. 9, we can see that the communication scenario is similar with that in Fig. 6 except a proxy server. Therefore how to pass through the HTTP proxy imperceptibly is the crucial issue in our LiHB channel.

The encoding and decoding scheme are operated on the sender and receiver sides, respectively. Those are not changed in the proxy-based LiHB channel. The main differences in the transmission model are described as follows.

5.2.1 On Sender Side

Based on the webpage resources, the encoder and decoder agree on the number of N and M beforehand. When internal network is equipped with proxy server, the proxy-based LiHB channel works as follows:

a) Under proxy mode, the sender and receiver don't have direct communication. During three-way handshake, there is a process of user authentication and authorization between the sender and proxy server. Then as the encoding algorithm 1 shows, sender operates the covert messages, calls the $Unrank()$ function, and distributes the request packets over the HTTP flows.

b) Once HTTP requests firstly arrive the HTTP proxy, the proxy server replaces the source IP and source port of the request packets with IP of proxy and new external port. Then the proxy puts the mapping relationship into its cache, and forwards it to the Internet.

5.2.2 On Receiver Side

According to the handshake sequence between proxy and web server, the decoder distinguishes the M HTTP flows by different external ports. Based on NAPT technique, the mapping table $\mathbb{T}$ composed of IP addresses and ports, guarantees the N requests dispatched to M flows arrive the receiver in the another M flows.

Monitoring each flow, the decoder counts the number of requests and the server responds each request with a ACK. The ACKs return to the sender according to the mapping table $\mathbb{T}$. After receiving N requests, the decoder calls the decoding function $Rank(\boldsymbol{F})$, converts the request-flow distribution to a *rank*, and decodes the original covert message.

It is important to note that, when encoder sends the requests persistently, the resources may be hit in the cache of proxy server. Based on the investigation in [15], it can be assumed that every time the object that the client applies for is cache hit, the proxy adopts to send a revalidation request to the web server. If it has been changed, the server will return new resource, otherwise, the server returns a small "304 Not Modified" packet. Note that the revalidation requests are also counted as the requests from the encoder, thus the amounts of requests from client dispatched to each HTTP flow remains unchanged. In this way, covert messages from encoder can be transferred to the receiver by proxy-based LiHB channel. Furthermore, the security mechanism of LiHB channel, especially the synchronism and reliability mechanism are also applicable to proxy-based LiHB.

6. EXPERIMENTS AND EVALUATION

6.1 Experimental Setup

In the experiments, we implement the LiHB and proxy-based LiHB channel in C language on Windows 7 with Intel's Pentium Dual-Core CPU 3.20GHz. We conduct the experiments in a test bed which allows us to study the impact of custom network conditions on the channel performance.

Some parameters should be determined before experiment. Regarding the encoding mechanism (N, M), we are to try different number of webpage objects, N, from small to large. Considering the browsers have limits on number of concurrent connections, i.e. the *maximum concurrent connections (MCC)*, the range of M is limited. Although the default number of MCC can be modified arbitrarily, we adopt to follow the normal usage and set the number at 6, because current browsers, e.g., Internet Explorer 10, Chrome and Firefox usually set it like this. Thus in this experiment M is set to 6 as a constant, but can be modified according to actual requirements.

Data collection of legitiamte and covert HTTP flows is also a necessary preparation. We collect $102,200$ HTTP requests from $2,000$ LiHB flows on the border gateway of a campus network and $82,000$ HTTP requests from $1,800$ proxy-based LiHB flows on a company's proxy server, which both are as covert HTTP flows. Meanwhile, we collect $100,000$ HTTP packets from $2,400$ normal HTTP flows as our legitimate HTTP flows. The HTTP envelope and the time series (i.e., IRDs and IPDs) are all obtained from the legitimate and covert HTTP packets. Additionally, we employ the SBD and FBD detection method as the adversary, and deploy them on the gateway or proxy server of the LAN.

6.2 Capacity Experiment

For evaluating the channel capacity, we should consider the encoding mechanism of LiHB and analyze the impact of N, M and IPDs. As mentioned above, M is a constant. The IPDs are generated by Poisson generator with the expectation parameter λ. Thus there are two factors, i.e. N and λ influencing the channel capacity.

In this experiment, we adopt the variable-controlling approach to test the transmission rate of LiHB channel. First, we transmit a 24-KB file on the channel ten times, in which N is set from small to large, and λ is set to 40 as a constant.

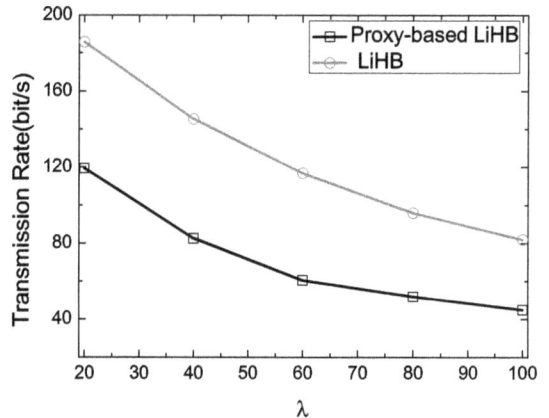

Figure 10: Correlation between transmission rate and λ

The average transmission rate is shown in Table 3. Secondly, we transmit the same file on another channel ten times, in which N is set to 50 based on first experiment, and λ is set from small to large. The average transmission rate is illustrated in Fig. 10.

Table 3: Transmission Rate with Different N

Covert Channel Rate(bit/s)	Number of Objects N				
	20	50	80	100	120
LiHB	92	145	178	196	201
Proxy-based LiHB	63	97	119	124	129

From the Table 3, it can be seen that the transmission rate increases logarithmically with the growth of N. Compared to the LiHB channel, the proxy-based LiHB has a lower transmission rate, because when requests pass through proxy server, this process takes some time. As shown in Fig. 10, the transmission rate decreases with the growth of λ, because λ is expectation and variance of the IPDs. When λ is less than 40ms, both the LiHB channels achieve a good performance in transmission rate. By setting appropriate values of the parameters, our LiHB channel can achieve a controllable transmission rate.

6.3 Reliability Experiment

For evaluating the channel reliability, we conduct the experiment under different network environment. In the testbed, we control network delay δ to test the reliability of LiHB channel. To evaluate the reliability, we introduce one assessment criteria, the *segment error rate (SER)*. The SER is defined in the formula:

$$SER = \frac{\sum_{i=1}^{size} h(Seg_i, Seg_i')}{size} \quad (3)$$

where Seg_i is the encoded covert messages, Seg_i' is the received messages, $size$ is the amounts of covert segments, and $h(Seg_i, Seg_i')$ is computed based on the levenstein distance.

In this experiment, the N is 50, M is 6 and λ is 40 based on capacity experiment. Regarding the impact of RTT, we

Table 4: Results of Reliability Experiment

Covert Channel	δ (ms)	SER Text	SER Word	SER PDF
LiHB	50	0.00	0.00	0.00
	200	0.00	0.00	0.00
	500	0.00	0.00	0.01
Proxy-based LiHB	50	0.00	0.00	0.00
	200	0.00	0.00	0.00
	500	0.00	0.00	0.01

vary the network delay δ in test-bed. With the LiHB and proxy-based LiHB, we transmit a 20-KB text file, a 20-KB word file and a 24-KB PDF file with different delay jitters. The transmission results are shown in Table 4. It can be seen that, the SER of both channels are almost zero under any network jitters. Hence the LiHB channel keeps a high reliability under poor network environment.

6.4 Undetectability Experiment

In this experiment, we evaluate the undetectability of Li-HB channel from two tests: shape test and regularity test. The former is to examine whether the distribution of LiHB channel is different from the normal, whereas the latter is to check whether the LiHB can be detected by the adversary detection methods.

First, we analyze the distribution of normal communication and LiHB traffic. In one single transmission with Poisson generator, the time sequence $(\Delta_1, \Delta_2, \cdots, \Delta_{len})$ is applied for sending HTTP requests. In normal communication and LiHB communication, we depict the distribution of HTTP requests between a pair of hosts with the obtained IRDs. The request distribution of the two communications are shown in Fig. 11. Obviously, the request distribution of the two communications are similar without distinguishing features. The request distribution under proxy-based network is also similar. Therefore, the LiHB channel with a suitable Poisson generator mimics the sending behavior of normal communication nicely.

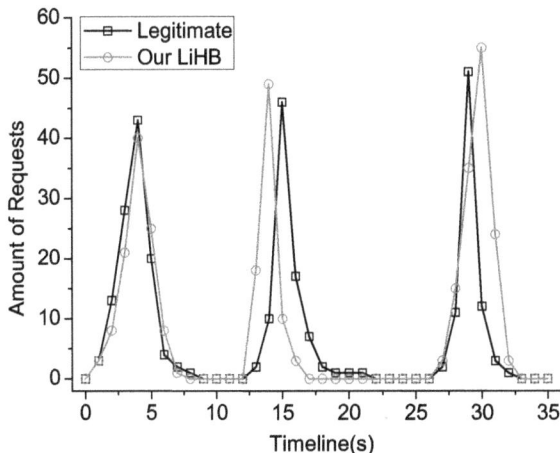

Figure 11: Request distribution of LiHB channel and legitimate channel

Secondly, we test our LiHB traffic against two main detection methods, the SBD and FBD method. Using SB-

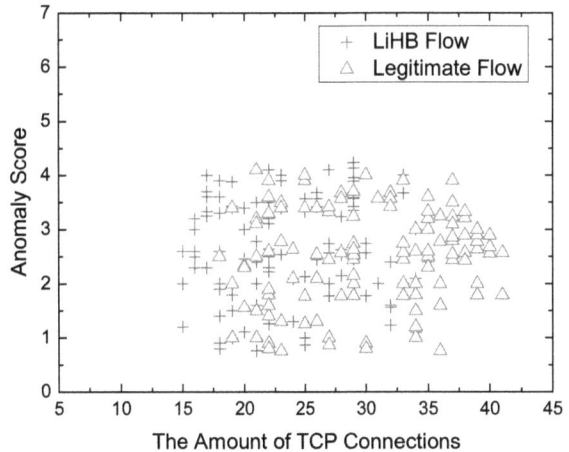

Figure 12: Anomaly scores of LiHB and legitimate channel with FBD Method

D method, we test the legitimate HTTP flows, LiHB and proxy-based LiHB HTTP flows. The detection results are shown in Table 5. It can be seen that the SBD cannot detect LiHB channel from the true positive rate (TPR), because it is a logical detection method and performs well in textual steganography. However, our LiHB channel is based on HTTP behaviors without changing any format of HTTP envelope.

Table 5: Detection Results using SBD Method

Channel	Flows	Alerts	TPR(%)
Legitimate	1,000	0	0.0
LiHB	2,000	0	0.0
Proxy-based Legitimate	1,000	1	0.1
Proxy-based LiHB	1,800	2	0.1

The FBD method focuses on the protocol fingerprint including the IPDs and packet size sequence in a flow. If anomaly score is much higher than that of legitimate flows, it will be identified as covert. Analyzing the coding mechanism, the number of resources N and M have little effect on undetectability. The expectation of IPDs, λ, is related with detection results of FBD. It is apparent that when λ is much bigger or smaller than normal level, the IPDs can be identified as covert. Thus λ is set to 40 empirically. The FBD model is trained with 1,000 legitimate and 1,000 LiHB HTTP flows to establish normal HTTP fingerprints. Next, we test the remaining legitimate and LiHB HTTP flows. The anomaly scores of legitimate and LiHB channel are depicted in Fig. 12. We can see that the scores of two channel mix together in the picture, and cannot be distinguished by the FBD method. The distribution of anomaly scores under proxy-based network is also the same case. Therefore, the two detection methods can hardly detect our LiHB covert channel so that LiHB channel achieves a high undetectability.

7. CONCLUSIONS

In this paper, we have proposed LiHB (Lost in HTTP Behaviors), a novel behavior-based covert channel in HTTP. Previous application-layer covert channels still had problems in undetectability. Based on the unsuspicious behaviors of browsers, we have designed LiHB channel through the combinatorial nature of distributing N requests over M HTTP flows. Besides, our channel has achieved a controllable capacity and operated well in a proxy-based network. Finally, we have implemented LiHB channel and evaluated its performance. Experimental results show that LiHB covert channel has achieved a good capacity, reliability and high undetectability.

8. ACKNOWLEDGMENTS

This work was supported by the Basic Perspective Project of SGCC (No. XXN51201304253).

9. REFERENCES

[1] M. Bauer. New covert channels in http: adding unwitting web browsers to anonymity sets. In *Proceedings of the 2003 ACM workshop on Privacy in the electronic society*, pages 72–78. ACM, 2003.

[2] K. Borders and A. Prakash. Web tap: detecting covert web traffic. In *Proceedings of the 11th ACM conference on Computer and communications security*, pages 110–120. ACM, 2004.

[3] E. Brown, B. Yuan, D. Johnson, and P. Lutz. Covert channels in the http network protocol: Channel characterization and detecting man-in-the-middle attacks. In *Proc. 5th Intern. Conf. Information Warfare and Security. Ohio, USA*, pages 56–65, 2010.

[4] S. Cabuk, C. E. Brodley, and C. Shields. Ip covert timing channels: design and detection. In *Proceedings of the 11th ACM conference on Computer and communications security*, pages 178–187. ACM, 2004.

[5] S. Castro. Covert channel and tunneling over the http protocol detection: Gw implementation theoretical design. *Gray World. net Team, Novembro*, 2003.

[6] M. Crotti, M. Dusi, F. Gringoli, and L. Salgarelli. Traffic classification through simple statistical fingerprinting. *ACM SIGCOMM Computer Communication Review*, 37(1):5–16, 2007.

[7] M. Dusi, M. Crotti, F. Gringoli, and L. Salgarelli. Tunnel hunter: Detecting application-layer tunnels with statistical fingerprinting. *Computer Networks*, 53(1):81–97, 2009.

[8] A. Dyatlov and S. Castro. Exploitation of data streams authorized by a network access control system for arbitrary data transfers: tunneling and covert channels over the http protocol. *Grayworld, USA, http://grayworld. net/projects/papers/html/ covert_paper. html*, 2003.

[9] K. Egevang and P. Francis. The ip network address translator (nat). Technical report, RFC 1631, 1994.

[10] R. Fielding, J. Gettys, J. Mogul, H. Frystyk, L. Masinter, P. Leach, and T. Berners-Lee. Hypertext transfer protocol–http/1.1, 1999.

[11] A. Galatenko, A. Grusho, A. Kniazev, and E. Timonina. Statistical covert channels through proxy server. In *Computer Network Security*, pages 424–429. Springer, 2005.

[12] S. Gianvecchio and H. Wang. Detecting covert timing channels: an entropy-based approach. In *Proceedings of the 14th ACM conference on Computer and communications security*, pages 307–316. ACM, 2007.

[13] S. Gianvecchio and H. Wang. An entropy-based approach to detecting covert timing channels. *Dependable and Secure Computing, IEEE Transactions on*, 8(6):785–797, 2011.

[14] S. Gianvecchio, H. Wang, D. Wijesekera, and S. Jajodia. Model-based covert timing channels: Automated modeling and evasion. In *Recent Advances in Intrusion Detection*, pages 211–230. Springer, 2008.

[15] D. Gourley and B. Totty. *HTTP: the definitive guide*. O'Reilly Media, Inc., 2002.

[16] D. L. Kreher and D. R. Stinson. *Combinatorial algorithms: generation, enumeration, and search*, volume 7. CRC press, 1998.

[17] Z. Kwecka. *Application layer covert channel analysis and detection*. PhD thesis, Edinburgh Napier University, 2006.

[18] Y. Liu, D. Ghosal, F. Armknecht, A.-R. Sadeghi, S. Schulz, and S. Katzenbeisser. Hide and seek in time₫robust covert timing channels. In *Computer Security–ESORICS*, pages 120–135. Springer, 2009.

[19] Y. Liu, D. Ghosal, F. Armknecht, A.-R. Sadeghi, S. Schulz, and S. Katzenbeisser. Robust and undetectable steganographic timing channels for iid traffic. In *Information Hiding*, pages 193–207. Springer, 2010.

[20] X. Luo, E. W. Chan, and R. K. Chang. Cloak: A ten-fold way for reliable covert communications. In *Computer Security–ESORICS 2007*, pages 283–298. Springer, 2007.

[21] X. Luo, E. W. Chan, P. Zhou, and R. K. Chang. Robust network covert communications based on tcp and enumerative combinatorics. *Dependable and Secure Computing, IEEE Transactions on*, 9(6):890–902, 2012.

[22] X. Luo, P. Zhou, E. W. Chan, R. K. Chang, and W. Lee. A combinatorial approach to network covert communications with applications in web leaks. In *Dependable Systems and Networks, 2011 IEEE/IFIP 41st International Conference on*, pages 474–485. IEEE, 2011.

[23] F. A. Petitcolas, R. J. Anderson, and M. G. Kuhn. Information hiding-a survey. *Proceedings of the IEEE*, 87(7):1062–1078, 1999.

[24] SINA. Sina homepage. *http://www.sina.com.cn/*, May 2014.

[25] P. Srisuresh and M. Holdrege. Ip network address translator (nat) terminology and considerations. 1999.

[26] R. P. Stanley. Enumerative combinatorics. vol. 2, volume 62 of cambridge studies in advanced mathematics, 1999.

[27] F. Wang, L. Huang, H. Miao, and M. Tian. A novel distributed covert channel in http. *Security and Communication Networks*, 7(6):1031–1041, 2014.

[28] H. Wang and S. Wang. Cyber warfare: steganography vs. steganalysis. *Communications of the ACM*, 47(10):76–82, 2004.

[29] S. Zander, G. Armitage, and P. Branch. A survey of covert channels and countermeasures in computer network protocols. *Communications Surveys and Tutorials, IEEE*, 9(3):44–57, 2007.

Visual Honey Encryption: Application to Steganography

Ji Won Yoon[*]
Center for Information Security
Technologies (CIST)
Korea University
Republic of Korea
jiwon_yoon@korea.ac.kr

Hyoungshick Kim
College of Information and
Communication Engineering
SungKyunKwan University
Republic of Korea
hyoung@skku.edu

Hyun-Ju Jo
Center for Information Security
Technologies (CIST)
Korea University
Republic of Korea
heyonjulove@naver.com

Hyelim Lee
Center for Information Security
Technologies (CIST)
Korea University
Republic of Korea
dream8933@naver.com

Kwangsu Lee
Center for Information Security
Technologies (CIST)
Korea University
Republic of Korea
guspin.lee@gmail.com

ABSTRACT

Honey encryption (HE) is a new technique to overcome the weakness of conventional *password-based encryption* (PBE). However, conventional honey encryption still has the limitation that it works only for binary bit streams or integer sequences because it uses a fixed distribution-transforming encoder (DTE). In this paper, we propose a variant of honey encryption called *visual honey encryption* which employs an adaptive DTE in a Bayesian framework so that the proposed approach can be applied to more complex domains including images and videos. We applied this method to create a new steganography scheme which significantly improves the security level of traditional steganography.

Categories and Subject Descriptors

E.3 [**Data**]: Data Encryption

Keywords

Honey encryption (HE), Password-based encryption (PBE), Steganography

1. INTRODUCTION

Password-based encryption (PBE) schemes have many practical applications, particularly when the encryption and decryption keys should be memorized by the user. For example, PBE is used to protect Android phone owners' sensitive data; the disk or volume encryption key is derived from a user's screen-unlock password and a salt value [13]. Unlike

---

[*]Yoon insisted his name be first and he is a corresponding author.

IH&MMSec'15, June 17–19, 2015, Portland, Oregon, USA.
Copyright ⓒ 2015 ACM 978-1-4503-3587-4/15/06 ...$15.00.
DOI: http://dx.doi.org/10.1145/2756601.2756606.

biometrics and cryptographic keys, passwords are easy to implement and do not require additional hardware support. However, passwords too have their own inherent limitations – namely, memorability and security. A password that is difficult to guess is also likely to be hard to remember.

Thus, as one would imagine, many users tend to choose passwords that are easy to remember without really paying close attention to the security implications. Trivial passwords such as 'password' and 'abcd1234' are often used by casual users. As a result, the real password space is much smaller than the theoretical one [4, 11], making brute-force and dictionary attacks possible and effective. For example, a study of $544,960$ passwords collected from real users showed that the average entropy of user passwords was approximately 40.5 bits, smaller than the 128 or 192 bit standard used by many systems [6]. That is, when a PBE scheme is used, attackers may search amongst only a small subset of the theoretically possible passwords, the most commonly used ones, and crack encrypted information by guessing the password used to derive the encryption key [7].

Honey encryption (HE) was introduced to overcome limitations of PBE schemes [9, 8]. *Honey encryption* generates a ciphertext that can be decrypted with not only the correct password but also wrong passwords. In this scheme, wrong passwords can yield fake but valid-looking plaintext to confuse an attacker who is trying to decrypt the ciphertext through a brute force attack. Thus, the attacker is unable to identify the original plaintext even after trying all possible password combinations. Juels and Ristenpart [9] presented a general framework to construct a honey encryption scheme using a new (randomized) message encoding using *distribution-transforming encoders* (DTE) for binary bit stream and integers only. However, the scheme still has practical limitations because it uses a fixed simple DTE for encoding and decoding. That is, Juels and Ristenpart [9]'s honey encryption scheme cannot be flexibly used for numerous application domains including natural language-based texts, sounds, and images since such data has its their own synthetic or semantic structure. For example, a lot of multimedia data transferred in the Internet can be interpreted as a spatial grid structured field. Because of this image structure neighboring pixels have more similar colour than distant ones. Since such complicated data cannot be directly encrypted with original honey encryption, a new honey encryption system is needed for such structured data. We simply name such data *multi-dimensional data* in that images are well-known as being a two-dimensional data type and films can be regarded as a three-dimensional one.

In this paper, we introduce a new variation of honey encryption which can be applied to such complicated multidimensional data using a two-dimensional Markovian process in a Bayesian scheme. The Markovian process for 2D images is a well-known mathematical model for designing and interpreting the synthetic structure of images. In this paper, to distinguish it from original honey encryption, we name this algorithm *visual honey encryption* since we mainly consider visual 2D images. For a specific application domain using images, we made a connection between multi-dimensional honey encryption and steganography since steganography is one of the best-known applications which deal with images in security area. From this perspective, we introduce a new type of steganography based on *visual honey encryption*. In this paper, for simplicity, we also name this new steganography *honey steganography*.

Eventually, there are three contributions in this paper. First, we introduce an adaptive scheme of DTE for honey encryption. Thus, we do not need to fix or predetermine the DTE as conventional honey encryption does. The second contribution is that we introduce a new variation of honey encryption which removes the practical limitation and weakness of the original using adaptive DTE and a Bayesian framework design. Thereby, we can apply honey encryption to more complicated data including natural language-based texts and multimedia data. We name this new flexible honey encryption *visual honey encryption*. The final contribution is that we introduce a new steganography based on *visual honey encryption* which improves on the security of conventional steganography in terms of time complexity.

2. BACKGROUND

2.1 Honey Encryption

Honey encryption (HE), introduced by Juels and Ristepart [9], is a symmetric encryption scheme such as password-based encryption (PBE). In HE, the encryption algorithm encrypts a message into a randomized ciphertext by using a key, and the decryption algorithm decrypts the ciphertext into the original message by using the key in a similar manner to normal encryption schemes. The notable difference between honey encryption and conventional symmetric encryption is the output of the decryption algorithm when an invalid key is used; whereas conventional encryption gives an error symbol, HE gives a plausible message.

HE provides two security properties. If the keys used with HE are sufficiently unpredictable, HE provides semantic security, in which computationally bounded adversary cannot recover meaningful information from ciphertexts. Additionally, HE provides message recovery security, so that a computationally unbounded adversary who can decrypt the ciphertext by trying all possible keys is still unable to distinguish whether the recovered message is valid or not. In this way, HE can provide security against brute-force attacks. A general methodology for building HE schemes is to apply a distribution-transformation encoder (DTE) to a message and then encrypt the results of the encoding using a key

such as a password. A DTE is a message encoding scheme and the DTE decoding algorithm can sample a message in the original distribution even when a random input value is given. Juels and Ristepart showed that credit card numbers and RSA private keys can be securely protected with HE.

2.2 Steganography

Cover modification is a well-known approach in steganography and a cover image embeds and conveys a desired secret message. Given the cover image, Alice modifies the cover image by embedding the hidden secret messages. The communication between Alice and Bob can be performed with the set of all possible cover images and the sets of the keys and messages. Let $\mathcal{C}$, $\mathcal{K}$, $\mathcal{M}$, and $\mathcal{S}$ denote a set of covers, a set of all stego keys, a set of all messages, and a set of stego images respectively. In general, since a steganographic scheme is a pair of embedding and extraction functions EMB and EXT, we have $EMB : \mathcal{C} \times \mathcal{K} \times \mathcal{M} \to \mathcal{S}$, and $EXT : \mathcal{S} \times \mathcal{K} \to \mathcal{M}$ such that $EXT(EMB(\mathbf{c}, \mathbf{k}, \mathbf{m}), \mathbf{k}) = \mathbf{m}$ for all $\mathbf{c} \in \mathcal{C}$, $\mathbf{m} \in \mathcal{M}$, and $\mathbf{k} \in \mathcal{K}$. Here, let $\mathbf{s} = EMB(\mathbf{c}, \mathbf{k}, \mathbf{m})$ be the stego image for $\mathbf{s} \in \mathcal{S}$. In steganography and steganalysis, much research has been focused on creating perfectly secure steganography in which the characteristics of the distribution of the stego images p_s is that of distribution of cover images p_c. Kullback Leibler (KL) distance is a well-known measure for perfectly secure steganography and is defined by $D_{KL}(p_c \| p_s) = \sum_{\mathbf{c} \in \mathcal{C}} p_c(\mathbf{c}) \log \frac{p_c(\mathbf{c})}{p_s(\mathbf{c})}$. Given the KL divergence, we can say that Alice's steganosystem is perfectly secure when $D_{KL}(p_c \| p_s) = 0$. In this case, the malicious person Eve cannot distinguish between cover images and stego images. However, it is often impractical to build such perfectly secure steganography and many practical stegano-systems are not perfectly secure. Nevertheless they are ϵ-secure with the constraint $D_{KL}(p_c \| p_s) < \epsilon$. In this paper, we show three additional measures to KL divergence: root mean square error (RMSE), peak signal to noise ratio (PSNR), and structural similarity (SSIM) [16].

2.3 Multi-dimensional Data

We define some terms related to multi-dimensional data for better understanding of the difference between conventional HE and our proposed scheme. Thus, in this paper, *One dimensional data* means both binary bit streams like '1011001' and integer sequences like '01028553945'. *Multi-dimensional data* means more complicated data including images, natural language based texts and films.

To date, HE handles only one dimensional data and generates one dimensional honeywords (fake data). However, as computer performance increases, multi-dimensional data becomes more popular. Multi-dimensional data, which include images and films, is the most common form of multimedia data, but cannot be encrypted with conventional honey encryption as it can only handle on-dimensional data. Thus, multi-dimensional honey encryption should be developed for honey encryption to become applicable to most multimedia data. In order to distinguish between conventional one dimensional honey encryption and our proposed approach, in this paper, we name the proposed approach *Visual honey encryption* (VHE).

In VHE, a honey multimedia data set generated via the encoding operation under encryption with incorrect passwords cannot be distinguished from the original multimedia datum, which can be decrypted and decoded with the correct key alone.

3. THREAT MODEL

In this section, we discuss the threat model and assumptions.

The adversary can access the encrypted data and has full knowledge of our encryption scheme, but lacks the key used for encrypting data. We assume a computationally bounded adversary running in a polynomial time, incapable of breaking the encryption algorithm without knowing the key used for encryption; however, the adversary is capable of breaking a steganographic scheme in a limited time $T(n)$ where n is the size of the image being used. This assumption is reasonable since most steganographic techniques have been broken by effective steganalysis given enough resources [1] while breaking advanced encryption algorithms (e.g., AES [5]) is computationally infeasible for even the most powerful supercomputers.

We also assume that the encryption key used for our scheme is derived from a user-chosen password. This is a common method in practice when using encryption algorithms for user applications. In particular, Password-Based Key Derivation Function 2 (PBKDF2) [10] is popularly used as a key derivation function that is part of RSA Laboratories' Public-Key Cryptography Standards (PKCS) series.

However, in practice, many users choose passwords that are easy to remember without paying close attention to the security implications. Therefore, the actual password space used is much smaller than the theoretical one [4, 11], and this dramatically increases the likelihood of attacker compromising a password through guessing attacks. That is, we assume the adversary can iteratively guess the user-chosen password and try to derive the encryption key to decrypt the encrypted data. We use Ψ to represent the actual password space which is much smaller than the theoretical password space. We note that $|\Psi|$ represents the size of the actual password space.

Given the above threat model and assumption, our goal is to protect the user's secret message in the encrypted image so that the adversary only knows the presence of the encrypted data and its characteristics (e.g., creation time, size, etc.) but not the secret message itself.

4. PROPOSED APPROACH

In this section, we first demonstrate the main concept and structure of VHE. Then, we present a new procedure to build VHE's DTE to accommodate multi-dimensional data. Afterwards, we show how to encode and decode the values using the VHE's DTE.

4.1 Concepts

VHE encodes and decodes senders' and receivers' data using a codebook that is extracted from the statistical properties of the multi-dimensional data. In this process, only authorized users with correct passwords or keys are able to obtain correct data (images/videos). In contrast, non-authorized users without correct passwords cannot obtain the information about the original data. Instead, they will obtain a wrong but valid-looking multi-dimensional datum that is generated by the rules of our statistical codebook and DTE.

Without loss of generality, in this paper, we particularly focus on applying VHE to images because they are representative of multi-dimensional data type. Note that our VHE does not encrypt and encode the header information of the multimedia but the internal pixel values only. From this point of view, our proposed VHE can be regarded as a file encryption system rather than channel encryption although VHE is also considered for communication channels. In addition, unlike text data, pixels have a high degree of similarity. That is, pixel values of real images are not random but highly connected with their neighbors. This neighboring property provides many useful mathematical properties of the image of practical use. For example, a Markov random field (MRF) is used for modeling such a neighboring structure in order to reduce the time complexity of image computation. In this paper, given this mathematical property, we make an adaptive DTE from the images using the Markovian rule.

4.2 Structure of VHE

VHE consists of a sequential processes: (1) selection of data, (2) construction of a codebook using statistical formula, (3) encoding and decoding using the codebook, (4) encryption with a key/password K_1, and (5) transmission of the encrypted message. Each process is described in details:

1. **Selection of data**: To begin with, we select two types of images for a plain image, **p** and d_c public images, **Y**s. The plain image has the same format and size as the fake images. The plain image is a hidden information while the fake images are in public. The public images are shared between Alice and Bob in order to use them to construct a DTE. This is known even to Eve who is a malicious subject. Since the encoder and decoder should use an identical DTE, the fake images should be shared between Alice and Bob before communication.

2. **Construction of a codebook using statistical formula**: Let $\mathbf{x}$, $\mathbf{Y}$, and θ denote the encoding space, a set of public images, and other public parameters of the model. In this stage, using the selected image $\mathbf{Y}$ and other known parameters, VHE constructs a full joint target posterior distribution $p(\mathbf{x}|\mathbf{Y}, \theta)$ for a statistical codebook and the distribution is used as a DTE is in conventional honey encryption. VHE systematically uses a conditional posterior distribution, $p(x_i|\mathbf{x}_{ne(i)}, \mathbf{Y}, \theta)$, rather than the full joint target distribution since every pixel is sequentially coded in a pixel-by-pixel order where $ne(i)$ denotes a set of indexes of the ith pixel's neighbors. As soon as the conditional posterior of the i-th pixel is constructed, VHE builds the corresponding cumulative mass function (CMF) of the conditional target posterior. Let $p_i \in \{0, 1\}^{d_p}$ and $c_i \in \{0, 1\}^{d_c}$ be the i-th plain image and the i-th encoded data respectively. For simplicity, d_c becomes either 8 for gray-scale images or 24 for true color images.

3. **Encoding and decoding using the codebook**: In the encoding and decoding stages, VHE uses the statistical codebook, CMF$(\cdot)$, to encode p_i into c_i or to decode c_i into p_i. This CMF works as a statistical

codebook by

$$c_i = \text{CMF}(p_i) \text{ , for encoding and } c_i \in \{0,1\}^{d_c}$$
$$p_i = \text{CMF}^{-1}(c_i) \text{ , for decoding } p_i \in \{0,1\}^{d_p} \quad (1)$$

where $d_p \leq d_c$. That is, input values with d_p binary digits are encoded into d_c binary digits via $\text{CMF}(\cdot)$ and $\text{CMF}^{-1}()$ is the inverse operation. Therefore, each pixel value in a plain image can be encoded or decoded in terms of the statistical properties of the shared public images.

4. **Encryption with an encryption key K_1 and decryption with a decryption key K_2:** Encryption is performed using conventional encryption algorithms like AES, RSA, and so on. If $K_2 = K_1$ in the symmetric crypto-system for an appropriate receiver, Bob, the encrypted cipher will be correctly decrypted and then decoded to the hidden plain image $\mathbf{p}$ via our DTE. Otherwise, the encrypted cipher will be decrypted to a random sequence which is different from the actual bit-streams because $K_1 \neq K_2$ and the malicious subject Eve obtains variations of fake images $\mathbf{h}$ which are decoded from the random sequence.

5. **Transmission of the encrypted data**

For instance, we have a hidden plain image $\mathbf{p}$ of Figure 1-(a) and a public image $\mathbf{Y}$ of Figure 1-(b). As shown in Figure 1-(c) and -(d), for a symmetric encryption system, the receiver can obtain a correct hidden image when K_1 and K_2 are identical. However, the receiver will obtain a number of fake images with some variation when $K_1 \neq K_2$. That is, there is only one $\mathbf{p}$ but there are $|\mathcal{K}_{enc/dec}|$ $\mathbf{h}$ where $|\mathcal{K}_{enc/dec}|$ is the cardinality of the key or password space for encryption or decryption for $K_1 \in \mathcal{K}_{enc}$ and $K_2 \in \mathcal{K}_{dec}$.

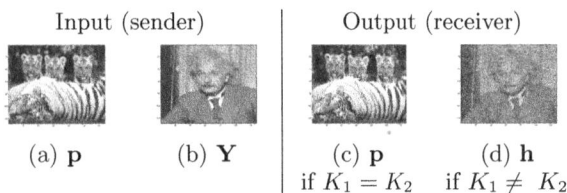

Input (sender)		Output (receiver)	
(a) $\mathbf{p}$	(b) $\mathbf{Y}$	(c) $\mathbf{p}$ if $K_1 = K_2$	(d) $\mathbf{h}$ if $K_1 \neq K_2$

Figure 1: Input and output of pseudo-VHE where K_1 and K_2 are the passwords for encryption and decryption in a symmetric crypto-system.

4.3 Connection to Steganography

Figure 1 shows that, when the cipher is decrypted and decoded with incorrect passwords, Eve obtains a false image which has similar properties to the desired real image. The power of visual honey encryption (VHE) is that Eve does not obtain meaningless random images at all. However, the VHE may not be useful in practice for two reasons: 1) Figures 1-(c) and -(d) are different, their histograms will be different so, a machine will be able to distinguish them; and 2) although there are various fake or deception images $\mathbf{h}$ as shown in Figure 1-(d), they are much closer to the public image $\mathbf{Y}$ than the original plain image $\mathbf{p}$ of Figure 1-(c). Therefore, our proposed visual honey encryption is not perfect honey encryption. However, we realized that there is a simple but practical solution to address this problem. The

solution is that $\mathbf{p}$ is replaced by $\mathbf{Y}$. In this case, the difference between the receiver's outputs $\mathbf{p}$ and $\mathbf{h}$ is dramatically reduced such that $|\mathbf{p} - \mathbf{h}|$ of Figure 2 is smaller than $|\mathbf{p} - \mathbf{h}|$ of Figure 1.

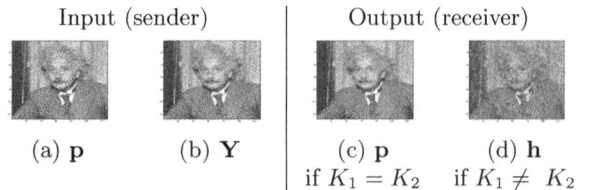

Input (sender)		Output (receiver)	
(a) $\mathbf{p}$	(b) $\mathbf{Y}$	(c) $\mathbf{p}$ if $K_1 = K_2$	(d) $\mathbf{h}$ if $K_1 \neq K_2$

Figure 2: Input and output of practical VHE

Figure 2 shows how to make practical VHE. However, in this case, we cannot select a hidden image to be sent by ourselves as shown in Figure 1 since $\mathbf{p}$ should be a variation of public images $\mathbf{Y}$, i.e., $\mathbf{p} \approx \mathbf{Y}$. Interestingly, we found that this practical shortcoming of VHE can be removed by combining it with steganography. We can embed a secret message $\mathbf{m}$ into $\mathbf{p}$ which now becomes a cover image $\mathbf{c}$, i.e., $\mathbf{s}=\text{Emb}(\mathbf{c}, \mathbf{m})$. In this case, $\mathbf{p} = \mathbf{s} \approx \mathbf{Y}$ and $\mathbf{m} =\text{Ext}(\mathbf{s})$ but $\mathbf{m} \neq \text{Ext}(\mathbf{h})$.

With this combination of steganography and practical VHE, a new powerful steganography algorithm is introduced as shown in Figure 3. The Figure presents three different models of steganography. Figure 3-(1) is the traditional steganography model in which the stego-image is directly transmitted to Bob without any encryption. The attacker performs only steganalysis to extract the hidden message with the stego-image. Figure 3-(2) is more complicated model than (1) since an encryption process is added during communication. Although in practice many systems follow this model as communication channels are increasingly encrypted, it contains no theoretical improvements in either steganography or encryption, and has therefore not been widely discussed in the literature. Figure 3-(3) depicts our proposed model which is a variation of Figure 3-(2) in which the traditional ASCII encoder and decoder are replaced by our proposed DTE based encoder and decoder.

4.4 Construction of Encoding/Decoding Distribution

Before describing the main algorithm of the new steganography scheme based on VHE as depicted in Figure 3-(3), we define the symbols which are used in the algorithm.

In this table, $\mathbf{p}$ for a stego image and $\mathbf{Y}$ for a fake image are matrices of $L_1 \times L_2$ size, and $\mathbf{x}$ and $\mathbf{y}$ are their corresponding vectorized forms with $L_1 L_2 \times 1$ for $L = L_1 L_2$.

The underlying concept behind our proposed approach is the use of statistical coding schemes instead of the traditional ASCII coding schemes. Given a stego-image $\mathbf{s}$ and a fake image $\mathbf{Y}$, we can make encoding or decoding procedures by reconstructing the underlying probability density function. In this paper, denote $p(\mathbf{x}|\mathbf{Y}, \theta)$ by the density function, similar to the DTE of Honey Encryption. This distribution can be interpreted well in a Bayesian framework. For a simplified representation, we vectorized the matrices to build $\mathbf{x}$ and $\mathbf{y}$, transforming $\mathbf{x} = \mathcal{V}(\mathbf{s})$ and $\mathbf{y}^{(n)} = \mathcal{V}(\mathbf{Y}^{(n)})$, which are more familiar forms for conventional Bayesian statistics. In this vectorized form $\mathbf{x}$ denotes $\mathbf{x}_{1:L_1 L_2} = \{x_i\}_{i=1}^{L_1 L_2}$. By

(1) Steganography without encryption module

(2) Steganography with encryption module

(3) Proposed Honey steganography

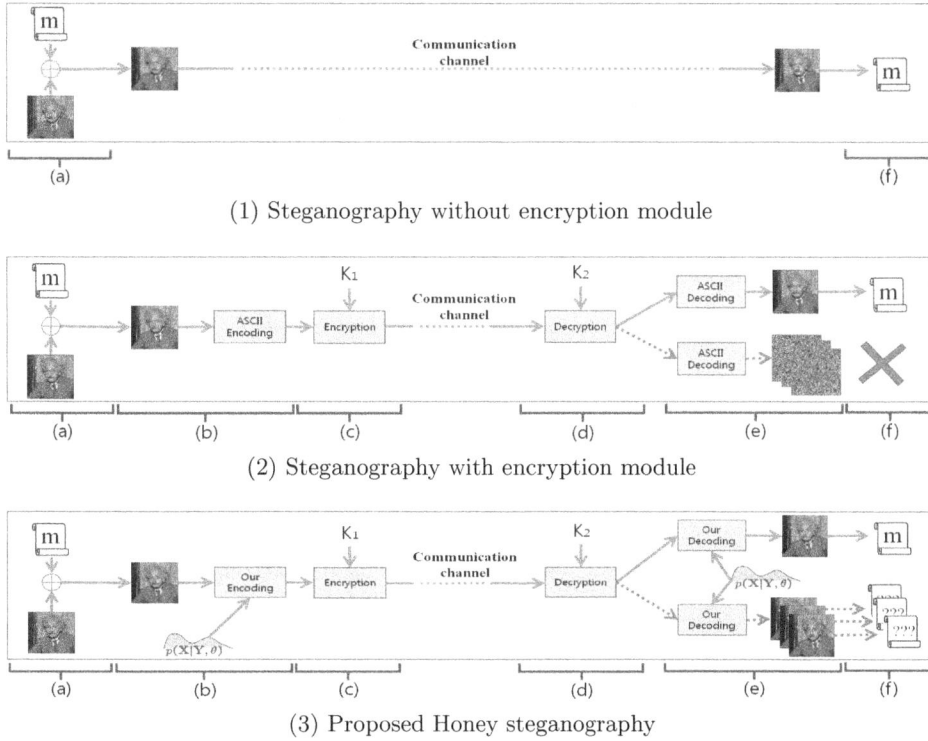

Figure 3: Various steganography schemes: (1) Steganography without an encryption module, (2) Steganography with an encryption module, (3) Proposed Honey steganography. In this Figure, green solid arrows represent the flow of appropriate communication between Alice and Bob while red dotted arrows represent an inappropriate flow between Alice and Eve. There are six steps in the Figure: (a) embedding messages to cover image, (b) encoding, (c) encryption, (d) decryption, (e) decoding, and (f) extracting messages.

Table 1: Definition of the used symbols

Symbols	Definition
N	the number of public images or duplicates of a public image
d_p	the number of binary bits of plain texts for each operation
d_c	the number of binary bits of cipher texts for each operation
$\mathbf{m}$	a secret message to be sent
$\mathbf{c}$	a cover image in which the secret message will be embeded
$\mathbf{s}$	Stego-image with $\mathbf{c}$ and $\mathbf{m}$
$\mathbf{z}$	Encoded data from $\mathbf{s}$
$\mathbf{p}$	a hidden stego image to be sent, $\mathbf{p} = \mathbf{s}$
$\mathbf{Y}$	public image(s)
$\mathcal{V}(\cdot)$	a transformation function from matrix to vector
$\mathbf{x}$	a vectorized form that encodes $\mathbf{s}$
$\mathbf{y}$	a vectorized form that encodes $\mathbf{Y}$
$\mathbf{u}$	encrypted data

using the Bayesian chain rule, we now have

$$p(\mathbf{x}|\mathbf{y}, \theta) = \prod_{i=1}^{L} p(x_i|\mathbf{x}_{1:i-1}, \mathbf{y}, \theta) \qquad (2)$$

where $L = L_1 L_2$. In general, images have a special grid structure and this is often modeled with a two dimensional the Markovian structure because it can reduce the time and space complexity of the computation using Markovian blankets. Therefore, we have a target distribution and it is factorized as

$$p(\mathbf{x}|\mathbf{y}, \theta) = \prod_{i=1}^{L} p(x_i|\mathbf{x}_{MB(i)}, \mathbf{y}, \theta) = \prod_{i=1}^{L} p(x_i|\mathbf{x}_{ne(i)}, \mathbf{y}, \theta). \qquad (3)$$

Here, x_i is the i th pixel value. $MB(i)$ and $ne(i)$ denote Markov blanket and neighbors of the ith pixel for dependency. Note that our proposed approach performs the encoding and decoding procedures sequentially. Therefore, our immediate goal is to construct the conditional distribution of the ith pixel instead of the full joint distribution of a full image, $p(x_i|\mathbf{x}_{ne(i)}, \mathbf{y})$. This conditional distribution means that the ith pixel is influenced by neighboring pixels and values of the fake image.

The conditional density of the ith pixel can be further reduced by assuming independence of pixels in the fake image such that

$$p(x_i|\mathbf{X}_{ne(i)}, \mathbf{y}, \theta) = p(x_i|\mathbf{x}_{ne(i)}, y_i, \mathbf{y}_{\sim i}, \theta) \qquad (4)$$

where y_i is the ith pixel of the clean fake image corresponding to x_i and $\mathbf{y}_{\sim i}$ denotes the vectorized form of $\mathbf{y}$ except y_i. That is, $\mathbf{y} = y_i \cup \mathbf{y}_{\sim i}$ and $y_i \cap \mathbf{y}_{\sim i} = \{\}$. Now this

distribution can be rewritten by

$$
\begin{aligned}
p(x_i|\mathbf{X}_{ne(i)},\mathbf{y},\theta) &= p(x_i|\mathbf{x}_{ne(i)},y_i,\mathbf{y}_{\sim i},\theta) \\
&\propto p(y_i|x_i,\theta)p(x_i|\mathbf{x}_{ne(i)},\theta). \quad (5)
\end{aligned}
$$

In Equation (5), we now have two key factors: likelihood function $p(y_i|x_i,\theta)$ and the prior function $p(x_i|\mathbf{x}_{ne(i)},\theta)$. These are explained in a Bayesian framework. The first factor is the likelihood function $p(y_i|x_i,\theta)$ that is the probability of how x_i well fits the fake pixel y_i. The other factor is a prior term that is constructed with neighboring values. In the image application, this prior is often designed with a Markov random field [2, 3, 12].

Note that equations (2) and (5) are basically targeted to a single fake image $\mathbf{Y}$ and its vectorized form $\mathbf{y}$. In this single image case, the prior and likelihood can have exactly the same influence on building the posterior. However, we could have multiple fake images instead of a single one. In this case, the equations can be rewritten by $\mathbf{Y} = \mathbf{y}^{(1:N)} = \mathbf{y}^{(1)},\mathbf{y}^{(2)},\cdots,\mathbf{y}^{(N)}$:

$$
\begin{aligned}
p(\mathbf{x}|\mathbf{Y},\theta) &= \prod_{i=1}^{L} p(x_i|\mathbf{x}_{ne(i)},\mathbf{Y},\theta) \\
&\propto \prod_{i=1}^{L}\left[\prod_{n=1}^{N} p(y_i^{(n)}|x_i,\theta)\right] p(x_i|\mathbf{x}_{ne(i)},\theta) \quad (6)
\end{aligned}
$$

where $y_i^{(n)}$ represents the ith pixel value of the nth fake image. Returning to the conditional posterior of the ith pixel for the multiple fake images, we have $p(x_i|\mathbf{x}_{ne(i)},\mathbf{Y},\theta) = \left[\prod_{n=1}^{N} p(y_i^{(n)}|x_i,\theta)\right] p(x_i|\mathbf{x}_{ne(i)},\theta)$. In this paper, we define the likelihood and prior using well-known normal distribution by

$$
\begin{aligned}
p(y_i^{(n)}|x_i,\theta) &= \mathcal{N}(y_i^{(n)};x_i,r^2) = \mathcal{N}(x_i;y_i^{(n)},r^2) \\
p(x_i|\mathbf{x}_{ne(i)},\theta) &= \mathcal{N}(x_i;f(\mathbf{x}_{ne(i)}),\rho^2) \quad (7)
\end{aligned}
$$

where $\sigma \in \theta$ and $\rho \in \theta$ are the standard deviations of each distribution and $\mathcal{N}(\cdot;a,b)$ is the normal distribution with a mean a and a variance b. $f(\cdot)$ is any linear/nonlinear function.

It is known that the product of the normal distributions becomes a normal distribution as shown in appendix A. Therefore, $p(x_i|\mathbf{x}_{ne(i)},\mathbf{Y},\theta)$ from equation (7) is unified in a collapsed normal distribution by

$$
p(x_i|\mathbf{x}_{ne(i)},\mathbf{Y},\theta) = \mathcal{N}(x_i;\mu,\sigma^2) \quad (8)
$$

where

$$
\begin{aligned}
\sigma &= \sqrt{\left(\sum_{n=1}^{N}\frac{1}{r^2}+\frac{1}{\rho^2}\right)^{-1}} \\
\mu &= \sigma^2\left(\frac{\sum_{n=1}^{N} y_i^{(n)}}{r^2}+\frac{f(\mathbf{x}_{ne(i)})}{\rho^2}\right).
\end{aligned}
$$

In addition, one fake image can be used for multiple fake images by duplicating it to N copies. In this paper, we make N images using one fake image in this way. In the result section, we show that the degree of influence varies as N varies.

4.5 Encoding and decoding schemes

Each pixel has 8 bits for single channel or gray-scale images so $x_i \in \{0,1,\cdots,2^8-1\}$. The basic idea of honey encryption is to change the encoding and decoding rules from traditional ASCII to distribution based coding scheme. Each value can be encoded and decoded with different weights in the statistical coding scheme. This means that some values can have more weight than others. In order to provide these varying weights, the length of the encoded data should be increased. In other words, in order to encode values in a d_c bit system ($d_c = 8$ for image pixels), longer bits are required to encode the value, i.e. $d_p \leq d_c$. Now let's return to our single channel image. In this case, we encode 2^{d_p} values into 2^{d_c} binary codes. This also means that d_c bit images are quantized to d_p bit pixels. In the results section, we set $d_p = 4$ and $d_c = 8$. The set of 2^{d_p} values can be defined manually or automatically by $\mathcal{Z} = \{z_0 \cup z_1 \cup ... \cup z_{2^{d_p}-1}\}$. In general, $\min \mathcal{Z} \leq 0$ and $2^{d_c} > \max \mathcal{Z}$ for d_c bit images. We first discretize and quantize the conditional posterior distribution $p(x_i = z|\mathbf{x}_{ne(i)},\mathbf{Y},\theta)$ of equation (8) to represent the probability masses function (PMF) of the $2^d = 16$ discrete values for $z \in \mathcal{Q}$. Now the cumulative mass function of the ith pixel is defined by

$$
p_{cmf}^{(i)}(z_k) = \sum_{k=0}^{2^k-1}\frac{p(x_i = z_k|\mathbf{x}_{ne(i)},\mathbf{Y},\theta)}{\sum_{j=0}^{2^d-1} p(x_i = z_j|\mathbf{x}_{ne(i)},\mathbf{Y},\theta)}. \quad (9)
$$

Before encoding or decoding the values using the CMF of the equation (9), we need to modify the CMF to maintain the consistency of the encoders and decoders. As already mentioned, 2^{d_p} values(symbols) are encoded to corresponding d_c-digit values with different weights. Symbols with a higher PMF. will cover more values among 2^{d_c} values and some symbols with a relatively low PMF will cover less. These are the characteristics of DTE of honey encryption which cause its power. However, they cause inconsistencies in the encoding and decoding operations. If the PMF of some symbols are lower than $1/2^{d_c}$, then we cannot encode them. Therefore, we need to change the PMF and CMF to ensure that the PMF of any symbol is larger than $1/2^{d_c}$. In order to achieve this, we reduce the probability of symbols with dominant weights and the removed weights are added to other symbols with low weights.

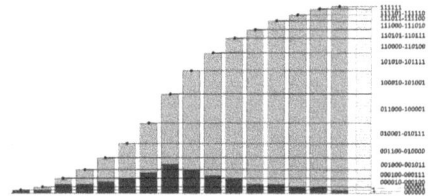

Figure 4: PMF (dark blue bars) and CMF (bright green bars) for encoding and decoding. For $d_p = 4$ and $d_c = 6$, 16 symbols with 4 bits digit are encoded into 6 bit digits.

Figure 4 displays three informative plots about an encoder from d_p bit digits to d_c bit digits and a decoder from d_c digits to d_p digits. The dark blue bars represent the probability mass function of $p(x_i|\mathbf{x}_{ne(i)},\mathbf{Y},\theta)$ of equation (8) and the green bars represent their corresponding CMF. Last, each bar of CMF indicates the d_c bit codes. That is, the 2^{d_p} values of $p(i)$ are encoded to 2^{d_c} binary digits of c_i via $c_i = CMF(p_i)$. For instance, we set $d_p = 4$ and $d_c = 6$ for simplicity in Figure 4.

4.6 Necessity of pre-processing

In the previous section, we described the process of the cumulative mass function (CMF) and the way to assign the bit array. Assigning the bit array to each case seems easy, but for exact encoding and decoding there is one problem to solve; every case must be matched with at least one bit array. In practice, there are various probabilities and some are really small values or extremely dominating. However even a small value has to be presented with at least one bit array. If a small value is not matched to one bit array then we cannot express it. Therefore, in this step, we need to assign a one bit array to even negligibly small probabilities. This step is necessary but it changes probabilities of cases and the CMF is also modified. The probabilities with smaller values than $1/2^{d_c}$ are reassigned to $1/2^{d_c}$ and dominating probabilities have their values reduced. Since small probability cases are assigned the probability $1/2^{d_c}$, an output image $\mathbf{h}$ that has been decrypted and decoded with an incorrect key has shot noise.Therefore, unfortunately, the attacker can distinguish between $\mathbf{p}$ and $\mathbf{h}$s easily. We tackle this problem, as shown in Figure 5, by adding a pre-processing step in which the sender's cover image $\mathbf{c}$ is replaced by one of $\mathbf{h}$s obtained by decoding a random image $\mathbf{r}$. Then, the receiver's $\mathbf{s}$ and $\mathbf{h}$ can be distinguished neither by human beings nor by machine, satisfying the property of honey encryption with ϵ-bound, i.e., $|\mathbf{s} - \mathbf{h}| - \epsilon < 0$ for an extremely small ϵ. Finally, we can make a pseudo-algorithm for our honey steganography, algorithm 1 for Alice and algorithm 2 for Bob and Eve as shown.

Algorithm 1 Sender's view of honey steganography

Require: Public: shared clean images $\mathbf{Y}$
Require: Private: a message $\mathbf{m}$ and an encryption key K_1.
1: Generate a random image $\mathbf{r} \in \mathcal{R}$.
2: **for** $i = 1$ to L **do**
3:     Infer a conditional posterior $p(x_i|\mathbf{x}_{ne(i)}, \mathbf{Y}, \theta)$.
4:     Obtain a CMF(i) by cumulating the posterior.
5:     Build DTE(i) for encoder and decoder using CMF(i).
6:     c_i =Decode(DTE(i), r_i) $\triangleright$ Decode $\mathbf{r}$ into $\mathbf{c} \in \mathcal{C}$.
7: **end for**
8: $\mathbf{s} = \mathbf{c} \oplus \mathbf{m}$ $\triangleright$ Make a stego-image $\mathbf{s} \in \mathcal{C}$ with $\mathbf{m}$ and $\mathbf{c}$.
9: $\mathbf{z}$ =Encode(DTE, $\mathbf{s}$) $\triangleright$ Encode the stego-image $\mathbf{s}$.
10: $\mathbf{u}$ =Encrypt($\mathbf{z}$, K_1) $\triangleright$ Encrypt the encoded sequence with a secret key K_1.

---

5. RESULTS

5.1 Description of Data

Top (Einstein), middle (Rome), and bottom (Lena) of Figure 6-(a) are the raw images used in this paper. We let $\mathbf{I}_{Einstein}$, $\mathbf{I}_{Rome}$, and $\mathbf{I}_{Lena}$ denote Einstein, Rome, and Lena images respectively. The size of every image is 128×128, i.e. $L_1 = 128$ and $L_2 = 128$ and they are all grayscale images because only the red channel of the true colors is used.

5.2 Parameters Used in Experiments

In the simulation, we simplify $f(\mathbf{x}_{ne(i)})$ to a running average filter for the Gaussian Markov random field (GMRF) by $f(\mathbf{x}_{ne(i)}) = \frac{1}{|ne(i)|} \sum_{j \in ne(i)} x_j$ to satisfy $x_i = \frac{1}{|ne(i)|} \sum_{j \in ne(i)} x_j + \epsilon_i$ where noise $\epsilon_i \sim \mathcal{N}(\cdot; 0, \rho^2)$ and $|\cdot|$ is the cardinality

---

Algorithm 2 Receiver's view of honey steganography

Require: Public: shared clean images $\mathbf{Y}$ and encrypted message $\mathbf{u}$
Require: Private: an decryption key K_2.
1: **for** $i = 1$ to L **do**
2:     Infer a conditional posterior $p(x_i|\mathbf{x}_{ne(i)}, \mathbf{Y}, \theta)$.
3:     Obtain a CMF by cumulating the posterior.
4:     Build DTE for encoder and decoder using CMF.
5: **end for**
6: **if** K_2 is a correct decryption key **then**
7:     $\mathbf{z}$ =Decrypt($\mathbf{u}$, K_2) $\triangleright$ Decryption
8:     $\mathbf{s}$ =Decode(DTE, $\mathbf{z}$) $\triangleright$ Decoding
9:     $\mathbf{m}$ =Extraction($\mathbf{s}$) $\triangleright$ Extraction from stego-images
10: **else**
11:     $\tilde{\mathbf{z}}$ =Decrypt($\mathbf{u}$, K_2) $\triangleright$ Decryption
12:     $\tilde{\mathbf{h}}$ =Decode(DTE, $\tilde{\mathbf{z}}$) $\triangleright$ Decoding
13:     Apply steganalysis to extract $\mathbf{m}$ from $\tilde{\mathbf{h}}$

    Extraction($\mathbf{h}$) $\triangleright$ Extraction from stego-images

14: **end if**

---

of a set. With this model, we fix $r \in \theta$ and $\rho \in \theta$ of equation (7) at $r = 1$ and $\rho = \sqrt{1/|ne(i)|}$ for simplicity. Then, the conditional posterior distribution of our interest is formed by $p(x_i|\mathbf{x}_{ne(i)}, \mathbf{Y}, \theta) = \mathcal{N}(x_i; \mu_i, \sigma_i^2)$ where $\sigma_i = (N + |ne(i)|)^{-1/2}$ and $\mu_i = (N+|ne(i)|)^{-1} \left(\sum_{n=1}^N y_i^{(n)} + \sum_{j \in ne(i)} x_j \right)$.

5.3 Evaluation Metrics

There is an important issue to be addressed to validate our proposed approach. Since this honey steganography also inherits the characteristics of honey encryption, for an ϵ-secure stegosystem, we need to check that the images obtained with incorrect keys or passwords are machine indistinguishable from one obtained with correct keys/passwords. There are various metrics to measure this based on similarities or differences between the images: Kullback Leibler distance (KLD), Peak Signal to Noise Ratio (PSNR), Root Mean square error (RMSE), and structural similarity (SSIM) [15, 14]. The details of the similarity measures are described in [16]. From now on we set $type \in \{KLD, PSNR, RMSE, SSIM\}$. Given these metrics, there are two different cases that should be evaluated:

- $\mathcal{D}_{type}(\mathbf{Y}, \mathbf{s})$ and $\{\mathcal{D}_{type}(\mathbf{Y}, \mathbf{h}^{(j)})\}_{j=1}^R$: this is the set of distance between a public image $\mathbf{Y}$ and a decoded stego-image with a correct decryption $\mathbf{s}$ and decoded honey images with R incorrect decryption, $\mathbf{h}^{(1:R)}$.

- $\{\mathcal{D}_{type}(\mathbf{s}, \mathbf{h}^{(j)})\}_{j=1}^R$ and $\{\mathcal{D}_{type}(\mathbf{h}^{(i)}, \mathbf{h}^{(j)})\}_{i,j=1, i \neq j}^R$: this is the set of the distance between decoded images.

Given this setting, we estimate the p-values of each metric to evaluate the distinguishability.

5.4 Steganography with Visual Honey Encryption (Honey Steganography)

Figure 6 demonstrates several input and output images obtained from honey steganography of three images. Figure 6-(a), (b), and (c) are handled by a sender, Alice. The other sub-figures can be obtained by two different types of receivers: an appropriate receiver Bob of Figure 6-(d) and a malicious receiver Eve of Figure 6-(e).

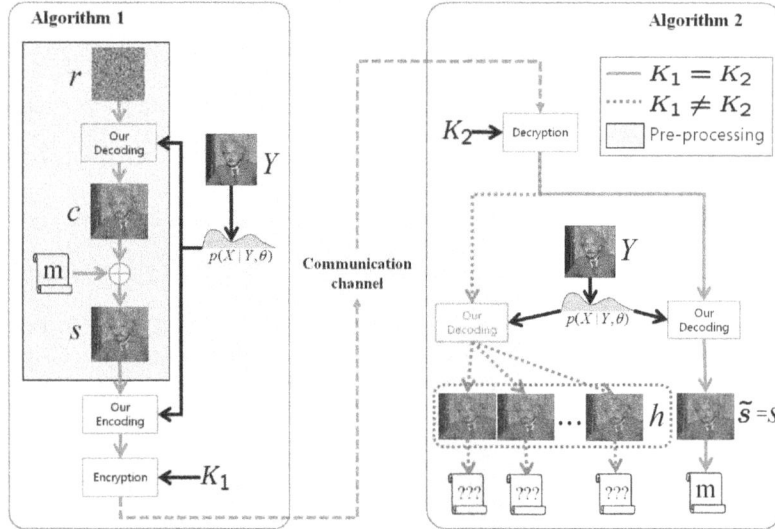

Figure 5: Proposed approach satisfies the indistinguishableness of images decrypted and decoded with a correct key and with incorrect passwords when a pre-processing procedure is adopted. Here, **Y** is a public image.

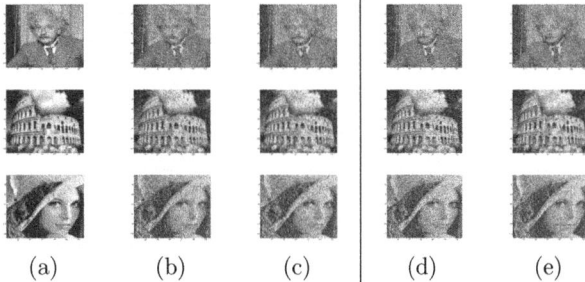

| | (a) | (b) | (c) | (d) | (e) |

Figure 6: Procedure of VHE for three examples: (a)→(b)→(c)→(d) with a correct key and (a)→(b)→(c)→(e) with an incorrect key. Each columns are (a) public image **Y**, (b) noisy cover image **c**, (c) noisy stego image **s**, (d) correctly decoded image $\tilde{\mathbf{s}}$, and (e) incorrectly decoded image **h**

The three images of Figure 6-(a) are the public clean images **Y** used to construct DTE with inferred conditional target posterior $p(x_i|\mathbf{x}_{ne(i)}, \mathbf{Y}, \theta)$ for $i \in \{1, 2, \cdots, L\}$. As we can see the images, clean images are used in this paper although, in practice, **Y** could be noisy or random images. In order to build DTE, **Y** is shared between Alice and Bob and it does not have to be shared privately. Therefore, **Y** is public information and even the malicious user Eve can access it. Figure 6-(b) demonstrates the three cover images obtained by decoding random images using our DTE. That is, we have **c** = Decode(DTE, **r**) where $\mathbf{c} \in \mathcal{C}$ and $\mathbf{r} \in \mathcal{R}$. These are used for embedding the hidden messages **m**. Through the steganographic process, we obtain steg-images **s** of Figure 6-(c), which consist of the cover images **c** and messages **m**. Figure 6-(d) and -(e) represent the images decrypted with correct passwords and with incorrect passwords respectively. By eye, it looks as if there is no difference betwen them. For a more scientific measurement, we calculated four different metrics to measure the similarity distances between **s**, $\tilde{\mathbf{s}}$ and

h. Table 2 shows the similarity distances and their p-values between images, $\mathcal{D}_{type}(\mathbf{Y}, \tilde{\mathbf{s}})$ and $\{\mathcal{D}_{type}(\mathbf{Y}, \mathbf{h}^{(j)})\}_{j=1}^{200}$. As can be seen in the table, all p-values are larger than 0.05, a standard significance level used for hypothesis testing. That is, we can say that the stego-images are ϵ-bound in their difference from public images, i.e., $|(\mathbf{Y} - \tilde{\mathbf{s}}) - (\mathbf{Y} - \mathbf{h})| < \epsilon$.

Table 2: Similarity distance and its p-value between images, $\mathcal{D}_{type}(\mathbf{Y}, \mathbf{s})$ and $\{\mathcal{D}_{type}(\mathbf{Y}, \mathbf{h}^{(j)})\}_{j=1}^{200}$

	$I_{Einstein}$	I_{Rome}	I_{Lena}
$\mathcal{D}_{KLD}(\mathbf{Y}, \mathbf{s})$	0.036	0.056	0.041
(p-value)	(0.685)	(0.055)	(0.735)
$\mathcal{D}_{PSNR}(\mathbf{Y}, \mathbf{s})$	1.02	0.911	0.974
(p-value)	(0.935)	(0.485)	(0.55)
$\mathcal{D}_{RMSE}(\mathbf{Y}, \mathbf{s})$	24.38	31.31	27.05
(p-value)	(0.895)	(0.465)	(0.555)
$\mathcal{D}_{SSIM}(\mathbf{Y}, \mathbf{s})$	0.762	0.876	0.833
(p-value)	(0.85)	(0.41)	(0.52)

However, table 2 is an indirect metric for the honey property. In theory, honey encryption is defined by $|\tilde{\mathbf{s}} - \mathbf{h}| < \epsilon$. Therefore, we calculate the distances between $\tilde{\mathbf{s}}$ and **h**s and present them in table 3. The average distance between $\tilde{\mathbf{s}}$ and **h**s and are closely located at the mode of the distribution, which means that expected p-values are larger than the significance level 0.05. Therefore, we have shown that $|\tilde{\mathbf{s}} - \mathbf{h}| < \epsilon$ and conclude that practically our proposed VHE becomes honey steganography.

5.5 Security Analysis of Honey Steganography

As already referred to, Figure 3 shows three different frameworks for steganography:1) steganography without encryption modules, 2) steganography in an encrypted channel, and 3) our proposed Honey steganography. The outstanding performance of our proposed Honey steganography is shown by its high security compared to the other two approaches. From the attackers' point of view, we first define four func-

Method	Time Complexity for attack
Steganography without encryption modules	$T_{stego}(n)$
Steganography in an encrypted channel	$\|\Psi\|\{T_{generate}(n) + T_{decrypt}(n) + T_{rand}(n)\} + T_{stego}(n)$
	$= \|\Psi\|\{T_{generate}(n) + T_{decrypt}(n)\} + \|\Psi\| \, T_{rand}(n) + T_{stego}(n)$
Our proposed honey steganography	$\|\Psi\|\{T_{generate}(n) + T_{decrypt}(n) + T_{stego}(n)\}$
	$= \|\Psi\|\{T_{generate}(n) + T_{decrypt}(n)\} + \|\Psi\| \, T_{stego}(n)$

Table 4: Time comparison of various steganography for attack, n is the parameter for the size of image and $\|\Psi\|$ is the possible number of passwords or keys

Table 3: Similarity distances between images, $\{\mathcal{D}_{type}(\mathbf{s}, \mathbf{h}^{(j)})\}_{j=1}^{R}$ and $\{\mathcal{D}_{type}(\mathbf{h}^{(i)}, \mathbf{h}^{(j)})\}_{i,j=1,i\neq j}^{R}$

	$I_{Einstein}$	I_{Rome}	I_{Lena}
$\mathbf{E}[\mathcal{D}_{KLD}(\mathbf{s}, \mathbf{h})]$	0.052	0.060	0.053
(E[p-value])	(0.523)	(0.552)	(0.528)
$\mathbf{E}[\mathcal{D}_{PSNR}(\mathbf{s}, \mathbf{h})]$	0.915	0.866	0.897
(E[p-value])	(0.593)	(0.570)	(0.527)
$\mathbf{E}[\mathcal{D}_{RMSE}(\mathbf{s}, \mathbf{h})]$	30.99	34.70	32.29
(E[p-value])	(0.5924)	(0.568)	(0.526)
$\mathbf{E}[\mathcal{D}_{SSIM}(\mathbf{s}, \mathbf{h})]$	0.584	0.807	0.716
(E[p-value])	(0.597)	(0.557)	(0.530)

tions which count the elapsed times: (1) $T_{generate}(n)$: Consumed time when generating a key from a password of which size is $\|\Psi\|$, (2) $T_{decrypt}(n)$: Consumed time when decryption, (3) $T_{rand}(n)$: Consumed time when checking the randomness of the images, and (4) $T_{stego}(n)$: Consumed time when using stegoanalysis to extract the hidden messages. In this paper, let $\|\Psi\|$ be the number of possible passwords, password space. In general, $T_{generate}(n)$ and $T_{stego}(n)$ are much larger than $T_{decrypt}(n)$ and $T_{rand}(n)$ since often several hashing operations are used when generating a key from the password and steganalysis is known to be a time consuming operation. We simply assume that $T_{rand}(n) < T_{decrypt}(n) << T_{generate}(n) << T_{stego}(n)$. Given this assumption, the time taken for steganalysis to identify the stego-images and to extract the hidden messages are compared in table 4. As shown in the table, our proposed honey steganography needs $(\|\Psi\| - 1)T_{stego}(n)$ times more execution time because all decoded images should be processed by steganalysis because of their indistinguishability. In traditional steganographic algorithms, this is unnecessary because all decrypted and decoded images with incorrect passwords or keys are random except for the image decrypted with correct passwords or keys. Figure 7 displays the results of simulating the execution time complexities in table 4. As expected, an attack on our proposed approach requires much more execution time and therefore our approach is more secure.

6. IMPLEMENTATION ISSUES

6.1 The Effects of Different N

Since we are using a single image instead of N multiple public images, Alice and Bob should share the correct value of N. If Alice and Bob have different N, then Bob will not be able to obtain the correct data. In addition, we simulated the system with varying N. As can be seen in Figure 8, the decoded image becomes closer to the original fake one since

the distribution is constructed with more fake images but the neighboured pixels' value is fixed.

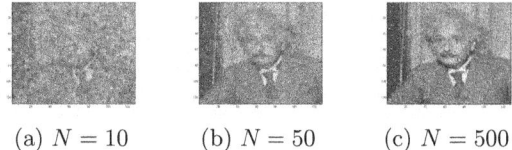

(a) $N = 10$ (b) $N = 50$ (c) $N = 500$

Figure 8: The clarity with various N

6.2 Simplified DTE for Honey steganography

With equation (3) for a single fake image and (6) for multiple fake images, the curvature space $\mathbf{x}$ is assumed to be a d-th order Markovian model in order to allow for the smoothness and reality of the physical images. That is, $p(x_i|\mathbf{x}_{1:i-1}, \mathbf{Y})$ can be reduced to $p(x_i|\mathbf{x}_{ne(i)}, \mathbf{Y})$ causing much lighter computation. However, we can still simplify the modeling by assuming the independence between $x_i \perp x_j$ although $x_j \in ne(i)$ and the prior of x_i may follow a uniform distribution. Then, the target distribution using N multiple fake images becomes $p(\mathbf{x}|\mathbf{Y}, \theta) = \prod_{i=1}^{L}\left[\prod_{n=1}^{N} p(y_i^{(n)}|x_i, \theta)\right] \times p(x_i|\theta) = \prod_{i=1}^{L}\prod_{n=1}^{N} p(y_i^{(n)}|x_i, \theta)$. In this case, the fake images are the significant factors to consider when constructing the distribution.

7. CONCLUSIONS

It is known that conventional honey encryption only works in limited domains such as binary bit streams and integer sequences. However, there are many more complicated data types which have a synthetic or semantic structure including natural language based texts, images, videos. In this paper, we introduced a new variation of honey encryption which can be applied to such complicated data types. The proposed approach has been designed in a Bayesian framework and can be applied to create a new steganography scheme which requires a high time complexity for stegano-analysis. Using this new steganography scheme, this new steganography is more secure than any conventional steganography.

8. ACKNOWLEDGMENTS

This work was supported by the Basic Science Research Program through the National Research Foundation of Korea (NRF) funded by the Ministry of Science, ICT and Future Planning (No. NRF-2013R1A1A1012797). This work was also supported by the National Research Foundation of Korea (NRF) grant funded by the Korea government (No. 2014R1A1A1003707).

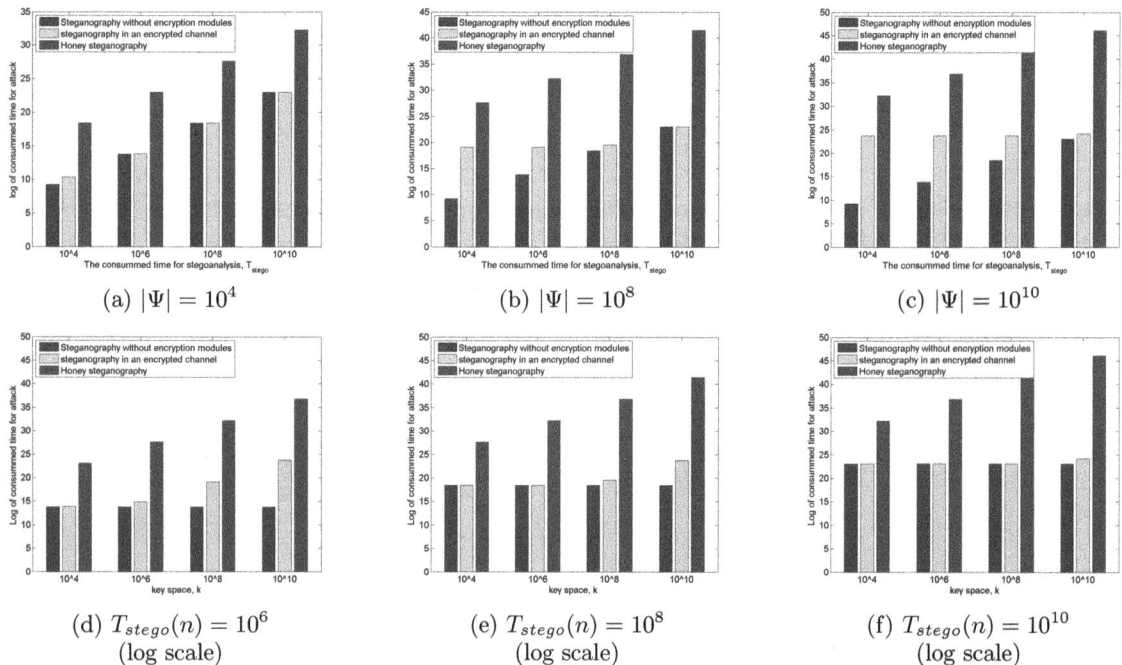

(a) $|\Psi| = 10^4$ (b) $|\Psi| = 10^8$ (c) $|\Psi| = 10^{10}$

(d) $T_{stego}(n) = 10^6$ (log scale)   (e) $T_{stego}(n) = 10^8$ (log scale)   (f) $T_{stego}(n) = 10^{10}$ (log scale)

Figure 7: Time comparison with varying a key size $|\Psi|$ and $T_{stego}(n)$

9. REFERENCES

[1] J. Barbier and S. Alt. Practical insecurity for effective steganalysis. In *Information Hiding, 10th International Workshop, IH 2008, Santa Barbara, CA, USA, May 19-21, 2008, Revised Selected Papers*, pages 195–208, 2008.

[2] J. Besag. Spatial interaction and the statistical analysis of lattice systems (with discussion). *Journal of Royal Statistical Society B*, 36:192–236, 1974.

[3] J. Besag. On the Staistical Analysis of Dirty Pictures. *Journal of the Royal Statistical Society. Series B (Methodological)*, 48(3):259–302, 1986.

[4] J. Bonneau. The science of guessing: analyzing an anonymized corpus of 70 million passwords. In *Proceedings of Security and Privacy (SP)*. IEEE, 2012.

[5] J. Daemen and V. Rijmen. *The Design of Rijndael*. Springer-Verlag New York, Inc., 2002.

[6] D. Florencio and C. Herley. A large-scale study of web password habits. In *Proceedings of the 16th International Conference on World Wide Web*, WWW '07, pages 657–666, 2007.

[7] C. Herley, P. C. Oorschot, and A. S. Patrick. Passwords: If we're so smart, why are we still using them? In *Proceedings of Financial Cryptography and Data Security*, pages 230–237, 2009.

[8] A. Juels and T. Ristenpart. Honey encryption: Encryption beyond the brute-force barrier. *Security & Privacy, IEEE*, 12(4):59–62, 2014.

[9] A. Juels and T. Ristenpart. Honey encryption: Security beyond the brute-force bound. In *Advances in Cryptology – EUROCRYPT*, pages 293–310, 2014.

[10] B. Kaliski. PKCS #5: Password-Based Cryptography Specification Version 2.0, 2000.

[11] H. Kim and J. H. Huh. PIN selection policies: Are they really effective? *Computers & Security*, 31(4):484–496, 2012.

[12] H. Rue and L. Held. *Gaussian Markov Random Field: Theory and Applications*. Chapman & Hall/CRC, 2005.

[13] A. Skillen and M. Mannan. On Implementing Deniable Storage Encryption for Mobile Devices. In *Proceedings of the 20th Annual Network & Distributed System Security Symposium*, NDSS '13, February 2013.

[14] Z. Wang and A. C. Bovik. A universal image quality index. *Signal Proc. Lett., IEEE*, 9(3):81–84, 2002.

[15] Z. Wang, A. C. Bovik, H. R. Sheikh, and E. P. Simoncelli. Image Quality Assessment: From Error Visibility to Structural Similarity. *IEEE Transactions on Image Processing*, 13(4):600–612, 2004.

[16] J. W. Yoon. Statistical denoising scheme for single molecule fluorescence microscopic images. *Biomedical Signal Processing and Control*, 10(0):11 – 20, 2014.

APPENDIX

A. COLLAPSING MULTIPLE NORMAL DISTRIBUTIONS

If we have two normal distributions $\mathcal{N}(x; \mu_1, \sigma_1^2)$ and $\mathcal{N}(x; \mu_2, \sigma_2^2)$ the collapsed normal distribution is as follows: $\mathcal{N}(x; \mu, \sigma^2) = \mathcal{N}(x; \mu_1, \sigma_1^2)\mathcal{N}(x; \mu_2, \sigma_2^2)$ where $\sigma = \sqrt{(1/\sigma_1^2 + 1/\sigma_2^2)}$ and $\mu = \sigma^2(\mu_1/\sigma_1^2 + \mu_2/\sigma_2^2)$.

For multiple normal distributions, we can generalize the product of the multiple normal distributions: $\mathcal{N}(x; \mu, \sigma^2) = \prod_{n=1}^{N} \mathcal{N}(x; \mu_n, \sigma_n^2)$ where $\sigma = \sqrt{\left(\sum_{n=1}^{N} \frac{1}{\sigma_n^2}\right)^{-1}}$ and $\mu = \sigma^2 \sum_{n=1}^{N} \frac{\mu_n}{\sigma_n^2}$.

Flicker Forensics for Pirate Devices Identification

Adi Hajj-Ahmad
University of Maryland
College Park, USA

Séverine Baudry
Technicolor R&D France
Cesson-Sévigné, France

Bertrand Chupeau
Technicolor R&D France
Cesson-Sévigné, France

Gwenaël Doërr
Technicolor R&D France
Cesson-Sévigné, France

ABSTRACT

Cryptography-based content protection is an efficient means to protect multimedia content during transport. Nevertheless, content is eventually decrypted at rendering time, leaving it vulnerable to piracy e.g. using a camcorder to record movies displayed on an LCD screen. Such type of piracy naturally imprints a visible flicker signal in the pirate video due to the interplay between the rendering and acquisition devices. The parameters of such flicker are inherently tied to the characteristics of the pirate devices such as the backlight of the LCD screen and the read-out time of the camcorder. In this article, we introduce a forensic methodology to estimate such parameters by analyzing the flicker signal present in pirate recordings. Experimental results clearly showcase that the accuracy of these estimation techniques offers efficient means to tell-tale which devices have been used for piracy thanks to the variety of factory settings used by consumer electronics manufacturers.

Categories and Subject Descriptors

[**Hardware**]: Input/Output and Data Communications—*Input/Output Devices*; [**Computing Methodologies**]: Image Processing and Computer Vision—*Digitization and Image Capture, General*; [**Computing Milieux**]: Computers and Society—*Public Policy Issues*

General Terms

Security, Algorithm.

Keywords

Passive forensics, piracy, LCD screen, back-light, camcorder, rolling shutter, read-out time, flicker.

IH&MMSec'15 June 17-19, 2015 Portland, OR, USA
©2015 ACM. ISBN 978-1-4503-3587-4/15/06 ...$15.00
DOI: http://dx.doi.org/10.1145/2756601.2756612.

Figure 1: Flicker artifact when recording an LCD screen displaying a uniformly gray frame with a camcorder.

1. INTRODUCTION

Movie piracy still remains a major concern for the Entertainment industry today. Disclosure on unauthorized sharing platforms prior to theatrical/Blu-ray releases holds the potential to significantly harm revenues. To address this risk, content owners routinely rely on cryptography-based content protection techniques to prevent consumers from easily accessing multimedia content [15]. Nevertheless, such protection has to be lifted eventually to render the content and a pirate then only has to place a camera in front of the screen to record a pirate copy of the movie.

A second line of defense then consists of embedding forensic watermarks within the rendered content, which can survive digital-analog-digital conversion [4]. As a result, when a pirate copy surfaces on unauthorized distribution platforms, it is possible to recover the underlying watermark identifier and trace it back to the user or device from which the piracy originated [7]. Such a traitor tracing mechanism has already been deployed in digital cinemas [5] and is anticipated to be soon extended to the consumer's home to protect ultra high definition content [12].

In this context, it is worth studying the piracy path when pirate video samples are obtained by camcording an LCD screen. As depicted in Figure 1, such a piracy scenario is known to yield a visible flicker signal due to the interplay between the camcorder and the screen. It is incarnated by typical dark/bright stripes that scroll up/down the pirate video. In prior work, research efforts have been dedicated to detect the presence of such flicker [13, 14, 11, 3]. Indeed, this tell-tale artifact provides clues about the piracy path and can be exploited by the forensic analyst to select which watermark detector to use. More recently, notable efforts have been spent to reverse the flicker distortion [16, 1] in order to improve watermark detection performances for instance.

In this paper, we intend to investigate whether the characteristics of the flicker signal present in a pirate copy could be exploited to infer which devices have been used to produce it. For instance, relying on some traitor-tracing evidence, police investigators may have raided the home of a suspect pirate and seized a collection of devices. It would therefore be useful to provide corroborating evidence that the flicker signal observed in the pirate movies could be produced using these devices. Moreover, in case watermark-based tracing mechanisms fail, it could provide a fall-back mechanism to link pirate samples together which originate from the same piracy workflow.

In Section 2, we start by reminding how the flicker signal is formed prior to deriving a mathematical identity that connects the read-out time of the camcorder and the back-light frequency of the LCD screen to some characteristics of the flicker signal, namely its vertical radial frequency. We detail two alternate methods in Section 3 to illustrate how this characteristic value can be estimated directly from the frames of a camcorded video sequence. We then review three forensic scenarios in Section 4 and detail how to identify the pirate devices in each case. Such analysis usually requires having access to the ground-truth parameters of the suspect devices and we therefore briefly describe a methodology to extract them in Section 5. Experimental results reported in Section 6 clearly indicate that the flicker signal present in camcorded movies is indeed useful to pinpoint which devices have been used in the piracy workflow. In Section 7, we summarize our findings, discuss the limitations of the proposed approach and outline directions for future work.

2. CONNECTING THE FLICKER SIGNAL TO THE PIRATE DEVICES

When placing a camcorder in front of an LCD screen, the interaction between the back-light of the screen and the acquisition mechanism of the camcorder is known to yield visible flicker in the video recording.

The image appearing on an LCD screen is formed by the light that is let through by an array of liquid crystal cells, each cell encoding a pixel of the image [2]. Each individual liquid crystal can be tuned by changing the electric potential applied to it in order to let more or less light pass. In other words, a key feature of an LCD display design is the presence of a source of light to illuminate the array of liquid crystal cells from behind. This so-called *back-light* is a periodical signal whose frequency is high enough to be imperceptible by the human eye, typically around 200 Hz.

On the other hand, camcorders have an array of built-in sensors which is exposed to light for a given period of time. The resulting electrical charge accumulated by each sensor is then converted to produce the pixel values of the video frame. With camcorders routinely operating between 24 and 60 frames per second (fps), several cycles of the back-light will be integrated during the acquisition period. Since the back-light of the screen and the shutter of the camcorder

are not synchronized, different frames of the video recording are associated to different sections of the back-light signal. As a result, the average luminance varies periodically at a frequency given by the aliasing of the high-frequency back-light signal by the low-frequency acquisition process.

Moreover, most camcorders commercially sold nowadays use CMOS sensors and a *rolling shutter* [8, 9]. In contrast with global shutters that acquire a whole frame at once, a rolling shutter captures each line sequentially e.g. from top to bottom. Consequently, each row of the image sees a different portion of the back-light and the average luminance of the recorded video now also varies along the vertical direction as exemplified in Figure 1. According to prior work [1], such spatio-temporal flicker can be modeled as follows:

$$\mathbf{f}[x, y, t] = (A \cdot \mathbf{c}[x, y, t] + B) \cdot \cos(\omega_t \cdot t + \omega_y \cdot y + \phi), \quad (1)$$

where x, y and t are respectively the column, row, and time indices and $\mathbf{c}$ is the luminance of the displayed video content. The first term of the equation indicates that the amplitude of the flicker scales linearly with the luminance of the camcorded content as given by the linear coefficients A and B. The second term captures the periodical nature of the flicker signal both in time and along the rows. The temporal radial frequency ω_t is given in radians/frame and the vertical radial frequency ω_y is given in radians/row. The phase ϕ accommodates for the absence of synchronization between the back-light and the shutter.

As mentioned earlier, a camcorder typically captures video frames at a rate f_c that is much smaller than the fundamental frequency f_{BL} of the back-light. In other words, the camcorder operates below the Nyquist rate and the flicker signal therefore ends up at an aliased frequency f_t of the back-light, i.e.

$$\exists k \in \mathbb{N}, \quad f_t = |f_{BL} - k \cdot f_c| < \frac{f_c}{2}. \quad (2)$$

The temporal radial frequency is then given by $\omega_t = 2\pi f_t / f_c$. In contrast, the read-out time T_{ro} taken by a camcorder to capture a video frame usually ranges between 10-35 ms. As a result, the vertical sampling rate is on the order of 10 kHz, i.e. much larger than the Nyquist sampling rate of a regular back-light signal. There is thus no aliasing and the vertical radial frequency can be written as:

$$\omega_y = 2\pi \cdot \frac{f_{BL}}{f_y}, \quad (3)$$

where $f_y = H/T_{ro}$ can be seen as the row acquisition rate if H denotes the number of rows in a video frame. It is then straightforward to establish the following mathematical identity:

$$T_{ro} \cdot f_{BL} = \frac{H \cdot \omega_y}{2\pi}, \quad (4)$$

that links some characteristics of the pirate devices, namely the read-out time T_{ro} of the camcorder and the back-light frequency f_{BL} of the LCD screen, together with some property of the flicker signal present in the video signal.

3. ESTIMATION OF THE VERTICAL RADIAL FREQUENCY

A straightforward investigation strategy consists of extracting the characteristic quantities appearing in the right-hand side of Equation (4) from the pirate sample and then

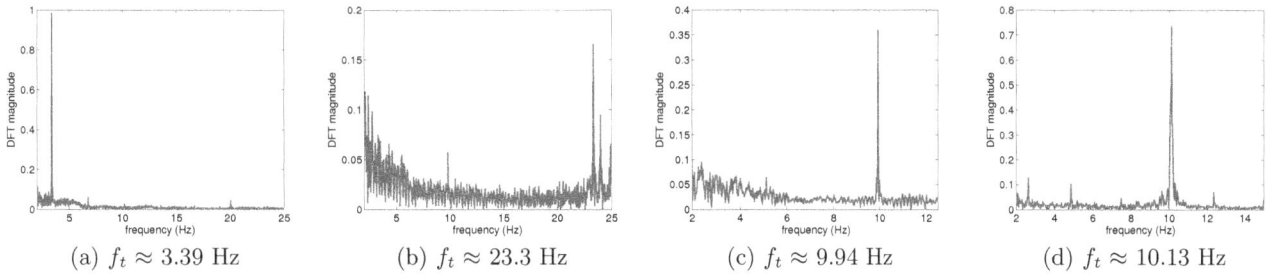

(a) $f_t \approx 3.39$ Hz (b) $f_t \approx 23.3$ Hz (c) $f_t \approx 9.94$ Hz (d) $f_t \approx 10.13$ Hz

Figure 2: Magnitude of the Fourier transform of one row average $\mathbf{r}[y^*, t]$ for several pirate samples of the *Wall-E* video using various combination of LCD screens and camcorders. The x-axis has been mapped to Hertz (Hz) using the knowledge of the frame rate f_c. The estimated temporal frequency f_t of the flicker signal is indicated for reference.

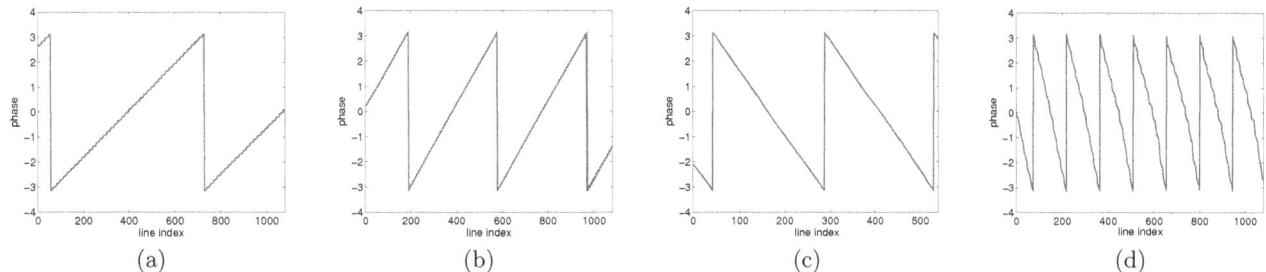

(a) (b) (c) (d)

Figure 3: Evolution of the flicker phase, computing using the Fourier coefficients $\mathbf{R}[y, \omega_t]$, with the row index in the video frame. The measurements have been extracted from camcorded recordings of the *Wall-E* video using different screen–camcorder pairs.

identifying which combination of screen–camcorder could produce such flicker. While the number of rows H in a video frame is readily available, estimating the vertical radial frequency ω_y of the flicker is more challenging. The task is complicated by the fact that the flicker signal has usually a much lower energy than the pirate video content. As a result, the video content is likely to interfere with the estimation process that only cares about the underlying flicker signal. In the next two subsections, we describe two alternate methods to estimate ω_y.

3.1 Flicker Phase Method

A first strategy to estimate the vertical radial frequency ω_y operates in two steps. The objective is to first get access to the temporal radial frequency ω_t in order to derive the vertical one from the evolution of the phase at this specific frequency.

To begin with, we first compute, for each frame, the average luminance of each row:

$$
\begin{aligned}
\mathbf{r}[y, t] &= \frac{1}{W} \sum_{x=1}^{W} \mathbf{p}[x, y, t] \\
&= \frac{1}{W} \sum_{x=1}^{W} \left(\mathbf{c}[x, y, t] + \mathbf{f}[x, y, t] \right), \quad (5)
\end{aligned}
$$

where W is the number of pixels per row in a frame of the pirate sample $\mathbf{p}$. Due to its horizontal nature, this operation attenuates the interference from the content while leaving the flicker signal untouched [14, 1]. According to the model

of the flicker given in Equation (1), the magnitude $\mathbf{R}[y, \omega]$ of the Fourier transform of the row average along the time axis is expected to feature a peak close to ω_t. For reference, Figure 2 illustrates this tell-tale flicker component for a variety of LCD screens and camcorder combinations. To estimate ω_t, we therefore record the radial frequency which maximizes the magnitude $\mathbf{R}[y^*, \omega]$ for any arbitrarily selected row y^*. In practice, we usually rely on a row toward the middle of the video frames to avoid unexpected behavior at the borders. To account for the fact that the low frequency range of the spectrum is likely to be dominated by the contribution of the visual content $\mathbf{c}$, the frequency range $[0, \alpha]$ is ignored during the estimation. Our empirical observations indicate that setting $\alpha = 0.4$ radians/frame manages to avoid interference from the video content in most cases.

According to Equation (1), the phase $\Phi_{\omega_t}[y]$ of the Fourier coefficients $\mathbf{R}[y, \omega_t]$ is given by $\omega_y y + \Phi_t$, with Φ_t being a time-dependent phase offset. In other words, the phase of the flicker is expected to evolve linearly along the rows, with a slope equal to the vertical radial frequency ω_y. Empirical observations reported in Figure 3 clearly indicated that it is indeed the case even if the modulo-2π operator disrupts the overall linear trend. To compensate for such undesired wrapping, the phase $\Phi_{\omega_t}[y]$ of $\mathbf{R}[y, \omega_t]$ is post-processed as follows:

$$
\Psi_{\omega_t}[y] = \begin{cases} \Phi_{\omega_t}[y], & \text{if } y = 0, \\ \Psi_{\omega_t}[y-1] + d_y, & \text{if } y > 0, \end{cases} \quad (6)
$$

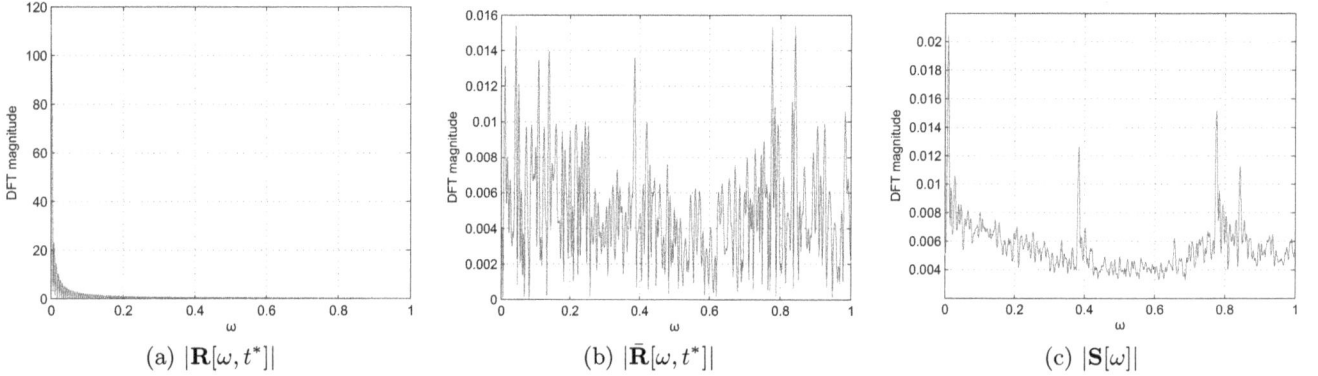

Figure 4: **Spectrum of the signal of interest at various stages of the content cancellation method.** The spectrum $|\mathbf{R}[\omega, t^*]|$ of the row luminance signature (a) is dominated by the visual content and the flicker signal is not visible. In contrast, the cleaning process (b) reveals the peak corresponding to the flicker at 0.009 rad/row although it lies hidden amongst other noise components. After aggregation, the flicker frequency peak clearly appears thanks to the signal-to-noise ratio reduction.

where

$$d_y = \left(\left(\Phi_{\omega_t}[y] - \Phi_{\omega_t}[y-1] + \pi \right) \mod 2\pi \right) - \pi. \quad (7)$$

Estimating the vertical radial frequency ω_y is then only a matter of applying linear regression to the *unwrapped* flicker phase $\Psi_{\omega_t}[y]$ and recording the slope. As exemplified in Figure 3, the slope of the flicker phase can be positive or negative. As a result, the vertical radial frequency ω_y is simply taken as the absolute value of the estimated slope of the flicker phase.

It should be noted that the regression error provides an efficient indicator to evaluate whether the selected temporal frequency ω_t is related to a flicker or not. In some cases, the largest frequency component in $\mathbf{R}[y^*, \omega]$ is not associated to the flicker signal, which may be present in the spectrum but with a lower amplitude. In this situation, the phase $\Phi_{\omega_t}[y]$ is unlikely to be linear and the linear regression yields large error. The algorithm can then either re-run the phase regression analysis for another secondary peak of the spectrum $\mathbf{R}[y^*, \omega]$ or fall back on the alternate estimation method described hereafter.

3.2 Content Cancellation Method

The phase flicker method presented in the previous section is essentially a two-step procedure that relies on the ability to estimate the temporal radial frequency ω_t to begin with. However, in practice, such estimation may prove difficult, if not impossible. For instance, when the back-light frequency of the display apparatus gets close to a multiple of the acquisition frame rate of the camcorder, the observed aliased temporal flicker frequency appears near zero which precludes accurate estimation due to the dominance of the content in the low frequency band.

In such cases, it is necessary to rely on a fall-back estimation technique to get access to the desired vertical radial frequency ω_y. In essence, the baseline idea is (i) to clean several observations of the vertical flicker to reduce the interference from the visual content, (ii) compute the vertical spectrum of the cleaned observations, (iii) aggregate these spectra to reduce the flicker signal-to-noise ratio, and (iv)

estimate the vertical radial frequency using frequency analysis.

The row luminance signatures $\mathbf{r}[y, t]$ are essentially dominated by content, thereby making the analysis of the subtle changes revealing the flicker difficult to analyze. Nevertheless, the content interference is expected to vary slowly along the rows. It is thus possible to cancel this component by applying a high-pass filter or removing the trend of the signal using some fitting tool, e.g.:

$$\bar{\mathbf{r}}[y, t^*] = \mathbf{h} \left(\mathbf{r}[y, t^*] \right), \quad (8)$$

where t^* is an arbitrarily selected time index and $\mathbf{h}(.)$ is any generic signal processing primitive to remove the low frequency components of a signal. Empirical observations indicate that this cleaning process is more efficient for uniform frames having more predictable row luminance signatures.

Still, significant content energy usually remains in individual cleaned row luminance signatures. As a result, estimating the vertical radial frequency ω_y based on the spectrum analysis of a single row luminance signature, even cleaned, may be unsuccessful. To improve the signal-to-noise ratio, it is common practice in multimedia security to aggregate several observations to reduce the interference introduced by uncorrelated noise components [6, 10]. Such aggregation can be performed directly in the Fourier domain:

$$|\mathbf{S}[\omega]| = \frac{1}{M} \sum_{i=1}^{M} |\bar{\mathbf{R}}[\omega, t_i]|, \quad (9)$$

where $|\bar{\mathbf{R}}[\omega, t^*]|$ is the magnitude of the Fourier transform of the cleaned row luminance signature $\bar{\mathbf{r}}[\omega, t^*]$, $|\mathbf{S}[\omega]|$ the magnitude of the vertical flicker spectrum, and the set of time indices $\{t_i\}_{1 \leq i \leq M}$ indicate which frames of the video sequence have been incorporated into the aggregation. In practice, we considered the $M = 40$ most uniform video frames, i.e. the M frames with the lowest variances, since empirical observations reveal that they provide better vertical flicker estimates $\bar{\mathbf{r}}[y, t^*]$.

Eventually, the vertical radial frequency ω_y is given by the frequency whose magnitude is maximal in the spectrum $|\mathbf{S}[\omega]|$. In this paper, to avoid false estimations, we also discard frequencies $\omega > \beta$ since they correspond to back-light frequencies that are never used in practice. Our empirical observations showed that using $\beta = 1$ radians/row provides good performances in general. For reference, Figure 4 depicts the added value of the cleaning and aggregation processes in a particularly difficult case.

4. FORENSIC INVESTIGATIONS

In this paper, a typical forensic scenario is that law enforcement forces have searched the homes of suspected pirates and seized camcorded movie samples as well as a collection of screens and camcorders. A key question is then to establish whether these suspect devices could have produced the collected pirate multimedia material. The charges against piracy consumers and piracy producers are indeed not the same.

In the remainder of the article, we investigate if flicker-based forensic analysis could successfully achieve this identification task. For completeness, we survey three alternate use cases corresponding to different a priori knowledge about the pirate devices. For the time being, we assume that we can have access to the read-out time T_{ro} of a camcorder and the back-light frequency f_{BL} of an LCD screen. We will detail in Section 5 how to retrieve these values in practice.

4.1 Camcorder Identification

In this scenario, the pirate LCD screen is assumed to be known and the forensic task therefore reduces to identifying the pirate camcorder within a collection of suspect devices. Based on the piracy identity given by Equation (4), it is immediate to write:

$$T_{\mathrm{ro}} = \frac{H \cdot \omega_y}{2\pi \cdot f_{\mathrm{BL}}}. \qquad (10)$$

The frame height H can be directly accessed from the pirate video and the vertical radial frequency ω_y can be estimated using any of the two methods described in Section 3. Since the pirate screen is assumed to be known, we have access to f_{BL} and we can compute the read-out time T_{ro} of the camcorder used to produce the pirate video sample. Pinpointing the pirate camcorder amongst the set of suspect devices is then simply a matter of identifying the device whose read-out time is the closest to this target value.

4.2 Screen Identification

Conversely, we can assume that the pirate camcorder is known and that the objective is to pinpoint the pirate screen amongst several suspect devices. Still reusing Equation (4), it is straightforward to express the back-light frequency as:

$$f_{\mathrm{BL}} = \frac{H \cdot \omega_y}{2\pi \cdot T_{\mathrm{ro}}}. \qquad (11)$$

As previously, we can rely on the parameters derived from the pirate video and camcorder to compute the pirate back-light frequency. The identification task then amounts to finding the screen whose back-light frequency is the closest to this target value.

While this strategy does provide an estimate of the back-light frequency f_{BL}, it relies on the estimation of the vertical radial frequency ω_y which may be very rough, especially when using the content cancellation method. As a result, the forensic identification accuracy may be jeopardized. In order to mitigate this limitation, instead of trying to identify the characteristic, it may be advantageous to simply verify

if a pair of suspect devices could produce the flicker signal observed in the pirate movie in a matter similar to what is done in biometrics.

For instance, considering a potential pair of pirate devices, it is possible to derive the theoretical aliased frequency f_t based on the back-light frequency f_{BL} of the screen and the sampling rate f_c of the camcorder. As a result, in the flicker phase method, instead of blindly looking for the temporal radial frequency ω_t in the spectrum $\mathbf{R}[y^*, \omega]$, we can restrict the search within a small range around the theoretical flicker aliased frequency. First, it allows to accurately lock on frequencies which may have been overlooked by mistake for not having the global maximum magnitude of the spectrum. Second, it provides means to quickly discard suspect pairs of devices when the phase $\Phi_{\omega_t}[y]$ is found not to be linear.

On another front, we could exploit the knowledge of the parameters of the suspect devices to improve the estimation accuracy of the back-light frequency. Based on the estimation of the temporal radial frequency ω_t, which has been empirically found to be more accurate than ω_y, it is possible to refine the estimation of the back-light frequency, e.g.:

$$f_{\mathrm{BL}}^{\dagger} = \left| f_t + f_c \cdot \arg\min_{k \in \mathbb{Z}} \left| f_{\mathrm{BL}} - |f_t + k \cdot f_c| \right| \right|. \qquad (12)$$

In other words, we exploit the aliasing phenomenon to identify which candidate frequency $|f_t + k \cdot f_c|$, $k \in \mathbb{Z}$, is the closest to the rough estimation obtained in Equation (11).

4.3 Blind Identification

In the most challenging scenario, neither the pirate screen nor the pirate camcorder have been yet identified and the forensic analyst has to investigate the pirate video in a completely blind manner. As a matter of fact, she is reduced to evaluating both sides of the piracy identity, duplicated here for convenience:

$$T_{\mathrm{ro}} \cdot f_{\mathrm{BL}} = \frac{H \cdot \omega_y}{2\pi}. \qquad \cdot$$

The product on the left-hand side can be evaluated using the ground truth back-light frequency and read-out time retrieved from the pirate devices. The left-hand side can be computed by analyzing the flicker signal present in the camcorded pirate video sequence. Identifying the pirate devices among a collection of suspect LCD screens and camcorders is then simply a matter of isolating the pair of devices which yields a difference between the two sides of the piracy identity that is the closest to zero.

5. PIRATE DEVICES CHARACTERISTICS

As described in the previous section, the proposed forensic protocol heavily relies on the ability of the analyst to have access to the characteristics of the suspect devices, namely the back-light frequency f_{BL} of the LCD screens and the read-out time T_{ro} of the camcorders. Unfortunately, such low-level characteristics are usually not indicated in the datasheets or manuals of consumer electronics products. Moreover, these parameters may differ along the production line and it is therefore preferable to extract the ground truth parameters from the suspect devices seized during the investigation. In contrast with the forensic analysis of the pirate video sequence, the extraction of these parameters is performed in a controlled environment e.g. devices can

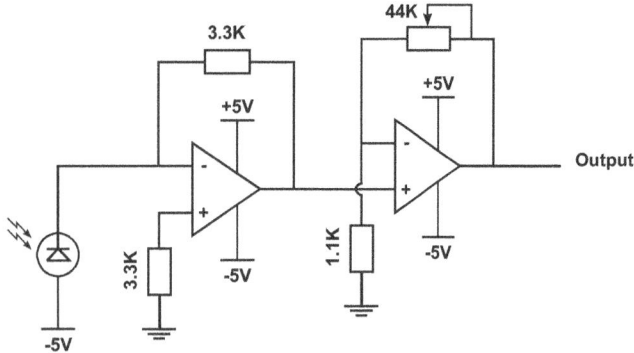

Figure 5: Custom-made light sensing probe. The photo-diode converts light into electric current, which is amplified by a first amplifier on the left-hand side. Namely, 0.1 mW/cm^2 yields a current of 0.8 μA and 2.64 mV. The adjustable gain amplifier on the right-hand side is then useful for accommodating to various light intensities of different screens. The gain can vary between 1 and 44.

Table 1: LCD screens used in our experiments

ID	Brand	Model	f_{BL} (Hz)
1	Dell	2209WA	240.06
2	Dell	U2410	180.43
3	Samsung	LE37B652T4WXXC	159.98
4	Samsung	UE32C6000RWXZF	120.00
5	Sony	KDL-32P3000	146.61
6	Sony	KDL-37P3000	226.70
7	Sony	KDL-32W5710	172.80

Table 2: Camcorders used in our experiments

Brand	Model	f_c (fps)	H	T_{ro} (ms)
JVC	GC-PX100BE	50	1080	13.5
Panasonic	HDC-SDT750	50	1080	16
Sony	HDR-CX200E	25	540	15
Toshiba	PA5081E-1C0K	29.97	1080	32.65

be fed with specific stimuli to facilitate measurements. The only constraint is to avoid tampering with the integrity of the device, i.e. breaking apart the device to examine its individual components.

5.1 LCD Screen Back-light Frequency

To reverse engineer the back-light frequency of an LCD screen in a non-invasive way, the first task is to get access to the raw signal with some kind of probe. To do so, we custom-made a sensing circuit that converts captured light into an electrical signal. In a nutshell, the reversed-current of a photo-diode is amplified with a regular transistor. The whole circuit is embedded within a pen-like casing that has a pin hole to let incoming light in as illustrated in Figure 5. The output of the sensing circuit can then be connected to a PC or an oscilloscope for live analysis or to some recording device, e.g. an audio recorder, for off-line analysis. By placing this apparatus on the surface of a screen which displays a static uniform gray frame, it gets direct access to the back-light signal without interference from other light sources or from the temporal dynamic of a motion picture. The recorded signal is typically a periodic signal whose fundamental frequency is equal to the back-light frequency f_{BL} of the LCD screen. Straightforward spectrum analysis then allows to efficiently extract the ground truth back-light frequency of the screen. In Table 1, we report on the measurements obtained on the seven LCD screens used in our experiments. The reverse-engineered back-light frequencies are within a 120-250 Hz which is in line with the known practices of the display industry.

5.2 Camcorder Read-out Time

Getting access to the read-out time T_{ro} of a camcorder is less direct than measuring the back-light frequency using a probe. The trick is to record a reference LCD screen displaying gray scale content, as depicted in Figure 1, with the suspect camcorder to obtain a short video sequence (e.g. 30 seconds) where the flicker is apparent. Based on our ability to extract the ground truth back-light frequency of the reference screen and thanks to the lack of visual content interference since we are using a neutral stimulus, the flicker phase method described in Section 3.1 provides access to the vertical radial frequency ω_y of the flicker which in turn yields the desired read-out time using Equation (10). To avoid corner cases where temporal aliasing may interfere with the estimation of ω_y, several reference screens may be considered to be more confident of the computed read-out time. The measurements that we obtained with the four camcorders used in our experiments are reported in Table 2 for reference. It should be noted that all camcorders are progressive, except the Sony camera which is interlaced. For convenience, we simply kept one of the two fields for this camera, thereby resulting in a vertical resolution of 540 rows although the camcorder has the ability to capture 1080 rows.

6. EXPERIMENTAL RESULTS

To validate our forensic protocol based on the analysis of the flicker signal present in camcorded pirate videos, we constructed a dedicated experimental dataset. For all combinations of LCD screens and camcorders from the pool of devices listed in Tables 1 and 2, we recorded a 1 minute long video sequence taken from the opening scene of the movie *Wall-E* displayed on a screen. Figure 6 depicts some screenshots for such camcorded video sequences. It is important

(a) Screen 2 and JVC

(b) Screen 3 and Panasonic

(c) Screen 7 and Sony

(d) Screen 1 and Toshiba

Figure 6: Screenshots of camcorded video sequences using various screen–camcorder pairs. Besides very different color changes, the flicker signal is more or less apparent depending on the pair of pirate devices.

Table 3: Aliased temporal frequency f_t either computed from the ground-truth measurement of the back-light frequency f_{BL} of the pirate LCD screen or estimated from the pirate video samples

	f_{BL} (Hz)	JVC		Panasonic		Sony		Toshiba	
		Theo.	Exp.	Theo.	Exp.	Theo.	Exp.	Theo.	Exp.
Screen 1	240.06	9.94	9.94	9.94	9.94	9.94	9.94	0.30	N/A
Screen 2	180.43	19.57	19.56	19.57	19.56	5.43	5.44	0.61	N/A
Screen 3	159.98	9.98	9.99	9.98	9.99	9.98	9.99	10.13	10.13
Screen 4	120.00	20.00	20.02	20.00	19.97	5.00	4.98	0.12	N/A
Screen 5	146.61	3.39	3.39	3.39	3.47	3.39	3.39	3.24	3.48
Screen 6	226.70	23.30	23.34	23.30	23.32	1.70	N/A	13.06	12.82
Screen 7	172.80	22.80	22.80	22.80	22.80	2.20	2.20	7.02	7.02

to note that the flicker is not always very visible but that, as will be detailed in the next sections, it can still be exploited to extract the desired forensic information. Overall, the experimental dataset amounts to 28 camcorded videos and we report hereafter the identification performances depending on the considered forensic scenario.

6.1 Camcorder Identification Scenario

When estimating the vertical radial frequency ω_y from the pirate video sample using the flicker phase method described in Section 3.1, a key intermediary step is the accurate estimation of the temporal frequency ω_t. For reference, we report in Table 3 the theoretical values obtained from the ground-truth measurements of the back-light frequency f_{BL} as well as the values obtained experimentally from the video samples. For ease of interpretation, these values are provided in Hertz, assuming knowledge of the camera acquisition rate f_c. Most of the aliased temporal frequency estimates are very close to the expected theoretical values, e.g. within a range of ± 0.02 Hz. This very high accuracy

validates the refinement procedure proposed in Section 4.2. Still, in four cases, the flicker phase method is unsuccessful. Essentially, the aliased temporal frequency f_t is too close to the content-dependent low-frequency components. Visually, it translates as a static flicker signal, i.e. horizontal strips of varying luminance with marginal vertical drift. In such cases ($\omega_t < \alpha$), there is no other choice but to fall back on the backup estimation method even if it yields less accurate estimates of the vertical radial frequency ω_y.

Once the vertical radial frequency ω_y is estimated, obtaining the read-out time T_{ro} of the pirate camcorder is simply a matter of applying Equation (10), using the back-light frequency f_{BL} of the known pirate LCD screen. The pirate camcorder is then the one whose ground truth read-out time is the closest to this estimated value. The experimental results reported in Table 4 indicate that the pirate camcorder is correctly identified in 25 out of 28 videos, i.e. 89% correct identification. One of the unsuccessful identification actually features an estimated read-out time much larger than the ground truth value, namely 63.77 ms vs. 16 ms. In this par-

Table 5: Back-light frequency f_{BL} computed either by leveraging on the piracy identity with Equation (11) or by exploiting frequency aliasing to refine the rough estimate with Equation (12). Figures in italic indicate LCD screen identification errors.

	f_{BL} (Hz)	JVC Rough	JVC Refined	Panasonic Rough	Panasonic Refined	Sony Rough	Sony Refined	Toshiba Rough	Toshiba Refined
Screen 1	240.06	243.22	240.06	238.18	240.06	240.46	240.06	241.26	N/A
Screen 2	180.43	177.74	180.44	178.46	180.44	181.08	180.44	179.68	N/A
Screen 3	159.98	159.36	159.99	158.33	159.99	156.90	159.99	159.94	159.98
Screen 4	120.00	115.67	120.02	*238.64*	*240.01*	112.69	120.01	119.12	N/A
Screen 5	146.61	145.49	146.61	136.73	146.53	146.60	146.61	147.57	146.37
Screen 6	226.70	225.83	226.66	227.67	226.68	226.32	N/A	227.02	226.94
Screen 7	172.80	173.48	172.80	172.39	172.80	173.00	172.80	171.82	172.80

Table 4: Frame read-out times T_{ro} estimated from pirate video sequences obtained using various pirate camcorder-screen pairs. Figures in italic highlight pirate camcorder identification mistakes.

	JVC	Panasonic	Sony	Toshiba
T_{ro} (ms)	13.5	16	15	32.65
Screen 1	13.68	15.87	15.03	32.81
Screen 2	13.30	15.82	15.05	32.52
Screen 3	13.45	15.83	14.71	32.64
Screen 4	13.01	*63.77*	*14.09*	32.41
Screen 5	13.40	*14.92*	15.00	32.86
Screen 6	13.45	16.07	14.97	32.70
Screen 7	13.55	15.96	15.02	32.47

Table 6: Identified pirate screen–camcorder pairs with the video sequences of our dataset. Pirate devices are represented by the format [J,P,S,T]–[1...7], where the letter indicates the camcorder and the number the LCD screen. Entries in italic highlight identification errors.

	JVC	Panasonic	Sony	Toshiba
Screen 1	J–1	P–1	S–1	T–1
Screen 2	*S–3*	P–2	S–2	T–2
Screen 3	J–3	P–3	*P–5*	T–3
Screen 4	J–4	*P–1*	*J–4*	T–4
Screen 5	J–5	*S–5*	S–5	T–5
Screen 6	J–6	P–6	S–6	T–6
Screen 7	*P–5*	P–7	S–7	T–7

ticular case, the back-light frequency of the screen is 120 Hz and is thus aliased to $|120 - 2 \times 50| = 20$ Hz when using the **Panasonic** camcorder. However, the fourth harmonic of the back-light also aliases at $4 \times 120 - 10 \times 50 = 20$ Hz. As a result, when the flicker phase method looks at the phase at frequency $f_t = 20$ Hz, it picks up the fourth harmonic and thereby overestimates the read-out time by a factor of 4. Should we divide the estimated value by 4, we would obtain $T_{ro} = 15.94$ ms and thus correctly estimate the **Panasonic** camcorder. The other two errors simply indicate the current limitation of the proposed forensic strategy when the visual content interferes with the estimation process.

6.2 Screen Identification Scenario

As discussed in Section 4.2, it is possible to estimate the back-light frequency f_{BL} of the pirate LCD screen by applying Equation (11) obtained by manipulating the piracy identity which links the vertical radial frequency of the pirate video sequence and the characteristic parameters of the pirate devices. Table 5 lists such rough estimates extracted from the video sequences in our experimental dataset. While the estimation is reasonably accurate, it sometimes yields notable deviation, e.g. the 10 Hz bias with the **Panasonic** camcorder and the **Screen 5**, which could result in identification mistakes. The a priori knowledge about the pirate camcorder grants the opportunity to leverage on the frequency aliasing mechanism to obtain a refined estimation of when an estimate of the aliased temporal frequency f_t is available. The refined estimates listed in Table 5 clearly showcase the improved accuracy of the estimation. All refined back-light frequency estimates are indeed within a 1 Hz

error margin around the ground truth except for a single combination of camcorder-screen pirate devices. In other words, pirate LCD screen identification is successful for 27 out of 28 pirate sequences.

As in a previous scenario, the combination of the **Panasonic** camcorder and the **Screen 4** appears to be a corner case. Interestingly, though, the problem does not only come from the fact that the fundamental and fourth harmonic of the back-light signal overlap at 20 Hz. When analyzing this pirate video sequence, each screen is successively tested as a potential pirate device. In particular, **Screen 1** and **Screen 3** are expected to have an aliased temporal frequency f_t close to 10 Hz with the **Panasonic** camcorder. On the other hand, 10 Hz is also the location of the second harmonic ($2 \times 120 - 5 \times 50 = 10$) for **Screen 4**. As a result, the forensic analysis will reveal two candidate f_t values at 10 Hz and 20 Hz, each one having a linear phase $\Phi_{\omega_t}[y]$ and associated to two estimates of ω_y corresponding to 240 Hz and 480 Hz respectively. It is common practice to eliminate higher harmonics and the algorithm therefore outputs 240 Hz, mistaking **Screen 1** for the pirate LCD screen.

6.3 Blind Identification Scenario

When there is no a priori information on the pirate devices, all potential screen–camcorder pairs have to be evaluated. The forensic protocol reduces in this case to the evaluation of the left-hand side and the right-hand side of the piracy identity given by Equation (4) and to isolate the pair of devices which yields the lowest difference. The results of such blind identification of the pirate devices are reported in Table 6. As could be anticipated, the lack of a priori in-

Table 7: Flicker forensics accuracy

Scenario	Accuracy
Camcorder Identification	89%
Screen Identification	96%
Blind Identification	79%

formation naturally translates in reduced identification accuracy. Still, the proposed forensic protocol is successful in 22 cases out of 28, i.e. a 79% correct identification rate.

When looking closely at the six identification mistakes, it is possible to isolate two main sources of error. First of all, the three entries with errors in Table 4, which are also the ones whose back-light frequency estimation error is among the largest in Table 5, produce errors in the blind identification scenario. In other words, pirate sequences which provide incorrect results in the non-blind scenarios, due to the limitations of the methods proposed to estimate the radial vertical frequency ω_y, also produce errors in more challenging forensic conditions.

The second source of error originates from the fact that screen–camcorder pairs are reduced to the product $\Pi = T_{\text{ro}} \cdot f_{\text{BL}}$ between the frame read-out time of the camcorder and the back-light frequency of the LCD screen. As a result, alternate screen–camcorder pairs may have very similar characteristic Π values. This is in particular the case for the pairs J–2, J–7, S–3, and P–5 which all have $\Pi \approx 2480 \pm 50$. These devices are thus considered close to equivalent during the forensic analysis and slight estimation errors for ω_y may lead to a screen–camcorder pair being confused for another one.

7. CONCLUSIONS AND FUTURE WORK

In this paper, we presented a passive forensic methodology to characterize pirate video sequences which have been created by placing a camcorder in front of an LCD screen displaying content. In essence, the idea is to isolate the flicker signal originating from the interplay between the screen's back-light and the camcorder's shutter and use it to verify which screen–camcorder pair, among a collection of devices, can produce such a visual artifact. To do so, we presented a number of estimation methods to characterize the flicker as well as some non-invasive measurement protocols to recover ground-truth parameters of the devices. Flicker-based pirate device attribution performances are summarized in Table 7 for the different forensic scenarios that we have considered in this study. While imperfect, they clearly demonstrate the potential for the flicker signal to serve as a powerful complementary tell-tale forensic indicator for pirate video samples. It could prove very useful for instance to establish piracy links between unrelated pirate video sequences for instance.

In future work, we intend to first focus on improving the estimation techniques to estimate f_t and ω_y since they have been found to significantly impact identification performances. For instance, we will investigate how to better exploit the harmonics of the flicker signal both to eliminate spurious peaks in the spectrum or to consolidate the estimation of the vertical radial frequency across various frequency bins. Although our preliminary investigations indicated that flicker forensics is barely affected by subsequent video processing, we will further benchmark the robustness

of the proposed estimation techniques to better appreciate the operating region of our system. Eventually, we will also look for additional statistical footprints in pirate movies that may involve other parameters of the screen/camcorder. This will be most helpful to introduce diversity among screen-camcorder pairs which have equivalent $\Pi = T_{\text{ro}} \cdot f_{\text{BL}}$ values that may be confused for one another.

An important thing to keep in mind, though, is that the parameters inducing the statistical footprint in the camcorded video should ideally be intrinsic to the device. Indeed, the beauty of the back-light frequency of an LCD screen and the frame read-out time of a camcorder is that they cannot be modified by the user. In contrast, while Moiré patterns present in camcorded videos may reveal information about the interaction between pirate devices, they are dependent on the acquisition geometry and are thus unlikely to be useful for device identification.

8. ACKNOWLEDMENTS

The authors would like to thank Mario de Vito for designing and building the custom-made sensing probe that we used in our experiments.

9. REFERENCES

[1] S. Baudry, B. Chupeau, M. de Vito, and G. Doërr. Modeling the flicker effect in camcorded videos to improve watermark robustness. In *Proceedings of the IEEE Workshop on Information Forensics and Security*, pages –, December 2014.

[2] N. Chang, I. Choi, and H. Shim. DLS: Dynamic backlight luminance scaling of liquid crystal display. *IEEE Transactions on Very Large Scale Integration*, 12(8):837–846, August 2004.

[3] B. Chupeau, S. Baudry, and G. Doërr. Forensic characterization of pirated movies: Digital cinema cam vs. optical disc rip. In *Proceedings of the IEEE Workshop on Information Forensics and Security*, pages –, December 2014.

[4] I. Cox, M. Miller, J. Bloom, J. Fridrich, and T. Kalker. *Digital Watermarking and Steganography*. Morgan Kaufmann Publishers Inc., 2nd edition, 2008.

[5] Digital Cinema Initiatives, LLC. *Digital Cinema System Specification*, 1.2 edition, March 2008.

[6] G. Doërr and J.-L. Dugelay. Security pitfalls of frame-by-frame approaches to video watermarking. *IEEE Transactions on Signal Processing*, 52(10):2955–2964, October 2004.

[7] T. Furon and G. Doërr. Tracing pirated content on the internet: Unwinding Ariadne's thread. *Security & Privacy*, 8(5):69–71, September/October 2010.

[8] A. E. Gamal and H. Eltoukhy. CMOS image sensors. *IEEE Circuits & Devices Magazine*, 21(3):6–20, May/June 2005.

[9] C.-K. Liang, L.-W. Chang, and H. H. Chen. Analysis and compensation of rolling shutter effect. *IEEE Transactions on Image Processing*, 17(8):1323–1330, August 2008.

[10] J. Lukáš, J. Fridrich, and M. Goljan. Digital camera identification from sensor noise. *IEEE Transactions on Information Security and Forensics*, 1(2):205–214, June 2006.

[11] J. J. Moreira-Pérez, B. Chupeau, S. Baudry, and G. Doërr. Exploring color information to characterize camcorder piracy. In *Proceedings of the IEEE Workshop on Information Forensics and Security*, pages 132–137, November 2013.

[12] MovieLabs. MovieLabs specifications for next generation of video and enhanced content protection. Technical report, 2013. http://www.movielabs.com/ngvideo/.

[13] D. Poplin. An automatic flicker detection method for embedded camera systems. *IEEE Transactions on Consumer Electronics*, 52(2):308–311, May 2006.

[14] X. Rolland-Nevière, B. Chupeau, G. Doërr, and L. Blondé. Forensic characterization of camcorded movies: Digital cinema vs. celluloid film prints. In *Media Watermarking, Security, and Forensics*, volume 8303 of *Proceedings of SPIE*, January 2012.

[15] W. Rosenblatt, S. Mooney, and W. Trippe. *Digital Rights Management: Business and Technology*. John Wiley & Sons, Inc., 2001.

[16] Y. Yoo, J. Im, and J. Paik. Flicker removal for CMOS wide dynamic range imaging based on alternating current component analysis. *IEEE Transactions on Consumer Electronics*, 60(3):294–301, August 2014.

Enhancing Sensor Pattern Noise for Source Camera Identification: An Empirical Evaluation

Bei-bei Liu [*]
School of Computing Science
Newcastle University,UK
beibei.liu2@ncl.ac.uk

Xingjie Wei
School of Computing Science
Newcastle University,UK
xingjie.wei@ncl.ac.uk

Jeff Yan
School of Computing Science
Newcastle University,UK
jeff.yan@ncl.ac.uk

ABSTRACT

The sensor pattern noise (SPN) based source camera identification technique has been well established. The common practice is to subtract a denoised image from the original one to get an estimate of the SPN. Various techniques to improve SPN's reliability have previously been proposed. Identifying the most effective technique is important, for both researchers and forensic investigators in law enforcement agencies. Unfortunately, the results from previous studies have proven to be irreproducible and incomparable —there is no consensus on which technique works the best. Here, we extensively evaluate various ways of enhancing the SPN by using the public "Dresden" database. We identify which enhancing methods are more effective and offer some insights into the behavior of SPN. For example, we find that the most effective enhancing methods share a common strategy of spectrum flattening. We also show that methods that only aim at reducing the contamination from image content do not lead to satisfying results, since the non-unique artifacts (NUA) among different cameras are the major troublemaker to the identification performance. While there is a trend of employing sophisticate methods to predict the impact of image content, our results suggest that more effort should be invested to tame the NUAs.

Categories and Subject Descriptors

I.4 [**Image processing and computer vision**]: Miscellaneous

General Terms

Algorithms, Experimentation, Performance, Security

Keywords

Digital Image Forensics; Sensor Pattern Noise; Source Camera Identification

[*]Liu is also affiliated with the School of Electronic and Information Engineering, South China University of Technology.

1. INTRODUCTION

It is well known that the sensor pattern noise (SPN) intrinsically embedded in a digital image can be employed to identify the source camera with which the image was taken. The SPN based source camera identification is among the most promising digital forensic techniques. By extracting the SPN from a suspect image, the source camera can be tracked down, providing a critical clue or evidence for law enforcement agencies.

In their seminal work [9], Lukáš et al. have laid down the fundamental scheme for SPN based source camera identification, which consists of three parts: extracting the SPN from an image, composing the reference pattern noise (RPN) for a camera and establishing the relation between an image and a camera. Abundant studies are devoted to improving the performance of SPN based source identification. Some of them focus on finding the optimal denoising filter for SPN extraction [1, 4, 15, 5], while some others focus on increasing the reliability of the extracted SPN (SPN enhancing).

It is generally recognised that the deterioration in SPN is caused by two sources, one is the non-unique artifacts (NUA) shared among different cameras and the other is the interference from image content. There are various SPN enhancing methods proposed in the literature. Some of these methods aim at eliminating the NUA while others try to counteract contamination introduced by image content. Evaluating differences in performance between these methods is important, but currently unfeasible due to inconsistent evaluation conditions across various studies —in other words, it is not yet clear which method works the best. For example, most studies are based on self-built datasets, making it impossible to reproduce and intercompare the reported results. Apparently different selections of cameras and images have an impact on the results.

In this work, we conduct an extensive evaluation on a range of SPN enhancing methods using a third-party public database. To the best of our knowledge, our work is novel in several aspects. (1) It is the first and most comprehensive evaluation of SPN enhancing. We evaluate 13 different enhancing schemes,consisting of the most typical methods and their combinations. (2) The results are obtained on a third-party database with consistent evaluation procedures and conditions. The previously reported experimental results are hardly intercomparable, because most experiments are conducted on self-built datasets using different measurements. (3) The scale of our experiment is significantly larger than those of related works in terms of the number of cameras and images involved. Particularly, the wide range of camera brands and models provides valuable samples for investigating the inter-camera similarities. (4) Our evaluation strategy differentiates between the enhancement techniques applied to the RPN of the camera and that applied to the SPN of the test image. This strategy has the advantage of identifying which part of the enhancement is actually working. The mix of the two types of enhancements is a cause of ambiguity in extant literature.

The rest of this paper is organised as follows. Section 2 briefly examines the fundamental scheme of SPN based source identification and related enhancing methods. Section 3 describes the setup of our evaluation. The results are presented and analysed in Section 4. Section 5 concludes the paper.

2. BACKGROUND AND RELATED WORKS

In this section, we first review the fundamental scheme of SPN based source identification introduced in [9]. Then we briefly describe some typical enhancing methods that can be categorised into two groups: methods to enhance the RPN of a camera and methods to enhance the SPN extracted from a test image.

2.1 The fundamental scheme

In [9], Lukáš et al. established the function of SPN as an identification of its source camera. For an image $\mathbf{I}$, the SPN $\mathbf{n}$ of which can be approximated by the noise residual extracted from the original image:

$$\mathbf{n} = \mathbf{I} - F(\mathbf{I}) \tag{1}$$

where a wavelet based filter [14] is recommended as the denoising filter F. For a camera C, a reference pattern noise (RPN) $\mathbf{r}$ of which can be achieved by averaging the SPNs of multiple images captured by C.:

$$\mathbf{r} = \sum_{i=1}^{L} \mathbf{n}_i / L \tag{2}$$

where L is the number of images involved in composing the RPN and recommended to be no less than 50. It is also suggested that flat field images or blue sky images are preferred for producing the RPN. To decide whether an image is taken by a particular camera, normalised cross-correlation (NCC) between the SPN and the RPN is calculated:

$$\rho = corr(\mathbf{n}, \mathbf{r}) = \frac{(\mathbf{n} - \bar{\mathbf{n}}) \cdot (\mathbf{r} - \bar{\mathbf{r}})}{\|\mathbf{n} - \bar{\mathbf{n}}\|\|\mathbf{r} - \bar{\mathbf{r}}\|} \tag{3}$$

The image is considered as being captured by the camera if the correlation ρ exceeds a predefined threshold.

Note that in a later work from the same research team [3], Eq.(2) is replaced by a maximum-likelihood estimator to estimate the PRNU(photo-response non-uniformity) of a camera. The NCC measurement of Eq.(4) is also suggested to be replaced by the peak to correlation energy (PCE) ratio in [8]. However, since we exploit flat field images (image of approximately constant intensity) in our experiments to compose the RPN, there is no much difference between using the PRNU estimator of [3] and the simple averaging method of Eq.(2). Besides, probably due to its simplicity, the NCC measurement is still widely adopted in the literature, especially in the related studies that we are evaluating. Therefore, in this work, we stick to using Eq.(1)∼(3) as the baseline scheme. We leave it to the future work to find out

how the results are affected when using different detectors such as PCE.

2.2 Enhancing the RPN of a camera

The motivation of enhancing the RPN of a camera is to remove the linear pattern and non-unique artifacts shared among different cameras. Although the inter-camera similarities has been recognized earlier in [9], it is in [3] where two specific operations —zero-mean and Wiener filtering are first proposed to tackle these undesired artifacts.

Zero-mean (ZM) operation [3]: It is believed that linear pattern will be introduced into the RPN due to the color interpolation in cameras as well as the row-wise and column-wise operation of sensors and processing circuits. To remove such linear pattern, the RPN obtained with Eq.(2) is processed by zeroing out the means of its columns and rows.

Wiener filtering (WF) operation [3]: It is also observed that the blockiness artifacts caused by JPEG compression may affect the estimated RPN. As such, a Wiener filter in the Fourier domain is applied to the RPN $\mathbf{r}$ to suppress the peaks and ridges in its spectrum:

$$WF(\mathbf{r}) = \mathcal{F}^{-1}\{\mathcal{F}(\mathbf{r}) - W(\mathcal{F}(\mathbf{r}))\} \tag{4}$$

where $\mathcal{F}$ indicates the Fourier transform and W is a 3×3 Wiener filter.

The above two operations were introduced at a very early stage of the research of SPN. After an extensive review of related works, we observed that while the ZM operation has been adopted by many, the WF operation has been frequently neglected. However, as will be seen in Section 4, we show that the contribution of the WF operation has been largely undervalued.

Phase RPN [11]: Kang et al. propose to use a 'phase RPN'in order to eliminate the various artifacts [11]. Specifically, the SPNs of the reference images are first transformed to the Fourier domain, the whitened spectra are averaged before being transformed back to the spatial domain:

$$\mathbf{r}_{\text{phase}} = real(\mathcal{F}^{-1}(\frac{\sum_{i=1}^{L} \mathbf{w}_i}{L})) \tag{5}$$

where $\mathcal{F}$ denotes the Fourier transform, and $\mathbf{w} = \mathcal{F}(\mathbf{n})/\|\mathcal{F}(\mathbf{n})\|$ is the phase component of the SPN $\mathbf{n}$. The phase RPN and the WF operation share the spirit of spectrum flattening. Our study shows that the two operations indeed give very close performances.

2.3 Enhancing the SPN of a test image

Li first points out in [12] that the SPN of an image can be contaminated by the image content. Image details such as edges and textures are visible in the SPN. Believing that these content artifacts are harmful to the SPN, a number of methods have been proposed to counteract such scene interference.

Attenuation models [12]: Based on the assumption that for each component in the SPN $\mathbf{n}$, the larger magnitude it has, the more likely it is contaminated by scene details. As such, in [12], Li proposes five attenuation models to assign less significance weighting factors to the large components. In particular, Li reports the best result is achieved on the following model (the Model 5 in the source study):

$$\mathbf{n}_{\text{att}(i,j)} = \begin{cases} e^{-0.5\mathbf{n}^2(i,j)/\alpha^2}, & \text{if } \mathbf{n}(i,j) \geq 0 \\ -e^{-0.5\mathbf{n}^2(i,j)/\alpha^2}, & \text{otherwise} \end{cases} \quad (6)$$

where α is the model parameter. In our evaluation we follow the optimal value suggested by the original paper. We noticed that there is an ambiguity about in which domain the attenuation model should be applied. The original proposition of [12] is to conduct the attenuation in the wavelet domain. However, there also sees implementation in other studies that applies the attenuation model in the spatial domain. For completeness, we include both implementations in our experiments.

Confidence weighting [13]: While the attenuation model in [12] decides the weight of a component simply by its magnitude, there are a few works that propose to use the content adaptive weighting scheme. This scheme weights against those image regions that we have less confidence in its SPN, typically being edge and highly textured regions. For example, image gradient magnitudes are exploited in [13] while a pair of intensity and texture features are used in [2]. Since some critical information for implementation is implicit in [2], we are not including it in our evaluation but use [13] to represent this line of work. The weight w for each pixel p is calculated in [13] as:

$$w(p) = G(\sigma) * \frac{1}{(1 + \|\nabla I(p)\|)} \quad (7)$$

where $G(\sigma)$ is a Gaussian kernel and ∇ denotes the gradient operator.

Whitening operation [10]: Similar to the idea of phase RPN, Kang et al. also propose to whiten the SPN of a test image[10]. A whitened SPN $\mathbf{n}_{\text{wh}}$ is obtained by:

$$\mathbf{n}_{\text{wh}} = \mathcal{F}^{-1}\left(\frac{\mathcal{F}(\mathbf{n})}{\|\mathcal{F}(\mathbf{n})\|}\right) \quad (8)$$

3. EXPERIMENTAL SETUP

3.1 Database

Our experiments use the "Dresden" image database [6] which features over 14,000 images acquired under controlled conditions with a wide range of cameras (73 cameras of 25 different models).In addition to indoor and outdoor natural images, the database provides a number of flat field images for each camera, which can be used to compose the camera's RPN. The number of flat field images per camera varies, and this may influence the quality of the RPN obtained. For the sake of equality, we only use those cameras with 50 flat field images available. As such, 46 cameras are included in our experiments, spanning 15 models and with 9268 test images available in total.The details of the cameras are listed in Table 2 in the Appendix.

Three features, among others, make the "Dresden" database suitable for the purpose of our research. First, as a third-party public database, "Dresden" exhibits no preference for any particular algorithms, which enables an objective assessment. Second, for most models multiple devices are available, which serves as excellent specimens for studying the NUA shared among different cameras. Last, some images captured by different cameras have highly similar scene content, i.e. the images were taken at several fixed scenarios

with varying cameras. Such a setting is rare in the literature but crucial to tease apart different factors that affect the SPN.

3.2 Evaluation methodology

We use the flat field images in the database to compose the RPN of each camera. The indoor and outdoor images captured with each camera are used as test images. Following the most widely adopted practise in literature, we first convert each image, either flat field or natural, to grayscale and then cut from center for a 512×512 block. We acknowledge that the image size as well as the JPEG compression level may have an impact on the performance. We leave it to future work to include more varying factors in the evaluation.

We assess how well the test images are matched with their true source cameras when different enhancing methods are applied. The camera identification problem is generally formulated as a signal detection hypothesis and, in forensic scenarios, a low False Positive Rate (FPR) is particularly important. Thus, we employ the experimental TPR for a fixed FPR of 10^{-3} as the evaluation measurement. More specifically, for each camera, we first determine a threshold for the NCC of Eq.(3) so that no more than 0.1% of the non-matching images are falsely judged as matching images. We then caculate the True Positive Rate (TPR) under this threshold, i.e. how many matching images are correctly identified. Finally, an overall TPR is obtained by averaging over the 46 cameras.

We divide our tests into four groups consisting of different combinations of methods which have been examined in Section 2, as listed in Table 1. Group 1 is the baseline scheme where the SPN and the RPN obtained with Eq.(1) and Eq.(5) do not undergo any enhancing operation. In Group 2, the RPNs remain un-processed while the SPNs of test images are enhanced with different methods. In Group 3, the SPNs of test images remain un-processed while the RPNs undergo different operations. In Group 4, enhancing operations are applied to both the RPNs of cameras and the SPNs of test images.

4. RESULTS AND ANALYSIS

The overall TPR and the corresponding rank obtained with each enhancing scheme are given in the last two columns of Table 4. The results not only reveal the most effective enhancing scheme but also clarify some misconceptions in the literature.

4.1 Which is the most effective?

The results show that among the 13 schemes evaluated, the top scheme is G4-3 which combines the confidence weighting method proposed by McCloskey [13] and the ZM and WF operations proposed by Chen et al. [3], achieving a TPR of 84.79%. It is also clear from Table 4 that some other schemes (G2-4,G3-2,G3-3,G3-4,G4-1,G4-2,G4-4) also perform well, achieving TPRs between 82.27% and 84.79%. All the well-performing schemes share a common strategy: they all employ spectrum flattening. This suggests that the whitening methods proposed by Kang et al.[10, 11] and the Wiener filtering operation proposed by Chen et al.[3] are both effective. Interestingly, while spectrum flattening is effective, it does not make much difference when applied to both the RPN and the SPN at the same time (G4-4).

Table 1: The 13 schemes being evaluated and the TPRs obtained at a fixed FPR of 10^{-3}.

	Scheme ID	RPN of camera	SPN of test image	TPR for FPR=10^{-3}	Rank
Group 1	G1-1	Basic	Basic	63.65 %	11
Group 2	G2-1	Basic	Attenuation in wavelet domain	56.16 %	13
	G2-2	Basic	Attenuation in spatial domain	59.69 %	12
	G2-3	Basic	Confidence weighting	65.47 %	10
	G2-4	Basic	Whitening	83.94 %	2
Group 3	G3-1	Zero-mean (ZM)	Basic	71.06 %	9
	G3-2	Wiener filtering (WF)	Basic	83.43 %	4
	G3-3	ZM+WF	Basic	83.69 %	3
	G3-4	Phase RPN	Basic	82.27 %	8
Group 4	G4-1	ZM+WF	Attenuation in wavelet domain	83.09 %	7
	G4-2	ZM+WF	Attenuation in spatial domain	83.30 %	5
	G4-3	ZM+WF	Confidence weighting	84.79 %	1
	G4-4	ZM+WF	Whitening	83.13 %	6

Note that although G4-3 achieves the highest TPR among all, the confidence weighting operation of [13] does not work well alone (G2-3). This confirms our discovery that spectrum flattening is key to an effective enhancement. This demonstrates an advantage of our evaluation strategy, which differentiates between enhancements applied to the RPN and those applied to the SPN. This way, we are able to pinpoint the element that actually works.

Regarding to the zero-mean and the Wiener filtering operations, both proposed by Chen et al.[3], a close-up of Group 3 shows that Wiener filtering plays a more important role than the zero-mean operation in removing artifacts from the camera RPN. The TPR obtained by applying Wiener filtering alone (G3-2) is notably higher than the TPR obtained by applying zero-mean alone (G3-1). Moreover, applying both of them (G3-3) does not significantly increase the TPR on top of G3-2.

4.2 Is the baseline method the worst?

Table 1 shows that the baseline method (G1-1) achieves a lower TPR than most of the other methods, which confirms the necessity of enhancement. However, the attenuation models proposed by Li [12], applied either in the wavelet (G2-1) or the spatial domains (G2-2), produce slightly lower TPRs than the baseline method. A similar weak performance of the attenuation model is also observed in other studies [10, 11]. To explain this, we examine difference introduced by individual cameras. We find that the low TPR is mainly caused by the 8 Sony cameras (C39-C46, Table 2) for which inter-camera correlations exhibit a visible increase after application of attenuation. We conjecture that this is because Eq.(6) magnifies the small magnitude components. As a result, rather than being removed or compressed, the originally weak non-unique artifacts in the SPN have been reinforced, which leads to a worse source identification result.

4.3 The impact of non-unique artifacts

In this section we demonstrate why some enhancing methods work well while others do not. The ideal SPN for source identification should exhibit high correlation with the RPN of the true source camera but low correlation with the RPN of other cameras. We examine how the two types of correlation values are affected by different enhancing methods.

For the ith camera C_i, we average the correlation values computed between its RPN and the SPNs of test images from the jth camera C_j:

$$\bar{\rho}_{i,j} = \frac{\sum_{k=1}^{N_j} corr(\mathbf{r}_i, \mathbf{n}_j^k)}{N_j} \qquad (9)$$

where $\mathbf{r}_i$ is the RPN of camera C_i, $\mathbf{n}_j^k$ is the SPN of the kth test image of camera C_j and N_j is the total number of test images available for camera C_j.

The pairwise average values obtained with Eq.(9) are displayed as intensity images. The off-diagonal components, which indicate correlations between non-matching cameras and images, are supposed to be as dark as possible (close to zero). However, as can be seen from Fig.1, there exist apparent bright off-diagonal components when neither the RPN or SPN is enhanced. These stains illustrate the well-known non-unique artifacts shared among different cameras.

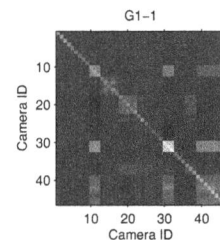

Figure 1: Intensity image displaying the average correlation values (Eq.9) for G1-1.

Fig.2 demonstrates what happens after enhancement. As can be seen, the off-diagonal stains hardly shift in (a),(b) and (c) which correspond to the two attenuation models and the confidence weighting method. Recall that these three methods all perform poorly in our evaluation (see Table 1). The reason of their poor performance turns out to be the failure to remove the NUAs. It is reasonable to deduce that the removal of NUA is most crutial to a reliable source identification. On the other hand, most of the off-diagonal stains vanish in (d) and (f)~(l) where at least one type of spectrum flattening operation is applied, indicating that the success of spectrum flattening is mainly attributed to the removal of NUAs across cameras. Note that the stains in (e) do not

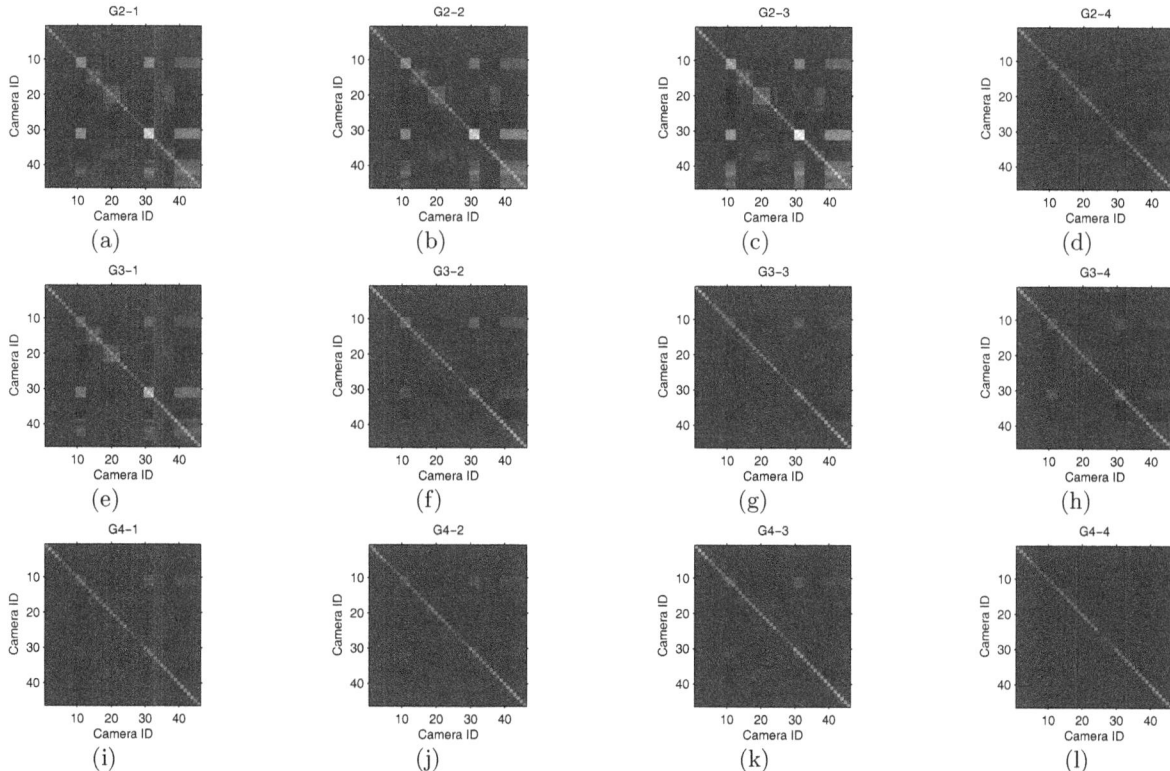

Figure 2: Intensity images displaying the average correlation values (Eq.9) for Group 2, 3 and 4.

vanish as much as those in (d) and (f)~(l), which tallies with our finding that the zero-mean operation is less effective than spectrum flattening.

4.4 Variability across different cameras

Our final observation is that the performances of individual cameras (not displayed due to space limitation) vary considerably. The individual TPR fluctuates dramatically from camera to camera. For some cameras (e.g. the Casio cameras in Table 2), the TPR is as low as about 33%, while for some others (e.g. the Canon cameras in Table 2), it can easily reach 100% without any form of enhancing. It is important to note that the observed variability cannot be attributed to other factors than the intrinsic characteristics of the individual cameras: the 'Dresden'database is specially designed so that each camera in the database captures almost the same scenes. On the one hand, the recognition of camera variations highlights the importance of reporting results on third-party public database for future studies. On the other hand, it also shows that we are far from comprehensively understanding the behavior of the SPN of various cameras. It deserves a further investigation into the reason for the observed variability across different cameras in the future.

5. SUMMARY

There are various methods to improve the reliability of the SPN based source camera identification technique, both for the SPN of an image and the RPN of a camera. However, the more methods on the shelves, the more difficult it is to pinpoint the best one. Unfortunately, the results reported in the literature are largely irreproducible and impossible to compare with each other because many factors vary from one study to another. This work is the first attempt to provide an independent assessment of the effectiveness of various SPN enhancing methods. We have evaluated a total of 13 schemes consisting of various combinations of representative enhancing methods. We explicitly differentiate between the enhancement applied to the camera RPN and that to the SPN of test image, hereby clarifying which of these enhancements actually work. Apart from revealing the most effective enhancing methods, our evaluation also clear up some misconceptions and identifies promising directions for future studies. We summarise our findings as follows:

(1) The combination of the confidence weighting method [13] and the zero-mean and Wiener filtering operations [3] achieves the best performance. Importantly, this result is primarily attributed to the effect of Wiener filtering, since neither the zero-mean operation nor weighting performs well alone.

(2) Our evaluation results demonstrate a clear division between the schemes that involve spectrum flattening and those that do not, suggesting that spectrum flattening is a very effective enhancing method. We also clarify that the Wiener filtering is more critical than the zero-mean operation, although the former has frequently been neglected in related studies. Besides, it does not seem to matter whether the spectrum flattening operation is applied to the RPN of camera, to the SPN of test image, or both. This suggests that we do not have to flatten the spectra of the two at the same time to guarantee a reliable results. This result is particularly relevant to large-scale forensic investigations, since spectrum manipulation is computationally expensive.

(3) Our evaluation shows that the major troublemaker to SPN based source identification is the non-unique artifacts, rather than the contamination introduced by image content. Low ranking schemes in our evaluation commonly failed to remove the NUAs across cameras. The image content influences the SPN mainly in the sense of squeezing out the useful SPN components, which is more likely to cause a true match to be falsely rejected than a wrong match to be falsely accepted. The NUAs, on the other hand, are mainly responsible for the false acceptance. Since a low false acceptance rate is critical in forensic investigations, it is more important to counter the influence of NUAs.

(4) Different cameras show varying responses to different enhancements. There is also a number of cameras on which none of the state-of-the-art enhancing methods can achieve satisfying results, which corroborates the observation in [7]. This variability reflects the complexity of camera making and highlights the further need for identifying novel artifacts and corresponding countermeasures.

6. ACKNOWLEDGMENTS

We thank Ahmet Emir Dirik for helpful comments. This research was supported by the EU programme on Prevention of and Fight against Crime (ISEC) —the Novel Image/photo Forensic Tools for fighting against child pornography (NIFTy) project (HOME/2012/ISEC/AG/INT/4000003892).

7. REFERENCES

[1] I. Amerini, R. Caldelli, V. Cappellini, F. Picchioni, and A. Piva. Analysis of denoising filters for photo response non uniformity noise extraction in source camera identification. In *Digital Signal Processing, 2009 16th International Conference on*, pages 1–7. IEEE, 2009.

[2] L.-H. Chan, N.-F. Law, and W.-C. Siu. A confidence map and pixel-based weighted correlation for prnu-based camera identification. *Digital Investigation*, 10(3):215–225, 2013.

[3] M. Chen, J.Fridrich, M.Goljan, and J.Lukas. Determining image origin and integrity using sensor noise. *IEEE Trans.Inf.Forensics Security*, 3(1):74 – 90, 2008.

[4] G. Chierchia, S. Parrilli, G. Poggi, C. Sansone, and L. Verdoliva. On the influence of denoising in prnu based forgery detection. In *Proceedings of the 2nd ACM workshop on Multimedia in forensics, security and intelligence*, pages 117–122. ACM, 2010.

[5] A. Cortiana, V. Conotter, G. Boato, and F. G. De Natale. Performance comparison of denoising filters for source camera identification. In *IS&T/SPIE Electronic Imaging*, pages 788007–788007. International Society for Optics and Photonics, 2011.

[6] T. Gloe and R. Böhme. The dresden image database for benchmarking digital image forensics. *Journal of Digital Forensic Practice*, 3(2-4):150–159, 2010.

[7] T. Gloe, S. Pfennig, and M. Kirchner. Unexpected artefacts in prnu-based camera identification: a'dresden image database'case-study. In *Proceedings of the on Multimedia and security*, pages 109–114. ACM, 2012.

[8] M. Goljan and J. Fridrich. Camera identification from cropped and scaled images. In *Electronic Imaging 2008*, pages 68190E–68190E. International Society for Optics and Photonics, 2008.

[9] J.Lukas, J.Fridrich, and M.Goljan. Digital camera identification from sensor pattern noise. *IEEE Trans.Inf.forensics Security*, 1(2):205 – 214, 2006.

[10] X. Kang, Y. Li, Z. Qu, and J. Huang. Enhancing roc performance of trustworthy camera source identification. In *IS&T/SPIE Electronic Imaging*, pages 788009–788009, 2011.

[11] X. Kang, Y. Li, Z. Qu, and J. Huang. Enhancing source camera identification performance with a camera reference phase sensor pattern noise. *IEEE Trans.Inf.Forensics Security*, 7(2):393 – 402, 2012.

[12] C.-T. Li. Source camera identification using enhanced sensor pattern noise. *IEEE Trans.Inf.Forensics Security*, 5(2):280 – 287, 2010.

[13] S. McCloskey. Confidence weighting for sensor fingerprinting. In *Computer Vision and Pattern Recognition Workshops, 2008. CVPRW'08. IEEE Computer Society Conference on*, pages 1–6, 2008.

[14] M. Mihcak, I. Kozintsev, and K. Ramchandran. Spatially adaptive statistical modeling of wavelet image coefficients and its application to denoising. In *Acoustics, Speech, and Signal Processing, 1999. Proceedings., 1999 IEEE International Conference on*, volume 6, pages 3253–3256, 1999.

[15] W. van Houten and Z. Geradts. Using anisotropic diffusion for efficient extraction of sensor noise in camera identification. *Journal of forensic sciences*, 57(2):521–527, 2012.

APPENDIX

Table 2: 46 cameras used in our evaluation

ID	Name	ID	Name
C1	Canon_Ixus55	C24	Pentax_W60
C2	Canon_Ixus70_0	C25	Praktica_DCZ5p9_0
C3	Canon_Ixus70_1	C26	Praktica_DCZ5p9_1
C4	Canon_Ixus70_2	C27	Praktica_DCZ5p9_2
C5	Casio_EXZ150_0	C28	Praktica_DCZ5p9_3
C6	Casio_EXZ150_1	C29	Praktica_DCZ5p9_4
C7	Casio_EXZ150_2	C30	Rollei_7325XS_0
C8	Casio_EXZ150_3	C31	Rollei_7325XS_1
C9	Casio_EXZ150_4	C32	Rollei_7325XS_2
C10	Fujifilm_J50_0	C33	Samsung_L74_0
C11	Fujifilm_J50_1	C34	Samsung_L74_1
C12	Fujifilm_J50_2	C35	Samsung_L74_2
C13	Nikon_S710_0	C36	Samsung_NV15_0
C14	Nikon_S710_1	C37	Samsung_NV15_1
C15	Nikon_S710_2	C38	Samsung_NV15_2
C16	Nikon_S710_3	C39	Sony_H50_0
C17	Nikon_S710_4	C40	Sony_H50_1
C18	Olympus_u1050_0	C41	Sony_T77_0
C19	Olympus_u1050_1	C42	Sony_T77_1
C20	Olympus_u1050_2	C43	Sony_T77_2
C21	Olympus_u1050_3	C44	Sony_T77_3
C22	Olympus_u1050_4	C45	Sony_W170_0
C23	Pentax_A40_3	C46	Sony_W170_1

ForeMan, a Versatile and Extensible Database System for Digitized Forensics Based on Benchmarking Properties

Christian Arndt[1], Stefan Kiltz[1], Jana Dittmann[1,2], Robert Fischer[3]

[1]Otto von Guericke University Magdeburg
Computer Science Dept., Research Group Multimedia and Security, P.O. box 4120, 39016 Magdeburg, Germany

[2]University of Buckingham
Applied Computing Dept., Buckingham MK18 1EG, United Kingdom

[3]Brandenburg University of Applied Sciences
Informatics & Media Dept., P.O. box 2132, 14737 Brandenburg, Germany

{christian.arndt | stefan.kiltz | jana.dittmann}@iti.cs.uni-magdeburg.de ; robert.fischer@fh-brandenburg.de

ABSTRACT

To benefit from new opportunities offered by the digitalization of forensic disciplines, the challenges especially w.r.t. comprehensibility and searchability have to be met. Important tools in this forensic process are databases containing digitized representations of physical crime scene traces. We present *ForeMan*, an extensible database system for digitized forensics handling separate databases and enabling *intra* and *inter trace type* searches. It now contains 762 fiber data sets and 27 fingerprint data sets (anonymized time series). Requirements of the digitized forensic process model are mapped to design aspects and conceptually modeled around benchmarking properties. A fiber categorization scheme is used to structure fiber data according to forensic use case identification. Our research extends the *benchmarking properties* by *fiber fold shape* derived from the application field of fibers (part of micro traces) and *sequence number* derived from the application field of time series analysis for fingerprint aging research. We identify matching data subsets from both digitized trace types and introduce the terms of *entity-centered* and *spatial-centered information*. We show how combining two types of digitized crime scene traces (fiber and fingerprint data) can give new insights for research and casework and discuss requirements for other trace types such as firearm and toolmarks.

Categories and Subject Descriptors

H.2.4 [**Systems**]: Multimedia databases, Object-oriented databases; H.2.8 [**Database Applications**]: Scientific databases, Image databases

General Terms

Design, Management, Documentation, Legal Aspects

Keywords

digitized crime scene forensics; forensic trace database; benchmarking properties

1. MOTIVATION

In traditional crime scene forensics there is a trend to include signal processing and pattern recognition, also based on contact-less acquisition of latent crime scene traces as *digitized forensics*, to relieve the various experts off tedious and error prone tasks. Digitized forensics [13] is the set of traditional forensic disciplines that utilize digital methods to acquire (digitize) and analyze the physical traces digitally. One means of support throughout is to provide searchable databases for comparison of traces against a collection of previously acquired traces, which can also support the chain of custody management with a documentation component. For some forensic trace types dedicated database systems exist (see also [3]), e.g. IAFIS [6] (or NGI [7]) for fingerprints or IBIS [9] for firearm and toolmark traces or FACID [1] for car carpets, but are nearly all company-supplied, operated by public authorities and thus, inaccessible to public research. They typically do not support multi trace types, e.g. sampled by the same sensing device. Since latent traces are invisible to the naked eye, the whole examination process and the resulting conclusions have to be comprehensible; also for non-experts (e.g. judge). Thus, in the USA and other mainly common-law countries the Daubert criteria [5] are used. These require answers to questions e.g. the forensic methods and potential or actual error rates, the acceptance in the relevant scientific communities, the publication and subjection to peer-review, as well as the potential for testing. Our work addresses the Daubert criteria by subjecting it to the scientific peer review process.

We present the conceptional design, the setup and testing with first results for *ForeMan*, a versatile, extensible database system for crime scene traces on the example of fiber data and fingerprint data and discuss further research and open questions. ForeMan needs to enable searching and comparing items *intra trace type* (in the fiber data set) but also an *inter trace type search* (different trace types - fiber and fingerprints) is exemplary demonstrated on the example of latent fingerprint aging series. A stringent criterion, however, is the option of separating those two trace type data sets, e.g. to meet data protection or privacy requirements, without a limitation of functionality for the trace types, respectively. Further, the database system has to comply with the requirements of the forensic process in digitized forensics [13] in general and the fiber examination process [2]. Benchmarking and its *benchmarking properties* [19] play a vital role in design decisions for the database system and its frontend and thus, supporting the compliance to the Daubert criteria, as well as further research. First results show the necessity of the extension of benchmarking properties by *fold shapes* for fiber data with its potential to detect forgery/fabrication and *sequence number* for time series data for research into fingerprint trace aging. Our research introduces the differentiation between *entity-* and *spatial-oriented examinations* and motivates the need to retain data for both types in the database system. Generally, we want to motivate the consideration / application of all available sensing-techniques for the acquisition and processing during digitized forensic examinations. Consequently, a database for forensic purposes should be able to store multiple arbitrary types of digital representations of single traces, respectively complete areas of crime scenes. A database for digitized forensics should allow to store generic types of annotation-data for each sample/representation. This should include "anticipated"/known annotation data like reference circles for firearm toolmarks. But this should also imply the possibility to store new or very specific data, which might be dependent on the specific case or sample. This also addresses the potential need of different annotations regarding different types of data representations.

This article is structured as follows: In section 2 selected aspects of the state of the art of the digitized forensic process in general and the fiber examination is outlined. The concept of ForeMan and the extension of the benchmarking properties are discussed in section 3. In section 4 the practical implementation of the database system and the frontend is described and a result discussion is conducted. The article closes with a conclusion and outlook on future work.

2. STATE OF THE ART

Selected aspects of the state of the art in crime scene forensics and fiber trace forensics are outlined in this section.

2.1 Digitized forensics & benchmarking

To be coherent with the demands according to the Daubert criteria, using a **model of the forensic process** (e.g. [13]) and to devise methods and actions accordingly, is beneficial. The forensic process can be broken down into the six examination steps of: *Strategic preparation* (all preparative actions taken prior to a particular incident incl. benchmarking), *Operational preparation* (all preparative actions taken after initiation of an examination but prior to acquisition), *Data gathering* (digitalization of physical objects), *Data investigation* (extraction of data from the trace carrier and the trace), *Data analysis* (separation and visualization of trace data and trace carrier data) and *Documentation* (process accompanying documentation and final report).

Benchmarking in forensics is part of the *Strategic Prepa-*

ration and serves the research into new methods and to provide environments, parameters during *Operational preparation* ([13]). To enable a methodical benchmarking it is broken down into six *categories* [20] and [19] with each category holding qualitative or quantitative **properties** and, if applicable, **sub properties**. The *forensic legal requirements L* include the protection of authenticity, integrity, privacy, evidential value, repeatability and documentation. The *technical properties T* benchmark e.g. the tolerated environmental factors, temperature and spatial resolution. With *application related aspects A* e.g. the required pre-processing time, fingerprint detection performance, separation of overlapping fingerprints is benchmarked. The *input sensory technology I* addresses the sensor and its properties e.g. the acquisition space, measurement method, mode of operation. With *processing algorithms P* particular algorithms for the support of the following investigations are benchmarked: e.g. Gabor filters or Sobel operators. The *tested objects and materials M* are very important for the performance of a particular sensor. Therefore, the main material characteristics of trace and trace carrier e.g. surface finish, absorbability, structure pattern are benchmarked.

2.2 Fiber taxonomy

In the forensic use case of identification (subsection 2.3) fibers are assigned to corresponding groups [16] (e.g. spinning of chemical fibers) based on certain *class characteristics* (i.e. traits, resulting from a controlled generation process, e.g. surface characteristics). One way to design such a categorization scheme in reference to grouping class characteristics is our proposed fiber taxonomy, which should also be supported by a fiber trace annotation mechanism in ForeMan. In [15] textile fibers are defined as unit of matter, either natural or manufactured, that forms the basic element of fabrics and other textiles [...]" with two main groups: natural (fiber in a natural state, i.e. originated from natural sources) or chemical/man-made/manufactured [15].

Natural fibers originate either from humans (e.g. body hair, scalp hair), animals (e.g. hair, wool, silk), minerals (e.g. Asbestos) or vegetables/plants (e.g. cotton, flax, sisal). Vegetable fibers can be further subcategorized regarding the part of the plant from which they are extracted.

Chemical fibers can be subdivided into organic and inorganic (e.g. carbon, glass, ceramic or metal fibers). Organic fibers can be categorized [23, 17] into fibers made from natural polymers (e.g. protein or cellulose) and into fibers made from synthetic polymers needing polymerization reactions (i.e. chainbuilding e.g. acrylic, polyester). Two selected branches of that taxonomy are also depicted in Figure 1.

2.3 Fiber examination process

The typical forensic fiber analysis process starts under laboratory conditions after the preservation of evidence at a crime scene. Trained experts analyze traces with the help of special microscopes or spectroscopic devices (depending on the examination objective) [15, 25]. Derived conclusions are based on subjective expert's opinions. Forensic experts pursue mainly two objectives (forensic use cases). During *identification* a fiber is tentatively assigned to a broad group (one-to-many comparison) to limit the amount of traces for the second objective. *Individualization* is considered as ultimate goal of forensics and is denoted by a one-to-one comparison to find the concrete textile originator. The identification objective varies accordingly to granularity of groups for the assignment [16]. The contactless acquisition of a digital representation of some aspects of the physical trace and its processing using pattern recognition techniques [2, 12] can support experts during the time-consuming and cost-intensive analysis by giving result indications.

3. CONCEPT OF FOREMAN

In this section the concept of ForeMan, as a versatile forensic database system based on the Mongo DBMS [22] is introduced. The main design objective of ForeMan is to be firmly rooted in the digitized forensics process, to incorporate all the requirements from the fiber examination process (section 2.3), the fiber taxonomy (see section 2.2) and to be extended for other forensic trace types (e.g. fingerprints, tool marks).

Our pursued database design should allow intra- and inter-trace type searches. Therefore, the data sets of different trace types needs to be stored independently in two or more separate databases. The trace types represent tested objects and materials M in the context of benchmarking, which are independently managed by the ForeMan frontend and separately stored in one singular Mongo DBMS. However, ForeMan is designed to handle the complete removal of other trace types (e.g. for reasons of data protection/privacy) and still function on the fiber trace database alone, which is addressed by $DO1$ in subsection 3.1. The concept and the extension of the benchmarking categories (see subsection 3.2) allow an **entity-centered** or a **spatial-centered** data examination and analysis. The latter is concerned with the location of different trace types at the crime scene, whereas the entity-centered view reflects on different (sub) types of traces, originating from the same entity (e.g. facial hair vs. scalp hair). The general idea is to prevent loss of context when entering the data into the frontend and the subsequent storage in the database system.

3.1 Pursued Design Objectives

This section supports our concept as sort of requirements analysis. Consequently, we define conceptual design objectives here and evaluate in section 4 if they could be achieved by our implementation. Selected steps of the generic forensic process model (section 2.1) are mapped onto corresponding design objectives:

DO1 - Separation of different traces
Independently managed and stored databases

DO2 - Strategic preparation support
Model internal data structures around benchmarking properties

DO3 - Data gathering support
Importability of measurement data

DO4 - Data Investigation support
Annotate, add information to stored data items

DO5 - Fiber taxonomy support
Include the fiber categorization scheme

DO6 - Intra trace searchability
Enable search among one singular trace type

DO7 - Inter trace searchability
Enable search over two or more different trace types

DO8 - Documentation
Provide process accompanying documentation

ForeMan is designed to assist the forensic process at the examination step of strategic preparation by supporting the benchmarking process (see section 2.1) - $DO2$. Therefore, a database controlling frontend and internal data structures are modeled around the benchmarking properties. Design objective $DO3$ refers to an acceptance (importability) of a wide range of data formats from contactless sensing (data gathering) devices such as the thin film reflectometer (FTR) [10], the chromatic white light sensor (CWL) [11] and the confocal laser scanning microscope (CLSM) [18].

In addition, the step of Data Investigation $DO4$ is supported by automatically extracting meta data stored from the acquisition process as well allowing the forensic experts to add data manually that is retained in the database system. Those automatically extracted and/or manually annotated data can represent a number of benchmarking categories (e.g. input sensory technology I but also technical properties T, see [13]). The phase of data analysis is assisted by two objectives providing searchability. $DO6$ offers an intra trace type search to find entries with matching properties. $DO7$ on the contrary enables an inter trace type search. $DO8$ refers to enabling a process accompanying documentation in order to realize a complete chain of custody.

These conceptual objectives serve as requirements for our implementation in section 4. Except $DO5$, which is considered to be trace-specific, the design objectives $DO1$-$DO8$ apply for all trace types in digitized forensic examinations. With regards to $DO5$, a taxonomy for firearm-related toolmarks is suggested in [8]. In the course of this work, we introduce a new fiber categorization scheme/taxonomy.

As benchmarking is an integral part of ForeMan, in the following newly identified properties are introduced.

3.2 Newly identified benchmarking properties

When dealing with fiber traces, the endings of a given piece of fiber can provide vital information when it forms **folds** as part of an enforced separation process through acts of perpetrator or victim. This information can be two-fold. At least it provides leads what activity was likely conducted. In very rare cases, matching folds (together with other matching fiber properties) can substantiate the presence of persons or objects at the crime scene according to the divisibility of matter as part of the Locard exchange principle [16]. The **fold shape** also allows for examinations into **forgery** and **fabrication** of traces. Folds that should be torn according to the situation at the crime scene should be very suspiciously examined if the fold of the fiber turns out to be clear cuts only.

Some digitized data is part of a larger set, e.g. fingerprint data that is used for research in trace aging and age determination (see [21]). With such research, the new benchmarking item **sequence number** of a given fingerprint data acquisition is vital information that needs to be retained and recalled in ForeMan. But also in the context of fiber examination, there is context information not contained in the original acquisition data that needs to be retained and to be recalled (see Figure 1).

A database for digitized forensics should allow to store multiple/arbitrary/(maybe concurrent) processing chains for each sample. This includes for example the sequence, the parameterization, and the results of individual (pre)processing steps and chains, e.g. the sequence, type, size of filter operations, or the parameterization of shape-detection steps.

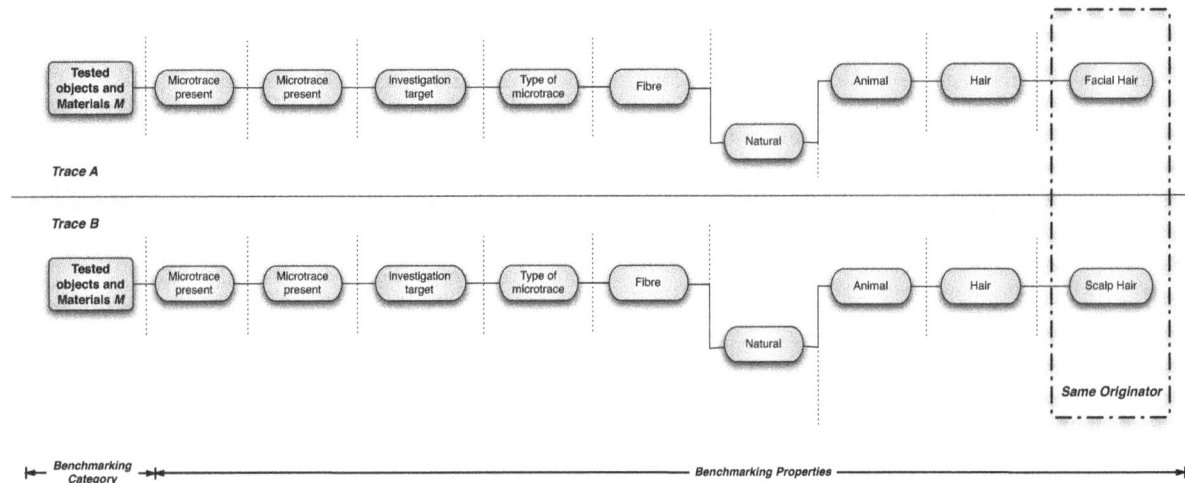

Figure 1: Example of two different benchmarking categories connected by the same originator (based on [23, 17]) in the context of benchmarking category and benchmarking properties from [19]

In the pictured example the benchmarking property "facial hair" provides a clear distinction to e.g. "scalp hair" and thus vital information. In the pictured example the benchmarking property "facial hair" provides a clear distinction to e.g. "scalp hair" and thus vital information. But also of very high importance is the information that two fiber data items (e.g. facial hair and scalp hair) originate from the same person (entity). It provides entity-centered information. Not recording and retaining this information would lead to a substantial loss of context, particular in the light of potential new findings, e.g. findings that allow for the identification of persons based on their hair. Similar information is the trace location at the crime scene (or for research purposes at the research facility). Recording and retaining such spatial-centered information also provides context and enables inter trace type searches.

Based on these newly identified benchmarking properties, we show the extensibility of ForeMan by the integration of them in our concrete implementation.

4. IMPLEMENTATION & EVALUATION

The implementation is described in this section and evaluated regarding the achievement of our pursued design objectives from subsection 3.1.

ForeMan consists of a MongoDB (version 2.4.10) and a controlling frontend, written in C# (MonoDevelop version 4.0.12, Mono version 3.2.8, also compatible to .Net version 4.5). Both are running on an up-to-date Debian Testing ("Jessie") Linux operational system. A Toshiba Tecra R10-111 notebook is used as portable hardware device to host the operational system and moreover, ForeMan. The main hardware specifications are: Intel Centrino® 2 CPU with 2.4GHz clock speed, 200GB HDD with 7,200RPM, NVIDIA® Quadro® NVS 150M graphic card, 4GB RAM. This setup was chosen to provide as far as possible a platform independent development environment and also portability. Our GUI application still uses the Windows® Forms graphical API, which is also available on Linux.

ForeMan's frontend main graphical user interface (GUI) is designed to enable the selection of a database from a drop-down menu in the upper left side. A listing of all stored data items of the currently connected database is shown in a scrollable menu. Every data set's identifier refers to the file name of the previously imported sensor measurement result. Meta information and added benchmarking properties for the selected data item is displayed. Each of the sensors used in our research (see also subsection 3.1) is capable of acquiring different types of trace representations (e.g. 2D intensity image, color photography, 3D topography), all of which are also displayed in ForeMan's frontend.

Every, via this frontend accessible database is handled individually by utilizing separate interface objects with their own connection information, as well - design objective DO1 fulfilled. Thus, all connectors remain independently and are stored inside lists to assure overall searchability.

Another design criterion from Section subsection 3.1 is to assist the examination step of data gathering - DO3, which is achieved by importing every measurement data of the FRT CWL, FRT FTR and Keyence CLSM sensing devices. Basically, each measurement result consists of a proprietary container format, including images, topography and meta information: FRT sensing devices [11, 10] - FRT data format; Keyence [18] - Vk4 suffix. Self-implemented external libraries are invoked to import images and meta information stored inside these containers, Based on the API of the respective sensing device, images and/or meta information can be extracted and thus, included inside ForeMan. Currently, 762 fiber data sets, consisting of all three sensor measurement results (see subsection 3.1), are stored inside ForeMan.

One fingerprint aging series, consisting of 27 intensity images and topography data, are stored exemplary inside a separate database, to enable and demonstrate inter trace search queries - DO7. In order to mark single aging series data as linked together, every piece of this particular data is related to an overall object identifier.

With the achievement of DO1, benchmarking properties have already been installed in our internal data structures. Each measurement data indwells a subset of benchmarking properties - DO2 (e.g. sensor parameter), which are automatically added during the data import - DO3. Consequently, benchmarking properties of a data item are realized editable and also extendable (see Figure 2) - *DO4*. Relevant data such as environmental conditions (e.g. acquisition area, acquisition time and duration, humidity, temperature) but also device settings (e.g. resolution) can be stored and compared with other acquisitions to derive a suitable parameterization depending on the piece of evidence and its environment. Next to supporting the training of experts in the acquisition of fiber traces, ForeMan thus supports active research for unknown fibers in unknown environmental conditions. In addition, newly identified benchmarking properties from subsection 3.2 are also integrated into ForeMan.

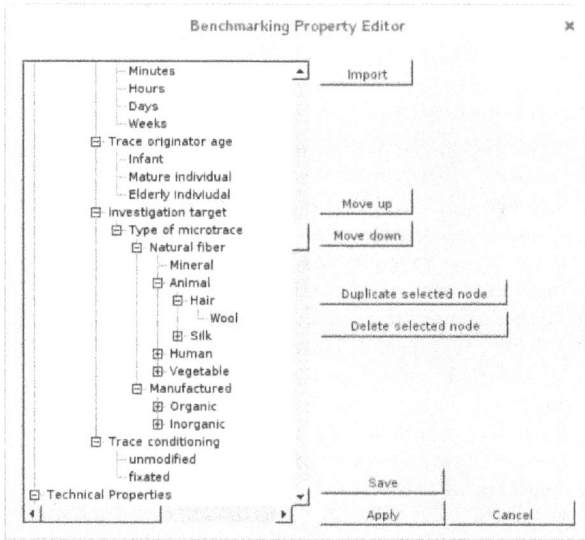

Figure 2: Screenshot of benchmarking properties editor, showing micro trace specific section

Different colors are utilized to visualize the state of an entry - *DO4*: red - default value (not edited yet), green - edited, qualitative benchmarking properties - blue, quantitative - beige. Due to different forensic trace requirements, investigation objectives, analysis processes and many more, the amount of relevant benchmarking properties differs between trace types. Hence, this is why the benchmarking list of fiber traces differs from the one of the fingerprint aging series. But there is always a matching subset of properties, which enables an inter trace type search - *DO7*.

Figure 2 shows the influence of the fiber taxonomy on the micro trace specific benchmarking properties section - *DO5*. This particular material properties M (see section 2.1) of a fiber trace are the result of the forensic use case *identification* [16], which should be annotated to structure the stored data.

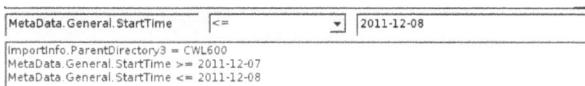

Figure 3: Merged search query: find all CWL 600 scans within a certain acquisition time range

One major benefit of Foreman is the searchability within connected databases - *DO6*/*DO7*. Automatically or manually annotated benchmarking properties favor such queries by structuring the data record - *DO3*. Moreover, the number of matching results can be limited by interlacing two or more queries. Figure 3 shows an exemplary query by searching for a specific sensor device (CWL 600) and also within a certain time range - *DO6*. By using comparison operators ($<$, $<=$, $>$ and $>$) on data items, it is possible to specify ranges. Interlaced queries, as well as multiple queries can be combined to achieve a better search performance.

Each pursued design objective from subsection 3.1 is met by our implementation. Nevertheless, some aspects remain future work, which is concluded in the last section.

5. CONCLUSION

With this paper, an existing benchmarking property scheme is extended by a fiber trace specific categorization taxonomy, fiber folds and sequence number of fingerprint aging time series. This benchmarking scheme and a model of the forensic process for digitized forensics form the conceptual basis for data structures of the "ForeMan" digitized forensic trace database and frontend. The current implementation of the database system stores over 700 different fiber traces of three acquisition devices and one exemplary latent fingerprint aging series, each in different databases and accessible by our frontend, enabling intra and inter trace type queries.

Beyond our implementation success, some requirements of the forensic and database community are not met, yet. During the examination process lots of data is generated, gathered and extracted - measurement data, sensor parameter, segmentation masks, feature vectors, classification models and results. The benchmarking properties as a set thereof serve as a vital foundation to maintain comprehensibility for both forensic research and forensic casework. Data needs to be saved according to the currently stored measurement results in order to achieve an overall process documentation and search-ability for both entity-centered, as well as spatial-centered information.

Integrity checking mechanisms, e.g. cryptographic hashes, and authenticity assuring mechanisms (i.e. provenance [24], [4]), e.g. digital signatures remain future work. With the integration of different user types (e.g. forensic expert, maintainer, scientific assistant) in the future, corresponding roles and views are needed. Analysis of fiber fold shapes as our proposed new benchmarking property describing features and images for template matching point towards interesting research into forgeability and fabrication at crime scenes but remains further work. Further, visual quality indices [14] could serve as a built-in image comparison component. More relevant forensic trace type data, as well as their specific benchmarking property profiles need to be imported into ForeMan. Future work should aim at a continuous extension of the database. This includes the integration of additional trace types, e.g. firearm- or locksmith-related toolmarks. Moreover, this also includes the integration of additional sensing-data, (pre)processing operations and the possibility to compare and evaluate different combinations. To provide an overall examination support/documentation all associated data should be stored inside this database based on the extended benchmarking scheme. To support the scientific community, content/parts of the database without data protection needs should be published. Results could be even more comprehensible, if intermediate results and the complete chain-of-custody is available.

6. ACKNOWLEDGMENTS

The work in this paper has been funded in part by the German Federal Ministry of Education and Science (BMBF) through the Research Program under Contract No. FKZ: 13N10816 and FKZ:13N10818.

7. REFERENCES

[1] L. C. Abendshien, C. J. Brown, D. K. Williams, and S. Shaw. Forensic Automotive Carpet Fiber Identification Database (FACID). [Online] http://projects.nfstc.org/trace/docs/final/williams_diane.pdf, last checked 24.11.2014, 06 2007.

[2] C. Arndt, C. Krätzer, and C. Vielhauer. First approach for a computer-aided textile fiber type determination based on template matching using a 3d laser scanning microscope. In *Proc. of the 14th ACM Workshop on Multimedia and Security*, MMSec '12, pages 57–66. ACM, New York, NY, USA, 2012.

[3] R. Bowen and J. Schneider. Forensic databases: Paint, shoe prints, and beyond. In *National Institute of Justice Journal Issue:258*, pages 34–38, 10 2007.

[4] N. J. Car. A method and example system for managing provenance information in a heterogeneous process environment - a provenance architecture containing the provenance management system (proms). In *20th International Congress on Modelling and Simulation*, pages 824–830, Adelaide, Australia, 2013.

[5] L. Dixon, B. Gill, and Institute for Civil Justice (U.S.). *Changes in the Standards for Admitting Expert Evidence in Federal Civil Cases Since the Daubert Decision*. G - Reference, Information and Interdisciplinary Subjects Series. Rand, 2001.

[6] Federal Bureau of Investigation (FBI). FBI - Integrated Automated Fingerprint Identification System (IAFIS). [Online] http://www.fbi.gov/about-us/cjis/fingerprints_biometrics/iafis/iafis, last checked 15.01.2015.

[7] Federal Bureau of Investigation (FBI). FBI - Next Generation Identification (NGI). [Online] http://www.fbi.gov/about-us/cjis/fingerprints_biometrics/ngi, last checked 15.01.2015.

[8] R. Fischer and C. Vielhauer. Forensic ballistic analysis using a 3d sensor device. In *Proc. of the 14th ACM Workshop on Multimedia and Security*, MMSec '12, pages 67–76, New York, NY, USA, 2012. ACM.

[9] Forensic Technology Inc. Integrated Ballistics Identification System (IBIS). [Online] http://forensictechnology.com, last checked 15.01.2015.

[10] Fries Research & Technology GmbH (FRT). Data sheet frt ftr - thin film reflectometer, 11 2010.

[11] Fries Research & Technology GmbH (FRT). Chromatic White Light Sensor FRT CWL. [Online] http://www.frt-gmbh.com/en/chromatic-white-light-sensor-frt-cwl.aspx, last checked 21.10.2014, 2014.

[12] M. Hildebrandt, C. Arndt, A. Makrushin, and J. Dittmann. Computer-aided fiber analysis for crime scene forensics. In C. A. Bouman, I. Pollak, and P. J. Wolfe, editors, *Proc. of SPIE 8296, Computational Imaging X, 829601*, volume 8296. 02 2012.

[13] M. Hildebrandt, S. Kiltz, I. Grossmann, and C. Vielhauer. Convergence of digital and traditional forensic disciplines: A first exemplary study for digital dactyloscopy. In *Proc. of the 13th ACM Workshop on Multimedia and Security*, pages 1–8, 2011.

[14] H. Hofbauer and A. Uhl. An effective and efficient visual quality index based on local edge gradients. In *3rd European Workshop on Visual Information Processing (EUVIP)*, pages 162–167, July 2011.

[15] M. M. Houck and J. A. Siegel. *Fundamentals of Forensic Science*. Academic Press, 2nd edition, 2010.

[16] K. Inman and N. Rudin. *Principles and Practice of Criminalistics - The Profession of Forensic Science*. CRC Press, 2001.

[17] A. R. Jackson and J. M. Jackson. *Forensic Science*. Pearson Education Limited, 3rd edition, 2011.

[18] Keyence Corporation. Vk-x100/x200 series 3d laser scanning microscope. [Online] available: http://www.keyence.com/products/microscope/laser-microscope/vk-x100_x200/index.jsp, last checked 21.10.2014, 2014.

[19] S. Kiltz, M. Leich, J. Dittmann, C. Vielhauer, and M. Ulrich. Revised benchmarking of contact-less fingerprint scanners for forensic fingerprint detection: challenges and results for chromatic white light scanners (cwl). In *Proc. of the SPIE*, volume 7881, pages 78810G–78810G–15, 2011.

[20] M. Leich, M. Ulrich, M. Hildebrandt, S. Kiltz, and C. Vielhauer. Forensic fingerprint detection: Challenges of benchmarking new contact-less fingerprint scanners – a first proposal. Workshop at DAGM 2010 on Pattern Recognition for IT Security, Darmstadt, Germany, September 2010.

[21] R. Merkel, S. Gruhn, J. Dittmann, C. Vielhauer, and A. Bräutigam. On non-invasive 2d and 3d chromatic white light image sensors for age determination of latent fingerprints. *Forensic Science International*, 222(1–3):52 – 70, 2012.

[22] MongoDB, Inc. Mongo db homepage. [Online] https://www.mongodb.org/, last checked 15.01.2015, 2013.

[23] H. L. Needles, editor. *Textile Fibers, Dyes, Finishes and Processes: A Concise Guide*. Noyes Publications, 1st edition, 12 1986.

[24] M. Schäler, S. Schulze, and S. Kiltz. Database-centric chain-of-custody in biometric forensic systems. In C. Vielhauer, J. Dittmann, A. Drygajlo, N. Juul, and M. Fairhurst, editors, *Biometrics and ID Management*, volume 6583 of *Lecture Notes in Computer Science*, pages 250–261. Springer Berlin Heidelberg, 2011.

[25] Scientific Working Group for Material Analysis (SWGMAT). Forensic fiber examination guidelines. [Online] http://www.swgmat.org/Forensic%20Fiber%20Examination%20Guidelines.pdf, last checked 15.01.2015, 1999.

Optimal Sequential Fingerprinting: Wald vs. Tardos

Thijs Laarhoven
Eindhoven University of Technology
P.O. Box 513, 5600 MB
Eindhoven, The Netherlands
mail@thijs.com

ABSTRACT

We study sequential collusion-resistant fingerprinting, where the fingerprinting code is generated in advance but accusations may be made between rounds, and show that in this setting both the dynamic Tardos scheme and schemes building upon Wald's sequential probability ratio test (SPRT) are asymptotically optimal. We further compare these two approaches to sequential fingerprinting, highlighting differences between the two schemes. Based on these differences, we argue that Wald's scheme should in general be preferred over the dynamic Tardos scheme, even though both schemes have their merits. As a side result, we derive an optimal sequential group testing method for the classical model, which can easily be generalized to different group testing models.

1. INTRODUCTION

In collusion-resistant fingerprinting, a distributor aims to embed fingerprints in digital content so that even if several users collude and mix their fingerprinted copies into a new copy, the resulting pirate version can still be traced back to the guilty parties. In 2003, the seminal work of Tardos [55] showed that in the non-adaptive setting, fingerprinting codes with this property must have a length ℓ quadratic in the number of colluders c and logarithmic in the total number of users n (i.e., $\ell \propto c^2 \log n$), and that such codes exist. These codes guarantee that with a proper decoding algorithm, at least one of the colluders can be found with high probability. Later, in 2013 it was shown [28] that in the adaptive setting, where code words are sent out symbol by symbol and the distributor is allowed to base future decisions on previous results, in fact *all* colluders can provably be found with a code length $\ell \propto c^2 \log n$, using a dynamic version of Tardos' scheme. Results in fingerprinting have recently found applications in other fields as well, including group testing [29, 35] and differential privacy [8, 13, 54, 57].

Over the years, various follow-up works to Tardos' milestone paper have allowed us to understand why Tardos' scheme is designed the way it is designed [15, 51], how the

scheme can be further improved theoretically [6, 31, 39, 40, 49, 50, 51] and practically [9, 11, 16, 17, 18, 19, 20, 26, 34, 36, 44, 48], what are the limitations of fingerprinting in general [2, 23, 37] and of the optimized (symmetric) Tardos scheme [27, 31], and how these limitations can be overcome by further modifying the scheme [24, 32, 41] to achieve asymptotic optimality [2, 23, 37, 42]. Most notably, connections were made between fingerprinting, game theory, channel coding, and statistical hypothesis testing, which ultimately allowed us to explain why the optimal non-adaptive designs are optimal [1, 23, 32, 36].

Although various of these insights directly carry over to the adaptive setting, in this area several questions remain:

- Is the "dynamic Tardos scheme" [28, 30] optimal?

- What motivates the design of this scheme?

Answering these and related questions may ultimately lead to the same level of understanding for the adaptive case as for the non-adaptive setting, allowing practitioners to make well-motivated design choices in the adaptive setting as well.

Contributions. In this paper we answer the second question by showing a connection with what is known in the literature as the *sequential probability ratio test (SPRT)*, invented by Wald in the 1940s [59]. As a result, we are also able to take a first step towards answering the first question: within the class of *sequential* fingerprinting schemes, where the code book is not constructed adaptively, both the dynamic Tardos scheme and schemes built from Wald's SPRT are essentially optimal for the uninformed fingerprinting game. We discuss in detail how sequential fingerprinting schemes can naturally be constructed from Wald's SPRT, and how various results from the literature can be used to tune these schemes to different scenarios. We finally compare the dynamic Tardos scheme to Wald's SPRT, and highlight why in general Wald's scheme should be preferred.

Roadmap. First, in Section 2 we outline the fingerprinting model considered in this paper. In Section 3 we briefly review the dynamic Tardos scheme and its variants. Then, in Section 4 we describe Wald's sequential probability ratio test procedure, and how it can be applied to fingerprinting to obtain optimal sequential fingerprinting schemes. Next, in Section 5 we illustrate the similarities and differences between these schemes through explicit examples, on the way showing that both schemes are asymptotically optimal for the uninformed fingerprinting game. Finally, in Section 6 we give an overview of the main characteristics of both schemes, which may allow practitioners to make a well-informed choice between the two schemes.

2. MODEL

The collusion-resistant fingerprinting problem is often modeled as the following two-person game between the distributor $\mathcal{D}$ and the coalition of pirates $\mathcal{C}$. The set of colluders is assumed to be a random subset of size $|\mathcal{C}| = c$ from the complete set of n users $\mathcal{U}$, and the identities of these colluders are unknown to the distributor. The distributor might not know c either, and he may only have a (crude) upper bound $c_0 \geq c$ on c. The aim of the game for the distributor is to discover the identities of the colluders without accidentally accusing innocent users, with as little effort as possible. The colluders want to prevent this and remain hidden. The game consists of the following three phases: the distributor uses an *encoder* to generate fingerprints; the colluders employ a *collusion channel* to generate pirate output; and the distributor uses a *decoder* to map pirate output to a set of accused users. We describe these three phases below.

a. Encoder.

The distributor generates a code $\mathcal{X} = \{\mathbf{x}_1, \ldots, \mathbf{x}_n\}$, consisting of binary code words $\mathbf{x}_j \in \{0,1\}^\ell$ for each user $j \in \mathcal{U}$, and each column $i \in \{1, \ldots, \ell\}$ corresponds to a different segment of the content.[1] A common restriction on the encoding process is to assume that $\mathcal{X}$ is created by first generating a *bias vector* $\mathbf{p} \in [0,1]^\ell$, by choosing each entry p_i independently from a certain distribution F, and then generating $\mathcal{X}$ using $P((\mathbf{x}_j)_i = 1) = p_i$. Schemes with this property are sometimes called *bias-based schemes*.

As initially suggested by Tardos [55] and later proven by Huang and Moulin [23], the best way to build bias-based encoders (for large coalitions, in the uninformed setting) is to use the arcsine distribution for generating p_i's. For this distribution, we have the following distribution function F:

$$F(p) = \frac{2}{\pi} \arcsin \sqrt{p}. \qquad (p \in (0,1)) \qquad (1)$$

Unless stated otherwise, throughout the paper we will assume that this encoder is used for generating biases.

b. Collusion channel.

Given $\mathcal{X}$, the entries can be used to select and embed watermarks in the content, and the content is sent out to the users. The colluders get together, compare their copies, and use a *collusion channel* or pirate strategy Θ to select the pirate output $\mathbf{y} \in \{0,1\}^\ell$. If the pirate attack is symmetrical both in the colluders and in the positions i, then the collusion channel can be modeled by a vector $\boldsymbol{\theta} \in [0,1]^{c+1}$, with entries $\theta_z = P(Y_i = 1 \mid Z = z)$ indicating the probability of outputting a 1 when pirates receive z ones and $c - z$ zeros.

c. Decoder.

After the pirate output has been distributed, the distributor intercepts it and applies a decoding algorithm to $\mathcal{X}, \mathbf{y}, \mathbf{p}$ to compute a set $\mathcal{C}' \subseteq \mathcal{U}$ of accused users. This is commonly done by assigning scores to users, and accusing those users whose scores exceed a predefined threshold η. The distribu-

tor wins the game if $\mathcal{C}' = \mathcal{C}$ and loses[2] if $\mathcal{C}' \neq \mathcal{C}$, which could be because an innocent user $j \notin \mathcal{C}$ is falsely accused (a false positive error), or because a guilty user $j \in \mathcal{C}$ is not accused (a false negative error). We often write ε_1 and ε_2 for (upper bounds on) the false positive and false negative probabilities.

Finally, the differences between non-adaptive (static) fingerprinting, adaptive (dynamic) fingerprinting, and sequential fingerprinting can be explained by showing in which order these phases take place. Denoting by a_i, b_i, c_i the three phases corresponding to the ith segment of the content, we can order the phases as follows:

- Non-adaptive: $a_{[1,\ldots,\ell]}; b_{[1,\ldots,\ell]}; c_{[1,\ldots,\ell]}$.

- Sequential: $a_{[1,\ldots,\ell]}; b_1; c_1; b_2; c_2; \ldots; b_\ell; c_\ell$.

- Adaptive: $a_1; b_1; c_1; a_2; b_2; c_2; \ldots; a_\ell; b_\ell; c_\ell$.

In other words: in the adaptive setting the code can be adjusted and accusations can be made after every symbol; in sequential fingerprinting only users can be accused between rounds; and in non-adaptive settings the distributor is only allowed to make a final decision at the end of the game.

While most work in the literature focuses on the non-adaptive setting, some work has also been done on sequential [46] and adaptive fingerprinting [5, 14, 28, 30, 45, 56]. In this paper we will mostly deal with the sequential setting.

3. TARDOS' SCHEME

3.1 Non-adaptive scheme

In Tardos' original scheme [55] and many of its subsequent variants, decoding in the non-adaptive setting is done as follows. First, for each segment i and user j, scores $S_{j,i} = g(x_{j,i}, y_i, p_i)$ are assigned using a score function g. Then, in the non-adaptive setting, a user $j \in \mathcal{U}$ is accused iff $S_j = \sum_{i=1}^{\ell} S_{j,i} > \eta$ for some well-chosen threshold η. Choosing a suitable score function is crucial, and it was long thought that the following symmetrized version [50] of Tardos' original proposal was the best choice:

$$g(x, y, p) = \begin{cases} \sqrt{p/(1-p)} & \text{if } (x,y) = (0,0); \\ -\sqrt{p/(1-p)} & \text{if } (x,y) = (0,1); \\ -\sqrt{(1-p)/p} & \text{if } (x,y) = (1,0); \\ \sqrt{(1-p)/p} & \text{if } (x,y) = (1,1). \end{cases} \qquad (2)$$

This function turns out to work quite well against arbitrary pirate attacks, and it has the convenient property that regardless of the pirate strategy, one always has $\mathbb{E}(S_{j,i} \mid H_0) = 0$, $\mathbb{E}(S_{j,i}^2 \mid H_0) = 1$, and $\mathbb{E}(S_{j,i} \mid H_1) \approx \frac{2}{\pi}$, where the hypotheses H_0 and H_1 correspond to:

- H_0: user j is innocent ($j \notin \mathcal{C}$).

- H_1: user j is guilty ($j \in \mathcal{C}$).

As convenient as this decoder may be, it is known to be suboptimal [23, 27], with code lengths which are up to a factor $\frac{1}{4}\pi^2 \approx 2.47$ longer than required. Using various different approaches (e.g. Lagrange optimization [41, 42], Neyman-Pearson decoding [32], Bayesian decoding [11], MAP decoding [18], empirical mutual information decoding [37]) it was

---

[1]More generally $\mathcal{X}$ is a code with entries from an alphabet of size q, but here we restrict our attention to the case $q = 2$.

[2]In this paper we consider the catch-all scenario, where not *at least one* colluder (the catch-one scenario) but *all* colluders should be found for the distributor to win the game.

later found that there are various ways to construct decoders for the uninformed setting in fingerprinting with a better performance than the symmetric score function. Various of these decoders were recently benchmarked in [20], indicating that different decoders work better in different settings. For comparison with Wald's SPRT we will continue the description of Tardos' scheme using Neyman-Pearson-motivated decoders, as considered in e.g. [17, 32], but other decoders considered in [20] may be used as well.

After obtaining the "evidence" $\mathbf{x}_j, \mathbf{y}, \mathbf{p}$, the distributor wants to distinguish between whether user j is guilty or not[3]. The Neyman-Pearson lemma tells us that the most powerful test to distinguish between H_0 and H_1 (minimizing one error probability, when the other is fixed) is to test whether the following likelihood ratio exceeds an appropriately chosen threshold η'. We write $f_A(a) = \mathbb{P}(A = a)$ for random variables A.

$$\Lambda(\mathbf{x}_j, \mathbf{y}, \mathbf{p}) = \frac{f_{\mathbf{X}_j, \mathbf{Y}|\mathbf{P}}(\mathbf{x}_j, \mathbf{y}|\mathbf{p}, H_1)}{f_{\mathbf{X}_j, \mathbf{Y}|\mathbf{P}}(\mathbf{x}_j, \mathbf{y}|\mathbf{p}, H_0)}. \tag{3}$$

Taking logarithms, and noting that different positions i are i.i.d., testing whether a user's likelihood ratio exceeds η' is equivalent to testing whether his score $S_j = \sum_i g(x_{j,i}, y_i.p_i)$ exceeds $\eta = \ln \eta'$ for g defined as follows. Here we omit subscripts on X, Y and P, as the random variables are i.i.d. for different i, j.

$$g(x, y, p) = \ln \left(\frac{f_{X,Y|P}(x, y|p, H_1)}{f_{X,Y|P}(x, y|p, H_0)} \right). \tag{4}$$

Results of Abbe and Zheng [1] have shown that in certain applications, a (generalized) linear decoder designed against the worst-case attack is asymptotically optimal. Since the worst-case attack for finite c is somewhat hard to compute, but is known to be close to the interleaving attack [18, 22] (and asymptotically equal to it [23]), an approximation of this optimal decoder may be obtained by assuming the colluders used the interleaving attack $\boldsymbol{\theta} = \boldsymbol{\theta}_{\text{int}}$, defined by

$$(\boldsymbol{\theta}_{\text{int}})_z = \frac{z}{c}. \qquad (0 \le z \le c) \tag{5}$$

In that case, working out the probabilities for fixed c leads to the following score function g [32]:

$$g(x, y, p) = \begin{cases} \ln \left(1 + \frac{p}{c(1-p)} \right) & \text{if } x = y = 0; \\ \ln \left(1 - \frac{1}{c} \right) & \text{if } x \neq y; \\ \ln \left(1 + \frac{1-p}{cp} \right) & \text{if } x = y = 1. \end{cases} \tag{6}$$

To sketch the situation of cumulative user scores and the accusation procedure, Figure 1 outlines the scores $S_j(i_0) = \sum_{i=1}^{i_0} S_{j,i}$ against i_0, for $i_0 = 0$ up to the final moment of decision $i_0 = \ell$. Assuming a colluder-symmetric collusion channel, scores of users $j \notin \mathcal{C}$ follow a certain random walk with a negative drift $\mu_0 < 0$ and a relatively large variance σ_0^2, while scores of guilty users $j \in \mathcal{C}$ follow a random walk with a positive drift $\mu_1 > 0$ and a smaller variance σ_1^2.

3.2 Sequential scheme

The improvement described in [28] for the adaptive setting does not change the code generation phase at all, so although

---

[3]Note that we only consider $\mathbf{x}_j$ to be part of the evidence, instead of $\mathcal{X}$. Using all of $\mathcal{X}$ for decoding would correspond to joint decoding; this is discussed later on.

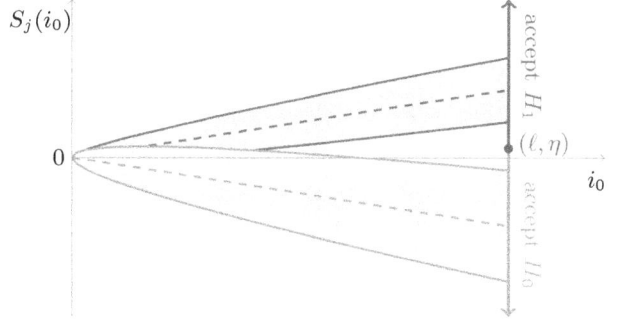

Figure 1: Tardos' scheme with log-likelihood decoding. The green and red marked areas (dashed lines) indicate the range (average) of innocent and guilty user scores respectively. Accepting H_0 or H_1 is based on whether $S_j(\ell) > \eta$, i.e., whether a user's score ends up above or below the blue point (ℓ, η).

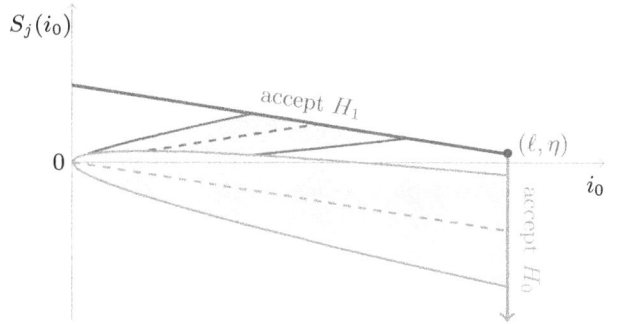

Figure 2: Laarhoven et al.'s sequential Tardos scheme with log-likelihood scores. The red decreasing line, which runs parallel to the dashed green line, shows when users are accused and disconnected.

it was coined the *dynamic* Tardos scheme, it may more suitably be called the *sequential* Tardos scheme. The modification compared to the non-adaptive scheme described above, to make better use of the sequential setting, is the following: instead of only cutting off users from the content at the very end, when their scores exceed η, we disconnect users as soon as their normalized scores exceed the normalized threshold η. This prevents the colluder from contributing to the remaining parts of the content, and allows the distributor to find the remaining colluders as well. Here by normalization we refer to translating the scores by $+\ell\mu_0$, so that innocent users are expected to have an average final score of 0.

To illustrate the effect of this change to the scheme, Figure 2 sketches the cumulative user scores in the sequential setting *without normalization*, and the new accusation criterion. Without normalization, the scores follow the same general path as in Figure 1, and the red accusation threshold becomes a decreasing line, rather than a horizontal line as in [28, 30]. As discussed in [28], with this modification one can provably find all colluders rather than only one with a similar provable code length as in the non-adaptive setting. The central result of [28] can be stated as follows.

THEOREM 1. *[28] Suppose ℓ and η are chosen in the non-adaptive Tardos scheme to guarantee that*

(i) with prob. at least $1 - \varepsilon_1$ no innocent users are accused;

(ii) with prob. at least $1 - \varepsilon_2$ at least one colluder is accused.

Then, using almost the same scheme parameters as before[4], with this sequential construction we can guarantee that

(i) with pr. at least $1 - 2\varepsilon_1$ no innocent users are accused;

(ii) with prob. at least $1 - 2\varepsilon_2$ all colluders are accused.

In practice, this means that to turn a non-adaptive scheme into a sequential scheme that provably finds all colluders, we just have to replace ε_1 and ε_2 by $\frac{1}{2}\varepsilon_1$ and $\frac{1}{2}\varepsilon_2$ in the formulas for ℓ and η of the non-adaptive setting. Since ℓ only depends logarithmically on ε_1 and ε_2, for large n and c the resulting increase in the code length is negligible.

3.3 Sequential variants

While the above sequential scheme deals well with the setting where c is known and users can be accused after every position i, the paper [28] also discussed slight variations of this setting, which may well appear in practice. In particular, the two problems of not being able to cut off users after every segment i, and not knowing c, were addressed in [28, Sections IV and V].

3.3.1 Weakly sequential decoding

To make tracing harder, pirates may delay the pirate output, so that a user whose score exceeds η at time i_0 can only be disconnected at time, say, $i_0 + B$. As we are now quite certain that he is guilty, and since he contributed to segments $i_0 + 1, \ldots, i_0 + B$, we could consider these segments *tainted* and disregard them completely for tracing the remaining colluders. This solution was proposed in [28, Section IV.A] and it was shown to lead to a moderate increase in the code length of $(c-1)B$. A different analysis in [28, Section IV.B] showed that one can also perform a new study of the possible overshoot over the boundary η, due to the increase B, leading to a higher increase in the code length. Therefore the solution from [28, Sect. IV.A] should be preferred.

3.3.2 Universal sequential decoding

As for the setting where c is unknown and only a crude estimate c_0 is known (or no bound is known at all), [28, Section V] proposed a method where each user is assigned several scores $S_j^{(1)}, \ldots, S_j^{(c_0)}$ based on how large the coalition is estimated to be, and disconnecting a user as soon as one of his scores crosses one of the corresponding boundaries $\eta^{(1)}, \ldots, \eta^{(c_0)}$. It was noted in [28] that the scores are very similar and the boundaries seem to correspond to a continuous function $\eta(i_0) \propto \sqrt{i_0}$. One of the open problems posed in [28, Section VII.B] was therefore whether schemes with single scores and curved boundaries are provably secure.

3.3.3 Joint decoding

Finally, another topic often considered in the fingerprinting literature is joint decoding [2, 4, 9, 23, 34, 36, 37, 43,

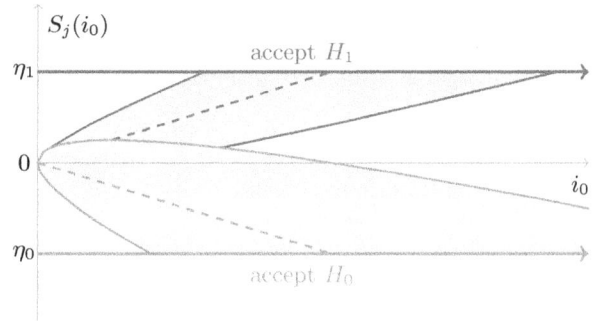

Figure 3: Wald's SPRT construction. As soon as a user's score leaves the interval $[\eta_0, \eta_1]$, he is marked innocent (below η_0) or guilty (above η_1).

52]: using the entire code $\mathcal{X}$, rather than only the user's code word $\mathbf{x}_j$, to decide whether user j should be accused. Assigning scores to tuples of users was considered before in e.g. [43], but no explicit decision criterion with provable results was provided, and it was left as an open problem.

4. WALD'S SCHEME

4.1 Sequential scheme

To understand the motivation behind the sequential Tardos scheme, and to see how the design can possibly be improved, we now turn our attention to what has long been known in statistics literature to be a solution for hypothesis testing in sequential settings: Wald's sequential probability ratio test (SPRT). This scheme originated in the 1940s [58, 59], and countless follow-up works have appeared since, which have been summarized in many books on this topic [3, 10, 21, 25, 38, 47, 59, 61].

Let us recall the formulation of the fingerprinting problem in terms of hypothesis testing, where we want to distinguish between the following two hypotheses:

- H_0: user j is innocent ($j \notin \mathcal{C}$).

- H_1: user j is guilty ($j \in \mathcal{C}$).

Now, to decide between these two hypotheses in sequential settings, Wald proposed the following procedure. Let η_1 and η_0 be two constants, with $\eta_1 > 0 > \eta_0$, and again let us use the optimal log-likelihood score function g from (6). Now we decide in favor of H_1 as soon as a user's cumulative score exceeds η_1, and we decide to accept H_0 as soon as the user's score drops below η_0. As long as a user score stays in the interval $[\eta_0, \eta_1]$, we continue testing. This accusation procedure is sketched in Figure 3.

Choosing the thresholds. To understand how the parameters η_0 and η_1 should be chosen, a connection is often made with the continuous-time analog of random walks, Brownian motions. Assuming that user scores are continuous, so that when a score crosses one of the boundaries it really *hits* the boundary (rather than jumping over it, in the discrete model), then to guarantee that an innocent user is acquitted with probability at least $1 - \varepsilon_1'$ and a guilty user is accused with probability at least $1 - \varepsilon_2'$, the following choice is optimal:

$$\eta_0 = \ln\left(\frac{\varepsilon_2'}{1 - \varepsilon_1'}\right), \qquad \eta_1 = \ln\left(\frac{1 - \varepsilon_2'}{\varepsilon_1'}\right). \qquad (7)$$

---

[4]This disregards a small technical detail regarding the overshoot over the boundary η; see the discussion of Z and $\tilde{Z}$ in [28, Section III.C]. To be sure that the scheme still works we can disregard scores right after a user is removed from the system [30, Section II] with a negligible increase in ℓ. We omit details here, and only present the simplified result.

To guarantee that all innocent users are acquitted and all guilty users are found, we need to let $\varepsilon_1' = O(\frac{1}{n})$ and $\varepsilon_2' = O(\frac{1}{c})$, which for large c, n means $\eta_0 \sim -\ln c$ and $\eta_1 \sim \ln n$. For instance, writing $\varepsilon_1' = \varepsilon_1/n$ and $\varepsilon_2' = \varepsilon_2/c$, so that the probability of not accusing innocents (accusing all guilties) is at least $1 - \varepsilon_1 (1 - \varepsilon_2)$, this corresponds to taking

$$\eta_0 = \ln\left(\frac{\varepsilon_2/c}{1 - \varepsilon_1/n}\right), \qquad \eta_1 = \ln\left(\frac{1 - \varepsilon_2/c}{\varepsilon_1/n}\right). \quad (8)$$

There are two important issues that we need to address, the first of which is that we are not dealing with continuous user scores but discrete scores. One of the effects of having discrete jumps in the scores is that there may be a slight *overshoot* over one of the boundaries when a user is accused or acquitted; a score may cross one of the lines at a non-integral point so to say, and at the next measurement the score may significantly exceed η_1 or drop below η_0. As a result the error probabilities for the above choice of thresholds are not exact. A useful property of the above choice of parameters is that if by $\tilde{\varepsilon}_1'$ and $\tilde{\varepsilon}_2'$ we denote the *real* probabilities of accusing innocent and guilty users, when using these thresholds η_0 and η_1, we have [58, Equation (3.30)]

$$\tilde{\varepsilon}_1' + \tilde{\varepsilon}_2' \leq \varepsilon_1' + \varepsilon_2'. \quad (9)$$

In other words, the total error probability does not increase, and at most one of ε_1' and ε_2' might increase. Alternatively, exact bounds on the error probabilities can be obtained, showing that the following slightly conservative choice of parameters guarantees that the error bounds are satisfied:

$$\eta_0 = -\ln\left(1/\varepsilon_2'\right), \qquad \eta_1 = \ln\left(1/\varepsilon_1'\right). \quad (10)$$

The second issue that we should address is that having a threshold η_0 only makes sense if all colluders have an increasing score. If the colluders know about the tracing algorithm, and use an asymmetric pirate strategy, e.g. by letting one colluder be inactive at the start and letting him join in later, this colluder will incorrectly be acquitted early on. In this setting one could say that innocence is virtually impossibly to prove, while it is possible to prove that someone is guilty. To deal with this problem, a simple solution is not to use a lower threshold η_0 at all. This is equivalent to setting $\varepsilon_2' = 0$, as that way we will never acquit a colluder. In that case, the conservative choice of thresholds from (7) can be stated as

$$\eta_0 = -\infty, \qquad \eta_1 = \ln\left(1/\varepsilon_1'\right). \quad (11)$$

Note that in this case, the aggressive and conservative expressions from (7) and (10) match, i.e., ε_1' is a tight bound on the probability of incorrectly accusing a single innocent user. This more realistic implementation of the sequential probability ratio test in the uninformed fingerprinting game is again sketched in Figure 4.

Optimality of the SPRT. Although reaching a decision with this procedure may theoretically take a very long time, Wald proved that his test procedure always terminates [59, Appendix A], regardless of ε_1 and ε_2. Furthermore, if by μ_0 (μ_1) and σ_0^2 (σ_1^2) we denote the expected score in one segment for innocent (guilty) users, then we know that with high probability, the procedure will terminate not long after $i_0 \cdot \mu_0 + O(\sigma_0)$ ($i_0 \cdot \mu_1 + O(\sigma_1)$) crosses the boundary η_0 (η_1).

More formally, Wald analyzed the expected time by which his procedure terminates, under either H_0 or H_1, and together with Wolfowitz he proved [60] that his SPRT is op-

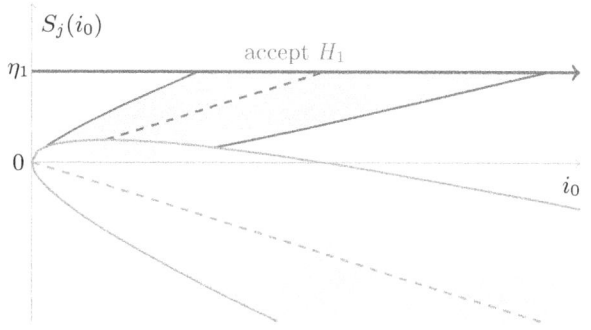

Figure 4: **Wald's SPRT with no early innocent decisions.** Setting $\eta_1 = \ln(1/\varepsilon_1')$ guarantees that innocent users are never accused with probability at least $1 - \varepsilon_1'$, while this design guarantees that $\varepsilon_2 = 0$.

timal in that it minimizes the expected time before a decision is reached, both under H_0 and under H_1. Ignoring overshoots over the boundary (i.e., assuming we are dealing with continuous random walks), he further derived explicit expressions for both these expected termination times, which are stated below. In the following theorem, we write $d_{\mathrm{KL}}(a\|b) = a \ln(\frac{a}{b}) + (1-a)\ln(\frac{1-a}{1-b})$ for the Kullback-Leibler divergence or relative entropy (in nats) between a and b.

THEOREM 2. *[59, 60] Suppose we have a sequential test procedure, for which*

- *an innocent user is accused w.p. at most ε_1';*

- *a guilty user is acquitted w.p. at most ε_2';*

- *the probability of termination is 1.*

Let T denote the time at which a decision is reached. Then:

$$\mathbb{E}(T|H_0) \geq \frac{1}{-\mu_0} d_{\mathrm{KL}}(\varepsilon_1'\|1 - \varepsilon_2') \approx \frac{\ln(1/\varepsilon_2')}{-\mu_0}, \quad (12)$$

$$\mathbb{E}(T|H_1) \geq \frac{1}{\mu_1} d_{\mathrm{KL}}(\varepsilon_2'\|1 - \varepsilon_1') \approx \frac{\ln(1/\varepsilon_1')}{\mu_1}. \quad (13)$$

Furthermore, the sequential probability ratio test is a sequential test simultaneously minimizing both $\mathbb{E}(T_0)$ and $\mathbb{E}(T_1)$, and assuming that there is no overshoot over the boundaries, both inequalities above are equalities for the SPRT.

For large n, the per-user false positive error probability scales as $\varepsilon_1' = \Theta(1/n)$ while $\varepsilon_2' = \Theta(1)$ based on the argument that if the average pirate score exceeds η_1, all pirate scores exceed η_1 [28]. We further have that

$$\mu_1 = \mathbb{E}(S_{j,i}|H_1) \quad (14)$$

$$= \mathbb{E}_P \sum_{x,y} f_{X,Y|P}(x,y|p,H_1) \ln \frac{f_{X,Y|P}(x,y|p,H_1)}{f_{X,Y|P}(x,y|p,H_0)} \quad (15)$$

$$= (\ln 2)\mathbb{E}_P I(X_1; Y|P), \quad (16)$$

where $I(X_1, Y|P = p)$ is the mutual information between a pirate symbol and the pirate output, as described in e.g. [23, 32]. This leads to the following corollary.

THEOREM 3. *For sequential tests satisfying the conditions stated in Theorem 2, we have:*

$$\mathbb{E}(T|H_1) \gtrsim \frac{\log_2 n}{\mathbb{E}_P I(X_1; Y|P)}. \quad (17)$$

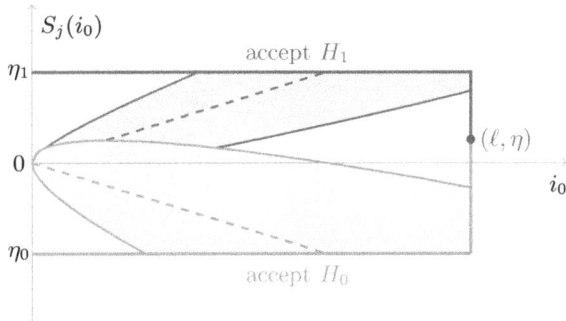

Figure 5: Wald's SPRT with truncated thresholds, guaranteeing a decision after at most ℓ segments. For small ℓ, both ε_1 and ε_2 will increase.

This result implies that in general, sequentiality does not lead to a decrease in the asymptotic code length; with non-adaptive schemes it is also possible to achieve this asymptotic code length [32]. The two gains of sequential testing are that (i) in fact *all* colluders, rather than at least one of them, can provably be caught with this asymptotic code length; and (ii) in practice, for finite c and n, the time needed to find and trace all colluders will generally be shorter than in the non-adaptive setting. Although the asymptotic code length are the same, the convergence to this limit is significantly faster for sequential schemes than for non-adaptive schemes.

While most of the analyses and results above are based on running this scheme with parallel infinite boundaries, it is not impossible to force an early decision. As already described by Wald [59, Section 3.8], one might ultimately prefer to *truncate* the test procedure at some fixed time ℓ, at which we make a decision similar to the sequential Tardos scheme, and similar to the non-adaptive setting. This may be done with and without a lower boundary; a sketch for the case with a lower boundary is given in Figure 5. Analyzing these variants rigorously seems difficult, even with Brownian approximations, but an interested reader may refer to e.g. one of the books on sequential testing listed at the beginning of this section. With truncation, one should ask the question whether forcing a decision by some fixed time ℓ is really important. After all, if the main goal is to minimize the *worst-case* code length ℓ needed to make a decision, then it is commonly best to wait until the very end and to take all evidence into account before making any decisions at all; which exactly corresponds to the non-adaptive setting.

4.2 Sequential variants

The SPRT has received extensive attention in the literature, with thorough analyses of the effects of the overshoot over the boundaries, slight modifications of the scheme (such as the truncated SPRT mentioned above), and the effects of using different boundaries than the horizontal lines in the figures above. We highlight two variants which we also considered for the sequential Tardos scheme, and we consider how joint decoding may be done with the SPRT. For further details we refer the interested reader to e.g. [3, 10, 21, 25, 38, 47, 59, 61].

4.2.1 Weakly sequential decoding

In the setting of weakly adaptive decoding, where pirates delay their rebroadcast of the content (or where content is sent out in blocks of size B), the results based on continuous approximations using Brownian motions become less and less accurate. For higher values of B, the overshoot over the boundary becomes more and more significant, which was also discussed in [28, Section IV.B]; there the possible overshoot was parametrized by $\tilde{Z}_B - Z$, and it was noted that exactly this overshoot causes problems.

To deal with this problem effectively, we can again use the method described in [28, Section IV.A]: ignore the tainted segments i to which a user who is now deemed guilty may have contributed. Then the increase in the code length may again only be $(c-1)B$, which in the uninformed fingerprinting game is negligible with respect to $\ell \propto c^2 \log n$.

4.2.2 Universal decoding

Recall that in the universal decoding setting, we assume that c is unknown, and only a crude bound $c_0 \gg c$ may be known. To deal with this, Laarhoven et al. [28] proposed to keep multiple scores per user, and multiple accusation boundaries. It was conjectured that using a single score for each user, and using a curved boundary function of the form $\eta_1(i_0) \propto \sqrt{i_0}$ may be possible.

In terms of hypothesis testing, testing whether $j \in \mathcal{C}$ or $j \notin \mathcal{C}$ for unknown coalition sizes c could be considered a test of a simple null hypothesis $H_0 : \mu = \mu_0$ against a one-sided alternative $H_1 : \mu > \mu_0$. In the informed setting, where the collusion channel is known, we might know exactly what μ_0 is, and so such a one-sided test may form a solution. In that case, curved stopping boundaries (in particular, having a boundary of the shape $\eta_1(i_0) \propto \sqrt{i_0}$) has been suggested before; see e.g. [47, Chapter IV]. When using the symmetric Tardos score function rather than the optimized log-likelihood ratios or MAP decoders, this approach may work well, although the issue remains that it seems that no single encoder and decoder can be used for arbitrary c and $\boldsymbol{\theta}$: in all known cases, either the decoder depends on c or c_0, or the encoder uses a cutoff which depends on c.

To work with different score functions than Tardos' score function [55] and Škorić et al.'s symmetric score function [50], where μ_0 may be considered fixed, we need to circumvent the issue that μ_0 may depend on c and the pirate strategy $\boldsymbol{\theta}$ as well. In the universal uninformed decoding setting we therefore do not even know what μ_0 is. Two hypotheses that may be more realistic to consider are $H_0 : \mu \leq 0$ against $H_1 : \mu > 0$: an innocent user will have a negative average score, while a guilty user will have a positive average score. However, depending on the collusion strategy, the values of μ_0 and μ_1 may both be small or large. This does not really help the colluders, as decreasing $|\mu_0|$ and $|\mu_1|$ also leads to a decrease in the variance of the scores, but it makes using a single linear decoder even more problematic.

To deal with these problems, the best solution for the universal setting may be to use a generalized linear decoder [1, 11, 36], and to normalize the scores during the decoding phase, as described in [30]. A generalized linear decoder is better suited for the setting of unknown c, and by normalizing user scores (which can be done based on $\mathcal{X}, \mathbf{p}, \mathbf{y}$) we know what μ_0 is. Then we can again use a hypothesis test of the form $H_0 : \mu = \mu_0$ against $H_1 : \mu > \mu_0$ as described above, where a curved boundary may be optimal.

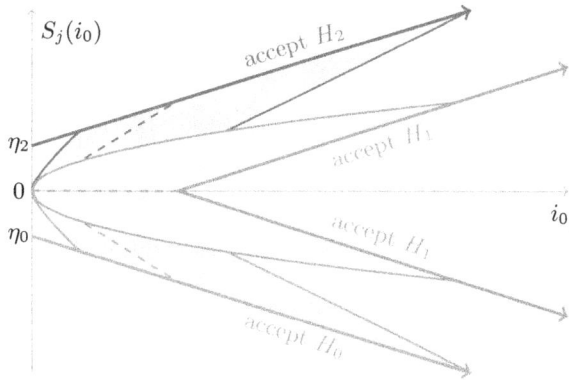

Figure 6: Sobel and Wald's decision procedure to decide between three hypotheses H_0, H_1, H_2. Letting H_i denote the event that a pair of users contains i colluders, this leads to a joint decoding method.

4.2.3 Joint decoding

Recall that in joint decoding the entire code $\mathcal{X}$ is taken into account to decide whether users should be accused. In [43] it was considered to assign scores to tuples $\mathcal{T}$ of $t \leq c$ users, after which one would like to distinguish between the following $t + 1$ hypotheses:

- H_0: tuple $\mathcal{T}$ contains no guilty users: $|\mathcal{T} \cap \mathcal{C}| = 0$;

- H_1: tuple $\mathcal{T}$ contains one guilty user: $|\mathcal{T} \cap \mathcal{C}| = 1$;

- ...

- H_t: tuple $\mathcal{T}$ contains t guilty users: $|\mathcal{T} \cap \mathcal{C}| = t$.

Although not quite as well studied as the case of two hypotheses, this topic has also received attention in SPRT literature, with the earliest work dating back to Sobel and Wald from 1949 [53]. They considered the problem of deciding between three simple hypotheses ($t = 2$), and provided a solution as sketched in Figure 6. Using joint Neyman-Pearson decoder to assign scores to pairs of users, they considered the use of several stopping boundaries, each corresponding to a decision of accepting one of the hypotheses. The distribution of scores then depends on whether the tuple contains 0, 1 or 2 colluders, as illustrated by the green, yellow, and red highlighted curves in Figure 6. This procedure can be generalized to multiple hypotheses as well, to deal with joint decoding with $c > 2$. For details on how to choose these stopping boundaries, see e.g. [53].

5. WALD VS. TARDOS: APPLICATIONS

In the previous two sections we saw how to construct sequential schemes based on the (dynamic) Tardos scheme, and based on Wald's SPRT. Here we briefly consider possible applications of both schemes, and how the two schemes compare. We consider three scenarios as follows:

1. Defending against the interleaving attack.

2. Defending against arbitrary pirate attacks.

3. The classical group testing model.

These settings are studied in the following subsections.

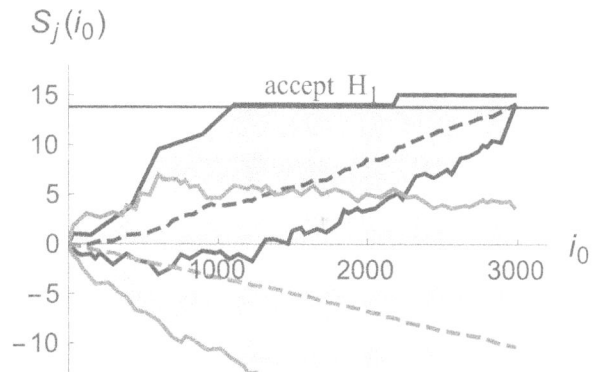

(a) Example of Wald's scheme: Interleaving attack

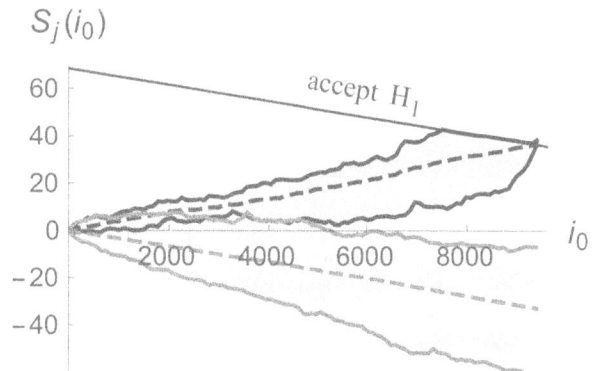

(b) Example of Tardos' scheme: Interleaving attack

Figure 7: A simulation of the interleaving attack in fingerprinting with Wald's SPRT (above) and the sequential Tardos scheme with log-scores (below). Even though it might be caused by not so tight parameter choices in the sequential Tardos scheme, with Wald's scheme we can more easily select tight parameters and trace colluders faster.

5.1 Defending against the interleaving attack

When defending against the interleaving attack, which may be the most practical pirate strategy due to its simplicity and its strength, the Neyman-Pearson decoder of (6) designed against the interleaving attack [32] may be a good choice, even when the tracer's estimate c_0 is not exact [20]. With this score function, in each segment the average pirate score increases by $\mu_1 \sim \frac{1}{2c^2}$, while for innocent users we have $\mu_0 \sim \frac{-1}{2c^2}$ which is proved in the appendix.

In Wald's scheme, recall that we may set $\eta_1 = \ln(1/\varepsilon_1')$ conservatively where ε_1' is the per-user false positive probability. Without using a lower threshold, setting $\varepsilon_1' = \varepsilon_1/n$, i.e., $\eta_1 = \ln(n/\varepsilon_1)$ (and $\eta_0 = -\infty$) guarantees that with probability at least $1 - \varepsilon_1$, no innocent users are ever accused, and with probability 1 all colluders are eventually found. We illustrate the scheme with a toy example in Figure 7a, where we set the parameters as $n = 1000$, $c_0 = c = 10$, and $\varepsilon_1 = 10^{-3}$, so that $\eta_1 \approx 13.82$. On average, it takes about 3000 segments to trace the colluders.

For large n and c, this corresponds to an asymptotic upper threshold of $\eta_1 \sim \ln n$ and an expected time of $\ell \sim 2c^2 \ln n$ until all pirates have been found. This thus corresponds to drawing a horizontal accusation threshold starting at $(0, \ln n)$, and the pirates are expected to be found around the point $(2c^2 \ln n, \ln n)$.

In the sequential Tardos scheme with log-likelihood scores, setting the parameters is more difficult. Various provable bounds on the error probabilities for given parameters are not tight, leading to pessimistic estimates and higher thresholds and code lengths than required. One could also estimate the actual required code length for a given set of parameters directly, leading to better scheme parameters, but this would have to be done for each instance separately; if any of the parameters $c, n, \varepsilon_1, \varepsilon_2$ then changes, one would have to redo the simulations or computations to find good practical parameters for the new setting.

To illustrate how far the provable parameters are off from reality, we again used the toy example of Figure 7a and used the provable bounds from [32, Theorem 3] and Theorem 1, to obtain the following parameters:

$$\mu_0 \approx 0.00382, \qquad \mu_1 \approx -0.00343, \qquad (18)$$

$$\ell \approx 17\,953, \qquad \eta_1^{(\ell)} \approx 6.9078, \qquad \eta_1^{(0)} \approx 68.41. \qquad (19)$$

Note that $\eta_1^{(0)}$, the value of the boundary at $i_0 = 0$, is significantly higher than when using Wald's SPRT. An illustration of how this scheme would then work in practice is given in Figure 7b. In most cases the scheme finds all pirates after roughly 9000 segments, which although much less than the provable code length of $\ell \approx 18\,000$ is much higher than the practical code length of the SPRT of $\ell \approx 3000$ segments.

For large n and c we can again compute what the parameters converge to. First, for this setting we also obtain an asymptotic code length of $\ell \sim 2c^2 \ln n$, and this again corresponds to the asymptotic point $(2c^2 \ln n, \ln n)$; see e.g. [32, Theorem 3, Corollary 3]. However, in the sequential Tardos scheme this accusation threshold is a decreasing line (cf. Figure 2) with a slope equal to $\mu_0 \sim \frac{-1}{2c^2}$. This means that at time $i_0 = 0$, the accusation line asymptotically starts at $\ln n - (2c^2 \ln n) \cdot \frac{1}{2c^2} = 2 \ln n$; the red line starts twice as high as in Wald's SPRT, at the point $(0, 2 \ln n)$. So although both schemes achieve the same asymptotic code length, even in the limit of large n and c these schemes are slightly different.

In this case there are several reasons to prefer Wald's SPRT approach: it is easier to choose good parameters, and asymptotically the accusation threshold lies lower than in the sequential Tardos scheme, allowing for a slightly faster tracing of the colluders.

5.2 Defending against arbitrary pirate attacks

For the general, uninformed fingerprinting game, where it is not known what collusion channel was used, the tracer has to use a decoder that works well against arbitrary collusion channels. Again, the paper of Furon and Desoubeaux [20] compares various of these candidate decoders, each of which were derived through different optimization techniques.

The decoder described in the previous subsection, designed against the interleaving attack, is capacity-achieving in the uninformed setting as well [32], and so a similar construction as in the previous subsection may again be used, both in the sequential Tardos scheme and in Wald's sequential scheme. As described in [30], with this score function it can only be guaranteed that $(\mu_1 - \mu_0)/\sigma_0$ is sufficiently

large regardless of the collusion channel, i.e., it is possible to distinguish between the innocent and guilty distributions. However, it could be that for different collusion channels, both μ_0 and μ_1 are smaller than when the interleaving attack is used. To cope with these difficulties, one could normalize the scores, i.e., based on y_i and p_i, compute μ_0 and σ_0 for segment i, and translate and scale the scores so that μ_0 and σ_0 are the same as for the interleaving attack.

Alternatively, one could use a wide range of different methods, such as using several score functions simultaneously; estimating the collusion channel and using this estimate to choose the score function [9, 17]; using a generalized linear decoder [1, 11, 36]; or settle for slightly less and use the suboptimal but 'universal' symmetric score function of Škorić et al. [50] which works almost the same for any collusion strategy. For small collusion sizes this score function does not perform that poorly [20, Figure 3], and it might make designing the scheme somewhat easier.

5.3 The classical group testing model

Let us further highlight how the sequential Tardos scheme and Wald's SPRT can behave very differently, by showing how both schemes apply to the classical group testing model. In group testing [12] one is tasked to identify the defective members $\mathcal{C}$ from a population $\mathcal{U}$ by performing group tests: testing a query group $\mathcal{Q} \subseteq \mathcal{U}$ returns a positive result if $\mathcal{Q} \cap \mathcal{C} \neq \emptyset$ and a negative result otherwise. Applications include blood testing for viruses, where pooling blood samples of several persons and testing this batch leads to a positive test result iff the virus is present in the tested batch. In terms of fingerprinting, this problem corresponds to dealing with the all-1 attack [29, 32, 34].

As described in [32], the Neyman-Pearson approach to the all-1 attack in fingerprinting leads to the following optimized decoder g:

$$g(x,y) = \begin{cases} \frac{1}{c}\ln(2) & \text{if } (x,y) = (0,0); \\ \ln\left(2 - 2^{-1/c}\right) & \text{if } (x,y) = (0,1); \\ -\infty & \text{if } (x,y) = (1,0); \\ \ln(2) & \text{if } (x,y) = (1,1). \end{cases} \qquad (20)$$

Note that this function does not depend on p anymore; to deal with the all-1 attack, it is best to replace the random bias generation using the arcsine distribution with a fixed bias $p \sim \frac{\ln 2}{c}$. In the non-adaptive, simple decoding setting, this leads to a required code length of $\ell \sim \frac{c \ln n}{(\ln 2)^2}$, while in the joint decoding setting the required code length becomes $\ell \sim c \log_2 n$, a factor $\ln 2$ less.

In Wald's scheme, choosing scheme parameters is done similarly as in Section 5.1. If we again consider the toy application of $c = 10$, $n = 1000$ and $\varepsilon_1 = 10^{-3}$ (with $\varepsilon_2 = 0$, not using a lower boundary), then we may again set $\eta_1 \approx 13.82$ and we are ready to use the scheme. Figure 8a shows an example simulation of this scheme with these parameters, using the all-1 score function from (20). For simplicity, we used the asymptotic approximation $p = (\ln 2)/c$ for generating the code.

In the sequential Tardos scheme, one would again first determine the point (ℓ, η) at which time a decision is taken(cf. Figure 2), and then draw the accusation threshold by drawing a line towards the y-axis, parallel to the line with the average innocent user scores. Note however that with this score function, the event $(x,y) = (1,0)$ is impossible for

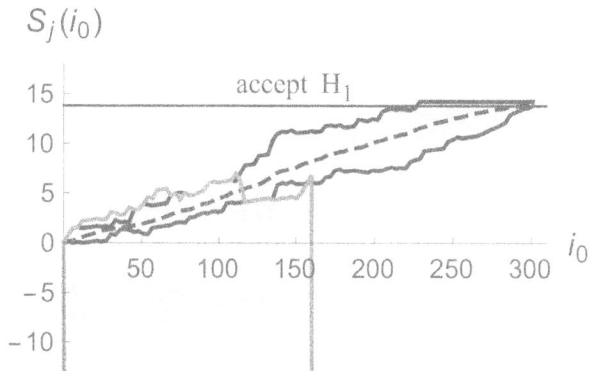

(a) Example of Wald's scheme: All-1 attack

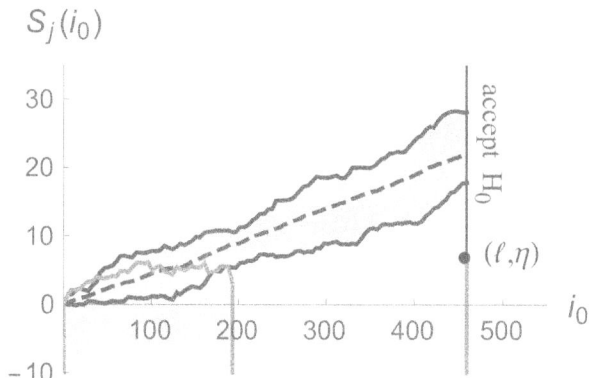

(b) Example of Tardos' scheme: All-1 attack

Figure 8: A simulation of the classical group testing model. The sequential Tardos scheme offers no improvement over non-adaptive group testing, and again Wald's scheme finds the defectives faster.

Characteristic	Wald	Tardos
Optimal (cf. Theorem 2)	✓	✗
Asymptotically optimal	✓	✓
No false negatives ($\varepsilon_2 = 0$)	✓	✗
Guaranteed decision at time ℓ	✗	✓
Parameters to choose	η_1	$\ell, \eta_1^{(0)}, \eta_1^{(\ell)}$
Simple relations for parameters	✓	✗
Better than non-ad. group testing	✓	✗

Table 1: A quick summary of various characteristics of Wald's SPRT and the sequential Tardos scheme. For Wald's scheme we assume we are not using a lower boundary η_0, i.e., we set $\varepsilon_2 = 0$ and $\eta_0 = -\infty$.

To compare some of the characteristics, Table 1 gives a quick summary of the various characteristics of both schemes. Here optimality refers to the optimality described in Theorem 2, and asymptotic optimality refers to the large n and large $c \ll n$ regime. Note that by setting $\varepsilon_2 = 0$ in Wald's scheme, we guarantee that eventually all colluders are always caught. This solution of an infinite accusation boundary comes at the cost of not knowing in advance how many segments are at most needed to reach a decision, although in practice this does not seem to be an issue. As we saw in Section 5, often choosing parameters is easier for Wald's scheme than for the sequential Tardos scheme; both because fewer parameters have to be chosen, and because there is a simple approximate relation between this single parameter η_1 and the error probability ε_1, which holds exactly if the scores behave like true Brownian motions. We further saw that for the sequential group testing setting, the sequential Tardos scheme offers no improvement over non-adaptive decoding (while Wald's scheme does).

Finally, as mentioned before, Wald's scheme has already been studied since the 1940s, with many books appearing on the topic ever since [3, 10, 21, 25, 38, 47, 59, 61], while the sequential Tardos scheme [28] was more of an ad-hoc construction to build a scheme that works well in adaptive settings as well. With Wald's scheme being easier to design, in many cases performing better than the sequential Tardos scheme (performing optimally well), and being backed by decades of research on the topic (allowing practitioners to tweak the scheme to their needs using known results from the literature), it seems that Wald's scheme is a more practical choice than the sequential Tardos scheme.

In this paper we further settled an important question on the optimality of these schemes (i.e., both schemes are asymptotically optimal in the sequential setting), but one important open question remains: is it possible to design truly adaptive fingerprinting schemes that perform even better than these sequential designs? Or are the sequential schemes discussed in this paper also optimal in the adaptive setting? This is left as an open problem for future work.

a guilty user (if a member $j \in \mathcal{C}$ has $(\mathbf{x}_j)_i = 1$, then by definition $y_i = 1$ as well), and so if this event occurs we know for sure that this user is innocent, and we assign the user a score of $g(1, 0) = -\infty$. Since the probability that this event occurs for innocent users is a positive constant, it immediately follows that $\mu_0 = -\infty$. As a consequence, the accusation threshold starting from (ℓ, η) with a slope of $-\mu_0 = \infty$ becomes a vertical line upwards. This is illustrated in Figure 8b which shows an example application of the sequential Tardos scheme with the same parameters as in Wald's scheme. The provable bounds from [32, Theorem 3] and Theorem 1 lead to $\ell \approx 459$ and $\eta_1^{(\ell)} \approx 6.91$.

6. WALD VS. TARDOS: AN OVERVIEW

Let us conclude with a brief overview of the two solutions for the sequential fingerprinting game. For simplicity, we will compare the sequential Tardos scheme with Wald's scheme without a lower boundary, as that seems to be the most convenient solution in fingerprinting. Note that although the sequential Tardos scheme is different from Wald's basic description of the sequential probability ratio test procedure, it could be considered a variant of the latter; truncating the thresholds was already considered by Wald himself, and using different shapes for the stopping boundary has been discussed extensively in various literature on the SPRT.

7. REFERENCES

[1] E. Abbe, L. Zheng. Linear universal decoding for compound channels. *IEEE Transactions on Information Theory*, 56(12):5999–6013, 2012.

[2] E. Amiri and G. Tardos. High rate fingerprinting codes and the fingerprinting capacity. In *SODA*, pp. 336–345, 2009.

[3] J. Bartroff, T. L. Lai, and M.-C. Shih. *Sequential experimentation in clinical trials*. Springer, 2013.

[4] W. Berchtold and M. Schäfer. Performance and code length optimization of joint decoding Tardos fingerprinting. In *MM&Sec*, pp. 27–32, 2012.

[5] O. Berkman, M. Parnas, and J. Sgall. Efficient dynamic traitor tracing. *SIAM Journal on Computing*, 30(6):1802–1828, 2001.

[6] O. Blayer and T. Tassa. Improved versions of Tardos' fingerprinting scheme. *Designs, Codes and Cryptography*, 48(1):79–103, 2008.

[7] D. Boneh and J. Shaw. Collusion-secure fingerprinting for digital data. *IEEE Transactions on Information Theory*, 44(5):1897–1905, 1998.

[8] M. Bun, J. Ullman, and S. Vadhan. Fingerprinting codes and the price of approximate differential privacy. In *STOC*, pp. 1–10, 2014.

[9] A. Charpentier, F. Xie, C. Fontaine, and T. Furon. Expectation maximization decoding of Tardos probabilistic fingerprinting code. In *SPIE Proceedings*, 7254:1–15, 2009.

[10] H. Chernoff. *Sequential analysis and optimal design*. SIAM, 1972.

[11] M. Desoubeaux, C. Herzet, W. Puech, and G. Le Guelvouit. Enhanced blind decoding of Tardos codes with new MAP-based functions. In *MMSP*, pp. 283–288, 2013.

[12] R. Dorfman. The detection of defective members of large populations. *The Annals of Mathematical Statistics*, 14(4):436–440, 1943.

[13] C. Dwork, K. Talwar, A. Thakurta, and L. Zhang. Analyze Gauss: Optimal bounds for privacy-preserving principal component analysis. In *STOC*, pp. 11–20, 2014.

[14] A. Fiat and T. Tassa. Dynamic traitor tracing. *Journal of Cryptology*, 14(3):354–371, 2001.

[15] T. Furon, A. Guyader, and F. Cérou. On the design and optimization of Tardos probabilistic fingerprinting codes. In *IH*, pp. 341–356, 2008.

[16] T. Furon, L. Pérez-Freire, A. Guyader, and F. Cérou. Estimating the minimal length of Tardos code. In *IH*, pp. 176–190, 2009.

[17] T. Furon and L. Pérez-Freire. EM decoding of Tardos traitor tracing codes. In *MMSec*, pp. 99–106, 2009.

[18] T. Furon and L. Pérez-Freire. Worst case attacks against binary probabilistic traitor tracing codes. In *WIFS*, pp. 56–60, 2009.

[19] T. Furon, A. Guyader, and F. Cérou. Decoding fingerprints using the Markov Chain Monte Carlo method. In *WIFS*, pp. 187–192, 2012.

[20] T. Furon and M. Desoubeaux. Tardos codes for real. In *WIFS*, 2014.

[21] Z. Govindarajulu. *Sequential statistics*. World Scientific, 2004.

[22] Y.-W. Huang and P. Moulin. Saddle-point solution of the fingerprinting capacity game under the marking assumption. In *ISIT*, pp. 2256–2260, 2009.

[23] Y.-W. Huang and P. Moulin. On the saddle-point solution and the large-coalition asymptotics of fingerprinting games. *IEEE Transactions on Inf. For. and Security*, 7(1):160–175, 2012.

[24] S. Ibrahimi, B. Škorić, and J.-J. Oosterwijk. Riding the saddle point: Asymptotics of the capacity-achieving simple decoder for bias-based traitor tracing. *EURASIP Journal on Information Security*, 1(12):1–11, 2014.

[25] C. Jennison and B. W. Turnbull. *Group sequential methods with applications to clinical trials*. Chapman and Hall, 2000.

[26] M. Kuribayashi. Bias equalizer for binary probabilistic fingerprinting codes. In *IH*, pp. 269–283, 2011.

[27] T. Laarhoven and B. de Weger. Discrete distributions in the Tardos scheme, revisited. In *IH&MMSec*, pp. 13–18, 2013.

[28] T. Laarhoven, J. Doumen, P. Roelse, B. Škorić, and B. de Weger. Dynamic Tardos traitor tracing schemes. *IEEE Transactions on Information Theory*, 59(7):4230–4242, 2013.

[29] T. Laarhoven. Efficient probabilistic group testing based on traitor tracing. In *Allerton*, pp. 1358–1365, 2013.

[30] T. Laarhoven. Dynamic traitor tracing schemes, revisited. In *WIFS*, pp. 191–196, 2013.

[31] T. Laarhoven and B. de Weger. Optimal symmetric Tardos traitor tracing schemes. *Designs, Codes and Cryptography*, 71(1):83–103, 2014.

[32] T. Laarhoven. Capacities and capacity-achieving decoders for various fingerprinting games. In *IH&MMSec*, pp. 123–134, 2014.

[33] T. Laarhoven. Asymptotics of fingerprinting and group testing: Non-adaptive channel capacities. *IEEE Transactions on Information Forensics and Security*, 2015.

[34] P. Meerwald and T. Furon. Towards joint Tardos decoding: The 'Don Quixote' algorithm. In *IH*, pp. 28–42, 2011.

[35] P. Meerwald and T. Furon. Group testing meets traitor tracing. In *ICASSP*, pp. 4204–4207, 2011.

[36] P. Meerwald and T. Furon. Toward practical joint decoding of binary Tardos fingerprinting codes. *IEEE Transactions on Information Forensics and Security*, 7(4):1168–1180, 2012.

[37] P. Moulin. Universal fingerprinting: Capacity and random-coding exponents. *arXiv:0801.3837v3*, 2011.

[38] N. Mukhopadhyay and B. M. de Silva. *Sequential methods and their applications*. CRC Press, 2009.

[39] K. Nuida, M. Hagiwara, H. Watanabe, and H. Imai. Optimization of Tardos's fingerprinting codes in a viewpoint of memory amount. In *IH*, pp. 279–293, 2007.

[40] K. Nuida, S. Fujitsu, M. Hagiwara, T. Kitagawa, H. Watanabe, K. Ogawa, and H. Imai. An improvement of discrete Tardos fingerprinting codes. *Designs, Codes and Cryptogr.*, 52(3):339–362, 2009.

[41] J.-J. Oosterwijk, B. Škorić, and J. Doumen. Optimal suspicion functions for Tardos traitor tracing schemes. In *IH&MMSec*, pp. 19–28, 2013.

[42] J.-J. Oosterwijk, B. Škorić, and J. Doumen. A capacity-achieving simple decoder for bias-based traitor tracing schemes. *Cryptology ePrint Archive, Report 2013/389*, 2013.

[43] J.-J. Oosterwijk, J. Doumen, and T. Laarhoven. Tuple decoders for traitor tracing schemes. In *SPIE Proceedings*, 2014.

[44] L. Pérez-Freire and T. Furon. Blind decoder for binary probabilistic traitor tracing codes. In *WIFS*, pp. 46–50, 2009.

[45] P. Roelse. Dynamic subtree tracing and its application in pay-TV systems. *Int. J. Inf. Security* 10(3):173–187, 2011.

[46] R. Safavi-Naini and Y. Wang. Sequential traitor tracing. *IEEE Transactions on Information Theory*, 49(5):1319–1326, 2003.

[47] D. Siegmund. *Sequential analysis, tests and confidence intervals*. Springer, 1985.

[48] A. Simone and B. Škorić. Asymptotically false-positive-maximizing attack on non-binary Tardos codes. In *IH*, pp. 14–27, 2011.

[49] B. Škorić, T. U. Vladimirova, M. U. Celik, and J. C. Talstra. Tardos fingerprinting is better than we thought. *IEEE Transactions on Information Theory*, 54(8):3663–3676, 2008.

[50] B. Škorić, S. Katzenbeisser, and M. U. Celik. Symmetric Tardos fingerprinting codes for arbitrary alphabet sizes. *Designs, Codes and Cryptography*, 46(2):137–166, 2008.

[51] B. Škorić, J.-J. Oosterwijk, and J. Doumen. The holey grail: A special score function for non-binary traitor tracing. In *WIFS*, pp. 180–185, 2013.

[52] B. Škorić. Simple-looking joint decoders for traitor tracing and group testing. *Cryptology ePrint Archive, Report 2014/781*, 2014.

[53] M. Sobel and A. Wald. A sequential decision procedure for choosing one of three hypotheses. *The Annals of Mathematical Stat.*, 20(4):502–522, 1949.

[54] T. Steinke and J. Ullman. Interactive fingerprinting codes and the hardness of preventing false discovery. *arXiv:1410.1228*, 2014.

[55] G. Tardos. Optimal probabilistic fingerprint codes. *Journal of the ACM*, 55(2):1–24, 2008.

[56] T. Tassa. Low bandwidth dynamic traitor tracing schemes. *Journal of Cryptology*, 18(2):167–183, 2005.

[57] J. Ullman. Answering $n^{2+o(1)}$ counting queries with differential privacy is hard. In *STOC*, pp. 361–370, 2013.

[58] A. Wald. Sequential tests of statistical hypotheses. *The Annals of Mathematical Stat.*, 16(2):117–186, 1945.

[59] A. Wald. *Sequential analysis*. John Wiley and Sons, 1947 (1st edition), Dover Publications, 2013 (reprint).

[60] A. Wald and J. Wolfowitz. Optimum character of the sequential probability ratio test. *The Annals of Mathematical Statistics*, 19(3):326–339, 1948.

[61] G. B. Wetherill and K. D. Glazebrook. *Sequential methods in statistics*. Chapman and Hall, 1986.

APPENDIX

LEMMA 1. *Suppose that:*

- *the encoder uses the arcsine distribution encoder;*
- *the collusion channel is the interleaving attack $\boldsymbol{\theta}_{int}$;*
- *the decoder is the interleaving log-likelihood decoder.*

Then the expected score of an innocent user (μ_1) in a single segment is asymptotically given by:

$$\mu_0 = \mathbb{E}_{x,y,p}\left[g(x,y,p) \mid H_1\right] \sim -\frac{1}{2c^2}. \qquad (21)$$

PROOF. For μ_0, we write out the expectation:

$$\mu_0 = \mathbb{E}_{x,y,p}\left[g(x,y,p) \mid H_1\right] \qquad (22)$$

$$= \int_0^1 \frac{\mathrm{d}p}{\pi\sqrt{p(1-p)}} \left[p^2 \ln\left(1 + \frac{1-p}{cp}\right)\right. \qquad (23)$$

$$\left. + 2p(1-p)\ln\left(1 - \frac{1}{c}\right) + (1-p)^2 \ln\left(1 + \frac{p}{c(1-p)}\right)\right]. \qquad (24)$$

Similarly, we can write out the definition of the average colluder score in a single segment as:

$$\mu_1 = \int_0^1 \frac{\mathrm{d}p}{\pi\sqrt{p(1-p)}} \left[p^2 \left(1 + \frac{1-p}{cp}\right)\ln\left(1 + \frac{1-p}{cp}\right)\right. \qquad (25)$$

$$+ 2p(1-p)\left(1 - \frac{1}{c}\right)\ln\left(1 - \frac{1}{c}\right) \qquad (26)$$

$$\left. + (1-p)^2 \left(1 + \frac{p}{c(1-p)}\right)\ln\left(1 + \frac{p}{c(1-p)}\right)\right]. \qquad (27)$$

Combining these results, and merging the logarithms into one term, we obtain the following expression for $\mu_1 - \mu_0$:

$$\mu_1 - \mu_0 = \int_0^1 \frac{\sqrt{p(1-p)}\,\mathrm{d}p}{\pi c}\ln\left(1 + \frac{c}{(c-1)^2 p(1-p)}\right). \qquad (28)$$

Since we know that $\mu_1 \sim \frac{1}{2c^2}$, we need to prove that the right hand side is asymptotically similar to $\frac{1}{c^2}$. Rearranging terms, we thus need to prove that

$$I \stackrel{\text{def}}{=} \int_0^1 \mathrm{d}p\,\sqrt{p(1-p)}\ln\left(1 + \frac{c}{(c-1)^2 p(1-p)}\right) \sim \frac{\pi}{c}. \qquad (29)$$

First, using $\ln(1+x) < x$ for all $x > 0$, we obtain:

$$I < \int_0^1 \frac{c\,\mathrm{d}p}{(c-1)^2\sqrt{p(1-p)}} = \frac{\pi c}{(c-1)^2} \sim \frac{\pi}{c}. \qquad (30)$$

To get a matching lower bound, we first reduce the range of integration from $[0,1]$ to $[\delta, 1-\delta]$ for some $\delta > 0$, noting that the integrand is strictly positive:

$$I > \int_\delta^{1-\delta} \mathrm{d}p\,\sqrt{p(1-p)}\ln\left(1 + \frac{c}{(c-1)^2 p(1-p)}\right). \qquad (31)$$

Choosing $\delta = \frac{1}{\sqrt{c}}$, the term inside the logarithm is small and the following bound is tight enough to obtain the result:

$$I \gtrsim \int_\delta^{1-\delta} \frac{c\,\mathrm{d}p}{(c-1)^2\sqrt{p(1-p)}} \sim \frac{\pi}{c} - \frac{4}{\pi c}\arcsin\sqrt{\delta} \to \frac{\pi}{c}. \qquad (32)$$

This proves that $I \sim \frac{\pi}{c}$, hence $\mu_0 \sim -\frac{1}{2c^2}$. $\square$

Universal Threshold Calculation for Fingerprinting Decoders using Mixture Models

Marcel Schäfer
Fraunhofer Institute for Secure
Information Technology SIT
Rheinstr. 75, 64295
Darmstadt, Germany
schaefer@sit.fraunhofer.de

Sebastian Mair
Technische Universität
Darmstadt
Department of Computer
Science
Darmstadt, Germany
sebastian.mair@stud.tu-darmstadt.de

Waldemar Berchtold
Fraunhofer Institute for Secure
Information Technology SIT
Rheinstr. 75, 64295
Darmstadt, Germany
berchtold@sit.fraunhofer.de

Martin Steinebach
Fraunhofer Institute for Secure
Information Technology SIT
Rheinstr. 75, 64295
Darmstadt, Germany
steinebach@sit.fraunhofer.de

ABSTRACT

Collusion attacks on watermarked media copies are commonly countered by probabilistically generated fingerprinting codes and appropriate tracing algorithms. The latter calculates accusation scores representing the suspiciousness of the fingerprints. In a 'detect many' scenario a threshold decides which scores are associated to the colluders. This work proposes a universal method to calculate thresholds for different decoders solely with knowledge of the accusation scores from the actual attack. Applying mixture models on the scores, the threshold is set up satisfying the selected error probabilities. It is independent from the fingerprint generation and can be applied at any decoder. Also no knowledge about the number of attackers or their strategy is needed.

Categories and Subject Descriptors

E.4 [**Coding and Information Theory**]: Nonsecret encoding schemes

General Terms

Algorithms, Security, Verification

Keywords

digital watermarking; traitor tracing; collusion attacks; fingerprinting codes; mixture models

1. INTRODUCTION

To counter copyright infringements, media watermarking is widely accepted. By embedding a unique identifier into every media copy sold, distributors are able to identify malicious customers that re-distribute their copies unauthorized. To prevent this, malicious customers unite and create fraudulent media copies by mixing their copies. Thus, the resulting copy does not contain a decent watermark identifying one or more of the originators, but a mixture of theirs. This manipulated watermark cannot be traced back. A solution is given by collusion secure fingerprinting codes. A fingerprinting code is a set of probabilistically generated codewords, called the fingerprints. Each fingerprint is embedded into the content as an individual identifier via watermarking techniques. Fingerprinting consists of three fingerprinting specific processes: The fingerprinting code generation, the collusion/attack channel, and the tracing algorithm. Integrated into watermarking applications in practice this gives the five processes that form the fingerprinting scheme: Fingerprint generation, watermark embedding, collusion/attack channel, watermark detection and tracing algorithm. The fingerprint generation is to be initiated before the watermark embedding process. The fingerprints are embedded as watermark messages into the media copies. The collusion channel mirrors the phase when the copies are purchased so that the distributor has no longer control of what happens with the copies, i.e. what attacks are made to them through fraudulent behavior. Once an attacked copy is found, the watermark detection process reads out the message contained. In case if no direct match was found within the fingerprint database, the tracing algorithm starts. It runs a decoder calculating accusation scores for each fingerprint (or tuple of fingerprints). These scores reflect probabilities of having contributed to the collusion. Finally the tracing algorithm outputs the most suspicious (tuple of) fingerprint(s).

The drawback of all probabilistic fingerprinting codes is their enormous code length compared to the limited payload provided by the media copy and the watermarking algorithm applied.

Hence, a lot of research was done in order to optimize fingerprinting codes and to shorten the code length. Optimizing means improving the fingerprint code generation and/or the tracing algorithm. For the latter one way is employing a more discriminative decoder, i.e. score functions that calculate accusation scores better isolating those of colluder-fingerprints from those of innocent-fingerprints.

Besides a discriminative decoder, many tracing algorithms utilize an appropriate threshold for distinguishing between the scores of innocent-fingerprints and colluder-fingerprints.

In this work we do not propose any optimization on the fingerprint generation or on the decoder. However, from a practical perspective, we introduce a new method to calculate the threshold. We solely consider the distribution of the accusation scores and apply two-component mixture models to distinguish the scores of innocents and those of colluders. The advantages of our proposed method are: (i) it can be applied at any code generation, (ii) it can be applied at any decoder/score calculation, (iii) it does not require knowledge of the collusion/attack strategy and (iv) it also works in cases in which the actual number of colluders strongly deviates from the maximum number the code was originally designed for.

2. RELATED WORK

Most approaches dealing with traitor tracing or active fingerprinting [4] follow the so called *marking assumption*, introduced by *Boneh* and *Shaw* [4] or a relaxed version of it. This assumption says that attackers in order to avoid perceptual artifacts in the media only manipulate in positions where their copies differ from each other, and leave all other positions untouched. Now downscaling to fingerprinting, this means, they only attack in positions in which their fingerprints have different symbols, referred to as *detectable positions*. With a strict interpretation of the marking assumption, the colluders decide between those symbols provided by the detectable positions (*restricted digit model* [22]). A relaxed interpretation of the marking assumption (*combined digit model* [21]), additionally allows symbols induced by averaging over symbols from the respective detectable positions[1] and erasure symbols for the manipulated fingerprint, i.e. positions not carrying any (useful) information at all [21], [13].

In literature most efforts are focused on the asymptotic (very large collusions) optimal code. That is, making the best of the two-party maxmin game between code designers and attackers. In other words: Generating the code that is the best *defense* against the best (in terms of most vicious) *attack*. This is known as the *fingerprinting-capacity* declared by *Moulin* and *O'Sullivan* [14]. The seminal work of probabilistic or bias-based fingerprinting codes is the well known *Tardos Codes* introduced by *Tardos* [19] proving that a fingerprinting scheme must satisfy $l \propto c^2 \ln n\varepsilon_1^{-1}$ for a large number of fingerprints n, with code length l, number of colluders c and upper bound on the probability of accusing a specific innocent ε_1. It followed a long list of descendants, that proposed optimizations by sharpening the bounds ([22], [15], [16], [9]), improving the distribution function ([5], [1],

[7]) or introducing a more discriminative or practical accusation score function ([20], [10], [6], [17]).

For very large collusions, the arcsine distribution for generating fingerprinting codes – as suggested by *Tardos* for binary fingerprints already in [19] – achieves the capacity bound as independently proven by *Amiri* and *Tardos* [1] and *Huang* and *Moulin* [7] for binary alphabets and is therefore the optimal choice. As they further prove the interleaving attack to be the asymptotic optimal attack [8], and as *Oosterwijk et al.* prove the score function in [17] to be the best *defense* against this attack, the game seemed solved[2]. In [16], they prove that this score function achieves capacity, which means with this choice of encoder [19] and decoder [17], they achieve asymptotic optimal code lengths for binary fingerprints of $l \sim 2c^2 \ln n\varepsilon_1^{-1}$. Recently, *Laarhoven* [11] published another score function also achieving capacity and additionally getting rid of the cutoff parameter. The two latter scoring functions among others serve as proof of the approach in section 5.

Other approaches in literature concentrate on more realistic (not asymptotically large) parameters in order to better match real world requirements. Many put their focus on the tracing algorithm (decoder). The standard decoder in most fingerprinting schemes (including the above mentioned) calculates scores per fingerprint that assesses its involvement in pertaining the generation of the manipulated fingerprint detected from the unauthorized media copy. As the score for each fingerprint is calculated independently of (the scores of) other fingerprints, this type of decoder is referred to as *single decoder*. Other decoders follow a *joint decoding* strategy, which means calculating scores for tupels of fingerprints, e.g. *Meerwald* and *Furon* [13]. Joint decoding is agreed upon to perform better than single decoders, but the increment in performance goes along with an increase in computational complexity. Some decoders estimate the collusion strategy or collusion size in order to include side information to the score calculation [12]. They also employed iterative single and joint decoding approaches [12], [13], both resulting in improved error rates. The downside of these approaches is the increase in complexity and its strong dependency on the correctness of the estimation of the collusion strategy.

This work also concentrates on the decoder. We follow the idea of *Furon* and *Pérez-Freire* [6] who made use of the Expectation-Maximization (EM) algorithm inside the decoder. Whereas [6] used the EM in order to gain knowledge of the collusion attack strategy, we focus on the accusation scores. Applying mixture models, we estimate the actual distribution of the accusation scores for a given model and thereby we are able to calculate feasible thresholds for every type of decoder. The benefit from this threshold calculation is, that it is adjusted to the actual case of collusion attack and that it does not depend on the collusion strategy.

3. SCENARIO DESCRIPTION

We follow the common assumption that the available watermark payload l equals the fingerprint length. Given this value l, we have to find the most appropriate trade-off between the desired false alarm rate ε_1 (we accuse an innocent) and no alarm rate ε_2 (we cannot accuse any colluder) and the chosen maximum number of colluders we want to resist c_0. From this we must choose an appropriate fingerprinting

---

[1]For binary fingerprints, both models are equal

[2]For the respective model and parameters

scheme. For simplification we will assume that the number of expected customers n is equal to the number of customers up to the time an unauthorized version is found.

Hence, the $n \times l$ fingerprint matrix X consists of n fingerprints $X_1, ..., X_n$, where each fingerprint is composed of l positions: $X_j = (X_{j,i})_{i=1,...,l}$ from $\{0,1\}^l$ for $j = 1, ..., n$. In biased-based fingerprinting, one decides between *continuous* generation and *discrete* generation, representing the selection of the distribution that prescribes the filling of the columns of X via a continuous distribution function [19], [5], or via discrete nodes respectively, as for instance [15].

In a collusion attack different copies of the same content, each containing an individual watermark, are compared in order to detect differences. These detected differences are assumed to be evoked by the individual watermark information contained in each copy. In order to generate a copy of high quality that carries untraceable watermark information, the new copy differs from its originator copies only in those detected positions (due to the *marking assumption*, see section 2). Note that we do not consider any specific watermarking operation and attack the attackers could run in addition after (or before) the collusion attack (see for instance [18]), because its impact on the detected watermark heavily depends on the underlaying watermarking system.

With X_c is denoted the $c \times l$ colluder matrix consisting of those rows of X that were associated to the colluders, namely the colluder-fingerprints. Its row indices represent the set of colluders C. Our method has been tested against the *majority vote attack*, where the attackers always chose the symbol appearing most in the respective column of X_c, against the *minority vote attack*, where the least appearing symbol is taken, and against the *interleaving attack*, for which the symbols are taken in turns from each colluder. Note that – due to lack of space – we only show results for the interleaving attack. Results for the other attack strategies differ only negligible.

A basic tracing algorithm is fed with y, X^3, and the fingerprinting parameters ε_1, ε_2 and c_0. Its output Ξ is either an empty set or a set of suspected fingerprints. We distinguish between three cases:

i) $C \cap \Xi = \emptyset$: No colluder fingerprint is suspected (false negative error). **ii)** $\Xi \setminus C \neq \emptyset$: There are innocent fingerprints among the suspected (false positive error). **iii)** $\Xi \neq \emptyset \wedge \Xi \subseteq C$: All suspected fingerprints pertained to the collusion. Note that if Ξ solely consists of innocent-fingerprints, we count it as false positive error only, although this is as well a false negative error.

The tracing algorithm applies a scoring function to measure the suspiciousness of single fingerprints (single decoder) or tuples of fingerprints (joint decoder). Thereby each fingerprint X_j or tuple of fingerprints X_T is associated a certain accusation score S_j or S_T. The higher the score, the higher its probability to have pertained to the collusion. Which fingerprints are sorted into the set of suspected fingerprints Ξ is frequently decided by means of a threshold Z ('detect many'). The fingerprints with scores larger than the threshold are suspected and sorted to Ξ. Other schemes consider solely the one fingerprint or the one tuple with the highest score ('detect one'). The scores can be grouped into two clusters, the one that is associated to the scores of innocent-fingerprints, and the one that is associated to the scores of colluder-fingerprints. In a detect many scenario, to reveal the colluder-fingerprints and not suspect innocents, the goal is to find the score function that best discriminates these clusters and to set up the threshold so that it clearly separates these according to the desired error probabilities.

However, in the majority of fingerprinting schemes, the threshold is calculated using the fingerprinting parameters the distributor selected in advance, ergo the threshold is fixed. This is suboptimal for several reasons. For instance, a pre-calculated threshold is always subject to statistical deviations within the scores that are likely to appear. Also, the scores achieved while applying the – asymptotic optimal – score functions of [17] or [11] vary with different attack strategies and so do their distributions [9]. For this reason it is not sound to apply a pre-calculated fixed threshold based on the expectation values. A threshold calculation based on the actual scores in the actual case of collusion attack seems beneficial. Recently, *Ibrahimi et al.* [9] proposed a threshold computation in case of – asymptotic optimal – interleaving attacks, and they show how the threshold has to be scaled with the variance of innocent-fingerprints' accusation scores. The threshold calculation yields proper results, even though it was tailored for the asymptotic behavior of the 'Oosterwijk' score function [17] utilizing expectation values of the moments of the scores. In section 5 we compare this approach to our threshold calculation.

4. THRESHOLD CALCULATION VIA MIXTURE MODELS

The threshold calculation as proposed in this section can be seen as a universal method for any decoder that aims at discriminating innocent-fingerprints' scores from colluder-fingerprints' scores. It solely works with the scores calculated in the actual case of collusion attack and is independent of the conducted attack. It does not need any information about the collusion strategy and its size.

In section 5 we evaluate our threshold calculation for some exemplary simple decoders [13], [20], [17] and [11]. The proposed tracing algorithm starts calculating the accusation scores applying the selected decoder. For distributors or copyright holders, the collusion strategy and its size is a priori unknown (but could be estimated, e.g. [13]). What is known is, that there are always two groups within the scores, colluder-scores and innocent-scores. It has to be at least one customer who uploaded the media copy containing the watermark message, i.e. containing the fingerprint. Based on this, we suggest a two-component mixture model. Such mixture models are linear superpositions of (two) arbitrary distributions that interfere with each other. We want one distribution to represent the scores of the innocent-fingerprints and the other distribution to represent the scores of the colluder-fingerprints.

4.1 Two-Component Mixture Model

A two-component mixture model is defined as

$$\rho(x|\Theta) = \alpha_1 \rho_1(x|\theta_1) + \alpha_2 \rho_2(x|\theta_2) \qquad (1)$$

for ρ_1, ρ_2 denoting static probability density functions with parameter sets θ_1 and θ_2 and where $\alpha_1 > 0$ and $\alpha_2 > 0$ are the associated weight parameters that satisfy $\alpha_1 + \alpha_2 = 1$. The total parameter set is denoted as $\Theta := \{\alpha_1, \theta_1, \alpha_2, \theta_2\}$.

---

[3]Knowing X, we also know the probabilities $p_1,..., p_l$ from the column generation

We decide for mixture models consisting of two normal distributions, referred to as *Gaussian Mixture Model* (GMM) [2]. These are adjusted to the two clusters that represent the scores of innocent-fingerprints and colluder-fingerprints. The choice for a Gaussian mixture model is assumed as sound. Already in [22] it was shown that by construction the *Tardos* codes yield curves for the scores of innocent-fingerprints and of colluder-fingerprints, that are assumed as normally distributed. Hence the probability functions of equation (1) are normal distributions $\rho_r(x|\theta_r) = \mathcal{N}(x|\mu_r, \sigma_r^2)$ with distribution parameters $\theta_r = \{\mu_r, \sigma_r^2\}$ for $r \in \{1, 2\}$. The goal is to determine the parameter set, containing the mean and the variance for each component. This is achieved applying the iterative *Expectation Maximization* (EM) algorithm. Thereby we are able to find a *maximum likelihood estimator* for the parameters of the mixture distribution that represents the accusation scores. The construction is as follows:

1. **Initialization:** Estimate the first parameter set: $\Theta^{(0)} = \{\alpha_1, \mu_1, \sigma_1^2, \alpha_2, \mu_2, \sigma_2^2\}$.

2. **Expectation step:** In step k, calculate $\tau_{1,j}^{(k)}$ and $\tau_{2,j}^{(k)}$ for all $j \in \{1, ..., n\}$ as

$$\tau_{r,j}^{(k)} := \rho(r|x_j, \Theta^{(k)}) = \frac{\alpha_r^{(k)} \mathcal{N}(x_j|\mu_r^{(k)}, \sigma_r^{2,(k)})}{\sum_{i=1}^{2} \alpha_i^{(k)} \mathcal{N}(x_j|\mu_i^{(k)}, \sigma_i^{2,(k)})}$$

3. **Maximization step:** In step k, calculate the weight parameters $\alpha_1^{(k+1)}$ and $\alpha_2^{(k+1)}$, the means $\mu_1^{(k+1)}$ and $\mu_2^{(k+1)}$ and the variances $\sigma_1^{2,(k+1)}$ and $\sigma_2^{2,(k+1)}$ as follows:

$$\alpha_r^{(k+1)} = \frac{1}{n} \sum_{j=1}^{n} \tau_{r,j}^{(k)}$$

$$\mu_r^{(k+1)} = \frac{\sum_{j=1}^{n} x_j \tau_{r,j}^{(k)}}{\sum_{j=1}^{n} \tau_{r,j}^{(k)}} \quad (2)$$

$$\sigma_r^{2,(k+1)} = \frac{\sum_{j=1}^{n} (x_j - \mu_r^{(k+1)})^2 \tau_{r,j}^{(k)}}{\sum_{j=1}^{n} \tau_{r,j}^{(k)}}$$

Update the parameter set $\Theta^{(k+1)}$.

4. **Abort criteria:** Check for convergence of the log-likelihood given by

$$\ln \rho(\mathcal{X}|\Theta) = \sum_{j=1}^{n} \ln \left[\sum_{i=1}^{2} \alpha_i \mathcal{N}(x_j|\mu_i, \sigma_i^2) \right].$$

4.2 Threshold determination

The parameter set Θ contains the estimated mean μ_1 of the scores of the innocent-fingerprints, now denoted as μ_{inn}, and the estimated mean μ_2 of the scores of colluder-fingerprints, now denoted as μ_C. Hence, the accordingly estimated parameters σ_1^2 and σ_2^2 are matched to the appropriate parameters for the variance of the innocent-fingerprints' scores $\sigma_1^2 = \sigma_{\text{inn}}^2$ and of the variance of colluder-fingerprints' scores $\sigma_2^2 = \sigma_C^2$. Note that, if applied in practice, these parameters come from the actual case of collusion attack. This is contrary to a priori computed expectation values, what is common sense in literature where the focus is on asymptotic (very large collusions) behavior of the code.

The crucial task is to suffice the selected bounds on false positive and false negative error, ε_1 and ε_2. In literature, ε_2 is frequently set to 0.5, e.g. [20], so it is in this work. Hence, the primary idea is to establish the estimated mean $\mu_2 = \mu_C$ of the second component of the mixture distribution as upper bound for the new dynamic threshold. Note that this choice of a threshold is motivated by the choice of Škorić *et al.* [20], where the probabilistic mean of the estimated colluder-fingerprints' scores was taken. On the other side, the threshold ought to be larger than the highest score among the innocent-fingerprints. Assuming a standard normal distribution an error of ε_1 is achieved at $\text{Erf}^{\text{inv}}(1 - \varepsilon_1)$. Mapped to the fingerprint construction analysis according to [20] this gives a lower bound for the threshold at $\Psi := \text{Erf}^{\text{inv}}(1 - \varepsilon_1) \cdot \sqrt{2} \cdot \sigma_{\text{inn}} + \mu_{\text{inn}}$. For lack of space we will not go into technical details here, but refer the reader to [20], where this has been widely studied. This means, if holds $\Psi < \mu_C$, the threshold satisfying ε_1 and ε_2 lies in the corresponding interval $[\Psi, \mu_C]$. Results for the limits of this interval, i.e. for $Z = \mu_C$ and $Z = \Psi$ are presented in section 5. To suffice ε_1 and ε_2, any choice within this interval is feasible. In practice, the distributor or copyright holder has the choice, for instance, to select a 'conservative' setting of the threshold (i.e. $Z = \mu_C$) in order to be sure not to suspect any innocents. Or he could select an 'offensive' setting (i.e. $Z = \Psi$), in order to catch as many colluders as possible. Scores exceeding the threshold Z are sorted into the set of suspicious fingerprints Ξ.

5. EVALUATION

Setting the threshold by means of mixture models solely requires the actual scores of the current collusion attack. Its application does not depend on the digit model or on the alphabet size. Therefore, we tested our method selecting the scenario most discussed in literature, which is also the *simplest* one: binary fingerprints that are traced by means of single decoders in the restricted digit model.

We tested our threshold calculation with the decoders of Škorić *et al.* [20], Oosterwijk *et al.* [17] and Laarhoven [11] by means of the Matlab toolbox for Tardos codes provided by *Furon*[4]. This choice is reasoned by the general acceptance of the decoder proposed in [20], and by the asymptotic optimality of the decoders in [17] and [11]. The results are depicted in table 1. The code length was set to $l = 12,248$, $22,912$ and $47,556$ for $c_0 = 15$, 21 and 31 respectively. The number of fingerprints was set to $n = 1,000$. The error bounds were set to $\varepsilon_1 = 1/n$ and $\varepsilon_2 = 1/2$. We ran 10,000 attacks per decoder and per selection of c, each with interleaving attack, minority vote and majority vote attack. The notation is as follows: Z^* refers to whether a threshold calculation according to [20] for the corresponding decoder in [20], or to a threshold calculation according to [9] for decoders proposed in [17] and [11]. FP stands for the average number of occurrences of the event of a false positive, i.e. an innocent that got accused. |C| denotes the average number of colluders accused in every attempt. Hence, the error bounds are satisfied if holds $\text{FP} \leq n\varepsilon_1$ and $|C| \geq c\varepsilon_2$.

For the sake of completeness and because of the eminent performance in practical settings we also specify results after 25 runs of each configuration for the iterative simple

---

[4] http://people.rennes.inria.fr/Teddy.Furon/website/software. html

Table 1: False positives (FP) and average number of colluders caught ($|C|$) for different decoders after interleaving attacks with $c_0 = 15$, 21 and 31 and varying actual collusion sizes c.

expected no. of colluders	actual no. of colluders	Threshold	Meerwald-Furon[13]		Škorić et al.[20]		Oosterwijk et al.[17]		Laarhoven[11]	
			FP	$|C|$	FP	$|C|$	FP	$|C|$	FP	$|C|$
$c_0 = 15$	$c = 13$	Z^*	0	1	0.21	12.82	0.05	9.74	0.00	9.83
		GMM^-	0	6.16	0.22	12.82	2.17	13.00	0.34	13.00
		GMM^+	0.32	13.00	0.00	6.38	0.05	7.51	0.00	6.47
	$c = 15$	Z^*	0	1	0.22	13.89	0.05	7.07	0.00	6.04
		GMM^-	0	7.44	0.23	13.88	2.20	14.98	0.34	14.99
		GMM^+	0.24	15.00	0.00	7.08	0.13	8.87	0.00	7.47
	$c = 18$	Z^*	0	1	0.21	13.21	0.05	3.66	0.00	1.83
		GMM^-	0	9.08	0.21	13.11	2.29	17.66	0.36	17.73
		GMM^+	0.28	17.76	0.02	7.80	0.37	11.18	0.00	8.95
$c_0 = 21$	$c = 18$	Z^*	0	1	0.24	17.70	0.01	14.15	0.00	14.37
		GMM^-	0	8.88	0.24	17.70	1.78	18.00	0.33	18.00
		GMM^+	0.36	18.00	0.00	8.86	0.00	9.55	0.00	8.94
	$c = 21$	Z^*	0	1	0.23	19.06	0.01	10.11	0.00	8.99
		GMM^-	0	10.32	0.23	19.04	1.80	20.97	0.33	20.98
		GMM^+	0.24	20.96	0.00	9.96	0.03	11.46	0.00	10.47
	$c = 24$	Z^*	0	1	0.23	18.43	0.01	6.22	0.00	4.09
		GMM^+	0	11.96	0.23	18.32	1.84	23.72	0.33	23.79
		GMM^-	0.52	23.68	0.01	10.88	0.10	13.60	0.00	11.92
$c_0 = 31$	$c = 24$	Z^*	0	1	0.24	23.88	0.00	22.48	0.00	22.81
		GMM^-	0	12.20	0.24	23.88	1.22	24.00	0.32	24.00
		GMM^+	0.40	24.00	0.00	11.92	0.00	11.69	0.00	11.93
	$c = 31$	Z^*	0	1	0.24	27.52	0.00	15.32	0.00	14.01
		GMM^-	0	15.28	0.24	27.46	1.23	30.95	0.31	30.97
		GMM^+	0.20	31.00	0.00	14.85	0.00	15.72	0.00	15.43
	$c = 38$	Z^*	0	1	0.23	24.21	0.00	6.69	0.00	3.92
		GMM^-	0	19.60	0.22	23.79	1.29	36.90	0.32	37.03
		GMM^+	0.28	37.16	0.05	16.93	0.03	20.25	0.00	18.82

decoder proposed in [13]. However, because of the computational complexity induced by the estimation of the collusion strategy, we stopped this decoder after the first iteration and accused the fingerprint with the highest score. Consequently, the false positive for Z^* is always zero and the number of colluders caught is always one. However, the discriminative nature of the decoder already separates colluder-fingerprints' scores out from innocent-fingerprints' scores such that a proper application of the GMMs is feasible.

We selected Ψ and μ_C as lower and upper threshold for the GMM, i.e. $GMM^- = \Psi$ and $GMM^+ = \mu_C$. As an initial guess of the parameter set $\Theta^{(0)}$ we considered the first component to be a standard normal distribution weighted with $\alpha_1 = (n - c_0)/n$, as most scores belong to innocent-fingerprints. The second component is therefore weighted with $\alpha_2 = 1 - \alpha_1$ and initialized with the maximal score to be the mean and with a variance of two.

Due to lack of space only results for the interleaving attack are depicted. Note that in the other attacks, the results for the GMMs are slightly better. The results achieved with the mixture models show competitive ability compared to the thresholds that are tailored to its scoring function. However,

the results for the decoder by *Oosterwijk et al.* [17] with $GMM^- = \Psi$ fall behind, as we cannot satisfy the requested bound on ε_1. Observations show that this is reasoned – for instance – by a skewness of the distribution of the scores. A reasonable approach to manage this problem would be to use mixture models of skew-normal distributions.

The false negative error rate (FN) is not listed in table 1 because the required upper bound ($\varepsilon_2 = 0.5$) was satisfied in all attacks and configurations for all tested decoders ($\varepsilon_2 = 0.5$). However, with the ordinary threshold calculation Z^* the FN rate was up to 0.14 (for $c > c_0$) for the 'Laarhoven'-decoder [11] and stayed below 10^{-3} for the 'Oosterwijk'-decoder [17], whereas the FN rate was zero in all parameter settings with GMM^+ and GMM^-.

6. CONCLUSION AND FUTURE WORK

In many scenarios, tracing of colluders in a fingerprinting scheme means calculating scores for all distributed fingerprints and deciding based on a threshold which fingerprints potentially belong to the colluders. We investigated a new method to calculate the threshold that separates the fingerprints identified as innocents from those that most likely pertained to the collusion. To do so, we employed two-component mixture models on the scores received from the current case of collusion attack. One component represents the distribution of innocent's scores, the other represents the distribution of colluders' scores. This way we provide an interval of possible thresholds that stay within the chosen error bounds ε_1 and ε_2. One major achievement of this work is a method that can be applied on any decoding function to separate innocents from colluders. It is independent of the conducted attack and of the fingerprint generation process. Moreover, the method does not need knowledge of the collusion strategy or its size, making it a universal threshold calculation. The tests show, that compared to ordinary threshold calculations especially tailored to the selected single decoders, our method shows slightly improved robustness against outliers. Especially in cases in which the actual collusion size c differs from the expected c_0, our method seems to meet the selected error bounds longer than with the other thresholds.

There is still a lot of work to do. The testset is still limited to some exemplary decoders. To prove universality, we plan to expand the testset to other decoders in literature. We claim that our method is feasible for any simple decoder, but we left out evaluations about joint (or tuple) decoders. The idea is, to integrate the mixture models into the decision making process also for joint decoders, e.g. [13], in order make use of its advantages and to expand the possibilities of that decoder. Also, a comparison to the threshold setting by rare event analysis as applied in [12] and [13] is – due to its computational complexity – still missing. The Gaussian mixture model works well for scores following a Gaussian distribution. However, in cases where the distribution deviates from Gaussian, other models might perform better.

7. REFERENCES

[1] E. Amiri and G. Tardos. High rate fingerprinting codes and the fingerprinting capacity. In *Proceedings of the twentieth Annual ACM-SIAM Symposium on Discrete Algorithms*, SODA 2009.

[2] J. A. Bilmes. A Gentle Tutorial of the EM Algorithm and its Application to Parameter Estimation for Gaussian Mixture and Hidden Markov Models. Technical report, U.C. Berkeley, 1998.

[3] O. Blayer and T. Tassa. Improved versions of Tardos' fingerprinting scheme. *Designs, Codes and Cryptography*, 48:79–103, 2008.

[4] D. Boneh and J. Shaw. Collusion-secure fingerprinting for digital data. *IEEE Transactions on Information Theory*, 44(5):1897–1905, Sept. 1998.

[5] T. Furon, A. Guyader, and F. Cérou. On the design and optimization of tardos probabilistic fingerprinting codes. *Information Hiding*, volume 5284 of *Lecture Notes in Computer Science*, pages 341–356. Springer Berlin Heidelberg, 2008.

[6] T. Furon and L. Pérez-Freire. EM Decoding of Tardos Traitor Tracing Codes. In *ACM Multimedia and Security*, Princeton, United States, Sept. 2009.

[7] Y.-W. Huang and P. Moulin. Saddle-point solution of the fingerprinting capacity game under the marking assumption. In *Information Theory, 2009. ISIT 2009. IEEE International Symposium on*, 2009.

[8] Y.-W. Huang and P. Moulin. On fingerprinting capacity games for arbitrary alphabets and their asymptotics. In *Information Theory Proceedings (ISIT), 2012 IEEE International Symposium on*, pages 2571–2575, July 2012.

[9] S. Ibrahimi, B. Škorić, and J.-J. Oosterwijk. Riding the saddle point: asymptotics of the capacity-achieving simple decoder for bias-based traitor tracing. *EURASIP Journal on Information Security*, 2014(1), 2014.

[10] M. Kuribayashi. Experimental assessment of probabilistic fingerprinting codes over awgn channel. *Advances in Information and Computer Security*, volume 6434 of *Lecture Notes in Computer Science*, pages 117–132. Springer Berlin Heidelberg, 2010.

[11] T. Laarhoven. Capacities and capacity-achieving decoders for various fingerprinting games. *CoRR*, abs/1401.5688, 2014.

[12] P. Meerwald and T. Furon. Iterative single tardos decoder with controlled probability of false positive. In *Multimedia and Expo (ICME), 2011 IEEE International Conference on*, 2011.

[13] P. Meerwald and T. Furon. Towards practical joint decoding of binary Tardos fingerprinting codes. *IEEE Transactions on Information Forensics and Security*, 2012.

[14] P. Moulin and J. O'Sullivan. Information-theoretic analysis of information hiding. *Information Theory, IEEE Transactions on*, 2003.

[15] K. Nuida, S. Fujitsu, M. Hagiwara, T. Kitagawa, H. Watanabe, K. Ogawa, and H. Imai. An improvement of discrete tardos fingerprinting codes. *Des. Codes Cryptography*, 52:339–362, September 2009.

[16] J.-J. Oosterwijk, B. Skoric, and J. Doumen. A capacity-achieving simple decoder for bias-based traitor tracing schemes. *IACR Cryptology ePrint Archive*, 2013:389, 2013.

[17] J.-J. Oosterwijk, B. Škorić, and J. Doumen. Optimal suspicion functions for tardos traitor tracing schemes. In *Proceedings of the First ACM Workshop on Information Hiding and Multimedia Security*, IH&MMSec '13, New York, NY, USA, 2013. ACM.

[18] F. Petitcolas, R. Anderson, and M. Kuhn. Attacks on copyright marking systems. In *Information Hiding*, volume 1525 of *Lecture Notes in Computer Science*, Springer Berlin Heidelberg, 1998.

[19] G. Tardos. Optimal probabilistic fingerprinting codes. In *Proceedings of the 35th Annual ACM Symposium on Theory of Computing (STOC), pp. 116-125*, 2003.

[20] B. Škorić, S. Katzenbeisser, and M. Celik. Symmetric Tardos fingerprinting codes for arbitrary alphabet sizes. *Designs, Codes and Cryptography*, 2008.

[21] B. Škorić, S. Katzenbeisser, H. Schaathun, and M. Celik. Tardos fingerprinting codes in the combined digit model. In *Information Forensics and Security, 2009. WIFS 2009. First IEEE International Workshop on*, 2009.

[22] B. Škorić, T. U. Vladimirova, M. Celik, and J. C. Talstra. Tardos Fingerprinting is Better Than We Thought. *Information Theory, IEEE Transactions on* 2008.

3D Print-Scan Resilient Watermarking Using a Histogram-Based Circular Shift Coding Structure

Jong-Uk Hou[1], Do-Gon Kim[2], Sunghee Choi[3], Heung-Kyu Lee[4]*

School of Computing, Korea Advance Institute of Science and Technology
291 Daehak-Ro, Yusong-Gu, Daejon, South Korea, 305-701
{juheo, dgkim2, hklee}@mmc.kaist.ac.kr[1,2,4], sunghee@kaist.edu[3]

ABSTRACT

3D printing content is a new form of content being distributed in digital as well as analog domains. Therefore, its security is the biggest technical challenge of the content distribution service. In this paper, we analyze the 3D print-scan process, and we organize possible distortions according to the processes with respect to 3D mesh watermarking. Based on the analysis, we propose a circular shift coding structure for the 3D model. When the rotating disks of the coding structure are aligned in parallel to the layers of the 3D printing, the structure preserves a statistical feature of each disk from the layer dividing process. Based on the circular shift coding structure, we achieve a 3D print-scan resilient watermarking scheme. In experimental tests, the proposed scheme is robust against such signal processing, and cropping attacks. Furthermore, the embedded information is not lost after 3D print-scan process.

Categories and Subject Descriptors

D.2.11 [**Software Architectures**]: Information hiding

General Terms

Security, Algorithms, Theory

Keywords

Digital watermarking; robust watermarking; 3D mesh model; 3D printer; stair-stepping effect

1. INTRODUCTION

Recently, the 3D printing content industry has grown rapidly due to the development of advanced 3D printing technology, the emergence of low-cost 3D printers and reduced production costs. As happened earlier in the music and video markets, copyright issues inevitably occur with the expansion of

*Corresponding author

IH&MMSEC'15, June 17 - 19, 2015, Portland, OR, USA
Copyright is held by the owner/author(s). Publication rights licensed to ACM.
ACM 978-1-4503-3587-4/15/06$15.00
DOI: http://dx.doi.org/10.1145/2756601.2756607

the content industry [11]. Therefore, copyright protection of content is very important in 3D printing environments, even though many challenges still remain to be resolved, such as the strength of printed materials and printing accuracy.

3D printing content is a new form of content, distributed in digital as well as analog domains. Content providers have attempted to protect their 3D models through finger-printing, encryption and access control based digital right management (DRM) and digital watermarking. However, content protection based on encryption and DRM are not effective since the 3D printing process disables those protections. As a result, 3D model content may not only be illegally copied though the Internet but also re-distributed in an offline market in printed form. This weak point of content protection is called the Analog hole [6], and a digital watermarking offers a robust method to close the analog hole piracy. For this reason, research to develop a digital watermark technology to protect 3D prints is needed to ensure the prosperity of the 3D content industry.

Digital watermarking is the process of hiding digital information in a noise-tolerant signal such as multimedia data. The watermark can be used to determine authorship when a copyright dispute occurs, and can be used as a fingerprint to track a distribution path when a prototype in the hands of a few people is leaked [5]. Furthermore, digital watermarking could be utilized as an active component of an automatic system to regulate unauthorized users in a content sharing environment. For this purpose, the 3D model watermark should be covertly embedded into the 3D model content before distribution. In addition, the embedded watermark has to resist possible attempts to infringe the copyright.

Watermarking systems for a 3D printing environment are faced with the following challenges.

1) A watermarked model completely loses its file and coordinate information after the 3D printing process.
2) The 3D printing process induces various signal processing and geometrical attacks.
3) Any obscured part of the mesh may be lost during the 3D scanning process.

Since the first publication of a 3D model digital watermarking method in 1997 [9], various 3D model watermarking methods have been continuously studied [2, 3, 7, 8, 12, 13, 15]. However, the offline distribution environments of 3D contents have rarely been considered. Yamazaki et al. [15] presented a framework for watermark extraction from 3D printed content. Instead of designing a robust watermarking domain, Yamazaki et al. used a mesh reconstruction process using the original mesh. We conducted a survey of the various watermarking algorithms, and found that no algorithm which is robust to the 3D print-scan process has been reported yet. Despite the contribution of Yamazaki et al., development of a robust watermarking domain for the 3D print-scan process is still necessary.

Therefore, the purpose of our research is to design a 3D model watermark that is robust to the 3D print-scan process. First of all, we organize possible distortions caused by 3D print-scan process with respect to the 3D mesh watermarking technology. Based on the results of our analysis, we construct a domain that would be minimally affected by 3D print-scan, and propose a 3D print-scan resilient watermarking using histogram based circular shift coding structure. As a result of our tests with various 3D mesh models and attacks, we experimentally demonstrate that the proposed method does not lose embedded information during the 3D print-scan process.

The paper is organized as follows. Section 2 analyzes the 3D print-scan process and classifies possible distortions. Section 3 describes the proposed watermarking method in detail. Section 4 shows the simulation results of the proposed watermarking method against various attacks. Section 5 concludes this paper and gives some future working directions.

2. ATTACKS DURING THE 3D PRINT-SCAN PROCESS

A 3D printer is a device that builds a three-dimensional object by moving the nozzle along not only the x, y and z axis. The 3D model designed by software, is converted to a stereolithography (STL) file which has become a defacto standard. The 3D printer modeling process, which is also called additive manufacturing, divides the STL data into a series of 2D cross-sections of a finite thickness. After that, these cross-sections are combined and added together in a layer-by-layer sequence to form the physical part. The output may require an additional amount of cleaning up before the final model is ready for use.

A 3D scanner is a device that measures a physical object to collect digital data, such as a STL file, on its shape. Multi-stripe laser triangulation (MLT) is a widely used method for this purpose. It obtains 3D data by sensing laser light reflected off an object at several angles, and merges them into a single 3D model. Due to duplicated and isolated vertices, a reconstruction and simplification as a post-processing is necessary.

Diverse distortions can disturb watermark extraction dur-

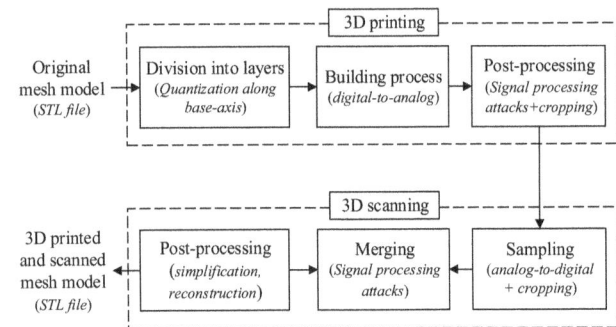

Figure 2: Theoretical stair stepping effect (left), real stair stepping effect of 3D printing content (right)

ing the 3D print and scan process. Fig.1 shows the overall process of 3D printing and scanning, and sources of distortions. Attacks are classified as follows.

1) DA-AD conversion: During 3D printing, the digital 3D data is converted into an analog form. The watermarked model completely loses its file, coordinates, and graph information after the 3D printing process. Surface information of the printed model is digitalized by 3D scanner. The sampling step of the 3D scanner is regarded as a remeshing attack.

2) Signal processing attack: The building process occurs as random noise in the building materials. In post-processing of the 3D print, coating and polishing can be considered to be a signal processing attack, such as smoothing. In the 3D scanning process, sampling error and powder from the pre-process is noise addition in an aspect of watermark. During merging of multiple scan data into a single dataset, geometric errors can occur. After that, in post-process, reconstruction, simplification and smoothing affects can appear to be signal processing attacks.

3) Cropping and local deformation: The supports of a printed model suffer local deformation in the bottom. Any obscured part of the mesh may be lost during the 3D scanning process because a laser or white light cannot reach it.

4) Stair stepping effect: A stair-stepping effect, which is a typical distortion in additive manufacturing [1], can occur in the process of dividing the layers. As shown in Fig.2, the surface is built in a stair shape because the building process is stacking single layers.

We summarize attacks from the 3D print-scan as follows.

- 3D printing: cropping, local deformation, stair-stepping effect, and noise addition
- 3D scanning: remeshing, cropping, signal processing attack, and noise addition

Because these attacks are complex distortions, providing robustness against them is a mandatory requirement for protecting 3D print content.

3. PROPOSED METHOD

3.1 Basic idea

In order to design a 3D print-scan resilient watermarking algorithm, first of all, we needed to determine which 3D model features were robust to the 3D print-scan process.

First, we consider the cropping and remeshing which occurs in the 3D scanning process. To cope with these attacks, we design a watermarking method based on the correlation of statistics. In addition, related information of the original mesh is kept, such as axis information.

We also notice the stair-stepping effect from 3D printing described in Section 2. Among various features of the 3D mesh, the specific component 'surface normal vector' is expected to be robust to the stair-stepping effect. Surface

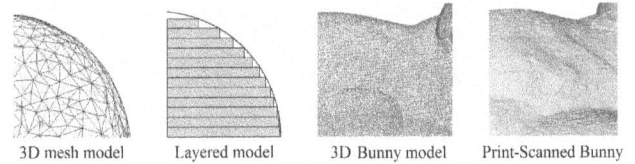

Figure 1: Overall process of 3D printing and scanning, and sources of distortions

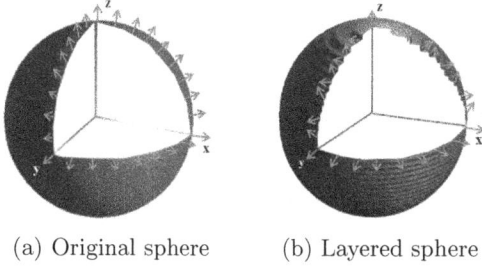

(a) Original sphere　　(b) Layered sphere

Figure 3: Change of the surface normal vector due to the stair stepping effect.

normal vector is a vector which is perpendicular to a given surface with a unit length. In Fig.3, we simulate the stair stepping effect and visualize the surface normal vector as the red arrows. The original sphere has radially uniform surface normal vectors in all directions based on the center (See Fig.3(a)). On the other hand, in the layered sphere most of the surface normal vectors are changed along the z-axis primary test not the x-y plane (See Fig.3(b)). Based on this observation, we assume that each layer preserves a statistical feature of surface normal vectors from the stair-stepping effect.

3.2　Watermark embedding algorithm

Fig.4 shows the proposed watermark embedding process. The whole process is divided into three steps: 1) pre-processing of an input model, 2) watermark pattern generation, and 3) watermark embedding. We now describe each step in detail.

3.2.1　Pre-processing

First, we determine the *base*-axis (or z-axis) for the watermark embedding, and we adjust the orientation of the watermarked mesh M. The *base*-axis should be determined as the orthogonal direction of the 3D printing layer. The *base*-axis information and the original mesh should be kept for registration for the watermark extraction. We conduct uniform remeshing on the input model not only to provide robustness against various attacks produced by the 3D scanning but also to remove irregularities of the vertex density.

3.2.2　Watermark pattern generation

The embedded watermark should carry a certain amount of data to indicate the copyright information. We design a

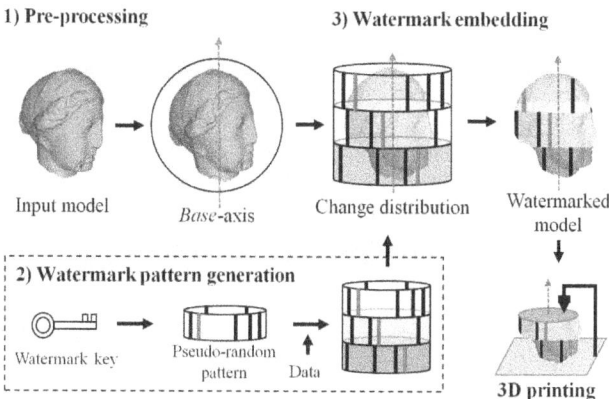

Figure 4: Overall process of embedding the watermark

data encoding based on the circular shift modulation along the z-axis. Details of the data encoding process are as follows.

First, a binary sequence R is generated as a reference pattern using a watermark key and a pseudo-random generator. R is a length λ pseudo-random binary sequence which has low auto-correlation. Input data is divided into n fragments x_j $(1 \leq j \leq n)$, and each x_j is encoded into data pattern P as obtained by a circular shift of the reference pattern R, as follows:

$$P_m = \begin{cases} P_1[i] = R[i], \\ P_{j+1}[i] = R[mod(i + \lambda \lfloor \frac{x_j}{2^k} \rfloor, \lambda)], \end{cases} \quad (1)$$

where mod denotes a modular operation, k denotes the length of each fragment, and data x_n is assigned as an unsigned integer. Data patterns x_n have the same pattern as the reference pattern, but they are shifted with $\lfloor \frac{x_n}{2^k} \rfloor^\circ$ degree.

Fig.5 shows the resulting watermark pattern of the encoded data. The proposed data encoding has an appearance similar to a multiple-dial combination lock. The pattern consists of several rotating disks which represent the watermark data. The relative rotation degree of each disk is used as payload for the watermark data.

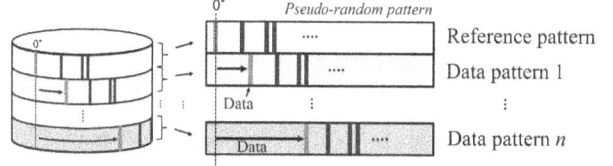

Figure 5: The circular shift coding structure consists of several rotating disks. The rotation degree of each disk is used as the payload for the watermark data.

3.2.3　Watermark embedding

The proposed watermarking is performed by modifying the input model in a way that changes its histogram. Fig.6 shows the overview of the histogram modification process along the data pattern. We use a histogram of the x-y plane projected face normal vector from the input model. We now describe the process for calculating the histogram.

For all faces f in input model M, we calculate face normal vectors $\vec{f}$ and project them onto the x-y plane to obtain $\vec{f'}$. In order to convert $\vec{f'}$ into a 1-dimensional vector, the x and y components of $\vec{f'}$ are converted into the relative angle with $\vec{b} = (1, 0)$ using the following equation.

$$\theta_f = mod(atan2(\vec{b} \times \vec{f'}, \vec{b} \cdot \vec{f'}), 2\pi) \cdot \frac{180}{\pi}, \quad (2)$$

where $atan2(y, x)$ is the arctangent function with two arguments. We calculate the distribution of θ_f to obtain the histogram H with λ bins, which is the same size as the R.

Algorithm 1 shows the detailed process of embedding the watermark pattern based on histogram H, where i denotes the index of the partition, and j denotes the index of histogram H. For the m pattern embedding, M is divided into m partitions along to the *base*-axis. The division interval is determined to have the same surface area of the each partition. HistChange(M_i, j, α) is a function for changing the j-th bin of the H obtained from M_i with a watermark strength

Algorithm 1 Watermark embedding process

$n \leftarrow 32/k$ // the number of data fragments
$m \leftarrow n + 1$ // the number of partitions
$\lambda \leftarrow$ length of the reference pattern
$\alpha \leftarrow$ watermark strength

input model M partitioning
$M \leftarrow \{M_1, M_2, ..., M_m\}$ // partitioned model set
$P \leftarrow \{P_1, P_2, ..., P_m\}$ // watermark pattern set
ForAll $i \leq m$ **do**
  ForAll $j \leq \lambda$ **do**
    If $P_i(j) == 1$ **then**
      $M_i \leftarrow \text{HistChange}(M_i, j, \alpha)$
    end if
  end for
end for
$M' \leftarrow$ merging the partitioned model
Return M'

α. As shown in Fig.6, the j-th value of the watermark pattern P corresponds to the j-th bin of the H. To change the variance of the histogram, we change the x, y components of a vertex $v = (x, y, z)$ as follows:

$$v' = v + v \cdot (\varepsilon, \varepsilon, 0) = (x + \varepsilon x, y + \varepsilon y, z), \qquad (3)$$

where $v \in \{v | \text{a vertex } v \text{ from a face } f \in F\}$, and F and ε denotes the set of faces included in the j-th bin of H and small value (=0.001). This changing process is repeated until $\frac{H_i(j) - \mu_i}{\sigma_i}$ is larger than α, where μ_i and σ_i is the mean and standard deviation of H_i, respectively.

Through this process, we finally obtain the watermarked model M'. For effective protection, the 3D prints provider should print the watermarked model along the *base*-axis, which is determined as the orthogonal direction of the 3D printing layer.

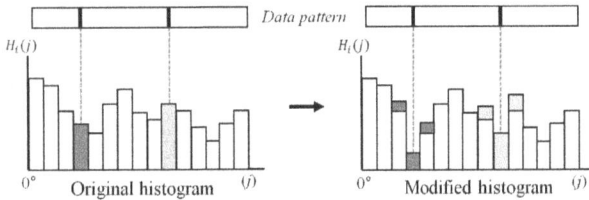

Figure 6: Watermark pattern embedded into the histogram. Variance around the changed point is increased.

3.3 Watermark extraction

Extracting the embedded watermark requires the following priori information: the watermark key, remeshing information, *base*-axis information, and the original model. Fig.7 shows the overall process of the watermark extraction. The whole extraction process is divided into two steps: 1) pre-processing of the input model, and 2) watermark extraction. We now describe each process in detail.

3.3.1 Pre-processing

First, we determine the *base*-axis for embedding the watermark using the following priori information: *base*-axis information, and the original model. Then, we align the orientation of the watermarked mesh. We conduct uniform remeshing on the input model using the same parameters used in the embedding process.

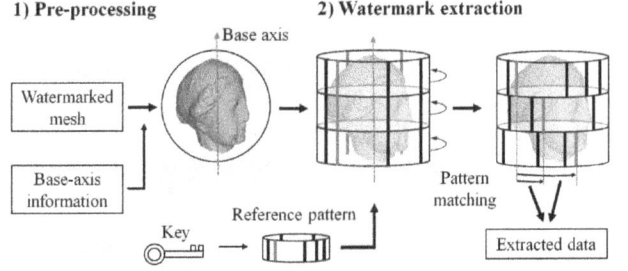

Figure 7: Overall process of watermark extraction

3.3.2 Watermark extraction

For the watermark extraction, we first obtain a watermarking domain of the input model. Then, we detect the watermark patterns using the cross-correlation between the reference pattern and the watermarking domain. After the detection of the pattern, we decode the watermark data using the shifted degree of each detected pattern. The detail description of each process is as follows.

(a) *Generate reference pattern*: We generate a length λ pseudo-random sequence as a reference pattern R using the same watermark key and the generator used in the embedding process.

(b) *Obtain H_i from the input model*: To detect the m number of the embedded pattern, the input model is divided into m partitions in a direction perpendicular to the *base*-axis. Then, the histograms H_i with λ bins are calculated from each partition.

(c) *Calculate a watermarking domain*: In the watermark embedding process, we embed the watermark into the variance of the histograms H_i. Therefore, to obtain a watermarking domain, the histograms H_i are converted to a variance domain $\sigma_{i,j}^2$ using the following equation.

$$\mu_{i,j} = \frac{1}{\lambda} \sum_{j' \in W} H_i(j'), \qquad (4)$$

$$\sigma_{i,j}^2 = \frac{1}{\lambda} \sum_{j' \in W} (H_i(j') - \mu_{i,j})^2, \qquad (5)$$

where w is the range for the variance calculation (*e.g.* $5 \cdot 360/\lambda$), and W denotes the range $[j - \frac{w}{2}, j + \frac{w}{2}]$, and i, j denotes the index of the partition and the index of histogram H, respectively.

(d) *Calculate a correlation map ρ_i*: To detect the watermark pattern in $\sigma_{i,j}^2$, we calculate the cross-correlation between reference pattern R and $\sigma_{i,j}^2$ for all shifting angle $0 \leq j^* < \lambda$.

$$\rho_i(j^*) = corr(R, \sigma_{i,j+j^*}^2). \qquad (6)$$

(e) *Watermark data decoding*: We decode the watermark data using the correlation map $\rho_i(j^*)$. First, we select θ_i in $\rho_i(j^*)$ as a reference angle as follows:

$$\theta_i = \underset{j^*}{\text{argmax}}[\,\rho_i(j^*)\,]. \qquad (7)$$

θ_1 represents the rotation degree of the reference pattern, and the rest of θ_i represents the rotation degree of the data patterns. Embedded data x_n is decoded by the relative differences between θ_1 and θ_i.

$$x_n = \lfloor mod(\theta_{n+1} - \theta_1, \lambda) \cdot 2^k / \lambda \rfloor. \qquad (8)$$

118

Merging the data fragments x_n, we finally obtain the watermark information.

4. EXPERIMENTAL RESULTS

To assess the proposed scheme, we tested its robustness under a wide set of attacks including the 3D print-scan process. Experiments were carried out on four 3D triangular mesh models obtained from 3D watermark benchmark project [14] as shown in Fig. 8: Bunny (34,835 vertices), Dragon (50,000 vertices), Venus (100,758 vertices), Hand (36,619 vertices).

The test environment was as follows. A desktop computer consisting of an Inter(R) i7-3770 CPU, 16GB main memory was used to measure the performance. The watermarking algorithm was implemented in MATLAB 2012b using the mesh toolbox developed by Gabriel Peyre [10], and we used the parameter $n = 4$ with 24bits payload, and $\lambda = 720$ to implement the algorithm. The geometric distortion was measured using maximum root mean square error (MRMS) [4].

Fig.9(b) shows the watermark with MRMS = 0.0070%, and no visual difference can be perceived between Fig. 9(a) and Fig. 9(b). In addition, we embedded the watermark with high strength factor ($\alpha = 6$) to show the visual shape of the watermark (MRMS = 5.506%). The embedded watermark appears as noise strongly represented on certain areas of the model's surface. We assumed that the watermark embedding and extracting time was proportional to the number of vertices, and confirmed this assumption from the experimental results (See Table 1).

	Bunny	Venus	Hand	Dragon
Embedding (second)	0.83	2.52	0.81	1.21
Extracting (second)	0.17	0.37	0.22	0.22

Table 1: Process time of the proposed method

4.1 Robustness test for online watermark

For testing the robustness of the digital contents watermark, we conducted several experiments with signal processing and geometry attacks, as follows: file attack, remeshing, noise addition, simplification, smoothing, quantization, and three types of cropping. Fig.10 presents the three types of cropping used in our experiment: (a) a direction parallel to the base axis, (b) the direction orthogonal to the base axis, (c) random cropping as a local deformation attack. The MRMS of the watermarked models are around 0.02%.

Table 2 shows the experimental result of robustness for the proposed method with the above attacks. Examining the results, the proposed method has robustness to the signal process and the geometry attacks. Our method shows good results in cropping attacks because our watermark is

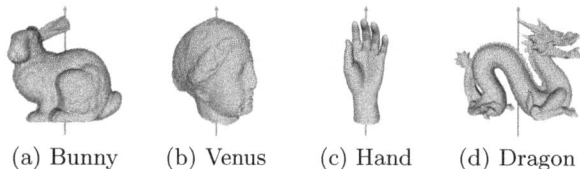

(a)   (b)   (c)

Figure 9: Comparison between the original and the watermarked model: (a) original Bunny model, (b) watermarked model, (c) strongly watermarked model

based on the angle of the surface normal vector, which is not changed by a loss of the other surface. Moreover, a correlation based pattern extraction provides a robustness to the small portion of cropping. Note that, even when the removed area was more than about 10%, our method performed with a relatively low bit error rate (BER).

4.2 Robustness test for offline watermark

We also conducted a test of offline 3D content. For the test, we used four types of models, as follows: watermarked Bunny and Venus with MRMS around 0.050%, and watermarked Bunny and Venus with MRMS around 0.50%. We printed these models using an Object Eden250 which creates 3D objects using resin. The spatial resolution in the height direction is around 0.2mm on average. Fig.11 shows the printed models of the watermarked Bunny and Venus using our method. The printed models were scanned by Maestro3D MDS400, which has 0.07mm spatial resolution.

To compare this method against the performance of a conventional scheme, we used the watermarking method of Cho et al. [3] which modified the statistical features of the distribution of the vertex norm. In our experiment, we used the second method of Cho et al. which employed the variance as a statistical feature. In contrast to the proposed method, Cho's method is a blind watermarking that does not require any related data of the original mesh. Therefore, for a similar comparison environment, the orientation of the scanned models for Cho's method was adjusted using a registration algorithm.

Table 3 presents the results of watermark extraction after the 3D print-scan process. The proposed method succeeded in extracting the embedded watermark from two test cases. In contrast, the method of Cho et al. did not extract the embedded watermark. As explained in [12], Cho et al. did not work against cropping attacks since the range of histogram cannot be synchronized after cropping. The print-scan process affected not only the geometry distortion but also the

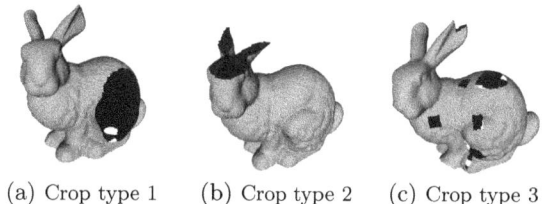

(a) Crop type 1   (b) Crop type 2   (c) Crop type 3

Figure 10: Cropping attacks used in the test: (a) a direction parallel to the base axis, (b) the direction orthogonal to the base axis, (c) random cropping

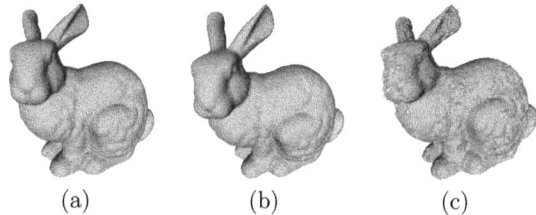

(a) Bunny   (b) Venus   (c) Hand   (d) Dragon

Figure 8: Test models for our experiment. *Base*-axis of the each model is represented as a red arrow.

	Bit error rate (BER)			
Attack type	Bunny	Venus	Hand	Dragon
Similarity transform	0	0	0	0
Resampling (x4)	0	0	0.02	0
Noise (0.01%)	0	0	0	0
Noise (0.1%)	0	0	0	0
Noise (1%)	0.11	0.09	0.10	0.08
Simplification (20%)	0	0	0	0
Simplification (40%)	0.07	0	0.01	0
Simplification (60%)	0.07	0	0.06	0
Smoothing (N=1)	0.11	0.04	0.12	0.05
Smoothing (N=2)	0.09	0.03	0.13	0.11
Smoothing (N=3)	0.10	0.04	0.14	0.08
Quantization (11bits)	0.03	0.06	0.06	0.10
Quantization (10bits)	0.07	0.06	0.04	0.06
Quantization (9bits)	0.16	0.07	0.10	0.08
Crop type 1 (5%)	0	0	0	0.01
Crop type 1 (10%)	0.04	0	0.06	0.01
Crop type 1 (15%)	0.05	0	0.12	0.03
Crop type 2 (5%)	0.03	0	0.03	0
Crop type 2 (10%)	0.05	0.05	0.07	0.05
Crop type 2 (15%)	0.09	0.09	0.12	0.09
Crop type 3 (5%)	0	0	0	0
Crop type 3 (10%)	0	0	0.08	0
Crop type 3 (15%)	0	0	0.08	0
Average BER	0.046	0.023	0.058	0.032

Table 2: Performance of the proposed method with various signal processing attacks.

Model MRMS	Bunny 1 (0.05%)	Bunny 2 (0.5%)	Venus 1 (0.05%)	Venus 2 (0.5%)
Ours BER	0.13	**0.00**	0.08	**0.00**
Cho's BER	0.43	0.47	0.50	0.46

Table 3: The results of watermark extraction following 3D print-scan

various complex attacks such as cropping and remeshing. For this reason, the conventional watermark scheme, which does not consider the print-scan process, has difficulty operating during the print-scan process.

5. DISCUSSION AND CONCLUSION

The main contribution of our method is considering the attacks on the 3D print-scan environment. We proposed the circular shift coding structure of the 3D model which provides robustness to various attacks. When the rotating disks of the coding structure are aligned in parallel to the layers of the 3D printing, the structure preserves the statistical feature of each disk from the layer dividing process.

However, there are some limitations in our method. For

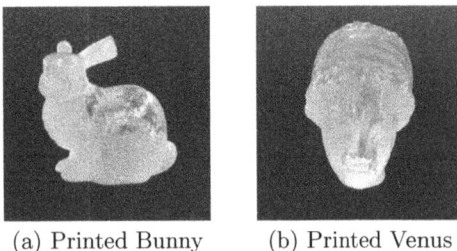

(a) Printed Bunny   (b) Printed Venus

Figure 11: The printed model using Object Eden250.

effective protection, the 3D prints provider must print the watermarked model along the *base*-axis, which is determined as the orthogonal direction of the 3D printing layer. When the watermarked model is printed along a different direction, the circular shift coding structure cannot guarantee the protection for the 3D print-scan process. Extracting the embedded watermark requires information such as *base*-axis information and the original model. Note that the original mesh is only used to determine the *base*-axis in our method.

Future works are as follows. First of all, we plan to design a blind algorithm for the 3D printing environment by an algorithm that determines the *base*-axis based on template matching. We also plan to model the distortion of the whole 3D print-scan process into one system, and the distortion will be analyzed to design an improved algorithm. We will test the method in comparison to previous watermarking schemes expected to be robust to 3D print-scan process such as [8,13]. In addition, assessments with diverse 3D printers and scanners will be conducted to enhance the reliability of our result. Lastly, considering the optimized process of watermarking imperceptibility [2,7], we will design the proposed algorithm to be a more imperceptible shape.

6. ACKNOWLEDGEMENTS

This work was supported by Samsung Research Funding Center of Samsung Electronics under Project Number SRFC-IT1402-05.

7. REFERENCES

[1] D. Ahn, H. Kim, and S. Lee. Surface roughness prediction using measured data and interpolation in layered manufacturing. *Journal of materials processing technology*, 209(2):664–671, 2009.

[2] A. G. Bors and M. Luo. Optimized 3d watermarking for minimal surface distortion. *Image Processing, IEEE Transactions on*, 22(5):1822–1835, 2013.

[3] J.-W. Cho, R. Prost, and H.-Y. Jung. An oblivious watermarking for 3-d polygonal meshes using distribution of vertex norms. *IEEE Transactions on Signal Processing*, 55(1):142–155, 2007.

[4] P. Cignoni, C. Rocchini, and R. Scopigno. Metro: Measuring error on simplified surfaces. Technical report, Paris, France, France, 1996.

[5] I. Cox, M. Miller, J. Bloom, J. Fridrich, and T. Kalker. *Digital Watermarking and Steganography*. Morgan Kaufmann Publishers Inc., San Francisco, CA, USA, 2 edition, 2008.

[6] I. J. Cox, G. Doërr, and T. Furon. Watermarking is not cryptography. In *Digital Watermarking*, pages 1–15. Springer, 2006.

[7] K. Kim, M. Barni, and H. Z. Tan. Roughness-adaptive 3-d watermarking based on masking effect of surface roughness. *Information Forensics and Security, IEEE Transactions on*, 5(4):721–733, 2010.

[8] Y. Liu, B. Prabhakaran, and X. Guo. Spectral watermarking for parameterized surfaces. *Information Forensics and Security, IEEE Transactions on*, 7(5):1459–1471, 2012.

[9] R. Ohbuchi, H. Masuda, and M. Aono. Watermarking three-dimensional polygonal models. In J. D. Hollan and J. D. Foley, editors, *ACM Multimedia '97: proceedings: November 9–13, 1997, Seattle,*

Washington, USA, pages 261–272, pub-ACM:adr, 1997. ACM Press.

[10] G. Peyré. The numerical tours of signal processing - advanced computational signal and image processing. *IEEE Computing in Science and Engineering*, 13(4):94–97, 2011.

[11] R. Stern. Napster: a walking copyright infringement? *Micro, IEEE*, 20(6):4–5, 95, Nov 2000.

[12] K. Wang, G. Lavoue, F. Denis, and A. Baskurt. A comprehensive survey on three-dimensional mesh watermarking. *Multimedia, IEEE Transactions on*, 10(8):1513–1527, Dec 2008.

[13] K. Wang, G. Lavoué, F. Denis, and A. Baskurt. Technical section: Robust and blind mesh watermarking based on volume moments. *Comput. Graph.*, 35(1):1–19, Feb. 2011.

[14] K. Wang, G. Lavoué, F. Denis, A. Baskurt, and X. He. A benchmark for 3D mesh watermarking. In *Proc. of the IEEE International Conference on Shape Modeling and Applications*, pages 231–235, 2010.

[15] S. Yamazaki, S. Kagami, and M. Mochimaru. Extracting watermark from 3d prints. In *Proc. International Conference on Pattern Recognition*, pages 4576 – 4581, August 2014.

End-to-Display Encryption

A Pixel-Domain Encryption with Security Benefit

Sebastian Burg
University of Tuebingen
Tuebingen, Germany
sebastian.burg@uni-tuebingen.de

Dustin Peterson
University of Tuebingen
Tuebingen, Germany
dustin.peterson@uni-tuebingen.de

Oliver Bringmann
University of Tuebingen
Tuebingen, Germany
oliver.bringmann@uni-tuebingen.de

ABSTRACT

Providing secure access to confidential information is extremely difficult, notably when regarding weak endpoints and users. With the increasing number of corporate espionage cases and data leaks, a usable approach enhancing the security of data on endpoints is needed. In this paper we present our implementation for providing a new level of security for confidential documents that are viewed on a display.
We call this End-to-Display Encryption (E2DE).
E2DE encrypts images in the pixel-domain before transmitting them to the user. These images can then be displayed by arbitrary image viewers and are sent to the display. On the way to the display, the data stream is analyzed and the encrypted pixels are decrypted depending on a private key stored on a chip card inserted in the receiver, creating a viewable representation of the confidential data on the display, without decrypting the information on the computer itself. We implemented a prototype on a Digilent Atlys FPGA Board supporting resolutions up to Full HD.

Categories and Subject Descriptors

H.4 [**Information Systems Applications**]: Miscellaneous; K.6.5 [**Management of Computing and Information Systems**]: Security and Protection Authentication—*Physical Security*

Keywords

Multimedia, Security, Encryption, Physical Security

1. INTRODUCTION

The protection of information has become an important issue in several fields of our everyday lives. While in the last decade, hackers and vigilantes have been the primary source for security attacks, today's governments emerge to become a huge source of attacks. Especially in the field of corporate espionage this may lead to massive, quantifiable losses – for example the damage for the German economy is estimated to be 12 billion euros every year [16].

While the security of servers and the network infrastructures is improved by the corresponding administrators, the main blind spot – the computers of employees – is still the primary and most promising target for attacks due to the lack of fitting security technology on the market. Notably when looking at the defense against unknown Trojan horses, this statement holds. We conclude that currently the transmission channel, which normally is protected by end-to-end-encryption mechanisms, is not the main weak point but the endpoints themselves are.

In this paper, we focus on closing this security hole by regarding endpoints as not trustworthy, so preventing the storage of sensitive data on them. We introduce an approach, which allows users to automatically display encrypted sensitive data on a display while not having them unencrypted anywhere on their machine, making data unreadable for any trojan horse. We call our approach **End-to-Display Encryption (E2DE)**.

As the name suggests the approach focuses on the extension of the secure data transmission beyond the boundaries of the **End-to-End Encryption (E2EE)**, whose main feature is the protection of the communication channel, neglecting the endpoints. Unfortunately, current E2EE implementations such as IPSec force a traffic decryption on the communication endpoints, thus making sensitive data being unencrypted and readable by trojan horses. E2DE extends the channel beyond the communication endpoint by using pixel-domain (image) data instead of raw application data, facilitating the decryption behind the endpoint between computer and display.

So, data encrypted using E2DE is never unencrypted on the computer, neither in any storage nor in main memory. This also improves user's compliance to security guidelines. [4] have shown that the security risks in corporations could be reduced by 80% if the users would comply to security guidelines – due to ease of the user and the existence of circumventions, currently these guidelines are not very effective. E2DE closes a lot of circumventions attacking the security guidelines by simply preventing the storage of unencrypted data on computers or other storage media. For example it is impossible for a user to just forward unencrypted data by email to a third person. The only way for the user to send data to a third person is to do it via the official way, i.e. a document management system, which then can control and log the access to certain data.

IH&MMSec'15 June 17 - 19, 2015 Portland, Oregon USA
Copyright is held by the owner/author(s). Publication rights licensed to ACM.
ACM 978-1-4503-3587-4/15/06. . . $15.00
DOI: http://dx.doi.org/10.1145/2756601.2756613.

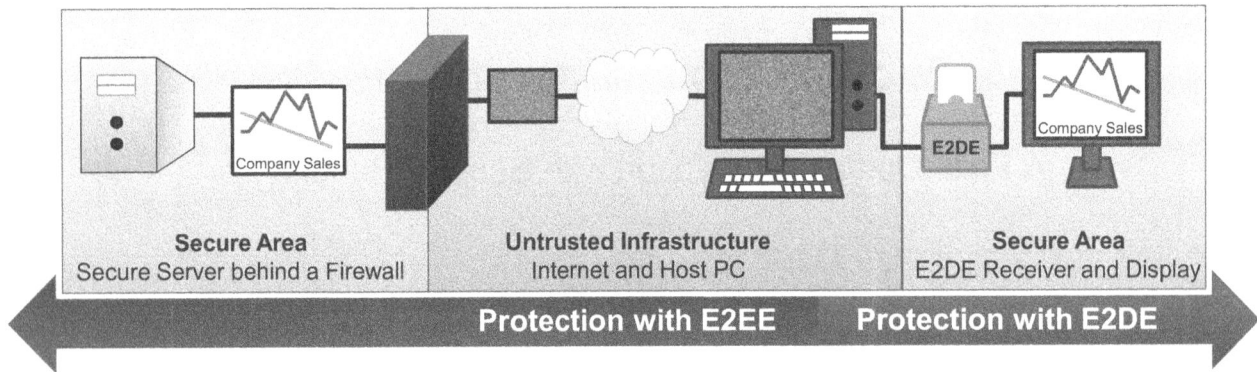

Figure 1: Comparison of End-to-End and End-to-Display Encryption

There have been similar ideas to enhance the endpoint security, but none have been introduced in the market yet. The approach, presented in this paper, outlines a first step towards a marketable and easy to use endpoint security solution with a smaller footprint and lower cost components.

The paper is structured as follows: In section 1.1 we focus on current state of the art in this research area. In the subsequent section the preliminaries are summed up. Section 2 describes our approach, while section 3 deals with our current prototypical implementation. Furthermore, we will outline and discuss the results of our current implementation in section 4. Finally, we conclude this paper and the presented results while illustrating the future work.

1.1 Related Work

The decryption of pixel-domain data is subject of several recent work. Hogl [8] and Staring et al. [15] first introduced the idea of pixel-domain data encryption. Borchert et al. [3] illustrated an application of their encryption approach in 2008 by using an encrypted pinpad for a two-factor authentication whilst being save from Trojan horses and non interceptable by man-in-the-middle attacks.

In 2009 Craver et al. [5] and Atakli et al. [2] introduced BLINK (brief lifetime ink) which has been a first implementation of a pixel-domain data decryption using an Altera Cyclone III FPGA Board and a DVI Daughterboard with several limitations. In their implementation a rudimentary pseudo-random number generator (PRNG) has been used. The key and seed for the PRNG are stored on the board itself, therefore restricting decryption to the installed device. Their proposed solution is limited to symmetric cryptography, and would require an extensive centralized infrastructure to maintain and update keys on installed devices. Furthermore, the implementation in [5] uses a trivial PRNG in place of encryption, and does not demonstrate the feasiblity of pixel-domain decryption with modern encryption algorithms. Additionally is their prototype limited to a maximum resolution of 1024x768 because of the reduced clock speeds, supported by their implementation.

In 2010 Patil et al. [13] test multiple circuits for encrypting and decrypting fullscreen VGA signals. In 2014 Kotel et al. [10] use AES to encrypt fullscreen VGA signal from a camera with the resolution of 720x480 pixels at 60Hz. Both these apply to fullscreen vga signals and have fixed AES keys.

To the best of our knowledge, there is no further work in the area of processing pixel-domain data to secure sensitive data.

1.2 Main Contributions

We enhance the approach of BLINK [5] [2] with strong encryption primitives achieving selective screen decryption at realistic screen resolutions. Using public key cryptography for key management, we improve the security and usability compared to the centralized symmetric key system in BLINK.

2. END-TO-DISPLAY ENCRYPTION

For the transmission of secret information, which is save against eavesdropping by trojan horses or similiar attacks, it is crucial to mistrust the receiving computer. The standard end-to-end encryption does not include the mistrust of the receiving computer in any security policy. We do include this in our approach by avoiding to store unencrypted sensitive data on an endpoint.

Figure 1 illustrates the differences between E2DE and E2EE in terms of endpoint security. The main difference is the decryption location, which resides on the endpoint, in case of E2EE, and behind on a so-called **E2DE Receiver** in terms of E2DE. The E2DE Receiver is connected to the HDMI outlet of the computer and to the HDMI input of the display, only working with the HDMI data sent by the computer. There is no other connection to the computer, making it necessary to transport each necessary information like metadata and key information in the visible pixel-domain data.

This is achieved by translating all documents and data to the pixel-domain storing them in the form of images. These images are then encrypted in the pixel domain, resulting in viewable images containing pseudo random pixels. Finally, the images are enhanced by an additional header line, containing metadata and key information and sent to the user via HTTP, mail or other means of communication.

Opening such an encrypted image on a computer that is not equipped with the E2DE Receiver will lead to an image with pseudo random pixels displayed. When equipped with the E2DE device and a chip card containing the correct key information, the E2DE Receiver is able to successfully decrypt the image leading to a viable image displayed on the monitor.

For image en-/decryption, illustrated in the following chapter, we use a hybrid cryptographic system [12] consisting of the two well known cryptographic ciphers RSA [14] and AES [6]. By using public-key cryptography, we facilitate the distribution of the user's public key to several content distributors without disclosure of the private key. E2DE makes it possible to use the same setup for multiple distributors without the need to disclose the private key. Therefore E2DE provides a real security benefit in comparison to BLINK.

2.1 Pixel Encryption

Downstream to the translation of a document into an image, its pixel domain data is encrypted using AES. Here, we generate an AES matrix using a random chosen key and seed pair. The image data is XOR'd pixel by pixel with the generated AES matrix, then. The data needed for encryption – the AES key and seed – is then encrypted and stored in the header line of the image.

We keep the generated numbers randomized by using the counter mode of AES, which means that after every generated set of values, the seed is incremented. Other AES modes may require to look ahead/behind which could result in distorted images due to overlays from other windows or by the interference from the mouse cursor.

For the encryption process we use the Portable Network Graphics(PNG)[1] format, which supports a lossless data compression. This is crucial for the decryption process – otherwise compressions may lead to decryption errors due to e.g. the reduction of the available color set.

2.2 Header Definitions

The additional header line added to the encrypted image contains a marker for recognizing the encrypted part on the screen, as well as information on the size of the encrypted images. Furthermore it contains the AES key and seed in an RSA encrypted container. Figure 2 illustrates the structure of the header.

The container is created using the public key of the intended recipient. Therefore the key and seed can only be extracted knowing the private key of the recipient. This key will be stored on an external storage medium like a chip card.

2.3 Pixel Decryption

Posterior to the encyption, the image needs to be decrypted when displaying it on an end user's computer. The computer sends the encrypted image as pixel stream through its HDMI output to the E2DE Receiver, which passes all the pixels through as long as no marker for the encrypted image is found.

Finding a marker causes the receiver to extract the metadata (height and width) as well as the key and seed information from the header line using the private key of the user supplied by the chipcard. Whenever the current pixels are in the encrypted area, the pixels are XOR'd with a generated AES matrix, again using the counter mode, and passed to the display.

3. IMPLEMENTATION

In the following sections we will illustrate the implementation of our working prototype featuring E2DE with varying

---

[1]http://www.libpng.org/pub/png/

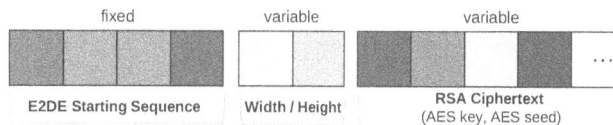

Figure 2: Structure of the E2DE Header

keys stored on chip cards. The circuit design was made using VHDL and Verilog – both, synthesis and implementation were done using Xilinx ISE 14.6.

3.1 Hardware Setup

We implemented the concept on the FPGA board Atlys from Digilent Inc[2]. The board is based on a Xilinx Spartan-6-LX45 FPGA which, on the one hand, is a good alternative to the more expensive Virtex prototyping boards, but also involves special capabilities to feature high-quality video processing, especially required in this work. Therefore it provides two HDMI input ports as well as two HDMI output ports – these are connected directly to the high-speed input and output TMDS converters of the FPGA board. Furthermore, there is an expansion panel, which in this work is used to communicate with an external chip card reader over the I^2C-bus.

3.2 Chip Card Reader

The decryption phase requires two keys, as described in the concept section. One key is necessary to decrypt the RSA-encrypted part in the header line. The second key, stored in this header line, is the AES key which is necessary for the image data decryption. While the RSA key is a fixed user-specific key which does not change at all, the AES key may change over time.

In the first prototype, the RSA key has been implemented as a register with a fixed key. Of course, this was not safe at all but fulfilled our first prototyping requests. In the current version, the fixed key is replaced by a variable key stored on a chip card. We implemented an I^2C-based chip card reader component on the FPGA which communicates to the chip card using a generic chip card reader interface which is directly connected to the expansion panel.

By integrating the chip card reader interface component into the RSA decryption component, our prototype now features support for multiple end-users utilizing multiple chip cards with various keys.

3.3 Pixel Stream Decryption

The pixel stream analysis and decryption breaks down into five functional requirements, implemented by corresponding components in the digital circuit. The implementation is illustrated in figure 3.

First, the differential data stream has to be transformed into a pixel data stream, in order to facilitate a pixel-based AES decryption. For the video stream transformation we used the TMDS decoder provided by the XAPP495 package [7] which converts the serial input data stream into a stream of RGB pixels.

Then, the pixel stream needs to be analyzed in order to detect the E2DE header and to perform the right decryption at the right position. Therefore we use a position marker, storing metadata about the currently analyzed pixel, that

---

[2]http://www.digilentinc.com/atlys/

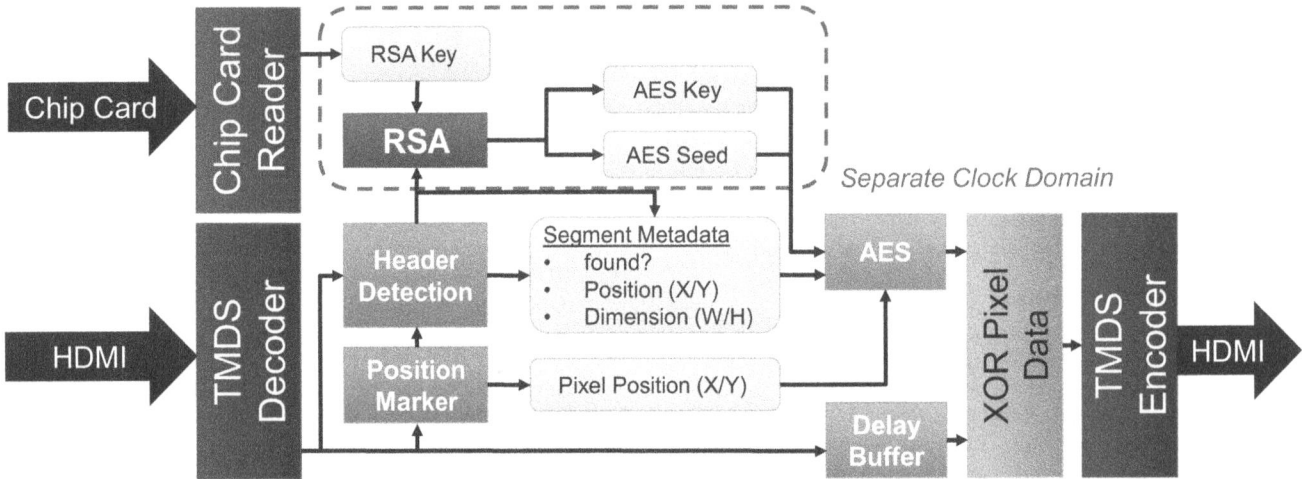

Figure 3: Structure of our FPGA Prototype

feeds the decryption components (RSA and AES) on the one hand and the detection unit on the other hand. The detection unit checks for a given succession of pixel values and informs the RSA component, where the header has been found.

Based on the input of the detection unit and the position marker, the RSA component decrypts the header and stores the decrypted AES key as well as the start coordinates, the width and the height of the encrypted segment into corresponding registers. Due to the laziness property of the window position and the AES key – they normally do not change every frame or every second – the RSA decryption, whose implementation is more timing-critical than all other components, is performed in a separate clock domain. For the current prototype version, we use the RSA implementation provided by [11].

Using the metadata from a previously done RSA decryption stored into corresponding registers, the AES decryption unit performs the image decryption based on the pixel data stream. The AES decryption unit that we use is provided by [9] and outputs an adjusted pixel stream. This stream is finally transformed into a digital HDMI-stream using a TMDS encoder [7].

3.4 EDID

The Extended Display Identification Data (EDID) is a sub protocol in the HDMI standard[3] which enables the computer and the display to exchange data in packages of sizes up to 256 byte. EDID data are transmitted over the I^2C bus via the SDA and SCL lines of the HDMI interface.

We explicitly note, that the channel from the display back to the computer poses no security risk as it is used only for data unrelated to the content of the display images.

Our implementation supports two options for handling these data. One is the plain forward of EDID data between display and computer. This mode may be used to hide the existence of the E2DE Receiver from possible attackers on the computer. The other option is the integration of an EDID Master/Slave core [1]. An EDID core enables a computer to detect the presence of an E2DE Receiver. One

---

[3]http://www.hdmi.org/manufacturer/specification.aspx

Resource Type	# Resources		Utilization
	Used	Total	
Slice Registers	15,628	54,576	28.64%
Slice LUTs	11,726	27,288	42.97%
Slices	4,250	6,822	62.30%
8-bit Block RAM	180	232	77.59%
16-bit Block RAM	0	116	0%

Table 1: Resource Allocation on Spartan-6 LX45 of Prototypical Implementation

can change between both options switching jumpers on the Atlys board.

4. RESULTS

In the following sections we describe the results regarding FPGA resource allocation, real-time behaviour and the limitations of our current implementation.

4.1 FPGA Implementation

The video analysis decryption and the chip card communication unit have been implemented and synthesized prototypically for the Spartan-6 LX45, supporting HDMI streams with resolution dimensions of up to 1920x1080. Despite the smaller size of this FPGA, compared to state-of-the-art Virtex-FPGA used in [2], the prototype could be implemented successfully for this FPGA with a 512-bit-RSA and a 128-bit AES and a moderate area consumption, which is outlined in table 4.1. Due to the presence of more powerful devices in the Spartan-6 family (LX75, LX150), we plan the increase of the encryption key widths to the current state of the art.

4.2 Real-Time Behaviour

Our FPGA implementation for the Spartan-6 LX45 uses two clock domains – the RSA decryption unit resides in one domain, the other components in the other domain. The other domain is fed by the pixel clock and supports a frame rate of up to 60Hz with a Full-HD resolution, which leads to a pixel clock of about 148.5MHz.

Figure 4: Demonstrator for End-to-Display Encryption. Monitor with E2DE Receiver on the left, host computer in the middle, attacker on the right observing desktop of host computer.

A buffer is used to provide us with the pixel information for the header information. This leads to a latency of the size of the buffer. For the current implementation this is a delay of 4 pixel clock cycles. The time needed to calculate the key and seed information from the header takes less than one frame, which leads to the visibility of the encrypted image on the display for this frame. After the AES Key and Seed are calculated, even by changing the counter Information or moving the image the decryption process is stable and displays the image unencrypted.

Our implementation leads to a prototype which supports a real time video decryption – there are no noticeable frame delays – even on updating the keys or window coordinates.

In figure 4 we demonstrate our setup. The monitor on the left is connected to the laptop in the middle via HDMI and the E2DE Receiver shown in front of the monitor. The laptop on the right observes the session of the user in the middle through the desktop sharing application "Teamviewer"[4]. The key for the user is stored in the FPGA. The confidential data becomes readable to the user on the monitor on the left after it is decrypted by the Atlys board, but the observer on the right is only able to see the encrypted image even though it has full access to the host computer.

4.3 Limitations

Even though the results are promising, the concepts and implementations still have of some limitations.

First, the presented approach suffers from the fact, that the header needs to be fully displayed and is not allowed to be disturbed by something like a mouse cursor or another window. Otherwise, the header decryption and the subsequent image decryption will fail, causing the image to be displayed wrong. This leads to the further limitation, that vertical scrolling is not possible.

Furthermore, our approach does not involve a check for the validity of a decrypted image. This makes unencrypted image segments, overlaying into an encrypted area (such as overlaying windows), possibly be decrypted. The effect holds especially for horizontal scrolling or overlaying dialogs. Despite it also affects the mouse cursor, the cursor is still visible.

As illustrated before do we use a key size of 512 bits for RSA and 128 bits for AES, which is obviously not the state of the art in terms of security. This is one of the limitations which will be solved using the next bigger device from the Spartan-6 family.

In regards to the chip card used, we see the need to replace these with smartcards. Storage chip cards can be copied and are therefore unreliable. Smartcards can be secured against raw key access, but become part of the calculation process and are therefore timing relevant.

5. CONCLUSION

In this paper we presented a hardware pixel-domain encryption with security benefits for protecting the information on not trustworthy endpoints, improving the capabilities of the end-to-end encryption and existing work like BLINK[2][5]. Our working prototype is fully functional and can be realized with tools and materials which are at a lower price level than other known implementations. The installation process is done by simply connecting the monitor to the E2DE Receiver and the computer to it as well. After plugging in the chip card, the decryption process with E2DE may start. The eased installation and usage process makes E2DE applicable even for non-computer affine people.

---

[4]www.teamviewer.com

E2DE performs its decryption only in the wire, which causes unencrypted data to never be accessible on the computer and therefore saves against eavesdropping by Trojan horses. With corporate espionage on the rise we believe that this technology can be a benefit for corporations, not just because of the secure transmission of confidential data but also due to the support for implementation and compliance of security processes and guidelines – such a guideline may be to prevent printing sensitive documents or sending unencrypted data to third parties.

In the emerging market of mobile devices like notebooks, tablets and smartphones, the use of a desktop PC with an attached display declines. These devices are currently barred from the benefits of E2DE. Due to the modular design of these devices, an integration of E2DE in these devices is possible while keeping the form factor of the device intact.

With the limitations outlined in section 4.3, we plan to enhance this technology further in multiple directions of research. For improvements in hardware, we plan to improve the level of security by enlarging the key widths for the RSA encryption. Due to increasing need for FPGA resources, we also plan to compare implementations on other platforms such as the Zynq platform. As improvements for E2DE, we plan to eliminate limitations caused by the encryption process as well the enablement of new features such as vertical scrolling and zooming.

6. REFERENCES

[1] J. Ahmad. HDMI2USB. https://github.com/timvideos/HDMI2USB, 2013.

[2] I. Atakli, Y. Chen, Q. Wu, and S. Craver. BLINK: Pixel-domain Encryption for Secure Document Management. In *Proceedings of the 11th ACM Workshop on Multimedia and Security*, MM&Sec '09, pages 171–176, New York, NY, USA, 2009. ACM.

[3] B. Borchert, M. Fouquet, H. Niedermayer, and K. Reinhardt. Verfahren und System zur bidirektionalen, abhör- und manipulationssicheren Übertragung von Informationen über ein Netzwerk sowie Dekodiereinheit, June 24 2010. DE Patent App. DE200,810,062,872.

[4] D. E. Brink. The last Mile in IT Security: changing user behaviour. 2014.

[5] S. Craver, Y. Chen, H. Chen, J. Yu, and I. Atakli. BLINK: Securing Information to the Last Connection. In *Consumer Communications and Networking Conference, 2009. CCNC 2009. 6th IEEE*, pages 1–2, Jan 2009.

[6] J. Daemen and V. Rijmen. *The Design of Rijndael*. Springer-Verlag New York, Inc., Secaucus, NJ, USA, 2002.

[7] B. Feng. *Implementing a TMDS Video Interface in the Spartan-6 FPGA*. Xilinx, December 2010. XAPP495.

[8] C. Hogl. Computersystem und Verfahren zur Ausgabe von verschlüsselten Daten, Mar. 26 1998. DE Patent App. DE1,996,138,623.

[9] H. Hsing. Tiny AES - Crypto Core. http://opencores.org/project,tiny_aes, October 2013.

[10] S. KOTEL, M. ZEGHID, A. BAGANNE, T. SAIDANI, Y. I. DARADKEH, and T. RACHED. FPGA-Based Real-Time Implementation of AES Algorithm for Video Encryption . *Recent Advances in Telecommunications, Informatics and Educational Technologies*, pages 27–36, 2014.

[11] J. Liu and W. Qian. 1024 Bit RSA FPGA Component. http://www.arl.wustl.edu/~jl1/education/cs502/course_project.htm, 2003.

[12] V. Palanisamy and A. J. Mary. Hybrid Cryptography by the implementation of RSA and AES. In *Internation Journal of Current Research*, volume 3, pages 241–244, 4 2011.

[13] J. E. Patil and A. D. Shaligram. FPGA Implementation for Real Time Encryption Engine for Real Time Video. In *Proceedings of the 14th WSEAS International Conference on Circuits*, ICC'10, pages 62–69, Stevens Point, Wisconsin, USA, 2010. World Scientific and Engineering Academy and Society (WSEAS).

[14] R. L. Rivest, A. Shamir, and L. Adleman. A Method for Obtaining Digital Signatures and Public-key Cryptosystems. *Commun. ACM*, 21(2):120–126, Feb. 1978.

[15] A. Staring, P. Tuyls, and D. Van. Gesicherter Dateneingabedialog mittels visueller Kryptographie, Nov. 30 2005. EP Patent 1,472,584.

[16] C. Trust. Studie: Industriespionage 2014 Cybergeddon der deutschen Wirtschaft durch NSA & Co.? 2014.

Touch-based Static Authentication Using a Virtual Grid

William Bond
Alumnus, Western Washington University
516 High Street
Bellingham, WA 98225
United States
wbond.wwu@gmail.com

Ahmed Awad E. A.
Associate Professor
New York Institute of Technology
701 West Georgia Street
Vancouver, BC, V7Y 1K8
Canada
Ahmed.Awad@nyit.edu

ABSTRACT

Keystroke dynamics is a subfield of computer security in which the cadence of the typist's keystrokes are used to determine authenticity. The static variety of keystroke dynamics uses typing patterns observed during the typing of a password or passphrase. This paper presents a technique for static authentication on mobile tablet devices using neural networks for analysis of keystroke metrics.

Metrics used in the analysis of typing are monographs, digraphs, and trigraphs. Monographs as we define them consist of the time between the press and release of a single key, coupled with the discretized x-y location of the keystroke on the tablet. A digraph is the duration between the presses of two consecutively pressed keys, and a trigraph is the duration between the press of a key and the press of a key two keys later. Our technique combines the analysis of monographs, digraphs, and trigraphs to produce a confidence measure. Our best equal error rate for distinguishing users from impostors is 9.3% for text typing, and 9.0% for a custom experiment setup that is discussed in detail in the paper.

Categories and Subject Descriptors

D.4.6 [**Operating Systems**] Security and Protection – *authentication.*

General Terms

Algorithms; Measurement; Experimentation; Security; Human Factors; Theory; Verification

Keywords

Back-Propagation Neural Networks; Monographs; Digraphs; Trigraphs; Bayesian Fusion; Keystroke Dynamics; Static Authentication; Mobile Authentication; Receiver Operating Characteristic Curve; Discretization.

IH&MMSec'15, June 17–19, 2015, Potland, OR, USA.
Copyright © 2015 ACM 978-1-4503-3587-4/15/06...$15.00.
DOI: http://dx.doi.org/10.1145/2756601.2756602

1. INTRODUCTION

In the field of keystroke dynamics, the goal is to identify whether a user is valid or an impostor. There may be different individuals with nearly identical signatures [1]. However, the differences between most people are pronounced enough that keystroke dynamics is an effective method for stopping impostors [1].

There has been an influx of mobile phones and tablets onto today's market. Therefore, it becomes increasingly necessary to extend the keystroke dynamics security originally only available to desktop and laptop computers to these other devices.

In the past, attempts to achieve robust authentication with keystroke dynamics were hampered by a trade-off between the computational power of neural networks, and the cheap computation of statistical methods [1]. The accepted solution is to send the data to a server, where the neural network can be run, and then receive back the authentication results to the mobile device. Particularly new to the field of keystroke dynamics is authentication on soft keyboards, rather than mobile numeric keypads. This paper is one of several that addresses soft keyboards. Another is [2].

The rest of the paper is structured as follows. Section 2 outlines previous work in the field, Section 3 describes the two experiments we conduct and how they are conducted, as well as the methodology we use in authentication of experimental subjects. Section 4 presents the results, and section 5 provides concluding remarks. Section 6 provides references, and graphs and confusion matrices for the experiments are provided in Section 7.

2. LITERATURE REVIEW

Several papers have been published in the literature on mobile authentication based on touchscreen interaction dynamics. We review in this section a sample of these related works.

Crawford[1] provides an overview of recent work in the field of keystroke dynamics. It begins with a discussion of error rates such as FRR, FAR, and EER. Crawford notes that neural networks are a superior method of keystroke dynamics analysis. It is necessary to send the data to a server for analysis, because the mobile device itself lacks sufficient computational power.

The article goes on to cover issues with desktop and laptop keyboards, and then mobile keyboards separately. Key points to note, mentioned by the author, are to always record error rates for comparison with further work in the field, and to use neural networks rather than statistical analysis if at all possible. Neural networks are generally too computationally expensive to run directly on mobile devices.

In this survey paper, the distinction between static and dynamic authentication is made. In static authentication, users type a fixed phrase multiple times, and in dynamic authentication, users type as they use the computer or tablet in their normal work routine. They are evaluated as being the owner or impostor as they type.

Huang et al. [2] introduce a method of authentication for mobile phone soft screen keyboards. An EER below 7.5% is obtained. Keystroke latency and key hold time are measured for 40 experimental subjects. The authors make use of an "α" value to statistically analyze the subjects' typing patterns. This value is multiplied by a threshold to obtain an upper limit of duration timing for a subject to be accepted as a valid user. It is divided by a threshold to obtain a lower limit of duration for the subject to also be accepted. No neural networks are used. The "α" value corresponding to the EER was 7.5%.

Karnan and Akila [3] provide a way to analyze password typing data for authenticity by using multiple algorithmic techniques, including the one that they propose. These are particle swarm optimization, genetic algorithms, ant colony optimization (which they propose), and back-propagation neural networks.

Their method of combining these approaches is to use neural networks for typist verification after input feature extraction. The feature extraction is what uses either a genetic algorithm, particle swarm optimization, or ant colony optimization. After the features have been extracted via one of these techniques, the neural net is used for classification. The performance of their ant colony optimization is superior to the two other approaches with an EER of 0.077% and an average classification accuracy of 92.8%. Average classification accuracy deals with trying to identify the exact identity of a user out of more than 2 users, rather than simply excluding an impostor. Therefore, it can't be expressed in terms of FAR or FRR.

In [4], Karnan and Krishnaraj provide a study that covers many of the same topics as [3]. These topics include genetic algorithms, ant colony optimization, and particle swarm optimization. The proposed method of the paper has four phases. These are feature extraction, subset selection classification, and performance evaluation. Monographs and digraphs are collected from users for feature extraction. There are 25 users, and 50 samples collected per user. Mean, standard deviation, and median are calculated for each user's classification profile.

In the second phase, subset selection, each of three algorithms are tested against each others' performance. These algorithms are Ant Colony Optimization, Particle Swarm Optimization, and Genetic Algorithms. The results of the subset selection phase are fed to the classification phase, which utilizes a back-propagation neural network (BPNN). An ROC curve is generated for the fourth phase, performance evaluation. An EER of 0.006% is obtained. This study is conducted on a number of keyboards of mobile devices using one finger only. The study does not specify if a soft touchscreen or a keypad is used. The success of PSO as opposed to ACO contrasts with the results of [3].

In [5], the authors use an evolutionary algorithmic approach to enhance back-propagation in neural networks when they are applied to keystroke dynamics. This is known as evolutionary neural networks. The paper tests 7 algorithms combinations. These are standard back-propagation, genetic algorithms, back-propagation with genetic algorithms, Lamarkian genetic algorithms, clonal selection, clonal selection with back-propagation, and clonal selection based on Lamarkian evolution.

This last approach obtained the most balanced results, with an EER of about 7%. The paper evaluated the results from data collected and stored in the GREYC database.

Sluganovic et al.[6] presents an approach for keystroke dynamics that is designed for desktop keyboards, and does not target mobile devices. The method is, however, relevant to the method of this paper, because a neural network is used as the classifier. The architecture of the neural network is feedforward.

C# is used to collect the data and test the networks, which are trained with Matlab.

A ten-fold cross validation approach is used, in which 90% of valid user and impostor samples are used for training, and 10% are used for testing. The Matlab neural networks are required to have at least one hidden layer, but the exact number of layers is left to the neural network designer. The neural networks use the multilayer perceptron model for each of their neurons.

Trojahn and Ortmeier [7] make extensive use of the data available for collection on smartphones and tablets to decrease their error rates. Data collected in their study have 21 feature vectors, including pressure when typing, as well as location and finger size. Also included is handwriting recognition. The authors use the WEKA tool to apply competing machine learning classifiers to the keystroke dynamics problem. These eight classifiers are J48, KStar, Multilayer Perceptron, Radial Basis Function Network, BayesNet, and Naïve Bayes. 18 users between the ages of 25 and 45 have their keystroke dynamics data collected and evaluated.

Sander and Bayerer [8] explain Bayesian fusion, which we use in our method as well. While we use a similarity ratio, the authors of [8] describe in detail how the Bayesian fusion approach is able to handle unreliable sensors, and gives an example. We will defer discussion of their work Section 3, where we will explain how it relates to our method.

3. EXPERIMENTS
In Subsection 3.1 we will describe the first experiment, in which users type a text phrase. Then in Subsection 3.2 we will describe the second experiment, in which users touch a sequence of colored boxes to authenticate themselves.

3.1 Text Experiment

3.1.1 Participants
The 25 participants were in the age range between early twenties and 73. The ethnicities were Caucasian, Asian American, and African American.

3.1.2 Experiment Setup
The devices we used are Motorola Xoom devices, and the Android operating system version 4.03 is installed on the devices. The dimensions of each device is 9.81 inches by 6.61 inches by 0.51 inches. The screen resolution of each device is 1280 by 800 pixels.

The method we present in this paper takes as input the experimental subject typing a fixed phrase, and as output generates a prediction of whether that user is the valid owner of the phone or an impostor. The study is composed of two separate experiments. In the first of these, users type the phrase "tive knowledge bases for todays web" onto a custom coded Android soft keyboard, 60 times in total. The first word, "tive", is the last part of the word "effective". The first part of the word was cut off due to our decision to make the phrase at a length of 34 characters. This phrase is selected by an automated program from among many phrases, because it has certain statistical properties. No attempt was made to prevent cutoffs of the first and last words.

3.1.3 Our Method of Analysis

The first stage of the algorithm consists of approximate typo filtering. There are 25 subjects. The subjects have their typos filtered and are then analyzed by the algorithm. The typo filtering is simple – all characters within a 5-substring of the goal text are considered to not be typos, and all other characters are considered to be typos. After typo filtering is done, the monographs, digraphs, and trigraphs are collected based on box location for an 4 by 8 grid of boxes covering the android soft keyboard. Trigraphs are limited to those trigraphs whose first digraph fly time is less than 3 seconds and whose second digraph fly time is also less than 3 seconds. Digraphs are limited to those whose fly times are less than 3 seconds. Monographs are required to be less than 1.2 seconds (this may seem overly lenient, but this is not the only level of outlier filtering).

Sixty sessions are collected for every subject. All sessions are reordered before being divided into groups. These groups are used for neural network training, neural network error threshold determination, and subject identification testing based on the determined thresholds.

It is important for the purposes of the study to spread out the samples collected for neural network training over a large period of time, and this cannot be done when simply taking the first 8 samples. This is the reason that sample reordering is done. Threshold determination and testing also benefit.

The reordering is done based on the order of each training sample modulo 6. The indices are base one in R, but Figure 1 considers them as base 0 instead. All the samples whose index modulo 6 is 0 go first. After them, all of the samples whose index modulo 6 is 1 come next. This is done for all values 0 through 5. In this manner, temporal variation is maximized for training, threshold determination, and testing samples. See Figure 1.

After the reordering of the samples, all of the monograph, digraph, and trigraph durations for each subject which are for sessions 1 through 50 are collected into distinct arrays. One of the arrays is for monographs, one is for digraphs, and one is for trigraphs.

These arrays are used to approximate the CDFs for the distributions of each subject's keystroke durations. We assume that for each subject, their keystroke durations come from a unique probability distribution. The p-values of individual keystrokes are heavily influenced by the locations of those keystrokes. The purpose of the neural networks is to determine how the locations of the keystrokes relate to the p-values of those keystrokes' durations in each subject's unique distribution. Keystroke here refers to any of monograph, digraph, or trigraph keystrokes.

To approximate the p-value for a particular keystroke, we take the sorted array of keystroke durations, after it has been trimmed so that all of its values are between the 2nd and 96th percentiles, inclusive. Then, we find the closest number in that array to the keystroke duration whose p-value we are searching for. The p-value is approximated as the rank of this number divided by the length of the array (in other words, the rank of the number within the array, normalized to be between 0 and 1).

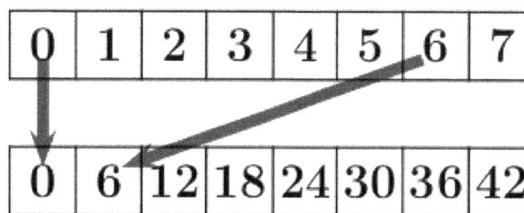

Figure 1

Sample reordering.

The locations of the boxes touched are normalized to the range from -1 to 1, inclusive, for the x location values. The locations are normalized to that same range for the y location values. The durations are normalized to the range 0 to 1, inclusive, using the CDF approximation array.

After normalization, the keystroke data for samples 1 through 8 are fed to three neural networks, in order to train them. One of the neural networks is for monographs, one is for digraphs, and one is for trigraphs. Each neural network has one hidden layer of 10 neurons each, and each neural network uses back-propagation as its algorithm. Different numbers of layers and different numbers of neurons per layer were tested, and we empirically determined that one hidden layer of 10 neurons was best.

After the neural networks have been trained, the algorithm proceeds to the error threshold determination phase. In this phase, the normalized box locations of the keystrokes, for samples 9 through 50 are fed to the neural networks on a sample by sample basis, and the trimmed mean of the errors for each sample are retrieved. The error vectors were obtained by comparing the outputs of the neural networks with the actual p-values of the durations of the keystrokes.

The error values are always between 0 and 1. In addition, the error values for each individual keystroke are stored in one of three hash tables, depending on whether it is a monograph, digraph, or trigraph, and depending on which subject it is. So at the end, because we have 25 subjects, we have 75 total hash tables.

Each hash table stores the vector of errors that have occurred for each keystroke location. This will later be used in the subject identification testing phase, which is done next.

In the testing phase, each neural network is fed all of the keystroke data from each subject for all of the testing sessions, except for keystroke locations which meet a condition. This condition is that during error threshold determination, this particular keystroke location is encountered. Also, it must be true that the 95th quantile of the error recordings for that location is lower than 0.8, for monographs, or 0.6, for digraphs, or 0.5, for trigraphs. If this is not the case, the keystroke in question is ignored.

This is the reason why the hash table is created in the error generation phase. If the error is too high for monographs, digraphs, or trigraphs coming from certain types of keystrokes, then it makes sense to ignore those types of keystrokes.

Otherwise, the keystroke's error level is computed and averaged with the other keystrokes in the same typing sample. In the testing phases, all of the mean error rates are computed for each sample, from samples 51 through 60. Gaussian distributions are generated from the mean and standard deviation of the threshold determination errors. There are 42 samples used for threshold determination for each subject. The cumulative distribution functions of these Gaussian models are evaluated at each testing error rate.

We choose to use a Gaussian model rather than a custom probability distribution, because we only have 42 data points (or 16 data points for box sessions), and that is not really enough to generate a reliable custom distribution, as we did when creating an array of keystroke durations for the purpose of generating a custom CDF with an approximation array. For the earlier case, we had 1448 data points to rank digraph durations for subject 1. The cumulative distribution functions were sampled for the monographs, digraphs, and trigraphs of a session, and were fused with the following Bayesian similarity ratio function:

$$final\ score = \frac{mdt}{mdt + (1-m)(1-d)(1-t)}$$

In this equation, m is the monograph score, d is the digraph score, and t is the trigraph score.

To explain what this equation means, let us now discuss the work of Sander and Bayerer [8], who discuss how Bayesian statistics contrast with classical statistics. Classical statistics interprets probabilities as frequencies of occurrences of a given outcome as the number of trials approaches infinity. Bayesian statistics, however, models probability as the Degree of Belief that a given outcome will occur within one trial.

The example explains how given an object z with two possible types A and B, the probability of the type being A or B given the reliability and types chosen by each of two sensors is equal to $\prod_{s=1}^{2}(\frac{1+r_s}{2}1_{\{z=t_s\}} + \frac{1-r_s}{2}1_{\{z\neq t_s\}})$. This Bayesian result is consistent with classical probability. In this case the sensors give values of either zero or one.

In this work, we use the Bayesian similarity ratio $\prod_{s=1}^{3}(\frac{p_s}{p_s(1-p_s)})$, where each of three sensors gives continuous values on the interval $(0, 1)$. These values are delivered by the p-values of a cumulative distribution function of neural net error rates for three neural networks dedicated to monograph, digraph, and trigraph analysis. The errors are modeled on a subject by subject basis with a Gaussian model.

Unlike in the equation from [8], the similarity ratio that we use does not take into account the differences in the reliability of the sensors. Referring to what happens after the Bayesian fusion function is executed, this final score is compared to values of 0.001 multiplied by the threshold, where the threshold varies between 0 and 1000, to generate the entire Receiver Operating Characteristic (ROC) curve of false acceptance rates and false rejection rates. ROC Curves generated in this way include Figures 2, 3, 4, 6, and 7.

We tried multiple configurations to see what different error rates we would get for each. Variations we used included different grid resolutions, voting fusion, weighted Bayesian fusion, and the unmodified Bayesian fusion. Voting fusion consists of comparing each of monograph, digraph, and trigraph error rates to the threshold and accepting the sample as valid only if at least 2 of 3 types of errors pass the threshold. Weighted fusion is when each of monograph, digraph, and trigraph error rates are raised to powers from 0.9 to 1.1 per user in a triple nested loop, to obtain the lowest error rates during the threshold determination phase. These same weights are then used during the testing phase.

3.2 Colored Box Experiment

3.2.1 Participants
There were 9 participants. The age range was from early twenties to 73 years old. The ethnicity of the subjects was Caucasian. Most of these participants, but not all, participated in the text experiment.

3.2.2 Experiment Setup
For this experiment, we used the same devices that we used for the text experiment. These are Motorola Xoom devices, with the Android operating system version 4.03 installed.

The second of these experiments has users touch 100 consecutively appearing boxes on a grid on the screen, where no soft keyboard is present. We will from this point refer to the second experiment as the "colored box experiment". Each user in the colored box experiment touches the same 100 boxes for 30 repetitions, for a total of 3000 boxes. This experiment is done as a proof of concept, and the first experiment is meant to be the practical application of the algorithm.

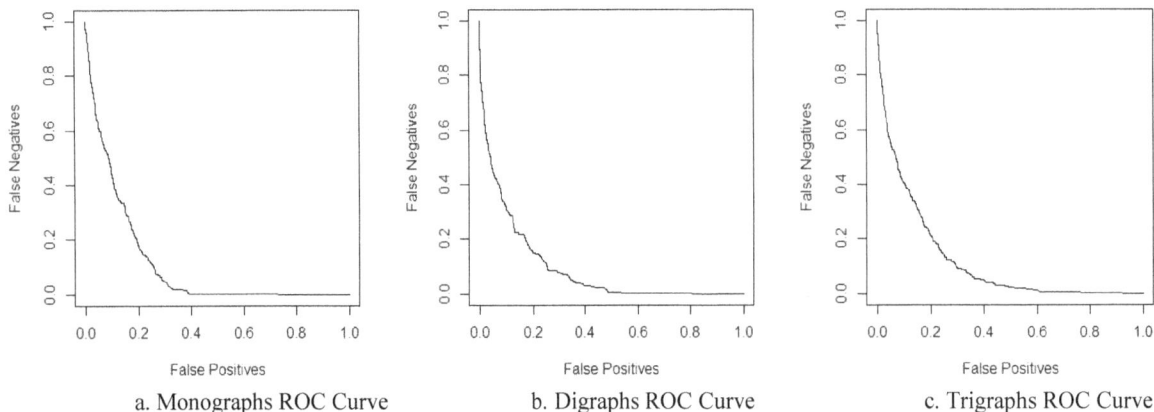

a. Monographs ROC Curve   b. Digraphs ROC Curve   c. Trigraphs ROC Curve

Figure 2

ROC curves for separate keystroke dynamics metrics without fusion. The EER for monographs is 19.3%. The EER for digraphs is 17.9%. The EER for trigraphs is 20.6%.

The keystrokes for both the text and the boxes are discretized into grids. For the text, the input keystrokes are discretized into a grid of 4 cells across in the y direction and 8 cells across in the x direction. An 8-by-8 grid is used for the colored boxes. So in this paper, when we refer to monographs, digraphs, and trigraphs, these are with the keystrokes being the time duration combined with the x locations and y locations on the discretized grid for each of the key presses.

For the text, it is empirically determined which combinations of number of rows and number of columns for the grids is best. Therefore, in our results section, we show results for grids with different numbers of rows and columns.

For the colored box experiment, we choose not to try any additional grids besides the 8 by 8 grid. We also do not use a custom mapping from visible boxes to actual boxes. This is due to the default grid being visible to the user as they touch the colored boxes, and also to the fact that the colored boxes each exactly fill one grid cell.

3.2.3 Our Method of Analysis

The colored box experiment is very similar to the text experiment, with key differences. The first of these differences is that the user touches colored boxes on a visible 8 by 8 grid, as opposed to typing on a visible touchscreen keyboard where an invisible 4 by 8 grid is used for algorithmic user identity verification. The setup is shown in Figure 6. Different subjects are used for the colored box sessions, and those subjects always have the correct typing patterns as a subset of what they type, unlike with the text session subjects. This is because a colored box session will not end until all necessary boxes have been touched in order (regardless of which boxes have been touched between any 2 of the correct boxes).

In the colored box experiment, the first 20 sessions are collected into distinct CDF approximation arrays instead of the first 50 sessions, because there are 30 sessions total instead of 60. The first 8 sessions are used for neural network training, and sessions 9 through 20 are used for threshold determination. Sessions 20 through 30 are used for testing.

For colored box sessions, typo filtering consists of discarding boxes that are not part of the goal sequence, in a start-to-finish fashion.

4. RESULTS

We present results in terms of ROC curves, which plot false positives on the x-axis against false negatives on the y-axis. For the best results, we also plot in terms of PR curves. PR curve means "precision recall curve". Recall is the number true positives divided by the total number of valid user authentication attempts. Precision is the number of true positives divided by the total number of authentication attempts in which the login system gave the user access to the system. This includes both valid and invalid users. For 25 subjects, the ROC curves of the unfused keystroke dynamics metrics looks like Figure 2 for the text experiment, evaluated using a 4 by 8 analysis grid. As the reader can see, the performance of the metrics without fusion to enhance them is very poor.

Section 7, the appendix shows the final results we obtained with our analysis technique. A 5 by 10 grid worked best for the text experiment. Only one grid size was attempted for the colored box experiment. The performance is significantly better using

fusion of monographs, digraphs, and trigraphs. We also include precision-recall (PR) curves in our final results. Precision is equal to true positives divided by the number of all positives. Recall is equal to true positives divided by the sum of true positives and false negatives.

5. CONCLUSION

The novel component of our work is the integration of a grid into keystroke dynamics analysis. This is a form of discretization to improve accuracy.

Possibilities for future work include the integration of pressure and finger size and shape from the Android Touch API into this analytic grid framework. Perhaps investigation of finer grids of boxes to touch may also be of value, such as a 10 by 10 grid instead of an 8 by 8 grid. Also, when given a user, it may be useful to identify a user out of many candidates when given a sample, rather than simply rejecting impostors. When you reject impostors, the problem statement implicitly only requires you to put the input into either of 2 categories: valid user or invalid user. With the addition of these Android Touch API data vectors, it may be also possible to obtain good results for identifying users out of a group of people.

6. REFERENCES

[1] Crawford, H. (2010), "Keystroke Dynamics: Characteristics and Opportunities", 2010 Eighth Annual International Conference on Privacy, Security, and Trust, pp. 205-212.

[2] Huang, Xuan; Lund, Geoffrey; and Sapeluk, Andrew (2012), "Development of a typing behavior recognition mechanism on Android", 2012 IEEE 11th International Conference on Trust, Security, and Privacy in Computing and Communications, pp. 1342 – 1347.

[3] Karnan, Marcus and Akila, M. (2010), "Personal Authentication based on Keystroke Dynamics using Soft Computing Techniques", 2010 Second International Conference on Communication Software and Networks, pp. 334-338.

[4] Karnan, Marcus and Krishnaraj, N. (2010), "Bio Password – Keystroke Dynamic Approach to Secure Mobile Devices"

[5] Henrique Pisani, Paulo; and Carolina Lorena, Ana (2012), "Evolutionary Neural Networks Applied to Keystroke Dynamics: Genetic and Immune Based", WCCI 2012 IEEE World Congress on Computational Intelligence

[6] Sluganovic, Ana Karlovic; Bosilj, Petra, Sare, Mislav; and Horvat, Sara (2012), "User Authentication Based on Keystroke Dynamics Analysis", MIPRO 2012, pp. 1719-1724

[7] Trojahn, Matthias; and Ortmeier, Frank (2013), "Toward mobile authentication with keystroke dynamics on mobile phones and tablets", 27th International Conference on Advanced Information Networking and Applications Workshops, pp. 697-702

[8] Sander, Jennifer, and Bayerer, Jergen (2013), "Bayesian Fusion: Modeling and Application", Sensor Data Fusion: Trends, Solutions, Applications (SDF), 2013 Workshop on, pp. 1-6

7. APPENDIX (NEXT PAGE)

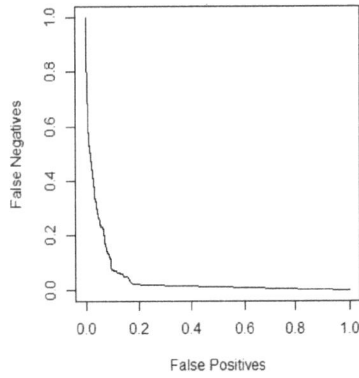

Figure 3

Best ROC curve for text experiment: EER 9.3%.
Weighted Fusion. Grid Size: 5 by 10.

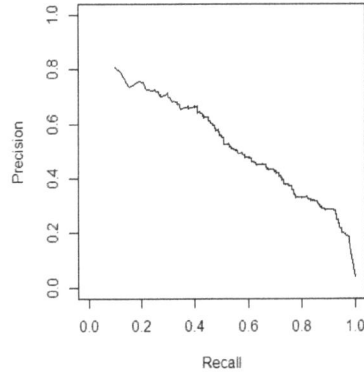

Figure 4

PR Curve corresponding to Figure 3.
Precision is 53.0% and Recall is 53.0% at breakeven point.

	1	2	3	4	5	6	7	8	9	10	11	12	13	14	15	16	17	18	19	20	21	22	23	24	25
1	9	8	5	5	8	8	1	5	10	10	1	5	8	2	3	9	0	9	2	0	6	10	5	8	8
2	0	8	0	0	0	0	0	0	0	0	0	0	0	0	0	0	0	0	0	0	0	0	0	0	0
3	5	0	7	1	3	0	0	3	0	0	0	1	1	0	0	0	0	5	0	0	1	6	1	0	7
4	0	0	0	9	0	0	0	0	0	0	0	0	0	0	0	0	0	0	0	0	0	0	0	0	0
5	6	0	1	8	8	4	0	0	8	7	0	1	0	1	0	9	0	2	4	0	4	5	2	0	3
6	0	1	0	0	1	9	0	0	0	0	0	0	0	0	0	0	0	0	0	0	0	0	0	0	0
7	0	0	1	0	0	0	8	6	0	0	3	0	0	0	0	0	0	0	0	0	0	0	0	0	3
8	7	0	2	1	2	1	0	9	5	3	1	0	1	0	0	0	0	0	0	0	0	4	0	0	4
9	0	0	0	1	0	0	0	0	9	1	0	0	0	0	0	0	0	0	0	0	0	0	0	0	1
10	2	0	0	3	1	0	0	0	5	10	0	0	0	0	1	4	0	0	0	0	2	0	0	0	3
11	0	0	1	0	0	0	0	0	0	0	9	0	0	0	0	0	0	2	0	0	0	0	2	0	1
12	0	1	1	0	1	3	0	0	2	1	0	9	1	0	1	0	0	1	0	0	0	6	0	7	1
13	0	0	1	0	1	0	0	0	0	1	0	1	10	0	0	0	0	0	0	0	0	0	0	10	2
14	0	0	0	0	0	0	0	0	0	0	0	0	0	9	0	0	0	0	0	0	0	0	0	0	0
15	5	0	1	3	0	3	0	0	2	6	1	0	2	0	8	3	0	7	0	0	1	7	4	2	7
16	1	0	0	0	3	2	0	0	5	5	0	0	0	0	0	9	0	0	0	0	1	1	0	0	0
17	0	0	0	0	0	0	0	0	0	0	0	0	0	0	0	0	10	0	0	0	0	0	0	0	0
18	6	0	3	3	2	0	0	1	3	0	0	0	1	0	3	1	0	9	0	0	0	8	6	2	8
19	1	1	0	1	6	10	0	0	4	1	0	2	0	0	0	7	0	0	10	0	4	1	0	0	0
20	0	0	0	0	0	0	0	0	0	0	0	0	0	0	0	0	0	0	0	10	0	0	0	0	0
21	0	0	0	1	2	1	0	0	1	0	0	0	0	0	0	7	0	0	3	0	10	0	0	0	0
22	1	0	0	0	0	0	0	0	0	0	0	0	0	0	0	0	0	0	0	0	0	10	0	0	1
23	4	0	2	5	1	0	0	0	2	1	1	1	0	0	1	1	0	7	0	0	0	2	9	0	5
24	0	0	0	0	0	0	0	0	0	0	0	0	0	0	0	0	0	0	0	0	0	0	0	10	0
25	1	0	0	0	3	0	0	0	0	1	0	1	0	0	0	0	0	0	0	0	0	0	0	0	9

Figure 5

Confusion matrix for text experiment applied to grid size of 5 by 10 using weighted fusion at EER threshold of 0.970.

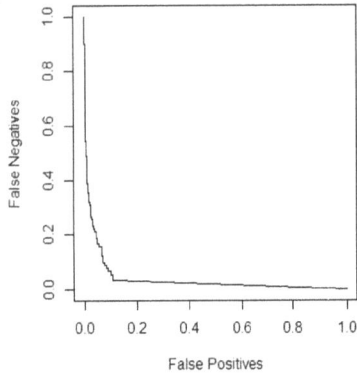

Figure 6

Best ROC curve for colored box experiment: EER 8.0%.
Unmodified fusion. Grid size: 8 by 8.

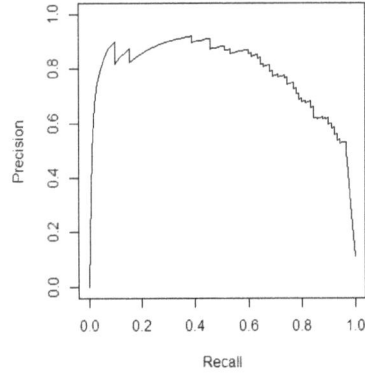

Figure 7

PR Curve corresponding to Figure 6.
Precision is 78.0%. and Recall is 78.0% at breakeven point.

	1	2	3	4	5	6	7	8	9
1	8	0	0	0	0	0	0	0	0
2	0	10	0	0	0	0	0	0	1
3	0	0	10	0	9	0	0	0	0
4	0	0	0	9	0	0	0	1	0
5	0	0	9	0	9	0	0	1	0
6	0	0	0	0	0	9	0	0	0
7	0	0	0	0	0	5	9	0	0
8	3	3	10	1	9	0	0	0	3
9	0	5	0	0	0	0	0	0	10

Figure 8

Confusion matrix for colored box experiment applied to grid size of 8 by 8 using weighted fusion at EER threshold of 0.9999.

SATTVA: SpArsiTy inspired classificaTion of malware VAriants

Lakshmanan Nataraj
Dept. of ECE
University of California, Santa
Barbara, USA
lakshmanan_nataraj
@ece.ucsb.edu

S. Karthikeyan
Dept. of ECE
University of California, Santa
Barbara, USA
karthikeyan
@ece.ucsb.edu

B.S. Manjunath
Dept. of ECE
University of California, Santa
Barbara, USA
manj
@ece.ucsb.edu

ABSTRACT

There is an alarming increase in the amount of malware that is generated today. However, several studies have shown that most of these new malware are just variants of existing ones. Fast detection of these variants plays an effective role in thwarting new attacks. In this paper, we propose a novel approach to detect malware variants using a sparse representation framework. Exploiting the fact that most malware variants have small differences in their structure, we model a new/unknown malware sample as a sparse linear combination of other malware in the training set. The class with the least residual error is assigned to the unknown malware. Experiments on two standard malware datasets, Malheur dataset and Malimg dataset, show that our method outperforms current state of the art approaches and achieves a classification accuracy of 98.55% and 92.83% respectively. Further, by using a confidence measure to reject outliers, we obtain 100% accuracy on both datasets, at the expense of throwing away a small percentage of outliers. Finally, we evaluate our technique on two large scale malware datasets: Offensive Computing dataset (2,124 classes, 42,480 malware) and Anubis dataset (209 classes, 36,784 samples). On both datasets our method obtained an average classification accuracy of 77%, thus making it applicable to real world malware classification.

Categories and Subject Descriptors

K.6.5 [**MANAGEMENT OF COMPUTING AND INFORMATION SYSTEMS**]: Security and Protection—*Invasive software*; I.5.4 [**PATTERN RECOGNITION**]: Applications—*Signal Processing*

Keywords

Malware Variant Classification, Sparsity based classification, Random Projections, Compressed Sensing

1. INTRODUCTION

Antivirus (AV) software vendor Kaspersky recently reported that they process on average 315,000 samples per day [1]. The main

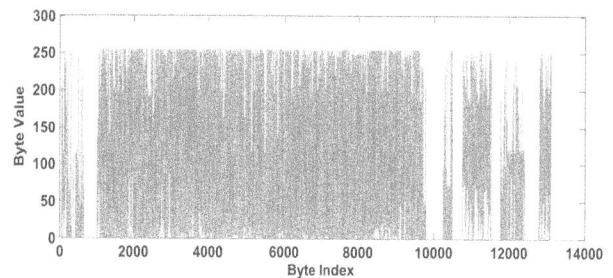

(a) Variant 1

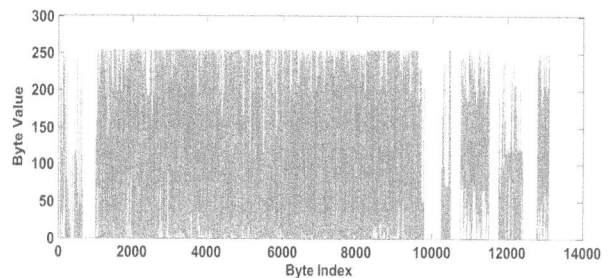

(b) Variant 2

Figure 1: Byte plots of the recently exposed Regin malware variants [3]. Variant (b) is created by making small change to Variant (a). They differ only in 7 bytes out of 13,284 bytes (0.0527 %).

reason for such a deluge is *malware mutation: the process of creating new malware variants from existing ones.* Variants are created either by making changes to the malware code or by using executable packers. In the former case, simple mutation occurs by changing small parts of the code. In the latter case, a more complex mutation occurs by encrypting (usually with different keys) the main body of the code and appending a decryption routine, which during runtime decrypts the encrypted payload. The new variants perform the same function as the original malware but their attributes would be so different that AV software, which use traditional signature based detection, would not work on them. Based on their function, these variants are classified into different *malware families*. Identifying the malware family of an unknown malware can play an important role in understanding and thwarting new attacks.

Although mutation techniques create a large number of malware variants, these variants have very small changes in the overall malware structure. Fig. 1 shows one such example of two malware variants of the recently exposed Regin malware [3], which has been

135

described as one of the most sophisticated malware discovered in recent times, and termed on par with Stuxnet, Flame and other advanced malware. In Fig. 1, variants are represented as byte plots where every byte is represented as a number. Despite their sophisticated design, the variants only differ in a few bytes (0.0527 %). Reports further observe that variants of Regin malware were used for diverse tasks such as cyber-espionage and secret surveillance against countries, companies and individuals. Although this example shows a case of simple mutation, this phenomenon is also true for variants created using executable packers, which are more common nowadays.

In this paper, we explore Sparse Representation based Classification (SRC) methods to classify malware variants into families. Such methods have been previously applied to problems where samples belonging to a class have small variations in them, for example, face recognition [31], iris recognition [27], background subtraction [6], and tracking [21]. We model a malware variant belonging to a particular malware family as a sparse linear combination of variants from that family using Random Projections. Since variants of a family have small changes in the overall structure and differ from variants of other families, projections of malware in lower dimensions preserve this "similarity".

The rest of the paper is organized as follows. The related works in malware classification are briefed in Sec. 2. Sec. 3 details the formulation of the sparse representation based classification framework. Sec. 4 details the experiments on various datasets. The limitations and conclusion are discussed in Sec. 5.

2. RELATED WORK

Typical malware features used for malware classification can be broadly grouped into either *static features* or *dynamic features* As the name suggests, static features are extracted from the malware without executing it. Dynamic features, on the other hand, are extracted by executing the code, usually in a virtual environment, and then studying their behavioral characteristics such as system calls trace or network behavior. We will focus more on static analysis which our proposed approach comes under. For more on dynamic analysis based methods, the readers are referred to [5, 28, 10, 8].

The most common static analysis method is control flow graph analysis [18, 11, 13]. After disassembling the code, the control flow of the malware is obtained and graphs are constructed to uniquely characterize the malware. However, these methods do not work well on packed malware since the control flow of a packed malware reveals only the unpacking routine. In contrast, our proposed method does not require any code analysis, unpacking or execution of malware.

Other Static features are based on n-grams [4, 16, 12, 13, 26], n-perms [14, 19], hashes [17, 30] and image similarity [22, 24, 23, 15]. The first two compute n-grams or n-perms on the binaries to characterize the malware. Among hash based methods, *ssdeep* [17] is a common technique to compute context triggered piecewise hashes on raw binaries. *Pehash* [30], however, uses the Portable Executable (PE) file structure to compute a hash. Image similarity based methods [22, 24] convert a malware binary to a digital image and apply image processing based techniques to compute features. These features have been used for malware classification [22], detection [15] and retrieval [23]. In contrast to these methods, we compute random projections on malware represented as numerical vectors. This results in compact features for malware classification. Although random projections have been previously used in [10, 8], these methods require dynamic analysis which is time consuming.

3. MALWARE CLASSIFICATION BASED ON SPARSE REPRESENTATIONS

3.1 Approach

Given a dataset of N labeled malware belonging to L different malware families with P malware per family, the task is to identify the family of an unknown malware $\mathbf{u}$. Similar to [22], we represent a malware as a numerical vector $\mathbf{x}$ of range $[0, 255]$, where every entry of $\mathbf{x}$ is a byte value of the malware. However unlike [22], we do not convert this vector to an image matrix. Since each malware sample can have a different code-length, we normalize all vectors to a maximum length (M) by zero-padding.

The entire dataset can now be represented as an $M \times N$ matrix $\mathbf{A}$, where every column represents a malware. Further, for every family k ($k = 1, 2, ..., L$), we define an $M \times P$ matrix $\mathbf{A}_k = [\mathbf{x}_{k1}, \mathbf{x}_{k2}, ...\mathbf{x}_{kP}]$ where $\mathbf{x}_{k\{.\}}$ represents a malware sample belonging to family k. Now, $\mathbf{A}$ can be expressed as a concatenation of block-matrices $\mathbf{A}_k$:

$$\mathbf{A} = [\mathbf{A}_1 \mathbf{A}_2 .. \mathbf{A}_L] \in \mathbb{R}^{M \times N} \qquad (1)$$

Let $\mathbf{u} \in \mathbb{R}^M$ be an unknown malware whose family is to be determined, with the assumption that $\mathbf{u}$ belongs to one of the families in the dataset. Since variants in a family have small differences, they will all be in the same linear span [1]. Then, following [31], we represent $\mathbf{u}$ as a sparse linear combination of the training samples as:

$$\mathbf{u} = \sum_{i=1}^{L} \sum_{j=1}^{P} \alpha_{ij} \mathbf{x}_{ij} = \mathbf{A}\alpha \qquad (2)$$

where $\alpha = [\alpha_{1,1}, ..., \alpha_{L,P}]^T$ represents the $N \times 1$ sparse coefficient vector ($N = LP$). α will have non-zero values only for samples that are from the same family as $\mathbf{u}$. The sparsest solution to (2) can be obtained using Basis Pursuit [27] by solving the following l_1-norm minimization problem:

$$\hat{\alpha} = \arg\min_{\alpha' \in \mathbb{R}^N} \|\alpha'\|_1 \text{ subject to } \mathbf{u} = \mathbf{A}\alpha' \qquad (3)$$

where $\|.\|_1$ is the l_1 norm.

Estimating the family of $\mathbf{u}$ is done by computing residuals for every family in the training set and then selecting the family that has minimum residue. Let $\mathbf{\Pi}_k$ be the characteristic function that selects the coefficients from $\hat{\alpha}$ that are only associated with family k. Then the residual function r_k can be expressed as:

$$r_k(\mathbf{u}) = \|\mathbf{u} - \mathbf{A}\mathbf{\Pi}_k(\hat{\alpha})\|_2 \qquad (4)$$

$$c = \arg\min_k r_k(\mathbf{u}) \qquad (5)$$

where c is the index of the estimated family associated with $\mathbf{u}$.

3.2 Random Projections

When a malware binary is represented as a numerical vector by considering every byte, the dimensions of that vector can be very high. For example, a 1 MB malware has around 1 Million bytes and this could make the calculations computationally expensive. Hence, we project the vectors to lower dimensions using Random Projections (RP). This also removes dependency on any particular feature extraction method. Previous works have demonstrated that SRC is effective in lower-dimensional random projections as well,

---

[1]Linear span means that any linear combination of a vector will be in the same subspace

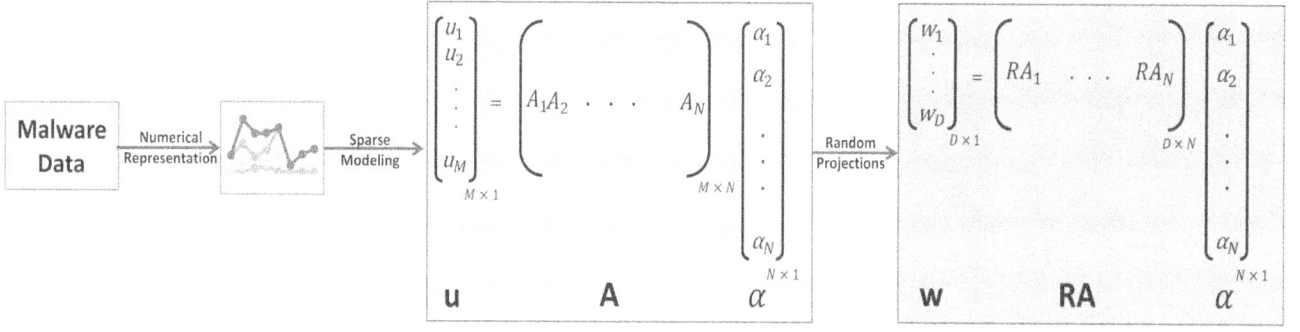

Figure 2: Overall Approach: Malware samples are represented as numerical vectors, projected to lower dimensions and then modeled using the Sparse Representation based Classification (SRC) framework

see [9, 31, 27]. Let $\mathbf{R} \in \mathbb{R}^{D \times M}$ be the matrix that projects $\mathbf{u}$ from signal space M to $\mathbf{w}$ of lower dimensional space D ($D << M$):

$$\mathbf{w} = \mathbf{R}\mathbf{u} = \mathbf{R}\mathbf{A}\alpha \qquad (6)$$

The entries of $\mathbf{R}$ are drawn from a zero mean normal distribution. The above system of equations is underdetermined and sparse solutions can be obtained by reduced l_1-norm minimization:

$$\hat{\alpha} = \underset{\alpha' \in \mathbb{R}^N}{\arg\min} \|\alpha'\|_1 \text{ subject to } \mathbf{w} = \mathbf{R}\mathbf{A}\alpha' \qquad (7)$$

The overall approach is shown in Fig.2.

3.3 Modeling Variants

When a new variant is created from existing an malware by making small changes, both variants share some common parts. The new variant is modelled as:

$$\mathbf{u}' = \mathbf{u} + \mathbf{e_u} = \mathbf{A}\alpha + \mathbf{e_u} \qquad (8)$$

where $\mathbf{u}'$ is the corrupted vector representing the new variant and $\mathbf{e_u}$ is the error vector. This can be reduced to matrix form using block matrices:

$$\mathbf{u}' = [\mathbf{A}, \mathbf{I}_M] \begin{bmatrix} \alpha \\ \mathbf{e_u} \end{bmatrix} = \mathbf{B_u}\, \mathbf{s_u} \qquad (9)$$

where $\mathbf{B_u} = [\mathbf{A}, \mathbf{I}_M]$ is a $M \times (N + M)$ matrix and $\mathbf{I}_M$ is an $M \times M$ Identity matrix and $\mathbf{s_u} = [\alpha, \mathbf{e_u}]^T$. This ensures that the system of equations (9) is always underdetermined and sparse solutions can be obtained. In lower dimensions, this reduces to:

$$\hat{\alpha} = \underset{\alpha' \in \mathbb{R}^N}{\arg\min} \|\alpha'\|_1 \text{ subject to } \mathbf{w}' = \mathbf{B_w}\, \mathbf{s_w}$$

$$r_k(\mathbf{w}') = \|\mathbf{w}' - \mathbf{B_w}\, \mathbf{s_w}\Pi_k(\hat{\alpha})\|_2$$

$$c = \underset{k}{\arg\min}\ r_k(\mathbf{w}') \qquad (10)$$

where $\mathbf{w}' = \mathbf{w} + \mathbf{e_w}$, $\mathbf{B_w} = [\mathbf{R}\mathbf{A}\alpha, \mathbf{I}_D]$ is a $D \times (N + D)$ matrix, $\mathbf{I}_D$ is a $D \times D$ Identity matrix and $\mathbf{s_w} = [\alpha, \mathbf{e_w}]^T$ We will use (10) to identify the malware family of an unknown test sample.

4. EXPERIMENTS

We test our technique on two public malware datasets: Malimg Dataset [22] and Malheur Dataset [28]. On both datasets, we select equal number of samples to reduce any bias towards a particular family [20]. The data is converted to numerical form and represented as a matrix as defined in (1) and then projected to lower dimensions using Random Projections (RP). For comparison, we use GIST features [25], which have been previously applied for malware classification [22]. We use the SRC framework (10) to identify the malware family of a test sample and compare with Nearest Neighbors (NN) classification that was previously used in [22]. We vary the dimensions from $\{48, 96, 192, 256, 384, 512\}$, which are consistent for both RP and GIST. In our experiments, we chose 80% of a dataset for training and 20% for testing.

4.1 Classification

4.1.1 Results on Malimg Dataset

The Malimg dataset contains 25 malware families with 9,342 samples, which we obtained from the authors of [22]. The dataset has a mixture of both packed and unpacked malware and the number of samples per family varies from 80 to 2,949. In our experiments, we select 80 samples per family (the minimum number present in all families). The size of the largest malware (M) was 840,960 bytes and all samples were zero padded to this size. The results are shown in Fig. 3a. First, we see that the classification accuracy increases as the dimensionality increased from 48 to 512. Beyond 512, there was no significant change in accuracy for both GIST and RP. The best accuracy of **92.83%** was obtained for RP with SRC as the classifier. At the same dimension, the lowest accuracy was for RP with NN as the classifier (84.45%). The accuracies for GIST for both classifiers were almost the same, in the middle range (88-89%).

4.1.2 Results on Malheur Dataset

The Malheur dataset consists of 3,131 malware binaries from 24 malware families, which we obtained from the authors of [28]. The malware binaries were labeled such that a majority amongst six different antivirus products shared similar labels. The number of samples per family varied between 20 and 300. We chose 20 samples from all families in our experiments. For this dataset, the value of M was 3,364,864. The classification results are shown in Fig. 3b. Here too, the best accuracy of **98.55%** was obtained for RP at 512 dimensions with SRC as classifier. However, unlike the Malimg dataset, RP with NN as classifier also had a high accuracy of 96.06%. This shows that the random projections of the variants in Malheur dataset are closely packed in lower dimensions. On the other hand, the accuracies for GIST features were around 93% for both classifiers.

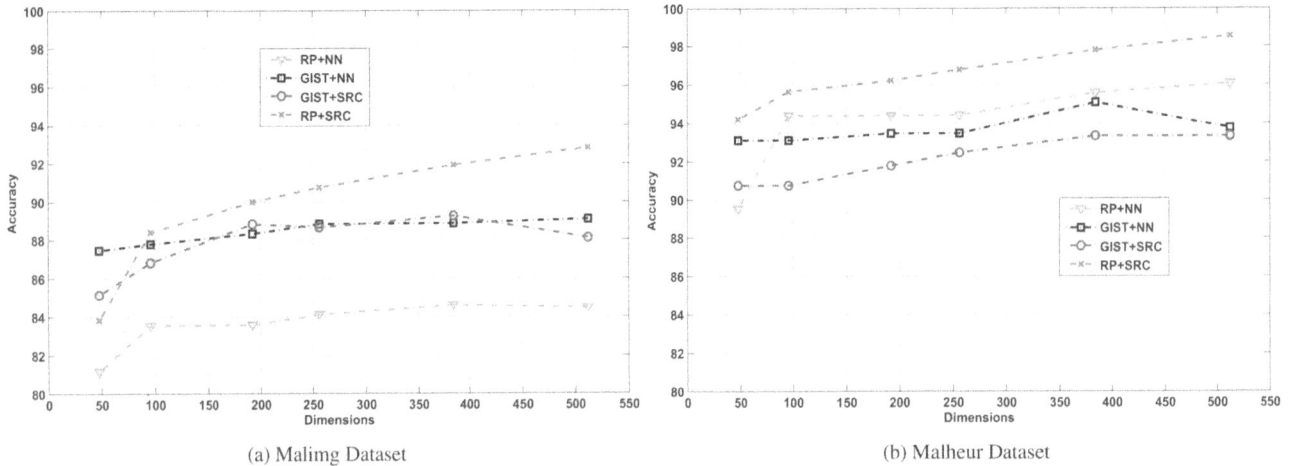

(a) Malimg Dataset

(b) Malheur Dataset

Figure 3: Experimental Results on (a) Malimg Dataset and (b) Malheur Dataset with features using Random Projections (RP) and GIST, and classification algorithm using Sparse Representation based Classification (SRC) and Nearest Neighbor (NN).

4.2 Comparison with Other Features

We compare our proposed approach with other relevant malware similarity features: *ssdeep* [17], GIST [22] and n-grams [16]. For n-grams, we chose $n = 2$ and computed a 2^{16} dimensional feature vector. The results are shown in Tab. 1. For both datasets, our proposed approach outperformed *ssdeep*, GIST and n-grams based features.

Table 1: Comparison of Classification Accuracies

Dataset	*ssdeep*	GIST	n-grams	RP
Malimg Dataset	67.63	89.08	91.75	**92.83**
Malheur Dataset	81.6	94.21	94.26	**98.55**

4.3 Rejecting Outliers

In order to reject test samples that do not belong to any family in a dataset, the Sparsity Coefficient Index (SCI) of a coefficient vector $\alpha \in \mathbb{R}^N$ is defined as:

$$SCI(\alpha) = \frac{\frac{L.max\|\Pi_i(\alpha)\|_1}{\|\alpha\|_1} - 1}{L - 1} \qquad (11)$$

The value of SCI varies between 0 and 1, 1 being the test sample can be represented as a linear combination of one family and 0 being the test sample is spread across all the families. It is common to have a threshold $\tau \in (0, 1)$ and reject outliers that are below τ.

For the Malimg Dataset, we vary τ for a fixed dimension ($D = 512$) as shown in Fig. 4a. At $\tau = 0.1$, the accuracy is 92.5% with no samples rejected. Accuracy of 100% is achieved when $\tau = 0.5$, at which 25% of the samples are rejected from the dataset. Similarly, for the Malheur dataset, we computed the accuracies and the percentage of samples dropped while varying τ. In Fig. 4b, we see that accuracy of 100% is reached when $\tau = 0.6$, but with only 5% of samples rejected.

4.4 Approximate l_1-norm

So far, we have used Basis Pursuit (BP) [7] for l_1-norm minimization and to recover the sparse coefficients. However, BP is computationally expensive and is not suitable for large scale data. Here, we compare the computation time and accuracy obtained using BP with an approximate l_1-norm minimization method, Orthogonal Matching Pursuit (OMP) [29]. OMP is a greedy algorithm that works by iteratively selecting a subset of columns from

the training data matrix that are almost orthogonal. We repeat the experiments on both datasets using OMP and report the time taken to identify the families of all samples in the test set. The results are shown in Tab. 2. We see that for both datasets, the computation time decreased by a factor of 18 (Malimg) and 30 (Malheur) respectively, at the cost of slight decrease in classification accuracy. This makes OMP suitable for large scale malware classification.

4.5 Large Scale Analysis

We evaluated our technique on two diverse large scale datasets. On both datasets, we randomly selected 20% of the data for testing and used Orthogonal Matching Pursuit to find the sparse coefficients. The results on both datasets show that our technique is applicable in large scale scenarios.

4.5.1 Results on Offensive Computing Dataset

We downloaded more than 1.4 Million malware from the Open Malware sharing platform [2] (formerly known as Offensive Computing). The samples were fed to different Antivirus software for labeling and the software that had minimum number of unknown labels was selected. This resulted in 2,124 malware families and we randomly selected 20 samples from each family to obtain a dataset of 42,480 samples (20 was the minimum number of samples present in some families). The size of the largest malware was 9.3 MB. We repeated the experiments using OMP and obtained an average classification accuracy of **66.34%**. The overall testing time was approximately 4 hours on a standard desktop machine. This time can further be reduced by using parallelization techniques. Out of 2,124 families, **927** families had an accuracy of **100%**. The average SCI value for these families was 0.97, with most values being 1. This shows that SCI can be used as a confidence measure during testing. At an SCI threshold of 0.6, 24.78% of the test samples were rejected and the classification accuracy was **77.08%**.

4.5.2 Results on Anubis Dataset

Next, we evaluated our technique on another large scale dataset that we obtained from the authors of Anubis [5]. The Anubis dataset had 36,784 samples divided into 209 clusters, with 176 samples per cluster. The clusters were labeled according to the behavioral pattern of a malware upon dynamic analysis [5]. This dataset is different from the Offensive Computing dataset in two aspects. First, the number of samples in a family/cluster is higher. Second, the labeling of clusters is based on dynamic analysis. This means there

138

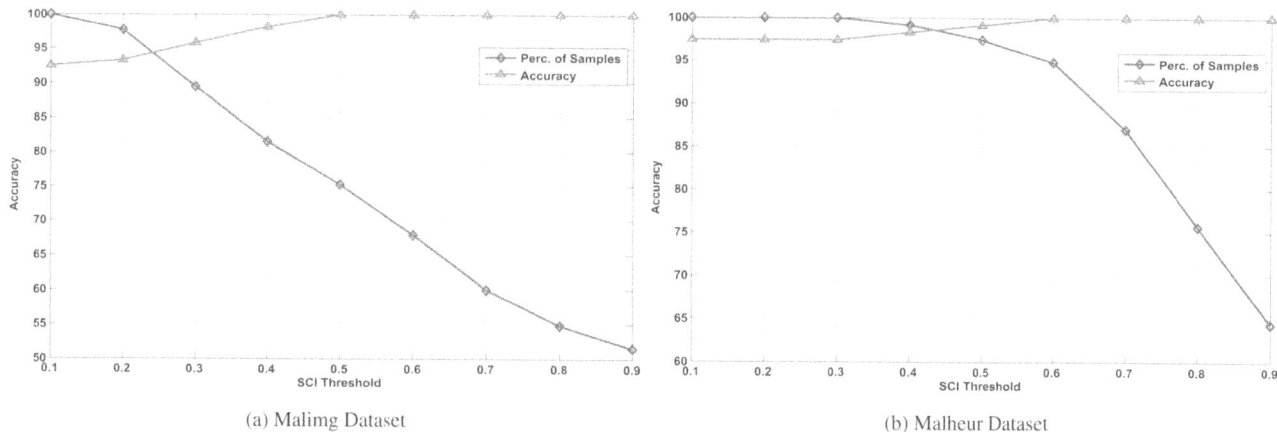

(a) Malimg Dataset   (b) Malheur Dataset

Figure 4: Rejecting outliers based on Sparsity Coefficient Index (SCI). Higher the value of SCI, higher the classification accuracy. Both datasets achieve 100% accuracies at an SCI value of 0.6. For the Mallheur dataset, only 5% of samples are rejected to achieve this accuracy. However, for the Malimg dataset, nearly 32% of samples are rejected for the same.

Table 2: Basis Pursuit (BP) vs Orthogonal Matching Pursuit (OMP)

Dataset	BP Accuracy	OMP Accuracy	BP Computation Time (secs)	OMP Computation Time (secs)
Malimg Dataset	92.83	89.25	420	**24**
Malheur Dataset	98.55	97.39	180	**6**

is a possibility that two samples that have very different structure but similar behavior can be assigned the same cluster, and our technique will not work on such samples. For this dataset, the maximum size of the malware was 8.1 MB. On repeating the experiment, we obtained an average classification accuracy of **57.36%**. This is much lower than the accuracy obtained for the Offensive Computing dataset, which had more number of classes (by a factor of 10). This perhaps shows that our method is better applicable to malware datasets that have finer labels. The overall testing time was approximately 3 hours on a standard desktop. For this dataset, **27** clusters had an accuracy of **100%** and 50 clusters had an accuracy of more than 90%. On setting the SCI threshold to 0.6, 34.64% of the test samples were rejected and we obtained an accuracy of **77.12%**.

5. DISCUSSIONS AND CONCLUSION

Our approach works well mainly on malware variants that have similar structure. However, we observe that most variants are those that are structurally similar (for example, Regin variants in Fig. 1). This is also evident from our large scale experiments. Further, previous works such as [24] have shown that the performance of structurally similar features and behavior based features are almost the same.

In future, we will explore using Random Projections as malware signatures and distinguish them from benign samples. While our current approach estimates the family of a malware, we will also focus on identifying the exact source from which a malware variant evolves.

In this paper, we proposed a novel method to identify families of malware variants using a combination of Sparse Representation based Classification (SRC) and Random Projections (RP). Experiments on two standard malware datasets, as well as large scale data showed promising results. We believe that our approach, that is based on representing malware binaries as numerical signals, will open the scope of malware analysis to broader fields.

6. ACKNOWLEDGEMENTS

This work has been supported by grants ONR # N00014-11-10111 and ONR # N00014-14-1-0027.

7. REFERENCES

[1] Kaspersky lab is detecting 325,000 new malicious files every day. http://usa.kaspersky.com/about-us/press-center/press-releases/kaspersky-lab-detecting-325000-new-malicious-files-every-day.

[2] Offensive Computing Dataset. http://offensivecomputing.net.

[3] Regin: Top-tier espionage tool enables stealthy surveillance. http://www.symantec.com/connect/blogs/regin-top-tier-espionage-tool-enables-stealthy-surveillance.

[4] T. Abou-Assaleh, N. Cercone, V. Keselj, and R. Sweidan. N-gram-based detection of new malicious code. In *Computer Software and Applications Conference, 2004. COMPSAC 2004. Proceedings of the 28th Annual International*, volume 2, pages 41–42. IEEE, 2004.

[5] U. Bayer, P. Comparetti, C. Hlauschek, C. Kruegel, and E. Kirda. Scalable, behavior-based malware clustering. In *Network and Distributed System Security Symposium (NDSS)*. Citeseer, 2009.

[6] V. Cevher, A. Sankaranarayanan, M. F. Duarte, D. Reddy, R. G. Baraniuk, and R. Chellappa. Compressive sensing for background subtraction. In *Computer Vision–ECCV 2008*, pages 155–168. Springer, 2008.

[7] S. S. Chen, D. L. Donoho, and M. A. Saunders. Atomic decomposition by basis pursuit. *SIAM journal on scientific computing*, 20(1):33–61, 1998.

[8] G. E. Dahl, J. W. Stokes, L. Deng, and D. Yu. Large-scale malware classification using random projections and neural networks. In *Acoustics, Speech and Signal Processing (ICASSP), 2013 IEEE International Conference on*, pages 3422–3426. IEEE, 2013.

[9] D. Donoho and J. Tanner. Counting faces of randomly projected polytopes when the projection radically lowers dimension. *Journal of the American Mathematical Society*, 22(1):1–53, 2009.

[10] J. Hegedus, Y. Miche, A. Ilin, and A. Lendasse. Methodology for behavioral-based malware analysis and detection using random projections and k-nearest neighbors classifiers. In *Computational Intelligence and Security (CIS), 2011 Seventh International Conference on*, pages 1016–1023. IEEE, 2011.

[11] X. Hu, T. Chiueh, and K. Shin. Large-scale malware indexing using function-call graphs. In *Proceedings of the 16th ACM conference on Computer and communications security*, pages 611–620. ACM, 2009.

[12] G. Jacob, P. Comparetti, M. Neugschwandtner, C. Kruegel, and G. Vigna. A static, packer-agnostic filter to detect similar malware sample. In *Proceedings of the 9th Conference on Detection of Intrusions and Malware and Vulnerability Assessment*. Springer, 2012.

[13] J. Jang, D. Brumley, and S. Venkataraman. Bitshred: feature hashing malware for scalable triage and semantic analysis. In *Proceedings of the 18th ACM conference on Computer and communications security*, pages 309–320. ACM, 2011.

[14] M. Karim, A. Walenstein, A. Lakhotia, and L. Parida. Malware phylogeny generation using permutations of code. *Journal in Computer Virology*, 1(1):13–23, 2005.

[15] D. Kirat, L. Nataraj, G. Vigna, and B. Manjunath. Sigmal: A static signal processing based malware triage. In *Proceedings of the Annual Computer Security Applications Conference (ACSAC)*, Dec 2013.

[16] J. Kolter and M. Maloof. Learning to detect and classify malicious executables in the wild. *The Journal of Machine Learning Research*, 7:2721–2744, 2006.

[17] J. Kornblum. Identifying almost identical files using context triggered piecewise hashing. *Digital Investigation*, 3:91–97, 2006.

[18] C. Kruegel, E. Kirda, D. Mutz, W. Robertson, and G. Vigna. Polymorphic worm detection using structural information of executables. In *Recent Advances in Intrusion Detection*, pages 207–226. Springer, 2006.

[19] A. Lakhotia, A. Walenstein, C. Miles, and A. Singh. Vilo: a rapid learning nearest-neighbor classifier for malware triage. *Journal of Computer Virology and Hacking Techniques*, 9(3):109–123, 2013.

[20] P. Li, L. Liu, D. Gao, and M. K. Reiter. On challenges in evaluating malware clustering. In *Recent Advances in Intrusion Detection*, pages 238–255. Springer, 2010.

[21] X. Mei and H. Ling. Robust visual tracking and vehicle classification via sparse representation. *Pattern Analysis and Machine Intelligence, IEEE Transactions on*, 33(11):2259–2272, 2011.

[22] L. Nataraj, S. Karthikeyan, G. Jacob, and B. S. Manjunath. Malware images: visualization and automatic classification. In *Proceedings of the 8th International Symposium on Visualization for Cyber Security*, VizSec '11, pages 4:1–4:7, New York, NY, USA, 2011. ACM.

[23] L. Nataraj, D. Kirat, B. Manjunath, and G. Vigna. Sarvam: Search and retrieval of malware. In *Proceedings of the Annual Computer Security Conference (ACSAC) Worshop on Next Generation Malware Attacks and Defense (NGMAD)*, 2013.

[24] L. Nataraj, V. Yegneswaran, P. Porras, and J. Zhang. A comparative assessment of malware classification using binary texture analysis and dynamic analysis. In *Proceedings of the 4th ACM workshop on Security and Artificial Intelligence*, AISec '11, pages 21–30, New York, NY, USA, 2011. ACM.

[25] A. Olivia and A. Torralba. Modeling the shape of a scene: a holistic representation of the spatial envelope. *Intl. Journal of Computer Vision*, 42(3):145–175, 2001.

[26] R. Perdisci and A. Lanzi. McBoost: Boosting scalability in malware collection and analysis using statistical classification of executables. *Computer Security Applications*, pages 301–310, Dec. 2008.

[27] J. K. Pillai, V. M. Patel, R. Chellappa, and N. K. Ratha. Secure and robust iris recognition using random projections and sparse representations. *IEEE Trans. Pattern Anal. Mach. Intell.*, 33(9):1877–1893, 2011.

[28] K. Rieck, P. Trinius, C. Willems, and T. Holz. Automatic analysis of malware behavior using machine learning. *Journal of Computer Security*, 19(4):639–668, 2011.

[29] J. A. Tropp and A. C. Gilbert. Signal recovery from random measurements via orthogonal matching pursuit. *Information Theory, IEEE Transactions on*, 53(12):4655–4666, 2007.

[30] G. Wicherski. pehash: A novel approach to fast malware clustering. In *2nd USENIX Workshop on Large-Scale Exploits and Emergent Threats (LEET)*, 2009.

[31] J. Wright, A. Y. Yang, A. Ganesh, S. S. Sastry, and Y. Ma. Robust face recognition via sparse representation. *Pattern Analysis and Machine Intelligence, IEEE Transactions on*, 31(2):210–227, 2009.

Thumbnail Preserving Encryption for JPEG

Charles V. Wright   Wu-chi Feng   Feng Liu

Portland State University
Portland, Oregon USA
{cvwright, wuchi, fliu}@cs.pdx.edu

ABSTRACT

With more and more data being stored in the cloud, securing multimedia data is becoming increasingly important. Use of existing encryption methods with cloud services is possible, but makes many web-based applications difficult or impossible to use. In this paper, we propose a new image encryption scheme specially designed to protect JPEG images in cloud photo storage services. Our technique allows efficient reconstruction of an accurate low-resolution thumbnail from the ciphertext image, but aims to prevent the extraction of any more detailed information. This will allow efficient storage and retrieval of image data in the cloud but protect its contents from outside hackers or snooping cloud administrators. Experiments of the proposed approach using an online selfie database show that it can achieve a good balance of privacy, utility, image quality, and file size.

Categories and Subject Descriptors

E.3 [**Data**]: Data Encryption; I.4.2 [**Image Processing and Computer Vision**]: Compression (Coding)

Keywords

Multimedia encryption; Image security; Privacy

1. INTRODUCTION

As network connectivity continues to increase, cloud services have become perhaps the most common tools for storing and sharing photos. As early as 2010, Facebook was already receiving tens of millions of new images every day [2]. The idea of moving all one's personal files to the cloud is increasingly popular because it offers a number of benefits over earlier approaches, including low cost, worldwide availability, built-in redundancy against hardware or network failure, and nearly infinite storage capacity.

At the same time, the security and privacy of today's cloud services leaves much to be desired. Users must trust the operators of the cloud infrastructure to protect their data against malicious outsiders seeking to steal secrets, as in the 2014 compromise of Apple iCloud accounts [7], in which intimate photos were stolen from hundreds of victims and posted to the Internet. Users must also trust that the cloud service itself (or its employees) will not misuse its access for its own ends, as when Facebook used its members' photos to build a face recognition database [13].

A simple way to secure one's multimedia data in the cloud would be to encrypt all files before uploading them into the cloud, using a key unknown to the cloud service. But the use of encryption presents its own challenges. First, traditional file encryption tools like PGP or `openssl` produce opaque binary byte streams as output, whereas the cloud photo services expect to receive only valid image files. Format-compliant encryption schemes can encrypt the image data while maintaining valid file formats. Recent work on P3 [12] and Cryptagram [17] has proposed using similar schemes to protect images posted to social networking sites. However, even format-compliant encryption still breaks much of the useful functionality that made the cloud services popular in the first place, because the cloud service can no longer perform meaningful computations on the data.

One particularly painful limitation that encryption creates for photo management services is that the service can no longer create useful low-resolution "thumbnail" versions of the images it stores. Each user may store hundreds or thousands of photos, each of which may be a few megabytes in size. Normally, the cloud service generates reduced resolution versions of each photo so the user can preview her collection without downloading hundreds of megabytes every time she visits the page. Without the thumbnails, even a simple task like finding a certain photo becomes much more difficult; it does not help that cameras tend to create images with non-informative filenames like `DSC0293.JPG`.

In other applications, it may be useful to allow the cloud service to perform some analysis on the uploaded images. For example, some security cameras can upload a snapshot to the cloud whenever they detect motion. The cloud service then uses its greater processing power to perform more intensive image processing to look for the presence of a human in the image. It would be nice if we could give the cloud service just enough information to do its job, while still allowing a user to log in from her mobile device to retrieve and decrypt the full-resolution image that triggered an alarm.

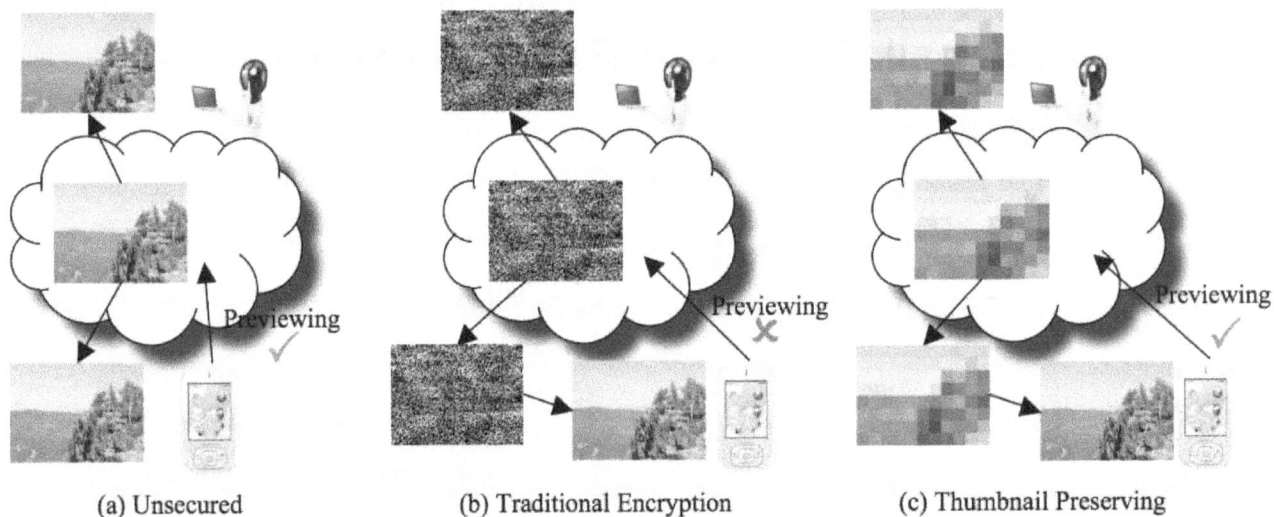

Figure 1: Different Approaches to Cloud Storage of Images. (a) Images stored in plaintext are available to both user and hacker. (b) Conventionally encrypted. Less usable for the client but secure from attackers. (c) Thumbnail-preserving. Attacker has access to the obscured version only. Users can preview thumbnails, then download at full resolution and decrypt locally.

In this paper, we propose an image encryption scheme for images that allows the cloud service to create accurate, reduced resolution thumbnails from the encrypted images, but prevents the extraction of more detailed information. Our goal is not to provide perfect security, but rather to protect privacy in images stored online, while still allowing convenient use of today's cloud services. To be useful in practice, any such scheme must:

1. Support the image formats used in popular cloud services like Flickr, Apple iCloud, Google Drive, and Facebook. In practice, this means support for JPEG.

2. Obscure the image data sufficiently to prevent the cloud service or an attacker from recovering fine details from the image, for example revealing the faces (or other body parts) of people in the photo.

3. Preserve coarse perceptual features of the image so that the user can effectively manage large photo collections online, using low-resolution versions of the images generated by the cloud service. A user who knows what the original photo looks like can recognize it trivially from the thumbnail.

4. Enable the user to reverse the encryption to recover a high-quality representation of the original image from the encrypted image.

5. Degrade gracefully when the cloud service compresses the obfuscated image to save on storage space. Facebook and other social networking services are known to apply aggressive compression to all uploaded photos.

Additionally, we would like to minimize the increase in file size incurred by the obfuscation, because many users access cloud services via mobile devices over slow or expensive wireless links. We also avoid reliance on trusted third parties as in P3 [12].

We experiment with and demonstrate the utility of the proposed approach with user-generated images from an online selfie dataset. Our results show that our approach can obscure interesting features in real user-generated images from the web, while maintaining acceptable image quality and file size. In the remainder of this paper, we provide some necessary background and related work. We then follow with a description of the proposed approach, some experimentation, and a discussion.

2. BACKGROUND AND RELATED WORK

2.1 Securing Data

Typically, to protect the confidentiality of sensitive data against a nosy third party, the best approach is to encrypt it using a rigorously vetted encryption scheme and a secret, hard-to-guess key. Many symmetric encryption schemes are built on block ciphers, for example AES-GCM is the block cipher AES [13] in Galois-counter mode [14].

There are a number of desirable properties for any encryption scheme. Most importantly, it should be computationally infeasible for anyone who does not have the key to recover the original data (the "plaintext") from the encrypted "ciphertext"; this is called *one-wayness*. Most current encryption schemes also aim to provide much stronger security, so that the adversary cannot learn anything at all—not even a single bit—about the plaintext from the ciphertext, even if he has access to a large number of (plaintext, ciphertext) pairs encrypted under the same key [15]; this is called *semantic security*.

In this work, our goal is a scheme that is one-way but not semantically secure. We want to prevent the adversary from learning the true values of our pixels, but we intentionally reveal coarser features, including the average color in each block of the image. We note that the approach presented here also reveals the set of pixel values in each block of the image. Because this technique reveals so much more information than a typical encryption scheme, the reader may find it more intuitive to think of this as a reversible *obfuscation* method.

2.2 Multimedia Cryptography

Multimedia cryptography techniques typically focus on taking advantage of the fact that the image data is (or is going to be) highly compressed and more or less random in byte distribution. As such, lighter-weight encryption techniques can be employed to encrypt and decrypt the stream [8, 14, 16].

More closely related to our approach is work on partial image encryption [3, 20, 19, 15, 10]. Stütz and Uhl's transparent encryption technique for JPEG2000 [15] is thumbnail-preserving and uses a traditional encryption method (AES) to achieve very good security; unfortunately it only works with the relatively rare JPEG2000 format. Unterweger and Uhl's bitstream encryption for JPEG [19] is also similar to our approach in many ways. Because they operate on the compressed JPEG bitstream rather than on the pixels, they incur no increase in file size. At the same time, their technique does create some visual artifacts, and it is not guaranteed to preserve an accurate thumbnail.

3. THUMBNAIL PRESERVING ENCRYPTION

Our encryption scheme is essentially a special purpose, wide block, tweakable block cipher [9] for image data. Given an image of MxN pixels, a secret key k, and a block size B, we divide the image spatially into blocks of neighboring pixels, ie BxB squares. The goal is to encrypt each block such that the cipher image reveals the average pixel value in the block but nothing more. This allows an untrusted third party who does not posess the key to re-construct an accurate M/B x N/B pixel thumbnail, where each block in the cipher image corresponds to a single pixel in the thumbnail. This has the desired effect of preserving coarse features of the image—those larger than the block size—while obscuring fine details smaller than the block size.

Naturally, a user who has the key can decrypt the cipher image to recover a full resolution MxN image. Our encryption scheme is carefully designed so that, even if the cipher image has been lossily compressed with JPEG, the decrypted image still maintains high fidelity to the original, and the image quality degrades gracefully as the level of JPEG quantization increases.

3.1 Key Derivation

Given an input image and a secret passphrase, we use the passphrase to derive a secret symmetric key K using a password based key derivation function [11]. We also use some public information about the image, such as its filename, as a "salt" in the key derivation function; this makes it more difficult for an adversary to guess our key and ensures that we derive a different key for each unique filename.

3.2 Color Space Transformation

In the following sections, we describe techniques for operating on images as two-dimensional arrays of greyscale pixel values. We treat a color images as a collection of three such 2-d arrays or "planes", one for each dimension of the color space, for example R,G,B or Y,U,V.

JPEG uses the YUV color space, where pixel values are represented by a luminance value, Y, and two chrominance values, U and V. Because the human eye is more sensitive to changes in brightness than in color, JPEG typically stores the U and V channels at half the resolution of the Y channel. Given a JPEG image as input, we simply decompress it to extract the Y, U, and V planes. If we are given an RGB image as input, we first convert it to the YUV colorspace and subsample the chrominance channels at 4:1:1 just like a JPEG encoder would.

We encrypt each plane independently using a unique key. We use the password-derived key K to compute a key for each color plane as a pseudorandom function (PRF) of the name of the plane. In our prototype implementation, we use HMAC-SHA1 as our PRF, so we compute the key for the Y plane as $K_Y = HMAC_K(\text{"Y"})$.

After encryption, we recombine the Y, U, and V planes to arrive at a raw uncompressed YUV representation of the cipher image. Finally, the cipher image YUV array (with its subsampled UV planes) is passed to the JPEG encoder, which then compresses the data in the regular way.

We take this approach to better align the encryption with the JPEG compression process. In early experiments, we investigated encrypting by operating on the full R,G,B or Y,U,V pixels as a single plane. While this produced acceptable results for lossless PNG images, with JPEG it led to significant artifacts and loss of color in the decrypted image. The reason was that dissimilar pixels in the original image were often placed next to each other in the permutation step. Then, when the JPEG encoder performed its subsampling on the U and V planes, much of the original color detail was lost.

3.3 Block Encryption

Then, if our block size is B, we divide the image into blocks of BxB pixels, and we encrypt the pixels in each block by first permuting the order in which they appear. Because each block can be encrypted independently of all the others, this design allows for a very fast implementation in the future using parallel processing on a GPU.

We use the (x, y) coordinates of the block as a "tweak" in our block encryption algorithm [9]. The tweak ensures that, even if the same block of pixel values appears at several different locations in the image, it will be encrypted differently at each location. For the block located at (x, y) in an image plane P having key K_P, we seed a cryptographically secure pseudorandom number generator with the seed $s = HMAC_{K_P}(x||y)$. (The $||$ operator denotes concatenation.) We then use the PRNG to permute the pixels in the block as follows.

We shuffle the locations of the pixels within the block, using our cryptographically secure PRNG to drive a random shuffle algorithm from Fisher and Yates [5]. We chose the Fisher-Yates shuffle because, when used with a good pseudo-random number generator, it makes all permutations of the input equally likely. As a result, the locations of the pixels in the cipher image give the adversary no information about their original locations. If he is to reconstruct the image, he must rely on the values of the pixels to infer which ones go where. With a sufficiently large block size, shuffling alone may actually give us some reasonable security (see Section 3.5). Figure 2 shows an example 320x320-pixel image encrypted with 32x32 blocks.

Figure 2: (left) Original and (right) 32x32 block-shuffled

3.4 Alternative: Recursive Block Encryption

As an alternative to the baseline approach above, we also propose the following scheme for use with large images, or in applications where efficiency and image quality are prioritized over high security.

As before, we first derive a secret symmetric key for the image and divide the image up into BxB-pixel blocks. Next, we divide each BxB block into a $(B/b)x(B/b)$ grid of smaller bxb-pixel sub-blocks. (Because JPEG uses 8x8-pixel blocks in its compression algorithm, we set $b = 8$.) We seed the PRNG as before and use the Fisher-Yates algorithm to permute the location of the sub-blocks within the block. Finally, we encrypt the pixels in each bxb sub-block using the algorithm from Section 3.3.

Figure 3 shows an example of this technique, using 32x32-pixel blocks and 16x16-pixel sub-blocks. Part (A) shows an intermediate result after the sub-blocks have been rearranged, but before the pixels have been encrypted. Part (B) shows the final encrypted image. Note that we chose a very large sub-block size for this image to illustrate the technique. In practice, the sub-blocks should be made much smaller to achieve good JPEG compression.

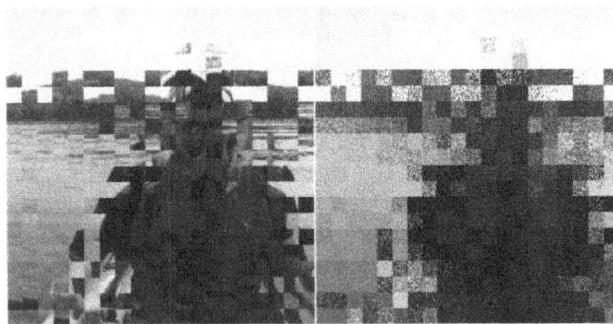

Figure 3: (left) After shuffling 16x16 sub-blocks within 32x32 blocks and (right) after shuffling pixels in sub-blocks

3.5 Security

It's not clear what is the best way to evaluate the security of our scheme. As a first approximation of the difficulty of reconstructing the image, we note that the number of possible permutations increases as the factorial of the number of pixels in the block. So for example, a 32x32 block contains 1024 pixels; there are therefore $1024! \approx 4 \times 10^{2567}$ ways to re-order its pixels. In comparison, there are only $2^{256} \approx 10^{77}$

possible AES-256 keys. This is the general approach used by Unterweger and Uhl for evaluating the security of their partial image encryption scheme in [19]. However, this approach is problematic because it focuses only on brute force attacks, ignoring the possibility of cryptanalytic or statistical attacks.

The most promising attack method may be to start with the low-resolution thumbnail and use super resolution techniques [6, 21] to increase its effective resolution. Super resolution can commonly be used to double the resolution of an image; if our attacker can do this, then he can replace each pixel in our thumbnail with a 2x2 grid of pixels. Then, he can go back to the ciphertext image and examine the pixels in the block corresponding to the given pixel in the thumbnail. He can then attempt to use the 2x2 grid of superresolution pixel values to place each pixel in the block back into the quadrant where it started. If he is successful, he can repeat this process several times to recover a much higher resolution version of the image.

Fortunately, it appears that this attack may be computationally quite hard. When the attacker attempts to put the pixels back into the correct quadrant of the block, for an NxN block he must find $N^2/4$ pixels whose average value is the value of the super resolution pixel for that quadrant. This is an instance of the d-SUM problem, a generalization of the more well-known 3SUM problem. The best known lower bound [4] for d-SUM given n numbers is approximately $O(n^{d/2})$. When $d = n/4$ as we have here, d-SUM is approximately $O(n^{n/8})$.

4. EXPERIMENTATION

Knowing that our techniques tend to create cipher images with more high frequency components than in natural images, we are interested in the impact of our encryption on the encrypted file size and the quality of decrypted images. In the remainder of this section, we describe the image dataset used and the results of our initial empirical evaluation.

4.1 Image Dataset

To study the performance impact of our techniques, we require an image dataset. Because the block size of permutation is currently fixed across the entire image, we sought an image set with roughly the same image content per pixel density. This allows us to look at the effect of encryption on images in a more meaningful way. For this reason, we chose an online database of "selfies" collected from Instagram by the Selfiecity project [18]. With selfies, the distance to camera and the object of the image (the person in this case) will be roughly constant. From this database, we randomly selected 50 images for this initial study. The selfies are 640x640 pixel JPEGs; 48 of the 50 are color images and 2 are black and white. Most were taken with mobile phones.

4.2 File Size and Image Quality

We encrypted each of the 50 images using the two techniques described in Section 3, with block sizes ranging from 8x8 up to 256x256. Each encrypted image was then JPEG compressed using the ImageMagick `convert` utility on Linux, with quality parameter ranging between 10 and 95. Finally, each cipher image was decrypted to recover the pixels of the original image, albeit with some loss due to JPEG.

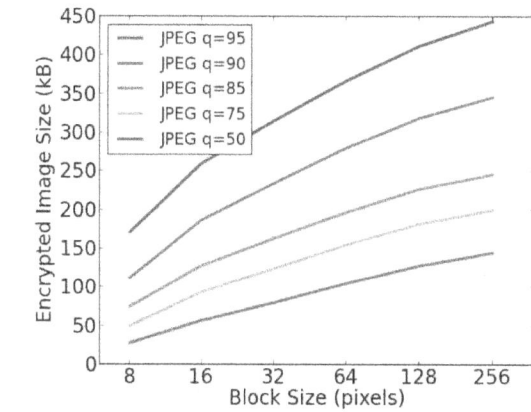

(a) File size for block-permuted images

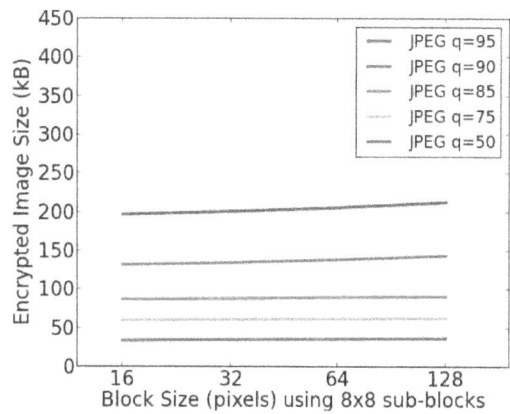

(b) File size for recursively permuted images

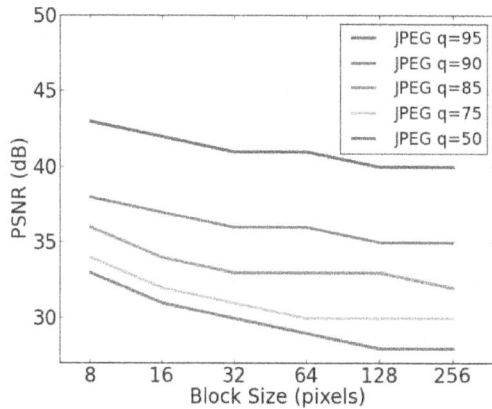

(c) Quality of decrypted images with block-based permutations

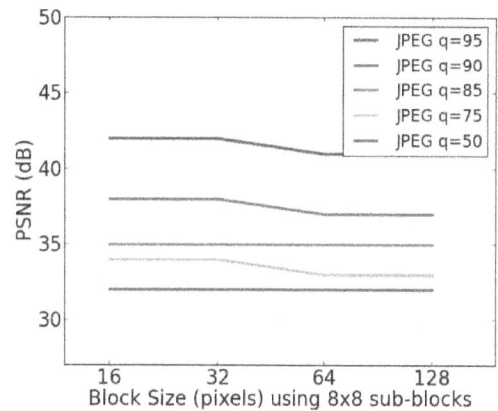

(d) Quality of decrypted images with recursive permutations

Figure 4: Experimental Results

4.2.1 Size of the Encrypted Images

Figure 4a and Figure 4b show the average size of images encrypted using the simple block encryption and the recursive encryption technique, respectively. The average file size of the original plaintext images was 56 kB.

With the simple block-based approach, as the block size increases, it becomes more and more likely that the permutation destroys spatial locality in the image by placing pixels from distant parts of the image next to each other. This creates high-frequency noise in the ciphertext image, which causes a large increase in file size, particularly for less-aggressive JPEG settings.

4.2.2 Quality of the Decrypted Images

Figure 5 shows two example images decrypted after the ciphertext was JPEG compressed with q=85. Figure 4c and Figure 4d show how the average peak signal-to-noise ratio (PSNR) for the decrypted images changes as the block size increases. When we use the simple block-based encryption scheme, doubling the block size tends to decrease the PSNR by about 1-2 dB. With the recursive block encryption scheme, the PSNR is relatively unaffected by changes in block size. This is because JPEG operates on 8x8 blocks, and the pixels within each 8x8 sub-block in the encrypted

image are still roughly similar to one another even after being permuted and perturbed.

Figure 5: Decrypted images (left) 16x16 blocks and (right) 64x64 blocks

5. CONCLUSIONS AND FUTURE WORK

We have presented a new image encryption algorithm for protecting JPEG image data stored in the cloud. It provides tunable privacy through an adjustable block size and allows the untrusted cloud service to reconstruct an accurate low-resolution thumbnail of the encrypted photo. Experiments with a data set of real selfie images from the web show that, by selecting an appropriate block size, we can achieve a good balance between convenience, privacy, image quality, and file size.

In future work, to make the adversary's job even more difficult, we will apply additional transformations to modify the pixel values after shuffling. The key property for these transformations is that they must (approximately) preserve the average value of the pixels in the block—otherwise the encryption will no longer be thumbnail-preserving. To achieve reasonable compression and high quality on natural images, we also approximately preserve the standard deviation of the pixels in each block. The simplest way to perturb pixel values without shifting the mean is to add some small noise to each pixel, where the noise is drawn from a statistical distribution with mean zero and relatively small standard deviation. For example, in additive white Gaussian noise (AWGN) with shape parameter σ, we set each pixel p_i equal to $p_i = p_i + n_i$, where $n_i \sim N(0, \sigma)$.

We will also investigate another approach, which also preserves the sample standard deviation. We first compute the mean value m of the pixels in the block and the difference between each pixel p_i and the mean, $d_i = p_i - m$. Then we set the new value for each pixel value to be:

$$p_i = \begin{cases} m + d_i, & \text{with probability } 0.5 \\ m - d_i, & \text{with probability } 0.5 \end{cases}$$

Each pixel has a 50% chance of being "reflected" across the sample mean and a 50% chance of staying the same. In either case, the mean is unchanged, and each value in the sample stays the same distance away from the mean, leaving the sample standard deviation unchanged. This way, blocks that are very uniform or low-frequency, e.g. a patch of clear blue sky, can still be compressed extremely efficiently, while blocks containing more interesting features are more strongly perturbed.

Finally, we will also develop a better understanding of the relationship between our encryption parameters (eg. block size) and the cloud service's ability to perform various analyses on the uploaded images. For example, work on using super resolution to improve face recognition [1] indicates that relatively large blocks may be required to prevent the recognition of people in our photos.

6. REFERENCES

[1] Simon Baker and Takeo Kanade. Limits on super-resolution and how to break them. *IEEE Transactions on Pattern Analysis and Machine Intelligence*, 24(9):1167–1183, September 2002.

[2] Doug Beaver, Sanjeev Kumar, Harry C Li, Jason Sobel, Peter Vajgel, et al. Finding a needle in haystack: Facebook's photo storage. In *OSDI*, volume 10, pages 1–8, 2010.

[3] H. Cheng and Xiaobo Li. Partial encryption of compressed images and videos. *Signal Processing, IEEE Transactions on*, 48(8):2439–2451, Aug 2000.

[4] Jeff Erickson. Lower bounds for linear satisfiability problems. In *Proceedings of the Sixth Annual ACM-SIAM Symposium on Discrete Algorithms*, SODA '95, pages 388–395, Philadelphia, PA, USA, 1995.

[5] Ronald Aylmer Fisher and Frank Yates. *Statistical tables for biological, agricultural and medical research.* 3rd edition, 1949.

[6] William T Freeman, Egon C Pasztor, and Owen T Carmichael. Learning low-level vision. *International Journal of Computer Vision*, 40(1):25–47, 2000.

[7] Andy Greenberg. The police tool that pervs use to steal nude pics from Apple's iCloud. *Wired*, September 2014.

[8] Lala Krikor, Sami Baba, Thawar Arif, and Zyad Shaaban. Image encryption using DCT and stream cipher. *European Journal of Scientific Research*, 32(1):47–57, 2009.

[9] Moses Liskov, Ronald L Rivest, and David Wagner. Tweakable block ciphers. In *Advances in Cryptology—CRYPTO 2002*, pages 31–46. Springer, 2002.

[10] Benoit M Macq and Jean-Jacques Quisquater. Cryptology for digital TV broadcasting. *Proceedings of the IEEE*, 83(6), 1995.

[11] Niels Provos and David Mazieres. A future-adaptable password scheme. In *USENIX Annual Technical Conference, FREENIX Track*, pages 81–91, 1999.

[12] Moo-Ryong Ra, Ramesh Govindan, and Antonio Ortega. P3: Toward privacy-preserving photo sharing. In *NSDI*, pages 515–528, 2013.

[13] Somini Sengupta and Kevin J. O'Brien. Facebook can ID faces, but using them grows tricky. *The New York Times*, September 2012.

[14] Changgui Shi and Bharat Bhargava. An efficient mpeg video encryption algorithm. In *Reliable Distributed Systems, 1998. Proceedings. Seventeenth IEEE Symposium on*, pages 381–386. IEEE, 1998.

[15] Thomas Stütz and Andreas Uhl. On efficient transparent JPEG2000 encryption. In *Proceedings of the 9th ACM Workshop on Multimedia & Security*, pages 97–108. ACM, 2007.

[16] Lei Tang. Methods for encrypting and decrypting mpeg video data efficiently. In *Proceedings of the Fourth ACM International Conference on Multimedia*, MULTIMEDIA '96, pages 219–229, 1996.

[17] Matt Tierney, Ian Spiro, Christoph Bregler, and Lakshminarayanan Subramanian. Cryptagram: Photo privacy for online social media. In *Proceedings of the First ACM Conference on Online Social Networks*, COSN '13, pages 75–88. ACM, 2013.

[18] Alise Tifentale and Lev Manovich. *Selfiecity: Exploring Photography and Self-Fashioning in Social Media*. Palgrave Macmillan, Forthcoming.

[19] Andreas Unterweger and Andreas Uhl. Length-preserving bit-stream-based jpeg encryption. In *Proceedings of the 14th ACM Workshop on Multimedia and security*, pages 85–90. ACM, 2012.

[20] Marc Van Droogenbroeck. Partial encryption of images for real-time applications. *Fourth IEEE Benelux Signal Processing*, pages 11–15, 2004.

[21] Qiang Wang, Xiaoou Tang, and Harry Shum. Patch based blind image super resolution. In *Tenth IEEE International Conference on Computer Vision*, volume 1, pages 709–716. IEEE, 2005.

On Elliptic Curve Based Untraceable RFID Authentication Protocols [*]

Eun-Kyung Ryu
School of Computer Science
and Engineering
Kyungpook National University
Daegu 702-701, Korea
ekryu@knu.ac.kr

Dae-Soo Kim
School of Computer Science
and Engineering
Kyungpook National University
Daegu 702-701, Korea
stairways@infosec.knu.ac.kr

Kee-Young Yoo [†]
School of Computer Science
and Engineering
Kyungpook National University
Daegu 702-701, Korea
yook@knu.ac.kr

ABSTRACT

An untraceable RFID authentication scheme allows a legitimate reader to authenticate a tag, and at the same time it assures the privacy of the tag against unauthorized tracing. In this paper, we revisit three elliptic-curve based untraceable RFID authentication protocols recently published and show they are not secure against active attacks and do not support the untraceability for tags. We also provide a new construction to solve such problems using the elliptic-curved based Schnorr signature technique. Our construction satisfies all requirements for RFID security and privacy including replay protection, impersonation resistance, untraceability, and forward privacy. It requires only two point scalar multiplications and two hash operations with two messages exchanges. Compared to previous works, our construction has better security and efficiency.

Categories and Subject Descriptors

C.2.0 [**General**]: Security and protection

Keywords

RFID, untraceability, privacy, authentication, ECC

1. INTRODUCTION

An untraceable RFID authentication scheme allows a legitimate reader to authenticate a tag, and at the same time it assures the privacy of the tag against unauthorized tracing. A common solution for supporting untraceable RFID authentication is that the tag refreshes its identifier by itself, relying on a challenge-response mechanism using a symmetric key cryptography. However, in order to identify only

one single tag, symmetric-key based schemes [13, 15, 21, 26, 2, 11, 14] have an inherent problem of requiring a linear computational complexity on the system side. Alternative approach is to use public-key cryptography for solving the inherent scalability problem with symmetric-key based schemes, as in [19, 20, 18]. In particular, recent studies in [27, 25, 3, 22, 5] showed that elliptic curve cryptography (ECC), a relatively new family of public-key algorithms, is applicable to resource-constrained RFID settings. For the same level of security, elliptic curve-based schemes can be implemented with much smaller parameters, leading to significant performance advantages [17].

In this paper, we revisit three elliptic-curve based untraceable RFID authentication schemes that were recently published in [7, 24, 6], and show they all are not secure against active attacks and do not support the untraceability for tags. We also provide a new construction that satisfies the requirements of security and privacy for RFID systems, including replay protection, impersonation resistance, untraceability, and forward privacy. It requires only two point scalar multiplications and two hash operations with two messages exchanges. Compared to previous works, our construction has better security and efficiency.

1.1 Related Work

Here we focus on elliptic-curve based untraceable authentication solutions for RFID tags, which are closely related to our work. Lee, Batina and Verbauwhede [19] introduced a randomized access control protocol for untraceable RFID authentication. The protocol adopts a commitment-challenge-response mechanism using the elliptic-curve discrete logarithm problem as an underlying primitive. However, the protocol is vulnerable to tracking and replay, which is shown in [4, 10]. To address the problems, a randomized Schnorr protocol was provided by Bringer, Chabannel and Icart in [4]. Lee, Batina and Verbauwhede [20] also introduced a revised version for the randomized access control protocol. However, Deursen and Radomirovic [9] showed that both the randomized Schnorr protocol and the revised protocol are vulnerable to man-in-the-middle attacks on untraceability. In [18], Lee et al. suggested another variant of the elliptic curve based randomized access control protocol, which we refer as EC-RAC III. The authors claimed that by non-linearity EC-RAC III is able to be resistant to the attacks in [9]. The protocol, unlike the author's claim, is still not secure against the man-in-the-middle attacks on traceability, as shown by Fan, Hermans and Vercauteren in [12]. A

---

[*]This work was supported by the IT R&D program of MSIP/IITP. [10041145, Self-Organized Software platform(SoSp) for Welfare Devices]

[†]Corresponding author: yook@knu.ac.kr.

Tag (x_i, Y) — **Reader (X_i, y)**

pick $r, k \in_R \mathbb{Z}_q$
$s = f(r, kY)$
$K = kP$
$T_1 = s x_i Y$

$\xrightarrow{\quad r, K, T_1 \quad}$

$s' = f(r, yK)$
$X'_i = y^{-1} s'^{-1} T_1$
check if X'_i is valid
$T_2 = y s' K$

$\xleftarrow{\quad T_2 \quad}$

check if $k^{-1} s^{-1} T_2 = Y$

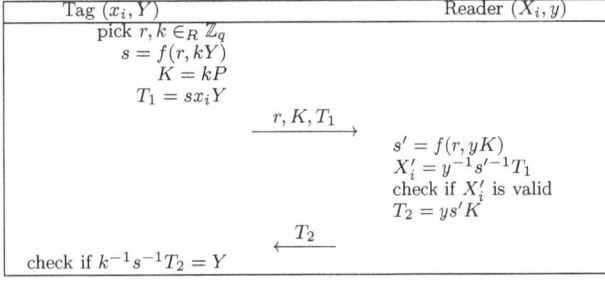

Figure 1: SPA Protocol [24]

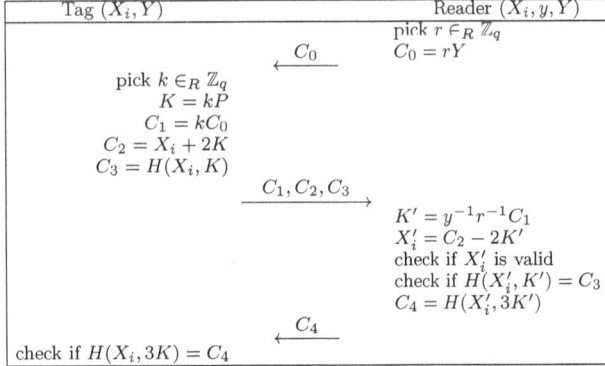

Tag (X_i, Y) — **Reader (X_i, y, Y)**

pick $r \in_R \mathbb{Z}_q$
$C_0 = rY$

$\xleftarrow{\quad C_0 \quad}$

pick $k \in_R \mathbb{Z}_q$
$K = kP$
$C_1 = kC_0$
$C_2 = X_i + 2K$
$C_3 = H(X_i, K)$

$\xrightarrow{\quad C_1, C_2, C_3 \quad}$

$K' = y^{-1} r^{-1} C_1$
$X'_i = C_2 - 2K'$
check if X'_i is valid
check if $H(X'_i, K') = C_3$
$C_4 = H(X'_i, 3K')$

$\xleftarrow{\quad C_4 \quad}$

check if $H(X_i, 3K) = C_4$

Figure 2: EMA Protocol [7]

Tag $(ID_i, H(ID_i), Y)$ — **Reader $(ID_i, H(ID_i), y, Y)$**

pick $r \in_R \mathbb{Z}_q$
$C_1 = rP, C_2 = rY$
$s = r + yH_1(C_2)$

$\xleftarrow{\quad C_1, C_2, s \quad}$

$V = C_1 + H_1(C_2) \cdot Y$
check if $sP = V$
pick $k \in_R \mathbb{Z}_q$
$C_3 = kC_2, K = kC_1$
$c = H(ID_i) + H_1(K)$
$d = H_2(ID_i, K)$

$\xrightarrow{\quad C_3, c, d \quad}$

$K' = y^{-1} C_3$
$H(ID_i)' = c - H_1(K')$
check if $H_2(ID'_i, K') = d$

Figure 3: PII Protocol [6]

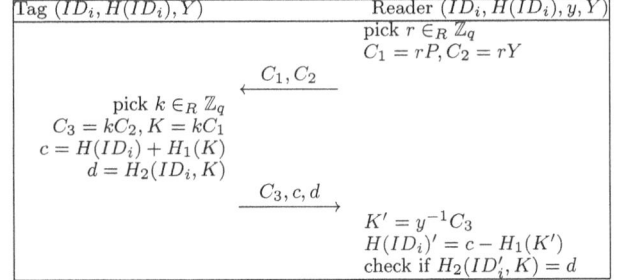

Tag $(ID_i, H(ID_i), Y)$ — **Reader $(ID_i, H(ID_i), y, Y)$**

pick $r \in_R \mathbb{Z}_q$
$C_1 = rP, C_2 = rY$

$\xleftarrow{\quad C_1, C_2 \quad}$

pick $k \in_R \mathbb{Z}_q$
$C_3 = kC_2, K = kC_1$
$c = H(ID_i) + H_1(K)$
$d = H_2(ID_i, K)$

$\xrightarrow{\quad C_3, c, d \quad}$

$K' = y^{-1} C_3$
$H(ID_i)' = c - H_1(K')$
check if $H_2(ID'_i, K) = d$

Figure 4: Reduced PII [6]

---

possible solution to remove the man-in-the-middle attacks is to apply a message authentication mechanism using a cryptographic hash function. Recently, several solutions in [7, 24, 6] (refer as EMA, SPA and PII, respectively) using both the elliptic-curve cryptography and the hash function have been proposed for untraceable RFID authentication. They, however, are not secure against active attacks and do not support the untraceability for tags, which we will analyze in more detail later.

The rest of this paper is structured as follows. In Section 2, we briefly review recently published three elliptic-curve based RFID authentication protocols. In Section 3, we demonstrate all three protocols have security pitfalls, so that they are not practical to use for untraceable RFID authentication. In Section 4, we introduce the communication model we consider and our design goals, and then describe our solution for supporting secure and untraceable RFID authentication. In Section 5, the analysis of our construction in regards to security and privacy is given along with the discussion of its advantages over previous ones. Finally we conclude in Section 6.

2. REVIEW OF THREE UNTRACEABLE AUTHENTICATION PROTOCOLS

Here we briefly review three elliptic-curve based untraceable RFID authentication schemes that were recently published in [24, 7, 6]. The system model we considered in this paper consists of RFID tags and a single reader (or multiple) connected to a server, where the reader and server are assumed as one single entity. We use both terms, reader and server, interchangeably when referring to the server or its corresponding readers.

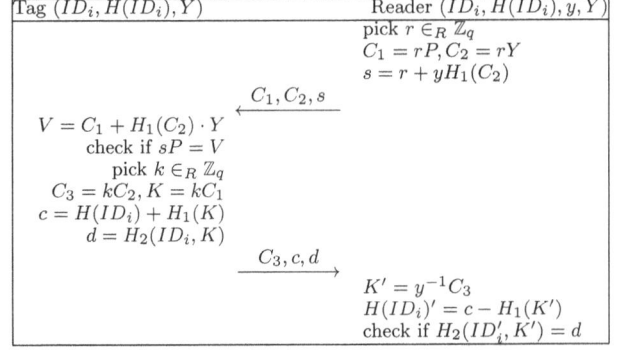

2.1 SPA

Songhela and Das [24] introduced a strong privacy preserving RFID authentication (SPA) protocol. The authors claimed that SPA provides mutual authentication with both forward and backward untraceability.

Let P denote as the base point, and y and $Y(= yP)$ are the server's private/public key pair, where yP denotes the point derived by the point multiplication operation on an elliptic curve group. x_i and $X_i = x_i P$ are tag's private/public key pair. A tag's public-key is also called a verifier, but it is kept secret in the server. The reader shares its public key Y with all the tags and each tag shares its public key X_i with the server. In SPA, the authentication procedure consists of three steps as depicted in Figure 1. In Step 1, a tag generates two random values r and k and computes $K = kP$ and $T_1 = sx_i T$, where $s = f(r, kY)$ and f is a pseudo-random function. The tag then sends $\{r, K, T_1\}$ to the reader. In Step 2, upon receiving the authentication message, the reader computes $s' = f(r, yK)$, derives $X'_i = y^{-1} s'^{-1} T_1$, and verifies the validity of X'_i. Then, the reader computes $T_2 = ys'K$, which is sent back to the tag. In Step 3, the tag verifies T_2 by checking if $k^{-1}s^{-1}T_2 = Y$. This completes the authentication procedure.

2.2 EMA

Chou [7] proposed an efficient mutual authentication (EMA) based on elliptic-curve cryptography. The design goal for EMA was to support forward privacy and resistance to various security attacks, such as replay, man-in-the-middle, and impersonation attacks.

EMA, unlike SPA, does not require a private/public key pair for tag, but uses only a secret identifier X_i which is shared with the server. For the server, it uses a private/public key pair, y and $Y(= yP)$, as usual. The authentication pro-

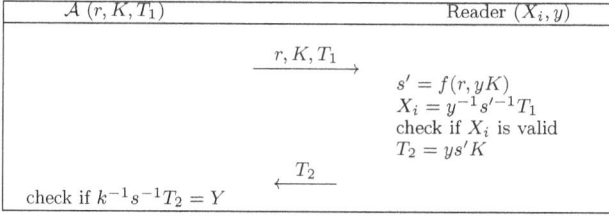

Figure 5: Attack (replay) on SPA

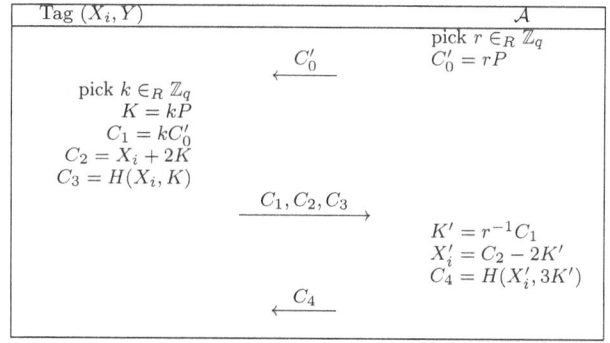

Figure 6: Attack (impersonation) on EMA

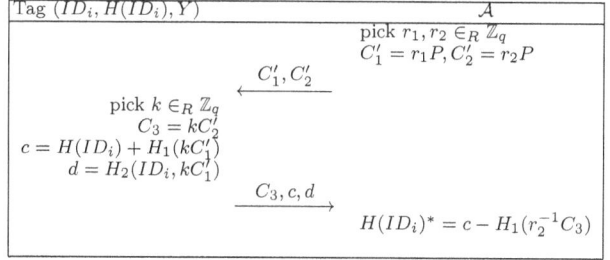

Figure 7: Attack (impersonation) on reduced PII

cedure consists of four steps as depicted in Figure 2. In Step 1, the reader picks a random value r, computes $C_0 = rY$, and sends C_0 to the tag. In Step 2, upon receiving the challenge message C_0, the tag picks a random k and computes $C_1 = kC_0, C_2 = X_i + 2K, C_3 = H(X_i, K)$, where $K = kP$ and H is a cryptographic hash function. The tag then sends $\{C_1, C_2, C_3\}$ to the reader. In Step 3, the reader computes $K' = y^{-1}r^{-1}C_1$, derives the tag's identifier $X'_i = C_2 - 2K'$, and checks if X_i is valid. It also checks if $H(X'_i, K') = C_3$. Then, the reader computes $C_4 = H(X'_i, 3K')$, which is sent back to the tag. Finally, the tag verifies the validity of C_4.

2.3 PII

Another protocol PII is described by Chen and Chou in [6], which uses the Schnorr identification mechanism over elliptic-curve. The goal for PII is the same as that in SPA and EPA.

Each tag is associated with a unique identifier ID_i and its hashed value $H(ID_i)$, which are shared with the server. For the server, it uses a private/public key pair, y and $Y(= yP)$. The protocol requires three cryptographic hash functions H, H_1, and H_2 (for more detail refer to [6]). The authentication procedure consists of three phases as depicted in Figure 3. In Step 1, the reader picks a random r, computes $C_1 = rP, C_2 = rY$ and $s = r + yH_1(C_1)$, and then sends $\{C_1, C_2, s\}$ to the tag. In Step 2, the tag computes $V = C_1 + H_1(C_2) \cdot Y$ and verifies the signature s by checking if $sP = V$. The tag picks a random k and computes $C_3 = kC_2, c = H(ID_i) + H_1(K), d = H_2(ID_i, K)$, where $K = kC_1$. The tag then sends back $\{C_3, c, d\}$ to the reader. In Step 3, the reader computes $K' = y^{-1}C_3$ and derives $H(ID_i)' = c - H_1(K')$. The reader verifies the validity of the identifier $H(ID_i)'$, and then checks if $d = H_2(ID'_i, K')$. This completes the protocol.

The author also suggested a version of unilateral authentication for reducing the computational overhead required to perform the PII protocol. As depicted in Figure 4, the reduced protocol eliminates the Schnorr signature mechanism embedded for achieving server-to-tag authentication. This enables the number of point multiplications to be reduced from four to two on the tag side.

3. SECURITY PITFALLS ON THE THREE UNTRACEABLE PROTOCOLS

The goal of untraceable RFID authentication protocols is basically to authenticate the tag to the reader and, at the same time, to protect the identity of the tag. It must be impossible for an adversary to impersonate a tag or a reader. It also must be impossible for the adversary to derive any information on the identity of tags involved. In this section we show that the three untraceable authentication protocols

described in the previous section do not satisfy basic security requirements for providing security and privacy in the RFID environment. We first show that SPA is not secure against a replay attack, by which an adversary can impersonate a tag to a reader by forwarding a past captured message. We also show that both protocols, EMA and reduced PII, are insecure against an impersonation attack. This causes for an adversary to obtain the private information on the identity of tags involved. We assume the security model from [1, 16] in which an adversary has the ability to perform various attacks ranging from passive eavesdropping to active interfering. It can influence all communication between tag and reader. It also gets the result of the authentication of a tag whether the reader accepts the tag or not.

Replay Attack on SPA: The SPA protocol was designed to provide security and privacy for tags. The tag's private key x_i in the SPA is combined with the server's public key Y, allowing only a legitimate reader to derive the tag's private identifier X_i. The SPA is, however, completely insecure against a replay attack, as shown in Figure 5. A replay attack is a form of network attack in which a past message is maliciously or fraudulently repeated or delayed to the same recipient. Suppose that an adversary $\mathcal{A}$ against the SPA intends to launch the replay attack by pretending an arbitrary tag to the reader. How the attack can be launched as follows.

1) $\mathcal{A}$ intercepts a valid message $\{r, K, T_1\}$ sent by a tag during legitimate authentication attempts.

2) At some later point in time, $\mathcal{A}$ simply replays the message $\{r, K, T_1\}$, without the need to modify it, to the reader.

3) This will force the reader perform an authentication procedure for the $\mathcal{A}$, computing $s' = f(r, yK)$ and $X'_i = y^{-1}s'^{-1}T_1$, and then verifies the validity of the

identity X_i'. The reader computes $T_2 = ys'K$ and sends back it to the $\mathcal{A}$.

Note that the replayed message is valid and thus successfully accepted by the reader. The security problem of the SPA is mainly due to that there is no mechanism to check the freshness of the authentication message. A way to avoid the replay attacks is to use of challenge-response techniques

Impersonation Attack on EMA and reduce PII: Impersonation resistance is one of core security properties that any authentication scheme must provide. However, we observed that for both EMA and reduced PII, there is lack of a mechanism for the tag to distinguish between a legitimate reader and a rogue one. This causes that both protocols, the EMA and the reduced PII, are insecure against rogue reader attacks. The problem is much worse in a fact that the private identifier X_i of any of tags is exposed by the attack. That is, it completely breaks the security and privacy of the system. Here we show how the attack can be launched against both protocols. Let us first consider the attack against EMA. As we see in Figure 6, an adversary $\mathcal{A}$, exploits the fact that the protocol does not verify the validity of C_0. In Step 1, $\mathcal{A}$ computes $C_0' = rP$ and sends it to the tag, where r is a random value chosen by $\mathcal{A}$. In Step 2, the tag computes $\{C_1, C_2, C_3\}$, as in a normal procedure, and then sends them back to $\mathcal{A}$. In Step 3, $\mathcal{A}$ now is able to derive K' and X_i' using only r. and In Step 4, $\mathcal{A}$ computes the valid response C_4 and returns it to the tag.

For the reduced PII, the protocol has a similar problem as in EMA. As we see in Figure 7, the protocol does not verify the validity of C_1 and C_2. How the attack works as follows. In Step 1, $\mathcal{A}$ picks two random values, r_1 and r_2. $\mathcal{A}$ computes $C_1' = r_1P$ and $C_2' = r_2P$, which are sent to the tag. In Step 2, the tag computes $\{C_3, c, d\}$ by following the procedure and then sends them back to $\mathcal{A}$. In Step 3, $\mathcal{A}$ derives the tag's identifier $H(ID)'$ using r_2. Consequently, the protocols, SPA, EMA and the reduced PII are not secure against replay or impersonation, meaning that they are not suitable to use for untraceable RFID authentication.

4. OUR SOLUTION

Here we provide our construction for elliptic-curve based untraceable authentication which is able to solve the problems above. We begin with the specification of the system model we consider and the design goals. We then demonstrate our construction that allows a legitimate reader to authenticate a tag, and at the same time it assures the privacy of the tag against unauthorized tracing.

4.1 System Model

An RFID system we consider consists of three entities, including tags, RFID readers, and the back-end server. A tag is a transponder, identified by a unique identifier with limited memory and computation capability, that can communicate with a reader using radio frequency communications. The readers are physical devices that supply energy to the tag, send a request, collect its response and send the latter to the back-end server. The server is assumed to be physically secure and not attackable. All communication between the server and readers is assumed to be over private and authentic channels. We use both terms reader and system, interchangeably when referring to the back-end server or its corresponding readers. The adversary in our context

can be either passive or active by controlling the communication between tag and reader. More specifically, it can observe and intercept any transmitted message. From the intercepted messages, it is able to replay the session at some later point in time. It is capable of adding or in some other way altering the messages transmitted on the channel. It can corrupt or, attempt to impersonate any entity. We assume that the adversary is computationally bounded and hence cannot break standard cryptographic algorithms.

4.2 Design Goals

We have three goals for untraceable authentication in RFID settings: security, privacy and efficiency.

4.2.1 Security

The primary objective of entity authentication is to allow that one party is assured of the identity of a second party involved in a protocol, and that the second has actually participated. From the point of view of the verifier, the outcome of an entity authentication is either acceptance of the claimant's identity as authentic, or termination without acceptance. In order to achieve this, our untraceable authentication protocol must provide the following security properties:

- *Correctness*: In the case of honest entities, tags and a reader, they are able to successfully authenticate each other by completing the authentication protocol.

- *Replay protection*: An adversary cannot reuse previously transmitted messages by an honest tag or reader, so as to successfully impersonate the same or a different recipient.

- *Impersonation resistance*: An adversary not belonging to legitimate entities cannot authenticate itself as a legitimate one to any other honest entity.

4.2.2 Privacy

For RFID systems, privacy is a significant concern to address the problem of unauthorized identification, tracking or linking tags. Privacy, in terms of anonymity and untraceability, is one of cryptographic properties distinguished from security. In general, untraceable privacy is a stronger notion than anonymous privacy, meaning that untraceability implies anonymity [8]. To date, privacy models for RFID are still being developed. These models differ mainly in their treatment of the adversary's ability to corrupt tags. We consider following privacy properties for our untraceable authentication scheme:

- *Untraceability*: The property of untraceability requires that an adversary who is given two transcripts of the protocol cannot determine whether the executions of the protocol were performed by the same participant or not. That is, an adversary is not able to distinguish whether or not it reads the same tag between any between two reads of the RFID tag.

- *Forward privacy*: Knowledge of a tag's internal state must not help the adversary to identify the tag from the past transcripts of the protocol. Forward privacy represents that an adversary is not able to break the property of untraceability, even if it is given all the internal state of a tag. This counteracts the adversary's attempt to corrupt the tags it chooses.

4.2.3 Efficiency

Due to the resource constraints of RFID tags, the performance of authentication schemes is a major challenge. The metrics used to evaluate the performance are computational and communication cost involved in the tag authentication process. Hence, another goal is to minimize the number of cryptographic operations, the number of message exchanges, and the total number of bits transmitted required to execute the authentication scheme, while at the same time providing strong security and privacy.

4.3 The Protocol

Our scheme uses the concept of the well-known Schnorr signature scheme [23] as the underlying cryptographic primitive. The Schnorr scheme is considered as the simplest to be provably secure in a random oracle model. It generates short digital signatures with appendix on binary messages of arbitrary length and requires a cryptographic hash function. The recent work in [25] shows that the elliptic curve version of Schnorr's scheme can be efficiently implemented for RFID tags. Table 1 lists the notations used throughout this paper to describe our construction.

Notation	Description
$\mathbb{G}$	A cyclic additive group
P	The generator of the group $\mathbb{G}$
q	The order of the group $\mathbb{G}$
x_i	tag's private key
X_i	tag's public key
y	server's private
Y	server's public key
H	Hash functions such as $H : \{0,1\}^* \rightarrow \{0,1\}^l$
$\oplus$	bit-wise exclusive or operation

Table 1: Notations

Let $\mathbb{G}$ be an additive cyclic group of prime order q, and let P be a generator of $\mathbb{G}$. Let H be a hash function such that $H : \{0,1\}^* \rightarrow \mathbb{Z}_q$. Recall that a Schnorr signature of a message m under public key $X \in \mathbb{G}$ is the pair $(R, s) \in \mathbb{G} \times \mathbb{Z}_q$ such that $sP = R + eX \in \mathbb{G}$, where e is the hashed value on $R\|m$. The signature can be publicly verified by using the sender's public key.

The underlying Schnorr technique inherently does not provide the privacy of the sender, as in any other public-key based scheme. To tackle this, the main idea of our scheme is to combine the sender's session secret with the receiver's public key. With such a mechanism, the signed message can be verified by the only intended receiver who knows the corresponding private key. Consequently, this makes our scheme achieve both the properties of authentication and privacy.

The protocol consists of two phases: the setup phase and the authentication phase. In the setup phase, the system generates the system-wide parameters and its own private and public key pair for the initial setup. Also every tag is independently associated to the system with a private and public key pair by the tag initialization. In the authentication phase, communication between tag and reader is initiated by the reader, which sends a challenge message to the tag. Upon receiving the message, the tag constructs a signature on the challenge message and an encrypted form of its verifier, and then sends them to the reader. Upon receiving the message from the tag, the reader derives the verifier

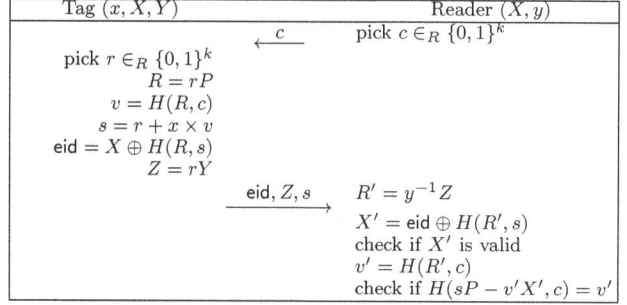

Figure 8: Untraceable authentication protocol

information using its private key, and accepts the tag as authentic if the received signature is valid. More specifically, each phase is described in following subsection.

4.3.1 Setup

The system generates an elliptic-curve group $\mathbb{G}$ of a prime order q. It chooses a generator P of group $\mathbb{G}$ and then publishes $\mathbb{G}$ and P as system parameters. For the server, it is associated with a private/public key pair (y, Y), where y is a random integer in $\mathbb{Z}_q^*$ and $Y = yP$. Similarly, a private/public key pair $(x, X = xP)$ is assigned to each tag. The public key X of each tag is also called a verifier. The tuple (x, X, Y) is stored on the tag. The system keeps the verifier X of each tag in its database.

4.3.2 Authentication Procedure

The authentication procedure works as follows. In Step 1, a reader chooses a random value c as a challenge and sends it to the tag. In Step 2, the tag responses by doing as follows: 1) Choose a random value r as the session secret, and compute $R = rP$ and $v = H(R, c)$. 2) Compute the schnorr-like signature (Z, s), where $Z = rY$ and $s = r + x \times v$. 3) Compute an encrypted verifier $\text{eid} = X \oplus H(R, s)$. 4) Send (eid, Z, s) to the reader. In Step 3, upon receiving the message (eid, Z, s), the reader do the following: 1) Compute $R' = y^{-1}Z$. 2) Derive $X' = \text{eid} \oplus H(R', s)$. 3) Check if X' is a registered verifier. 4) Compute $v' = H(R', c)$. 5) Accept the tag provided $H(sP - v'X, c) = v'$.

Correctness. If both the reader and tag are honest entities belonging to the system, they always successfully complete the protocol. That is, if the received message (eid, Z, s) was created by a registered tag, then $H(sP - v'X', c) = H((r + x \times v)P - v'X', c) = H(rP, c) = H(R, c) = v'$. This allows the reader to authenticate the tag. The Figure 8 shows how the protocol works in a pictorial form.

5. ANALYSIS OF OUR SCHEME

Here we show that our construction satisfies the requirements of security and privacy defined in Section 4. We also discuss its advantages over previous works in terms of communication and computational cost with other attributes.

5.1 Security

The security of the protocol relies on the well-known elliptic curve discrete logarithm problem. Let $\mathbb{G}$ be an elliptic curve group of prime order q. Let P be a generator of $\mathbb{G}$. The elliptic curve discrete logarithm problem (ECDLP) is as follows: given $\mathbb{G}, P, q$ and $R \in \mathbb{G}$, find the integer $r \in [0, q-1]$

	EC-RAC III	EMA	PII	Reduced PII	SPA	ours
Tag computation	3 pm	2 pm + 2 h	4 pm + 3 h	2 pm + 2 h	4 pm + 1 h	2 pm + 2 h
Transmission size	480	608	768	608	640	544
Number of passes	3	3	2	2	2	2
Tag hardware	ECC	ECC + Hash	ECC + Hash	ECC + Hash	ECC + Hash	ECC + Hash
(gates)	(8,214)	(10,214)	(10,214)	(10,214)	(10,214)	(10,214)
Replay protection	√	√	√	√	×	√
Impersonation resistance	√	×	√	×	×	√
Untraceability	×	×	√	×	√	√
Forward privacy	×	×	×	×	×	√

Table 2: **Comparisons of elliptic-curve based untraceable RFID protocols. For each scheme we show the number of cryptographic operations required on tags, the total size of all transmitted messages, the number of passes, the number of logical gates necessary for implementing the protocol in hardware, and the security features of each scheme. We denote by "pm" the point multiplication over an elliptic curve and by "h" the hash function. The size is in bits. The notations $\sqrt{}$ and $\times$ represent "satisfied" and "not satisfied", respectively.**

such that $R = rP$. The intractability of ECDLP forms the basis for the security of most elliptic curve based cryptographic schemes.

THEOREM 5.1. *The proposed protocol satisfies the property of security including replay protection and impersonation resistance under the ECDLP assumption.*

PROOF. Let us first consider a replay attack against our scheme. The attack will happen in either of following forms. One is that the adversary intercepts a valid message (eid, Z, s) previously transmitted by a registered tag, and then tries to retransmit it to a reader in the system. It is, however, easy to see that the attack does not work since the encrypted verifier eid and signature s are combined with the tag's private key x and a fresh challenge by the reader c in each session. The other case is that the adversary uses the only part of information from the past valid message (eid, Z, s). To do this, the adversary must calculate a valid signature s' associated with the challenge c' from the reader. Note that $s' = r + x \cdot v' \bmod q$, where x is the tag's private key and $v' = H(R, c')$. This means that the adversary, like in Schnorr scheme, must break the underlying ECDLP.

Now, consider an impersonation attack against our scheme. The attack is either of following cases. One is that an adversary tries to act as a registered tag to a reader. To do this, the adversary will be faced with the problem that it must reply to the reader with the valid response message (eid, Z, s). However, in our scheme it is clear that the adversary with no knowledge of the tag's private key x is not feasible to calculate the signature s such that $s = r + x \cdot v$. That is, the problem of impersonation attacks by the adversary is reduced to an instance of ECDLP for the verifier X of a registered tag. The other case is a reader impersonation attack against our scheme. Suppose that in our scheme an adversary pretends to be a valid reader by sending a challenge c to, and receiving the corresponding message (eid, Z, s) from a registered tag. There, however, is no information leakage of the tag since the eid is an encrypted verifier and the security of (Z, s) is inherited from that of the Schnorr scheme. These results assure that in our scheme the security against active replay and impersonation attacks relie on the ECDLP assumption. □

5.2 Privacy

THEOREM 5.2. *The proposed protocol satisfies the privacy requirements, untracebility and forward privacy.*

PROOF. The property of untraceability requires that it should be computationally infeasible for an adversary to determine whether two execution of the protocol were performed by the same tag or not. Suppose that an adversary is given a pair of valid messages $\{c, (\text{eid}, Z, s)\}$ and $\{c', (\text{eid}', Z', s')\}$ of the protocol. The challenge of the adversary is to determine the messages (eid, Z, s) and (eid', Z', s') performed by the same or different tags. However, in our scheme uniform random numbers r and r' are session independent, and Z and Z' are also uniform random elements in $\mathbb{G}$. It means that the only way for the adversary to break the untraceability is to obtain the server's private key y from publicly available information P and $Y(= yP)$. The problem of breaking the untraceability against our scheme, hence, is reduced to an instance of the underlying primitive. Now let us consider the property of forward privacy. Forward privacy, as discussed in Section 4.2, represents that the adversary should not be able to break the untraceability even if it is given all the internal state of a tag. Suppose that an adversary is given a tag's internal data, i.e. private key x and verifier X, and also given a pair of valid messages $\{c, (\text{eid}, Z, s)\}$ and $\{c', (\text{eid}', Z', s')\}$. The challenge of the adversary is to determine the messages (eid, Z, s) and (eid', Z', s') performed by the same or different tags. To do this, the adversary needs to know the session independent pair of values, R and R', which are hidden in Z and Z'. This means that the adversary should find the private key y of the server. Similarly as before, the problem of breaking the forward privacy against our scheme is reduced to an instance of the underlying ECDLP primitive. □

5.3 Advantages

Table 2 shows a comparison of our scheme to the previous ones in terms of computational and communication cost with some other features. The advantages of our scheme over previous schemes are summarized as follows:

- Our scheme satisfies all requirements of security and privacy for untraceable authentication, which include replay protection, impersonation resistance, untraceability, and forward privacy, while PII do not support the forward privacy. For EC-RAC III, it does not satisfy both privacy properties, untraceability and forward privacy, as demonstrated in [12]. For EMA, reduced PII and SPA, they do not support even the property of impersonation resistance that is one of the core security requirements any authentication scheme must satisfy.

- Our scheme requires only two point scalar multiplications and two hash operations, which is cheaper than in EC-RAC III, PII and SPA. The total size of transmitted message in our scheme is 544bits, which is shorter than other schemes, except EC-RAC III. Our scheme requires two communications between tag and reader, while three times in EC-RAC III and EMA. As in [6] when we assume that the ECC implementation for 160-bit key size takes 8,214 gates and the DM-PRESENT-80 hash function takes about 2,000 gates, our scheme requires 10,214 gates for a hardware implementation.

6. CONCLUSION

We have demonstrated that three elliptic-curve based untraceable RFID authentication schemes recently published, SPA, EMA, and reduced PII, are not secure against active attacks and do not support the untraceability for RFID tags. We have also provided a new construction that satisfies the requirements of security and privacy for RFID systems, including replay protection, impersonation resistance, untraceability, and forward privacy. It requires only two point scalar multiplications and two hash operations with two messages exchanges. Compared to previous works, our construction has better security and efficiency. We believe that our construction will provide a promising building block for security in RFID settings.

7. REFERENCES

[1] G. Avoine. Adversary model for radio frequency identification. In *No. LASEC-REPORT-2005-001*.

[2] G. Avoine and P. Oechslin. A scalable and provably secure hash-based RFID protocol. In *PerCom 2005 Conference Proceedings*, pages 110–114, 2005.

[3] L. Batina, J. Guajardo, T. Kerins, N. Mentens, P. Tuyls, and I. Verbauwhede. Public-key cryptography for RFID-tags identification. In *PerCom'07 Conference Proceedings*, pages 217–222, 2007.

[4] J. Bringer, H. Habanne, and T. Icart. Cryptanalysis of EC-RAC, a RFID identification protocol. In *CANS Conference Proceedings*, pages 149–161, 2008.

[5] S. Canard, L. Ferreira, and M. Robshaw. Improved (and practical) public-key authentication for UHF RFID tags. In *CARDIS 2012 Conference Proceedings*, pages 46–61, 2012.

[6] Y. Chen and J. Chou. ECC-based untraceable authentication for large-scale active-tag RFID systems. *Electronic Commerce Research*, pages 1–24, 2014.

[7] J. Chou. An efficient mutual authentication RFID scheme based on elliptic curve cryptography. *The Journal of Supercomputing*, 70(1):75–84, 2014.

[8] T. Deursen, S. Mauw, and S. Radomirovic. Untraceability of RFID protocols. In *WISTP'08 Conference Proceedings*, pages 1–15, 2008.

[9] T. Deursen and S. Radomirovic. Untraceable RFID protocols are not trivially composable: Attacks on the revision of EC-RAC. In *Cryptology ePrint Archive: Report 2009/332*.

[10] T. Deursen and S. Radomirović. Algebraic attacks on RFID protocols. In *WISTP Workshop Proceedings*, pages 8–51, 2009.

[11] T. Dimitriou. A lightweight RFID protocol to protect against traceability and cloning attacks. In *SecureComm 2005 Conference Proceedings*, pages 59–66, 2005.

[12] J. Fan, J. Hermans, and F. Vercauteren. On the claimed privacy of EC-RAC III. In *ACM RFIDSec'10 Conference Proceedings*, pages 66–74, 2010.

[13] M. Feldhofer, S. Dominikus, and J. Wolkerstorfer. Strong authentication for RFID systems using the AES algorithm. In *CHES 2004 Conference Proceedings*, pages 357–370, 2004.

[14] D. Henrici and P. Muller. Hash-based enhancement of location privacy for radio-frequency identification devices using varying identifiers. In *PerSec 2004 Conference Proceedings*, pages 149–153, 2004.

[15] A. Juels and S. Weis. Authenticating pervasive devices with human protocols. In *CRYPTO 2005 Conference Proceedings*, pages 293–308, 2005.

[16] A. Juels and S. Weis. Defining strong privacy for RFID. In *PerCom'07 Conference Proceedings*, pages 342–347, 2007.

[17] K. Lauter. The advantages of elliptic curve cryptography for wireless security. *IEEE Wireless communications*, 11(1):62–67, 2004.

[18] Y. Lee, L. Batina, D. Singerlee, and I. Verbauwhede. Low-cost untraceable authentication protocols for RFID. In *ACM WiSec'10 Conference Proceedings*, pages 55–64, 2010.

[19] Y. Lee, L. Batina, and I. Verbauwhede. Use of elliptic curves in cryptography. In *RFID Conference Proceedings*, pages 97–104, 2008.

[20] Y. Lee, L. Batina, and I. Verbauwhede. Untraceable RFID authentication protocols: Revision of EC-RAC. In *RFID Conference Proceedings*, pages 178–185, 2009.

[21] M. Ohkubo, K. Suzuki, and S. Kinoshita. RFID privacy issues and technical challenges. *Communications of the ACM*, 48(9):66–71, 2005.

[22] M. O'Neill and M. Robshaw. Low-cost digital signature architecture suitable for radio frequency identification tags. *Computers & Digital Techniques*, 4(1):14–26, 2010.

[23] C. Schnorr. Efficient signature generation by smart cards. *Journal of cryptology*, 4(3):161–174, 1991.

[24] R. Songhela and M. Das. Yet another strong privacy-preserving RFID mutual authentication protocol. In *SPACE 2014 Conference Proceedings*, pages 171–182, 2014.

[25] P. Tuyls and L. Batina. RFID-tags for anti-counterfeiting identification. In *CT-RSA 2006 Conference Proceedings*, pages 115–131, 2006.

[26] S. Weis, S. Sarma, R. Rivest, and D. Engels. Security and privacy aspects of low-cost radio frequency identification systems. In *SPC 2004 Conference Proceedings*, pages 201–212, 2004.

[27] J. Wolkerstorfer. Is elliptic-curve cryptography suitable to secure RFID tags. In *RFID and Lightweight Cryptography Workshop Proceedings*, 2005.

A Negative Number Vulnerability for Histogram-based Face Recognition Systems

Alireza Farrokh Baroughi
Electrical and Computer
Engineering
Binghamton University
Binghamton, NY USA
afarrok1@binghamton.edu

Scott Craver
Electrical and Computer
Engineering
Binghamton University
Binghamton, NY USA
scraver@binghamton.edu

Mohammed Faizan
Mohsin
Electrical and Computer
Engineering
Binghamton University
Binghamton, NY USA
mmohsin2@binghamton.edu

ABSTRACT

A popular method of face identification is the use of local binary pattern (LBP) histograms. In this method, a face image is partitioned into regions, and a histogram of features is produced for each region; faces are compared by measuring the similarity of their histograms through statistics such as χ^2 score or K-L divergence. Comparison of histograms, however, is particularly prone to exploitation via a negative-number bug if coded naively. This allows a surprisingly precise and powerful attack: if an adversary can alter a histogram to change a single zero to a negative number of appropriate magnitude, the change will induce a negligible difference in matching under ordinary use, but match an attacker to an intended victim if the attacker briefly displays a printed striped pattern to a camera.

This tampering is minor and can be inflicted long before the attack, allowing the insertion of a back door in a face recognition system that will behave normally until the moment of exploitation. We exhibit an example of this bug in the wild, in the OpenCV computer vision library, and illustrate the effectiveness of this attack in impersonating multiple victims.

Categories and Subject Descriptors

D.4.6 [**Security and Protection**]: Authentication

General Terms

Security,Biometrics

Keywords

Biometrics; Face Identification; Local Binary Pattern; OpenCV

IH&MMSec'15, June 17–19, 2015, Portland, Oregon, USA.
Copyright ⓒ 2015 ACM 978-1-4503-3587-4/15/06 ...$15.00.
DOI: http://dx.doi.org/10.1145/2756601.2756617.

1. INTRODUCTION

Biometric detectors commonly transform multimedia data into a feature set, which is then matched against known feature sets in a database to determine a user match. The choice of feature, and the choice of detection algorithm, have security as well as performance implications: a feature set that can be grotesquely amplified by an unusual input, or a detector structure that translates such a grotesque amplification into a false positive, can allow an attacker to subvert a detector with inputs engineered specifically to confuse it.

An interesting security question is that of the extent to which an insider can cause havoc with limited ability to alter or influence a feature stored in a biometric database. This may not at first seem interesting, since numerous mechanisms can limit an insider—contrariwise, an unimpeded insider can inflict so much harm as to render such an observation trivial. However, we find that the extent and sophistication of an insider attack, and the degree of insider access necessary to perform an attack, depends on the type of features used, and the method by which they are matched.

In this paper, we outline a vulnerability that arises in a detector that employs histogram comparison, i.e. face recognition with local binary pattern histograms. As we will show, common formulae for comparing histograms are particularly vulnerable to negative-number bugs—bugs in which a function is assumed to operate on non-negative input, and for which a naïve implementation does not strictly rule out negative values. Such a vulnerability manifests in detectors based on those formulae, and allows a far more sophisticated attack than the brute corruption of a biometric database.

2. AN OVERVIEW OF LOCAL BINARY PATTERN HISTOGRAMS

Local binary pattern (LBP) histograms are statistics drawn from an image that capture some essence of luminance gradients, which may then convey greater information about the three-dimensional shape of a subject's face [1].

A local binary pattern image is simply an image in which each pixel value is replaced with a code number reflecting the luminance gradient pattern about that pixel. In a simple LBP image, each pixel is compared in luminance to its eight immediate neighbors; each comparison results in a 1 if a neighbor's luminance is higher or equal, and a 0 if not. These eight bits are then combined into a byte value that replaces the pixel's luminance value. An image and its simple LBP image is displayed in figure 1. An extended local bi-

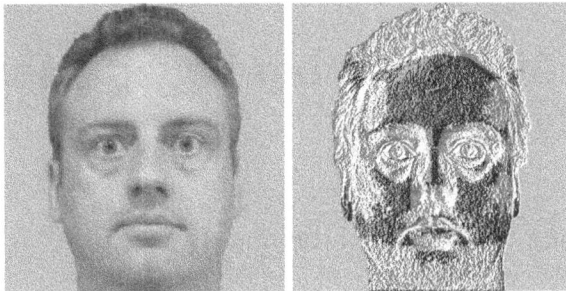

Figure 1: A face image and its corresponding extended LBP image. Each pixel is compared to eight neighbors within a radius of 2 pixels.

nary pattern compares a pixel to n neighbors evenly spaced around a circle of radius R from the pixel. For a pixel $p[i,j]$, we can write an n-bit string $b[i,j]$ as follows:

$$b_k[i,j] = \{p[i,j] < p[i + Rcos(2\pi k/n), j + Rsin(2\pi k/n)]\}$$

...where the real pixel coordinates on the right-hand side can be rounded to an integer value, or resolved by interpolating the image.

Once an LBP image is created, we can tally a histogram of the 2^n possible LBP values, essentially converting an image into a vector of 2^n numbers. In order to capture the local characteristics of a face image, an LBP image is first partitioned into a set of sub-images, for example 25 or 49 regions on a 5x5 or 7x7 grid, and a separate histogram is tallied for each sub-images. The user's face is ultimately transformed into an array of histograms.

2.1 Training and Testing of Histograms

A test image can be compared to a user's image by comparison of histograms in a straightforward way, for example using a Pearson chi-squared test to score the likelihood that a histogram at least as extreme as the test histogram may come from data distributed according to the user's histogram.

It is not immediately obvious, however, how a training dataset of m user images should be combined into a single detector statistic. Because these features are histograms rather than projections of an image on a basis set, it is not necessarily valid to average them into a single vector. Early papers on LBP histogram matching demonstrated their efficacy by training a classifier to distinguish between LBP histograms of one user versus another; however, a face recognition system that features hundreds of users would either require a multi-class classifier or a different approach to detection entirely.

The authors examined the source code used for LBP face recognition in the OpenCV library [6], and found that the `LBPHFaceRecognizer` class defines a training algorithm that simply translates m user training images into m histograms, and stores them in a training database without further processing. A test histogram is then compared to all histograms in the database by a chi-squared statistic, placing the database histogram in the denominator; and the nearest-neighbor classification of a query histogram is assigned to whatever user owned the histogram of closest match.

This initially attracted our attention because it implicitly models a user's biometric data as approximating one of m

vectors. Like more explicit multiple mixture models, such as Gaussian mixture models, this may allow a *sidestepping attack,* as described in [2]. In a sidestepping attack, one piece of a complex biometric model, such as one mixture in a Gaussian mixture model, is tampered with while leaving the remainder unaltered. The tampered mixture is designed to match an attacker only when that attacker takes on an unusual affect; in [2], for example, an attacker affects a cartoon voice to a speaker identification system. The presence of multiple mixtures allows the victim user to be correctly classified by a match to the unaltered mixtures, while the attacker is correctly classified to his or her own database entry in normal use. Only when the attacker affects the cartoon voice does a mismatch occur.

The vulnerability and attack outlined in this paper does not require a user to be represented by multiple histograms or mixtures; we instead observe that an insignificant alteration of a single histogram will result in a system where a victim and attacker are correctly matched to their respective histograms, but that an unusual affect—the presentation of a printed pattern at the moment of classification—will cause an attacker to match a victim's histogram.

3. NEGATIVE NUMBER VULNERABILITIES IN HISTOGRAM COMPARISON

Some formulae for histogram comparison entail summation over a histogram's support set with a term in the denominator, towit χ^2 and K-L divergence. These formulae are defined here as follows, between two histograms g and h. In each case, an element from one histogram lies in the denominator.

$$\chi^2(h,g) = \sum_{k=1}^{n} \frac{(h_k - g_k)^2}{h_k}$$

$$D(h\|g) = \sum_{k=1}^{n} h_k \log \frac{h_k}{g_k}$$

A second formula is sometimes used for χ^2 similarity, which we refer to as a "type 2" formula, versus the "type 1" defined above:

$$\chi^2(h,g) = \sum_{k=1}^{n} \frac{(h_k - g_k)^2}{g_k + h_k}$$

If a denominator would be zero, the corresponding term is typically excluded from the set. The file `facerec.cpp` in the OpenCV library uses the χ^2 comparison for LBP histograms, for example, and the relevant code is quoted in figure 2. This code only includes a value in the sum if the denominator's magnitude is reliably nonzero for a double-precision floating point variable (`DBL_EPSILON` is the smallest value ϵ for which 1.0 and $1.0 + \epsilon$ are distinct `double` values, roughly 2.22×10^{-16}.) When used for comparing LBP histograms, this code assigns `h1` as the histogram drawn from a biometric database, while `h2` is drawn from a test image.

3.1 Negative number bugs

A negative number bug occurs when data is assumed to be nonnegative, but is stored in a format and manipulated in a manner that allows a negative value. Perhaps the most famous example of a negative-number bug is the Hursti

```
if( method == CV_COMP_CHISQR )
{
    for( j = 0; j < len; j++ )
    {
        double a = h1[j] - h2[j];
        double b = h1[j];
        if( fabs(b) > DBL_EPSILON )
            result += a*a/b;
    }
}
```

Figure 2: χ^2 **comparison code from OpenCV 2.4.9, illustrating a negative number bug.**

hack [3], in which an electronic voting machine stored vote counts as (signed) integer variables, and concluded that no votes were yet cast if the sum of all vote totals was equal to 0. If a memory card is initialized to give one candidate N votes and another candidate $-N$ votes, the software would mistakenly conclude that 0 votes were cast, allowing an election to proceed with a head start of $2N$ votes for one candidate. The Hursti hack demonstrates that such bugs can occur in secure applications.

The above OpenCV code illustrates another negative number bug: the code must determine if a denominator b is suitably nonzero, and an obvious way to do this is to compare `fabs(b)` to the `DBL_EPSILON` threshold. However, since histogram values are nonnegative, no `fabs()` call is necessary; indeed, it allows a negative value for b to be included in the sum.

The admission of a negative denominator permits a dramatic and selective effect on the χ^2 value. Suppose that somehow a value `h1[j]` is set to -10^{-a} for some $a > 0$. If the corresponding value `h2[j]` is zero, the resulting sum includes a term of $(-10^{-a})^2/(-10^{-a}) = -10^{-a}$; the χ^2 sum is decreased, although by a negligible amount if a is large. If, on the other hand, `h2[j]` has a significant nonzero value, then the resulting sum includes a term of roughly $-10^a \times \mathtt{h2[j]}^2$. Here, a large a produces a large reduction in the χ^2 sum.

The primary consequence of this bug is that a negative value injected into a histogram can result in a term that decreases rather than increases a χ^2 sum, creating a closer match. However, there is a more sophisticated and nefarious property of this bug: a negative value of appropriately small magnitude will produce a negligible effect if compared to a zero, and a very large effect if compared to a nonzero value.

3.2 Exploitation of LBP histogram recognition

The aforementioned bug can be exploited in a face recognition as follows:

1. Identify an image sub-region where a certain LBP value does not commonly appear.

2. Find a printed pattern that exhibits that same LBP value.

3. Alter a histogram so that the corresponding LBP value is a negative number $-\delta$ of small magnitude.

The attacker then briefly displays this printed pattern at the moment of recognition, causing a low score when matched to the victim. This is possible if subsequent code chooses as a match the histogram of lowest χ^2 dissimilarity.

An example pattern that reliably exhibits certain LBP values in its histogram is a stripe pattern. Such a pattern can provide significant histogram mass across a small number of LPB values, which depend on the angle of the stripe and the ratio of the stripe width to ratio of the stripe width to the radius used by the face recognition program.

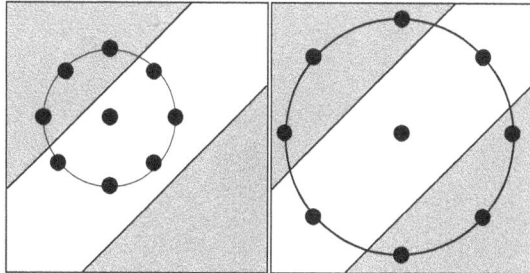

Figure 3: **A diagonal stripe pattern, illustrating some LBP indices that may be created.**

3.3 Selecting a negative value

In order for the attack to work, an injected negative number must be of a value that produces the intended effect without false matches between the victim and other users. To determine the appropriate δ value, consider an LBP histogram whose maximum value is $a\delta$ over all users in the database, but which can be raised to $A\delta$ with the presentation of a printed pattern, where $A > a$. The injection of a $-\delta$ for that LBP value will reduce the χ^2 distance to other histograms by at most $(a+1)^2\delta$, while the χ^2 distance during an attack is reduced by $(A + 1)^2\delta$. The value of δ is chosen so that the first reduction is negligible while the second is suitably large.

For example, suppose an LBP histogram has a maximum value of 0.01 while an attack can induce a value of 0.1 (these numbers reflect the degree of changes we can inflict in real systems.) A δ of 0.0005 will reduce inter-histogram matches by 0.2205, while allowing an atack that reduces a score by 20.2005. The score reduction possible by an attacker is roughly the square of the ratio (A/a), multiplied by the score reduction that one is willing to allow between enrolled users in the database. This analysis considers a single negative number; one can inject several negative numbers to match several LBPs induced by a printed pattern. If we do not expect all values to attain their maximum for a single user, then this can permit an injection with a lower inter-histogram score, and hence a lower effect in normal use.

4. RESULTS

We have tested our attack on OpenCV 2.4.9, where this negative number bug was observed. OpenCV computes LBP histograms with a default of $n = 8$ neighbors, and a division of each image into $8 \times 8 = 64$ sub-regions. We tested our attack with both 8×8 and 5×5 sub-regions.

Our test database consists of 102 high-resolution face images drawn from 9 users against a chroma-key backdrop. Face images feature subjects looking forward and slightly left and right with a neutral expression. These images were then scaled to 512 by 512 resolution and cropped using the same Haar cascade technique used by OpenCV's application `facerec_video.cpp` to identify test faces for detection. The resulting face images have variable sizes of roughly 350 by 350 pixels. Tests with OpenCV demonstrated that extended LBP features were effective for face recognition with a neighbor radius of 15 pixels. We then produced a series of

Figure 4: Several images from our test database.

test images in which various striped cards are displayed on one side of the user's face, covering half of the mouth. These were cropped similarly, and analyzed to identify conspicuous LBP values.

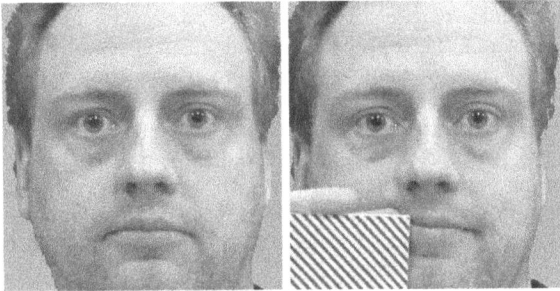

Figure 5: A face image with and without a striped card displayed.

4.1 Triggered LBP values

For face images with striped cards, we searched for LBP patterns reflecting a gradient, specifically those LBPs that have 3, 4, or 5 "1" bits in a row. We expect to see greater tallies for these LBPs corresponding to the type of card displayed. The values that we observed for different cards are displayed in table 1.

We chose these LBP indices as the focus of our initial investigation. Our indices are expressed in hexadecimal: since the LBP pattern is eight bits based on eight neighbors, the least significant byte reflects the pattern, while the most significant byte communicates the number of the sub-block where that index is found. The sub-block number is of the form ROW $\times N$ + COLUMN, where N is the number of rows or columns, and the row and column indices range from $0 \cdots N - 1$.

4.2 Unused LBP values

An analysis of images in the database showed several LBP values that were higher for card images and low for conventional images in the database. The statistics for those

Table 1: Selected LBP values with and without a diagonal striped card, using 8x8 sub-images

LBP index	Pattern	No card	Card
1ff7	{1,1,1,1,0,1,1,1}	0.0030450	0.0291955
27f7	{1,1,1,1,0,1,1,1}	0.00542175	0.025519
281f	{0,0,0,1,1,1,1,1}	0.000216263	0.0892445
291f	{0,0,0,1,1,1,1,1}	0.00408244	0.0645905
2ff7	{1,1,1,1,0,1,1,1}	0.0042071	0.02321223
3070	{0,1,1,1,0,0,0,0}	0.016804	0.000216263
37f7	{1,1,1,1,0,1,1,1}	0.0140826	0.0294118
3807	{0,0,0,0,0,1,1,1}	0.0	0.001513843
3870	{0,1,1,1,0,0,0,0}	0.000432524	0.00237889
3ff7	{1,1,1,1,0,1,1,1}	0.0145758	0.0126874

Table 2: Selected LBP value statistics over our user database

Index	pattern	mean	max	median
1ff7	{1,1,1,1,0,1,1,1}	0.012421	0.114218	0.004444
27f7	{1,1,1,1,0,1,1,1}	0.009280	0.072593	0.000000
281f	{0,0,0,1,1,1,1,1}	0.000621	0.014872	0.000000
291f	{0,0,0,1,1,1,1,1}	0.006943	0.112188	0.000816
2ff7	{1,1,1,1,0,1,1,1}	0.011437	0.076049	0.001250
3070	{0,1,1,1,0,0,0,0}	0.010917	0.055625	0.001875
37f7	{1,1,1,1,0,1,1,1}	0.013846	0.064198	0.005260
3807	{0,0,0,0,0,1,1,1}	0.016324	0.220250	0.000000
3870	{0,1,1,1,0,0,0,0}	0.005712	0.055000	0.000000
3ff7	{1,1,1,1,0,1,1,1}	0.013787	0.080868	0.005432

same LBP indices over the user database are shown in table 2. An examination of all LBP histograms in our database demonstrate that a great many values are little-used. Over all users, 78.6% of LBP indices had a median of 0.0, while 94.6% had maximum values under 0.1, and 52.8% had maximum values below 0.01. A median of 0.0 occurs because these bin values are zero over the majorith of histograms in the database.

For injection of a negative value, it is desirable to use a bin that is typically zero, and which, if nonzero, is of small magnitude, to minimize the likelihood of an attack being triggered by accident. We therefore target bins that rarely contain nonzero values in our database, in hopes that they reflect a similar rarity of large values in test users. Our examination shows that several indices, for example 0x281f, are an excellent candidate for insertion of a negative number. We use this bin in our subsequent experiments.

4.3 Exploitation

Guided by the above process, we amended histograms belonging to chosen victims in our database based on selected LBP indices. For 8x8 LBP partitions, we chose index 0x281f; for 5x5 LBP partitions, we used LBP index 0x1500 for one victim, and indices 0x18e1 and 0x181e for a second. Histogram values were set to -0.0008. To demonstrate exploitation, we changed these values directly in OpenCV's demonstration program `facerec_video.cpp`.

We were then able to trigger a mismatch reliably by holding the striped card at an appropriate angle, as illustrated in our screenshots below. An attacker can impersonate either of two users by positioning the card in one of two locations.

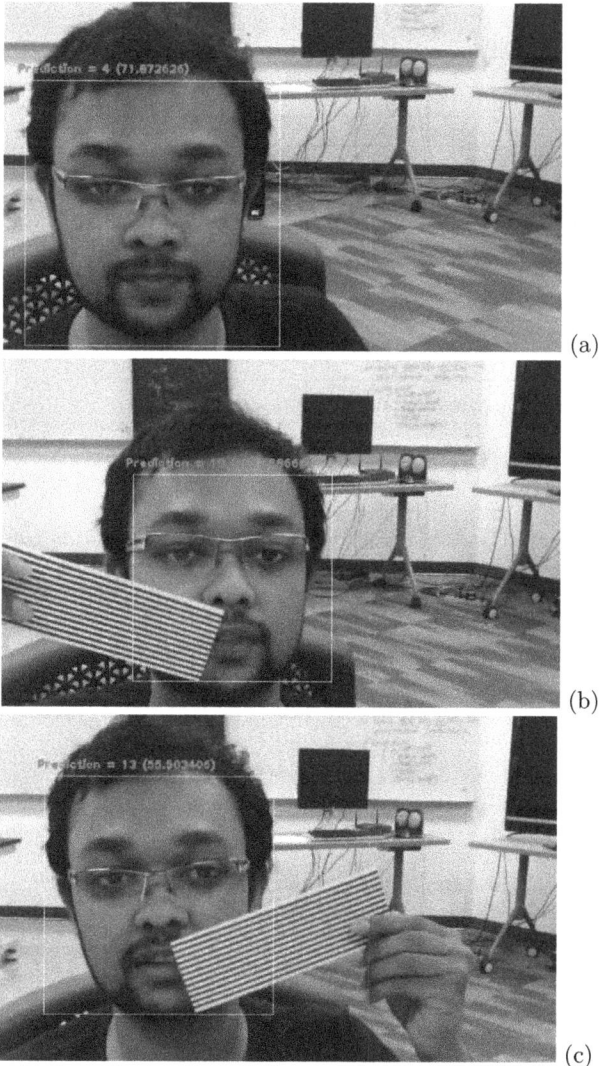

Figure 6: Screenshots from OpenCV face recognition program. In (a), user is correctly classified; in (b), a striped card matches a negative value in a target user; in (c), two negative values in a separate histogram matches a second victim.

5. DISCUSSION

5.1 Negative number bugs are widespread

The reader may initially discount these results on the grounds that we are exploiting a bug in OpenCV, and that a face recognition system can simply not use OpenCV. However, this is not a specific bug in one piece of software. Negative number bugs are a broader phenomenon than this one library, just as buffer overrun vulnerabilities and format specifier bugs are a broader phenomenon than any specific software application where they are found. Negative number bugs can occur anywhere that data is assumed to be nonnegative and therefore not checked.

We have examined several applications and code libraries that contain functions for computing chi-squared similarity, and observed that many implementations admit negative values while few forbid them. A summary is shown in ta-

ble 5.1. Of eleven examples of χ^2 similarity functions that we found in libraries and software applications, only three disallowed negative values. In one case, the popular library *Numerical Recipes in C* offered two separate χ^2 functions, of which one admitted negative values and one did not [5].

It is difficult to estimate the likelihood of a certain kind of bug, but this survey of software at least demonstrates that this specific vulnerability is not confined to OpenCV. Computer programmers occasionally forget to check for negative values, or opt not to do so; vigilance is required when such formulae are implemented in multimedia security applications.

5.2 Potential countermeasures

A great deal of effort has been spent on securing biometric templates both to preserve their privacy and to prevent various types of attack. We outline several countermeasures.

Use of cryptographic checksums. A hash of each histogram is computed and stored in another location so that tampering can be uncovered. If this is employed, then even a tiny change to a database will be noticed; an attacker would only be able to set a negative number when the histogram is first computed in enrollment.

Use of an encrypted database. Encrypting a biometric database is an obvious decision, and can limit insider attacks. Care must be taken, however, in the method of encryption. For example, if a histogram is stored in binary format (i.e., as an array of `int` or `double` variables) and encrypted using a stream cipher or a block cipher in OFB or CTR mode, a negative number of appropriate size can be injected without knowledge of the key by complementing bits in chosen locations.

Transformation of feature space. An approach to protecting privacy of biometric data is subjecting that data to a key-based transformation that preserves the salient characteristics of the data. An example of transforming LBP histogram data can be found in [4]: the authors project histograms as vectors into a subspace using a random projection matrix $R_{d \times n}$:

$$X_{d \times m}^{RP} = R_{d \times n} \times X_{n \times m}$$

where $X_{n \times m}$ is feature matrix (histogram), and $X_{d \times m}^{RP}$ is random projected features in subspace. The authors use a variant of the χ^2 dissimilarity measure, although it is not clear how they address negative denominator values in their transformed space.

If data is so transformed, and a χ^2 dissimilarity measure is still used, this attack would rely on the ability to find a coordinate in the transformed space that is normally close to 0, that can be made larger by presentation of a printed pattern. This may render the attack impractical, although one should not rely upon a privacy-preserving transformation to prevent this attack as a side-effect.

Testing templates upon enrollment and afterwards. A new template should be compared to other templates already enrolled in a biometric database, to ensure that no false matches will occur. If a system uses multiple histograms to represent a single user, it is also wise to test that the individual histograms match one another and do not closely match other users. In this way, a dramatically altered histogram can be identified. However, the goal of this attack is to produce a negligible change under normal use; a tampered histogram still resembles its target user.

Table 3: A sampling of libraries and applications with χ^2 distance functions.

Library or software	χ^2 type	command	Allows negative
OpenCV C++	type 1	`compareHist`	Yes
OpenCV Python	type 1	`cv2.compareHist`	Yes
BOB for Python	type 2	`bob.math.chi_square`	Yes
Matlab	type 2	`pdist2(x,y,metric='chisq')`	Yes
analogue for R	type 2	`distance((x,y,method="SQchi.square"))`	Yes
code.google.com (Java)	type 1	`computePearsonChiSquared`	Yes
SPSS	unknown	`Analyze>Correlate>Distances...`	No
Numerical Recipes in C	type 1	`chsone`	No
Numerical Recipes in C	type 2	`chstwo`	Yes
Microsoft Excel	type 1	`CHISQ.TEST`	Yes
iWork Numbers	type 1	`CHITEST`	No

Disallowing negative numbers. This may seem like the most obvious countermeasure: do not allow negative numbers. The OpenCV code in figure 2 can prevent exploitation by removing the `fabs()` call, for example. Code can likewise check for negative numbers upon input.

It should be pointed out, however, that disallowing negative number bugs is somewhat like disallowing buffer overrun vulnerabilites. One can mandate that the underlying coding mistake should not be made, but the mistake can be made nonetheless. We recommend a formal code review to look for this specific error. One can also include a check for negative numbers in a periodic check for anomalies in a histogram database.

5.3 A note on insider attacks

This paper describes an insider attack; one can make a compelling argument that an insider attack is not interesting, either because an attacker with insider access can obviously inflict all manner of harm, or because a properly designed system will prohibit insider attacks.

We would urge more careful consideration, for several reasons. First, there is no binary division between attackers who have, and who don't have, insider access. Rather, there is a spectrum of insider access ranging from broad editorial powers to a minor ability to alter or a small piece of information for a limited time. Different levels of tampering require different levels of access, and can be caught or prevented by different countermeasures. The attack described herein requires the alteration of a single number in a database, long before the attack is launched. Such an attack can even be launched against an encrypted database depending on how it is encrypted.

Secondly, it is good security practice to harden software against such an attack whether or not some other security measure can prevent it. The code that we quoted contains a vulnerability, and that vulnerability should be removed; any other code that implements χ^2 comparison for security purposes should also be examined to ensure that the same vulnerability is not present. Even if a system is so designed to prevent an attacker from exploiting such a vulnerability, it is important to observe the potential for that vulnerability and ensure that it is not present.

ACKNOWLEDGEMENT

This work was supported and made possible by grant FA9550-09-1-0666 from the Air Force Office of Scientific Research.

6. REFERENCES

[1] T. Ahonen, A. Hadid, and M. Pietikainen. Face description with local binary patterns: Application to face recognition. *Pattern Analysis and Machine Intelligence, IEEE Transactions on*, 28(12):2037–2041, 2006.

[2] S. Craver and A. Farrokh baroughi. The non-trusty clown attack on model-based speaker recognition systems. In *SPIE/IS&T Electronic Imaging: Media Watermarking, Security, and Forensics*, 2015.

[3] Z. Goldfarb. As elections near, officials challenge balloting security. *Washington Post*, January 22, 2006.

[4] Z. Lingli and L. Jianghuang. Security algorithm of face recognition based on local binary pattern and random projection. In *Cognitive Informatics (ICCI), 2010 9th IEEE International Conference on*, pages 733–738, July 2010.

[5] W. H. Press, S. A. Teukolsky, W. T. Vetterling, and B. P. Flannery. *Numerical Recipes in C (2Nd Ed.): The Art of Scientific Computing*. Cambridge University Press, New York, NY, USA, 1992.

[6] The OpenCV project. OpenCV (Open Source Computer Vision), July 2013. http://www.opencv.org/.

Automated Firearm Identification: On Using a Novel Multiple-Slice-Shape (MSS) Approach for Comparison and Matching of Firing Pin Impression Topography

Robert Fischer[1,2], Claus Vielhauer[1,2]

[1]Brandenburg University of Applied Sciences, Department of Informatics & Media,
PO Box 2132, 14737 Brandenburg, Germany
{robert.fischer,claus.vielhauer}@fh-brandenburg.de
[2]Otto-von-Guericke University of Magdeburg, Dept. of Computer Science, AMSL Research Group,
PO Box 4120, 39016 Magdeburg, Germany
claus.vielhauer@iti.cs.uni-magdeburg

ABSTRACT

The examination of firearm related toolmarks impressed to cartridges and bullets is a well known forensic discipline. The application of three dimensional imaging systems and pattern recognition techniques for automatic comparison and matching of topographic data is a central field of research in the domain of digital crime scene analysis. In this work, we introduce and evaluate a novel Multiple-Slice-Shape (MSS) approach with the objective to closer link the preprocessing and feature extraction stages and improve the automated examinations of firearm toolmark surface data. We employ two existing features which are applied to the topography of firing pin impressions and aim at an automatic matching of the shapes based on multiple line-profile measurement. We suggest several modifications of the original Multiple-Angle-Path (MAP) and Multiple-Circle-Path (MCP) features to achieve an optimal integration into the proposed processing pipeline. Our evaluation approach is three-fold. First, we aim at the determination of an initial parameterization for MSS processing and feature extraction. Second, we evaluate the accuracy of discrimination for two firearms of the same mark and model. Third, we evaluate the accuracy using six different weapons. The test set contains 72 cartridge samples including six guns and three ammunition manufactures. Regarding the first evaluation, the results indicate an improvement of the accuracy for both features. Regarding the second evaluation, the achieved accuracy ranges between 67% and 100% for the MAP feature, and between 92% and 100% for the MCP feature. With respect to the third evaluation, the best result is achieved for MAP_{32} with 73% and for MCP_{15} with 92% compared to 56% and 82% correct classification rate regarding the original versions. It is supposed that various 3D spatial features can be combined and maybe improved by using the proposed MSS approach. We motivate the evaluation of this question for future work.

Categories and Subject Descriptors

I.4 [**Image Processing and Computer Vision**]: I.4.1 [**Digitization and Image Capture**] Scanning, Segmentation, I.4.7 [**Feature Measurement**] Size and shape, Feature representation
I.5 [**Pattern Recognition**]: I.5.4 [**Applications**] Computer Vision

IH&MMSec'15, June 17-19, 2015, Portland, OR, USA.
© 2015 ACM. ISBN 978-1-4503-3587-4/15/06...$15.00.
DOI: http://dx.doi.org/10.1145/2756601.2756619

General Terms

Algorithms, Measurement, Design, Experimentation

Keywords

New forensic features, firearm identification, digital crime scene analysis, digitized forensics, topography processing, firing pin shape matching, pattern classification, multiple slice shape

1. INTRODUCTION

Within the field of multimedia security related research, the computer assisted evaluation of forensic evidence and toolmarks as well as the evaluation of systems for automated forensic examinations currently play an important role. This research is embedded into the overall context of digitized forensics and digital crime scene analysis. The application of three dimensional sensing techniques for contactless acquisition of firearm related toolmarks in combination with the implementation of pattern recognition systems for automated processing, extraction, and comparison of these traces are central fields of research.

Besides disclosed scientific studies and examinations, there also exist undisclosed commercial systems. Due to their proprietary nature, these systems must be considered as limited regarding reproducible scientific research. For that reason, undisclosed systems are out of the scope of this work. The manual examination of toolmarks impressed on spent cartridges and bullets is a well known and broadly accepted forensic discipline. These examinations are considered as a sub discipline of forensic ballistics and are generally called inner ballistics. The main objectives are to link toolmarks found on spent cartridges or bullets to a specific firearm, or to exclude that a specific weapon could have provoked the markings. Generally, the underlying concept is based on two hypotheses: First, the markings provoked by a weapon are consistent and reproducible. Second, it is possible to distinguish between the markings of two individual weapons [1].

The application of three dimensional sensing techniques for toolmark acquisition provides extended surface characteristics. This enables the design of features applicable to topographic data and is supposed to supplement the examinations. In this context, the use of confocal microscopy is considered a promising acquisition technique. At the same time difficulties are arising, e.g. large amount of data and noisy data. As a result, the direct comparison of the toolmark topography gathered with confocal microscopy is considered difficult [2]. This leads to two important scientific challenges: First, the design and evaluation of digital preprocessing concepts for topographic data and second, the design and evaluation of features applicable to topographic data. Prior work attempts to address these challenges for example by employing multiple line-profile-measurement features used for firing pin shape comparison and matching. In this paper we will seize and further extend this idea. We introduce a pattern recognition approach improved by more closely linked preprocessing and feature extraction stages. The main contributions of this paper are: (1) the design and evaluation of a novel Multiple-Slice-Shape (MSS) approach aiming at close coupling of preprocessing and feature extraction, (2) a detailed suggestion for the adoption and modification of two existing features based on multiple line-profile-measurement, and, (3) the suggested method enables the feature calculation in a way that does no longer depend on annotation data e.g. reference circles. Regarding the feature extraction and evaluation, we employ modified versions of the Multiple-Angle-Path and the Multiple-Circle-Path feature [3]. Our evaluation goal is three-fold:

E_1:   Determination of an initial parameterization for the MSS processing and the feature extraction steps

E_2:   Experimental determination of the accuracy of discrimination regarding two firearms of the same brand and model

E_3:   Experimental determination of the accuracy of discrimination regarding six firearms each two of the same brand and model

The test set contains cartridges shot by three different weapon systems, whereat two instances are used for each weapon model. Cartridges from three different ammunition manufactures are included. The test set consists of 72 digital cartridge scans. Regarding E_2, the achieved classification accuracy ranges between 67% and 100% for the MAP feature and between 92% and 100% for the MCP feature. With respect to E_3, the best achieved accuracy is between 73% correct classifications for the MAP, and 92% correct classifications for the MCP feature. Compared to the original results [3] of the features, the proposed MSS approach for coupled preprocessing and feature extraction leads to a notable improvement of the classification accuracy.

Hereafter, the paper is organized as follows; section two summarizes state of the art regarding 2D and 3D approaches. In section three, the detailed descriptions of our proposed processing chain, the preprocessing concept and the extracted features are given. Section four introduces the experimental setup, followed by the presentation of experimental results in section five. The discussion of results, conclusions, and prospects for future work are presented in section six.

2. RELATED WORK

With regard to the applied imaging technique, prior research on automated firearm identification can generally be categorized in 2D and 3D approaches.

Two dimensional acquisition includes for example ring-light illuminated microscopes, CCD sensors, or digital cameras. Xin et al. [4] introduce an approach based on three features (ratio between inner and outer firing pin circle, the firing pin diameter and a similarity measure) for the comparison of 150 digitally acquired cartridge bottoms. The result is given as a best hit list with a likelihood of 88.0% that the matched specimen appears in the top 5% of the hit list. Geradts et al. [5] suggest a method based on log-polar transformation and difference computation. The test set contains 49 cartridges shot by 19 different firearms. The authors state that it is possible to retrieve all images in the top 5%

of the hit list. Donguang Li [6] introduces an approach based on a morphological gradient for rim firing pin mark identification. The method achieves a classification accuracy of 97.0% using a test set of 150 rim-fire cartridges. Thumwarin [7] suggest the combination of a log polar transform, the calculation of Fourier coefficients, and the utilization of Fisher's linear discriminant. The test set consists of 166 cartridges fired by six different guns. The results are presented in a subjective fashion. An extension of this work is introduced by Thumwarin et al. [8]. The approach is expanded by using a Wiener filter for handling noise and fluctuation. Experimental evaluation is performed on a test set of 900 spent cartridges fired by six different weapons. The system achieves a correct classification rate of 87.53%. Leng et al. [9] introduce an extension of the original [6] approach by using a back-propagation neural network for classification. The author's state that based on 50 samples an accuracy of 98% is indicated.

Ghani et al. [10] introduce the application of different order geometric moments for automated firearm identification. Based on five different weapons, 747 intensity images of firing pin impressions are used as test data and 48 features are suggested. After feature selection the method achieves a correct classification rate of 96.7%. Another work by Ghani et al. [11] is based on the same test set, a selection of six features from [10], and a back-propagation neural network for classification. The best result is a correct classification rate of 96%. Two later publications [12, 13] of the authors describe the use of the same test set and different subsets of features from the original feature set [10]. The utilization of 16 features based on firing pin center images in [12] results in a correct classification rate of 75.4%. According to another publication [13], the use of 16 features applied to whole firing pin images leads to a correct classification rate of 65.7%.

Three dimensional acquisition includes for example line-scan imaging, laser conoscopic holography, photometric stereo, chromatic white light, or confocal microscopy. A comparative study of sensors for the topography acquisition of toolmarks is presented by Bolton-King et al. [14]. Regarding the sensor requirements, e.g. minimum lateral and depth resolution, the application of confocal microscopy is described as promising for forensic examinations. Smith et al. [15] suggest surface profile measurement for firearm identification. The authors introduce the application of line-scan imaging to retrieve two dimensional spatial distributions of cylindrical objects. Bachrach et al. [16] seize this suggestion and present a method for bullet identification based on line-scan imaging. The test set consists of six bullets shot by three different firearms of the same model. Regarding the worst case, the described evaluation indicates a discrimination ratio of 88%. Senin et al. [17] present an approach based on laser conoscopic holography and introduce an idea of a 3D virtual comparison microscope. No experimental evaluation is presented in this work. Sakarya et al. [18] suggest a system based on photometric stereo for surface measurement of cartridges. Suapang et al. [19] introduce an acquisition system based on a CCD camera and a rotary device to acquire 2D images as well as line-scans of specimens. Feature extraction is done based on a combination of a Sobel filter for contour and edge detection and a subsequent FFT-analysis.

In [3] the application of a confocal microscope for data acquisition and a combination of features from 2D and 3D spatial domain is suggested. Based on a test set of cartridge samples shot by six different weapons, the method achieves a correct classification rate of 86%. In [20], the utilization of multiple line-profile-measurement features for the comparison and matching of firing pin shapes based on topographic data is motivated. The application of a Multiple-Circle-Path feature achieves a correct classification rate of 86.1% in the best case. The application of a Multiple-Angle-Path feature leads to a correct classification rate of 55.6%. The authors assume that the performance of both features might be increased significantly when using more suitable and robust reference points for the calculations.

In this paper, we introduce and evaluate an improved pattern recognition approach for automated firearm identification based on firing pin topography. The concept is based on strongly coupled preprocessing and feature extraction stages for comparison and matching of firing pin impression topography. The introduced Multiple-Slice-Shape (MSS) approach consists of a preprocessing stage which aims at a combination of data preprocessing and localization of robust reference points in 3D spatial space. The subsequent extraction of the features from the topographic data is based essentially on the identified reference points. With regard to the evaluation of our suggested processing pipeline, we apply modified versions of two existing multiple line-profile features [3] and evaluate the classification performance.

3. THE PROPOSED METHOD

Our proposed concept is a combined approach which is aiming at the utilization of topographic data in the course of automated firearm identification. For high detail topography measurement of firing pin impressions on central fire cartridge bottoms, we use a data acquisition concept based on [20]. The following section provides a detailed description along with a formal description of the suggested Multiple-Slice-Shape approach. The suggested pattern recognition chain is based on the general biometric processing pipeline [21] as shown in Figure 1.

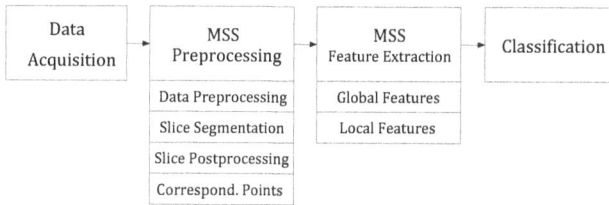

Figure 1. Simplified overview of the digital processing pipeline (based on the general biometric processing pipeline [21])

3.1 General Description of MSS Approach

The introduced MSS approach consists of two main parts. First, the preprocessing aims at data preprocessing and obtaining robust reference points from the topographic data. In the course of preprocessing a composition of multiple plane cuts (slices) through the topography of firing pin impressions is extracted. The number and the thickness (regarding z-dimension) of the slices can be freely defined by the parameters slice count sc and slice thickness st. With respect to different angles, the number of extracted corresponding points for each slice is defined by the angle count parameter ac.

Second, based on the identified reference points, the feature extraction aims at extracting a set of 3D spatial features for comparison and matching of firing pin shapes. We suggest distinguishing between *local* features to describe relations between pairs of slices and *global* features to describe characteristics of the complete set of slices. In the scope of this work, we apply two global features: the Multiple-Angle-Path and the Multiple-Circle-Path. We provide a detailed description of the

applied modifications which aim at an optimal integration of the MAP and MCP feature extraction into the MSS processing.

3.2 Data Acquisition

A confocal laser scanning microscope (CLSM) [22] is used for contactless topography acquisition of firing pin impressions on central fire cartridge bottoms. The sensor parameterization and positioning are applied manually for each scan. The acquisition device is not specifically adapted for forensic toolmark acquisition and there is no possibility of a physical registration. Scans of firing pin impressions cover an area of approx. 2.5 x 2.5mm and a height range between 500 and 1000μm. The microscope simultaneously acquires 16 bit laser intensity, 24 bit color, and 32 bit topographic data. Within the scope of this work, we exclusively use the topography dataset; color and laser data are used for illustration purposes only.

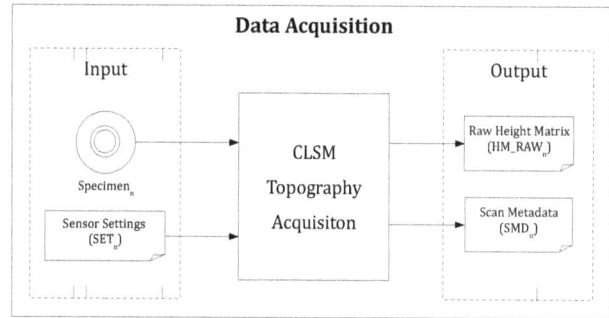

Figure 2. The proposed processing pipeline in detail: Data acquisition step

As shown in Figure 2, the data acquisition step requires a physical sample and a set of sensor settings as input and provides a digital representation of the sample and a set of scan metadata as output. The following sensor settings (SET) are used: magnification (mag) = 20, lateral resolution ($xyRes$) = 1.3μm (approx. 18000ppi), height resolution ($zRes$) = 0.5μm, and height range ($zRange$) between approx. 500 and 1000μm. The sensor parameterization and the positioning of the samples are done manually for each scan.

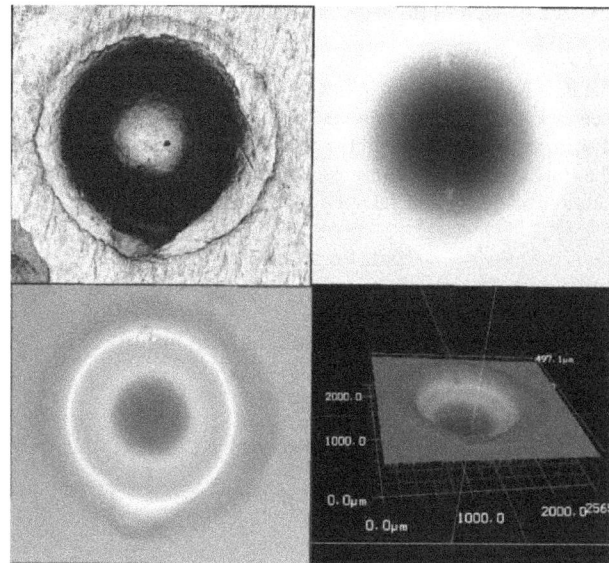

Figure 3. Example of acquired data: a) intensity image, b) height map, c) height map (false colored), d) 3D view (3D visualization Keyence Analysis Software [22])

Regarding the formal representation of topographic scan data, we suggest the following notation. Let M be a matrix $M \subset \mathbb{N}_0 \times \mathbb{N}_0 \times \mathbb{R}$, with each point p denoted by $p = (p_x, p_y, p_z) \in M$, we define the following functions for data access, $values(M) = \{p_z; p \in M\}$ returns the set of all point values of a given matrix M, $value(M, x, y) = p_z; p \in M, p_x = x, p_y = y$ returns a single value at the given index, and $polarMap(\alpha, r) = p; p_x = r \cdot \cos \alpha, p_y = r \cdot \sin \alpha$ returns a point in cartesian coordinates, given by angle α and radius r.

The data acquisition results in a set of scan metadata (SMD) and a corresponding raw height data matrix $HM_{RAW} \subset \mathbb{N}_0 \times \mathbb{N}_0 \times \mathbb{R}$. An illustration of the acquisition result is given in Figure 3. The scan metadata contains the applied sensor settings (*mag*, *xyRes*, *zRes*, *zRange*) as introduced earlier. Additionally, it contains a value indicating the data height zero (*zZero*) and a value defining the physical length of one digit in z-dimension (*zDigit*). The complete set of metadata is: $SMD = \{mag, xyRes, zRes, zRange, zZero, zDigit\}$.

3.3 MSS Preprocessing

As shown in Figure 1 the overall MSS preprocessing is split into four individual stages: 1) *Data Preprocessing*, 2) *Slice Segmentation*, 3) *Slice Postprocessing*, and 4) *Corresponding Point Estimation*. A detailed description of all stages is provided in the following sections. A complete example is shown in Figure 4. Please note, that all lines are emphasized to increase visibility.

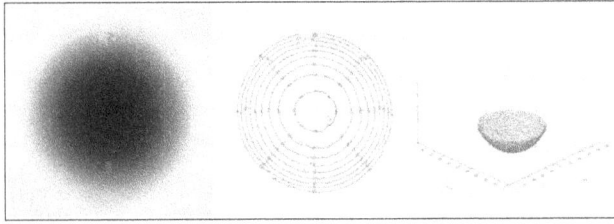

Figure 4. Example of entire MSS Preprocessing: a) height map, b) 2D top view of the segmented slices and extracted reference points (*sc*=10, *st*=1µm, *ac*=8), c) 3D view of the segmented slices (*sc*=25, *st*=1µm)

3.3.1 Data Preprocessing

The data preprocessing requires four input parameters, as can be seen in Figure 5: a raw data matrix HM_{RAW}, a filter size fs, a set of scan metadata SMD, and the outer firing pin reference circle c. The outer reference circle is automatically detected and, in addition, manually annotated for each sample.

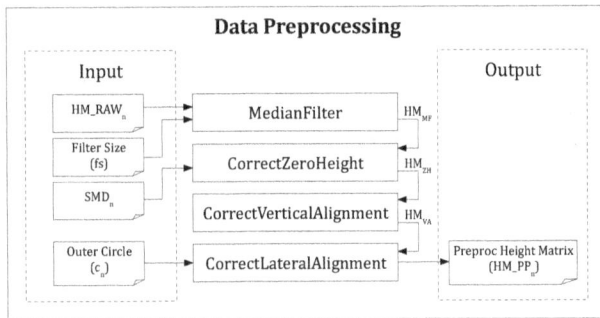

Figure 5. The proposed processing pipeline in detail: Data preprocessing step

The first challenge is to handle outliers and invalid measurement values. For this purpose, a median filter of size fs is applied to the raw data $HM_{MF} = MedianFilter(HM_{RAW}, fs)$. The filtered data HM_{MF} and the zero height value $zZero$ are used as input for the following height correction step. First, all values below $zZero$ are discarded $HM_Z = \{p; p \in HM_{MF}, p_z > zZero\}$. Second, the minimum value $zMin = min(values(HM_Z))$ is determined and all matrix values are decreased so, the minimum value matches 0 height again $HM_{ZH} = HM_Z - zMin$. Both operations are shown combined as $HM_{ZH} = CorrectZeroHeight(HM_{MF}, zZero)$ in Figure 5.

The vertical alignment of the surface is corrected based on an ideal plane and by using a least squares minimization approach [23] $HM_{VA} = CorrectVerticalAlignment(HM_{ZH})$. Next, the lateral alignment of the data is corrected by using the outer firing pin circle $c = (c_x, c_y, c_r)$ and a margin value m. The translations $x' = x - (c_r + m)$ and $y' = y - (c_r + m)$ are applied in order to shift the matrix index system. Afterwards, the resulting matrix is cropped to a size of N by N, with $N = 2c_r + m$. The margin is required to preserve a gap between the outer firing pin edge and the matrix borders for later processing tasks. The processing step $HM_{PP} = CorrectLateralAlignment(HM_{ZH})$ like shown in Figure 5 is a combination of alignment and cropping. The final result of the complete data preprocessing stage is a preprocessed height data matrix HM_{PP}.

3.3.2 Slice Segmentation

The slice segmentation stage aims at extracting a given number of slices from the data. Four input parameters are required as shown in Figure 6: a preprocessed height matrix HM_{PP}, the related set of scan metadata SMD, the number of slices to extract sc, and the thickness st of each slice in µm. Using the $zDigit$ value from scan metadata SMD all values can be transformed to physical dimensions in µm.

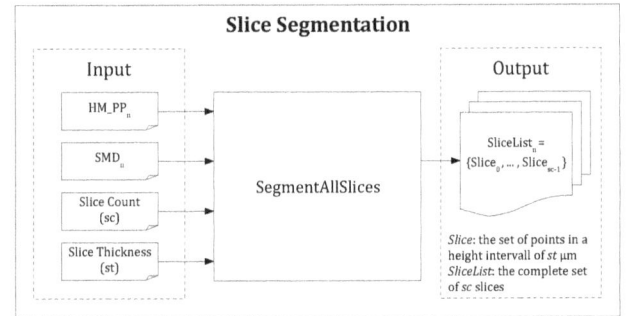

Figure 6. The proposed processing pipeline in detail: Slice segmentation step

Given the minimum $zMin = min(values(M))$ and the maximum $zMax = max(values(M))$ height values of a matrix M, a *Slice* is defined as the set of points lying within a height interval $[zLow, zHigh] := \{x; x \in \mathbb{N}, zLow \leq x < zHigh\}$. We define the following function to extract a single *Slice* from a matrix M

$$singleSlice(M, zLow, zHigh) = \{p; p \in M, zLow \leq p_z < zHigh\}.$$

The range of the height interval is given by the parameter slice thickness st and the amount of extracted slices is given by the parameter slice count sc.

Let the maximum height range be $zMax$ and let Δz be the height delta to equally divide the sc height intervals over the full height

$zMax$, with $\Delta z = \frac{zMax}{sc}$. Now, the complete set of slices can be defined

$$slice(i) = \left\{ \begin{array}{c} singleSlice(i \cdot \Delta z + \Delta z, i \cdot \Delta z + \Delta z + st) \\ , 0 \leq i < sc, i \in \mathbb{N}_0 \end{array} \right\}.$$

The final result of the slice segmentation stage is a set of sc slices, each of st μm thickness: $SliceList = \{slice_0, \dots, slice_{sc-1}\}$. An example of the slice segmentation using 7 and 25 slices of 1μm thickness is given in Figure 7.

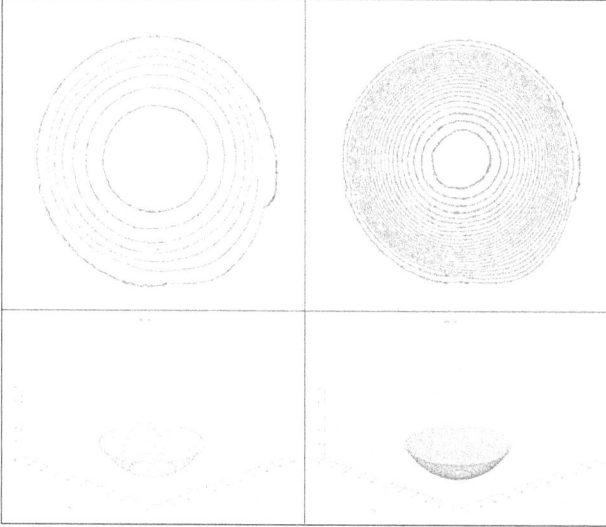

Figure 7. Examples of slice segmentation using 7 and 25 slices (sc=7, sc=25) of 1μm (st=1) thickness, in the first row the 2D top view, in the second row the corresponding 3D views

3.3.3 Slice Postprocessing

The goals of the slice postprocessing stage are: thinning of the slice to strokes that are a single pixel wide (regarding x-y dimension), removal of isolated points, determination of the bounding rectangle, and determination of a slice center point. The expected input for the stage is a single $Slice$ as shown in Figure 8.

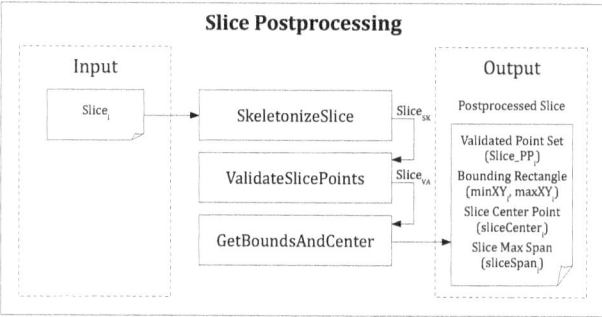

Figure 8. The proposed processing pipeline in detail: Slice postprocessing step

First, the thinning of the slice points is performed. For this purpose, we transform the slice to a two dimensional binary image and apply a morphological thinning operation based on [24]. Afterwards, the image is transformed back. The result is a new point set where all strokes of the slice are a single pixel wide $Slice_{SK} = SkeletonizeSlice(Slice)$. During the next step, the center of the thinned slice $Slice_{SK}$ is estimated based on the $sliceSpan$ which is given by the minimum $minX =$

$min(\{p_x; p \in Slice\})$, $minY = min(\{p_y; p \in Slice\})$ and the maximum $maxX = max(\{p_x; p \in Slice\})$, $maxY = max(\{p_y; p \in Slice\})$ x-y values

$$sliceCenter_x = minX + \frac{maxX - minX}{2},$$

$$sliceCenter_y = minY + \frac{maxY - minY}{2}.$$

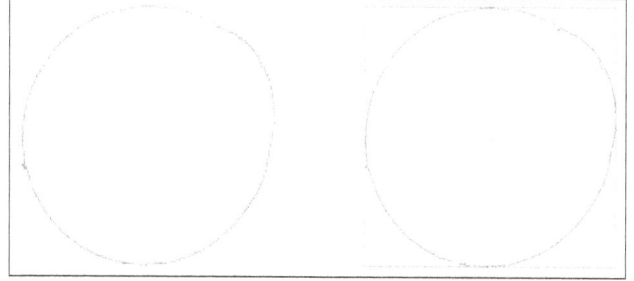

Figure 9. Example of slice postprocessing, on the left side: the original slice, on the right side: the postprocessing result with bounding rectangle and center point

The distance of a point $p \in Slice$ to the estimated $sliceCenter$ is

$$distToCenter(p) = \sqrt{\begin{array}{c}(p_x - sliceCenter_x)^2 \\ +(p_y - sliceCenter_y)^2\end{array}},$$

and the average distance of all points is

$$averageCenterDist = \frac{\sum_{i=1}^{|Slice_{sk}|} distToCenter(p_i)}{|Slice_{sk}|}.$$

A variance of 20% of the determined average distance is used as threshold. All points of the slice which exceed the threshold are discarded. Additionally, isolated points are discarded. The result is a validated point set $Slice_{VA} = ValidateSlicePoints(Slice_{SK})$. Finally, the center point and the minimum and maximum x-y dimension of the validated point set $Slice_{VA}$ are calculated again in the same way as described above.

The final result of the postprocessing stage is a validated slice point set $Slice_{PP}$, along with the corresponding bounding rectangle $minXY, maxXY$, the span $sliceSpan$ and the slice center $sliceCenter$. An example of the slice postprocessing stage is shown in Figure 9.

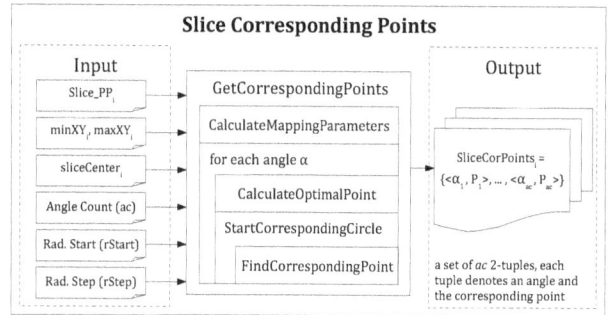

Figure 10. The proposed processing pipeline in detail: Corresponding point estimation step

3.3.4 Slice Corresponding Points

The goal of the corresponding point stage is to find reference points on a slice with respect to different angles. As shown in Figure 10: a post processed slice $Slice_{PP}$, the bounding rectangle $minXY, maxXY$, and the center $sliceCenter$ from the prior stage are required as input. Furthermore, the amount of considered angles ac, the starting radius $rStart$, and the radius step $rStep$ for the circle window are expected as input parameters.

We introduce and apply a 'corresponding circle window' algorithm. A simplified illustration of the algorithm is shown in Figure 12. First, the parameters for the polar mapping are calculated. Based on the angle count ac, the angle delta is determined by $\Delta\theta = \frac{2\pi}{ac}$.

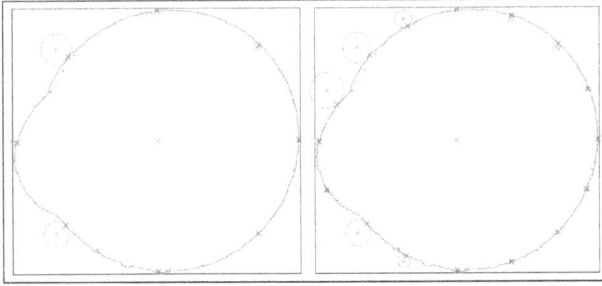

Figure 11. Examples of corresponding point estimation: rStart=5, rStep=1, on the left side ac=8 and on the right side ac=16 (Initial circle windows solid, final circle windows dotted, found corresponding points marked with a cross)

Let A be the complete set of considered angles $A = \{a \cdot \Delta\theta; 0 \leq a < ac, a \in \mathbb{N}_0\}$. Given the preprocessed point set $Slice_{PP}$, the $sliceSpan$, the bounding rectangle $minXY, maxXY$, and the $sliceCenter$, the algorithm can be described in the following way, with respect to each angle $\alpha \in A$ (also see Figure 12 I-III):

I. Use the $sliceCenter$ as point of origin of a polar coordinate system and calculate an optimal corresponding point
$$optimalPoint = polarMap\left(\alpha, \frac{sliceSpan}{2}\right)$$

II. Construct an initial circle window cc_1, defined by the $optimalPoint$ as center and $rStart$ as radius

III. Check for points inside the corresponding circle cc_n:

    a. *If* a point $p \in Slice_{PP}$ is located inside cc_n:
        Break and use it as corresponding point cp

    b. *Else*: Expand the radius of cc by $rStep$ and goto III

The algorithm results in an estimated corresponding point $cp \in Slice$ for each $\alpha \in A$. The overall result of the stage is a set of 2-tuples denoted by an angle α and the related corresponding point $< \alpha_i, cp_i >$, the set of all points is $SliceCorPoints = \{< \alpha_1, cp_1 >, \dots, < \alpha_{ac}, cp_{ac} >\}$. Two examples of the corresponding circle window algorithm and the estimated corresponding points using eight ($ac = 8$) and sixteen angles ($ac = 16$) are shown in Figure 11. Please note, that all lines are emphasized to increase the visibility.

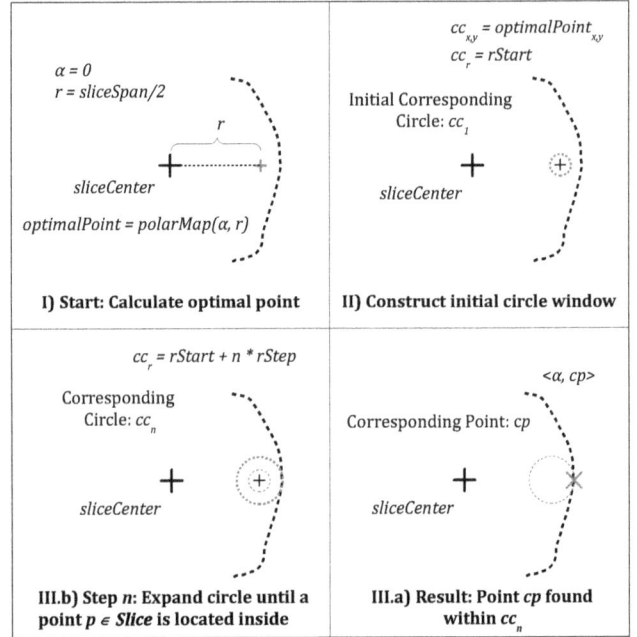

Figure 12. Illustration of the 'corresponding circle window' algorithm: I) start with optimal point, II) construct initial circle window, III.b) expand circle window, III.a) result: corresponding point found

3.4 MSS Feature Extraction

We suppose that various 3D spatial features can be combined with the introduced MSS preprocessing. We want to motivate a basic distinction between *local* and *global* features. Local features are meant to describe relationships between pairs of slices, e.g. change of local vertical gradient, or change of local lateral deviation in consideration of multiple angles. Global features are meant to describe the characteristics of entire slice sets, e.g. straight or circular path lines applied to the complete firing pin impression or statistical analysis considering all slices. Following this, the employed Multiple-Angle-Path (MAP) and the Multiple-Circle-Path (MCP) are both considered as *global* features.

3.4.1 Multiple-Angle-Path

In its original form [3], the MAP_n feature represents a composition of n straight path-lines regarding n different angles. First, multiple polar mappings are used to collect the height values along each of the path-lines. The reference points are defined by the outer firing pin circle c. The point of origin for the polar coordinate system is the center point $c_{x,y}$ and the radius for the mapping ranges between 1 and c_r, with that an angle path can be defined

$$anglePath(i) = \left\{ polarMap\left(i \cdot \frac{2\pi}{n}, r\right)_z ; 1 \leq r \leq c_r, r \in \mathbb{N} \right\}.$$

The height values for each $anglePath$ are collected in separate vectors. The length of each vector of height values equals c_r. Additionally, all vectors are concatenated to obtain one global path

$$anglePath_{global} = \left\{ \bigcup_{i=0}^{n-1} anglePath(i) \right\}.$$

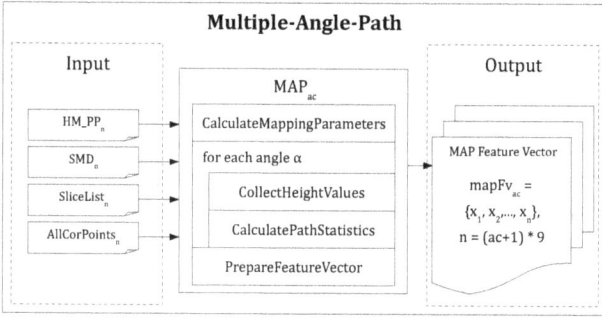

Figure 13. The proposed processing pipeline in detail: Multiple-Angle-Path feature

For the application of the MAP feature in combination with the introduced MSS approach, we make the following modifications: First, the parameter n is predefined by the angle count ac from the corresponding point estimation stage. Second, the reference outer circle c is not used anymore. Instead, the polar coordinate point of origin is defined by the center $sliceCenter$ of the lowest slice $Slice_0$. Third, the maximum radius r_{max} for the polar mapping is now determined based on the $slicSpan$ of $Slice_{sc-1}$, with $r_{max} = \frac{slicSpan}{2}$. The modified angle path is

$$anglePathMss(i) = \left\{ polarMap\left(i \cdot \frac{2\pi}{ac}, r \right)_z \atop ; 1 \leq r \leq r_{max}, r \in \mathbb{N} \right\},$$

and the global path

$$anglePathMss_{global} = \left\{ \bigcup_{i=0}^{ac-1} anglePathMss(i) \right\}.$$

The modified MAP step requires a preprocessed height matrix HM_{PP}, the scan metadata SMD, the set of slices $SliceList$, and the corresponding points of all slices $AllCorPoints$. As shown in Table 1, nine statistics are calculated for each path: *min*, *max*, *span*, *incremental length*, *cumulative length*, *mean*, *variance*, *standard deviation*, and *rms*. The feature results in $ac + 1$ straight path lines with nine statistical values each. The result of the step is a feature vector $mapFv_{ac} = (x_1, x_2, x_3, \ldots, x_n) \in X$, with $n = (ac + 1) \cdot 9$, as shown in Figure 13. A graphical comparison of the original and the modified MAP feature using example of 16 angles ($ac = 16$) is given in Figure 14.

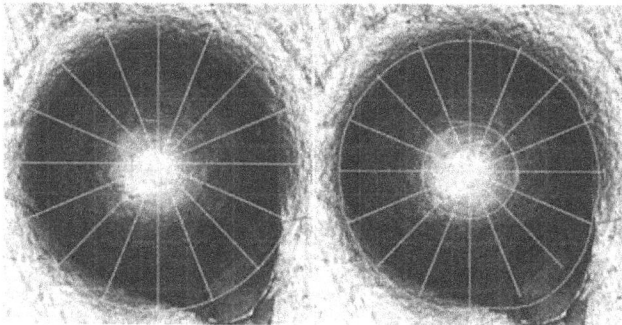

Figure 14. Comparison of MAP$_{16}$: On the left side the original version (outer reference circle in green), on the right side the MSS version (lowest and highest slice in green)

3.4.2 Multiple-Circle-Path

In its original form, the MCP$_n$ feature represents a composition of n circular path-lines regarding n different radii. Similar to the first feature, the reference points are based on the outer reference circle c. The point of origin of the polar system is given by the center point $c_{x,y}$. Instead of iterating over the angle, the MCP feature is iterating over different radii. Let the maximum radius be c_r and let Δr be the radius delta to equally divide the n radii over the full range of c_r, with $\Delta r = \frac{c_r}{n}$. In the original work [3], the formal description mistakenly limits the max length of a radial path to 360, a radial path was defined as

$$radialPath(i) = \left\{ polarMap\left(\frac{2\pi}{a}, (i+1) \cdot \Delta r \right)_z \atop ; 1 \leq a \leq 360, a \in \mathbb{N}_0 \right\}.$$

Additionally, all vectors are concatenated to obtain one global path

$$radialPath_{global} = \left\{ \bigcup_{i=0}^{n-1} radialPath(i) \right\}.$$

A graphical comparison of the original and the modified MCP feature using example of radius count 10 is given in Figure 15.

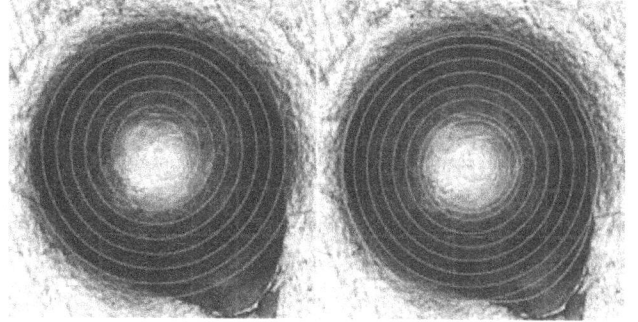

Figure 15. Comparison of MCP$_{10}$: On the left side the original version (most outer circle = outer reference), on the right side the MSS version (lowest and highest slice in teal)

For the application of the MCP feature in combination with the introduced MSS approach, we apply the following modifications: First, we rename the parameter n and instead of it use rc representing the radii count. Second, the outer reference circle c is not used anymore. Instead of this, the polar coordinate point of origin is defined by the average center point of all slices. Third, the maximum radius r_{max} for the polar mapping is now determined based on the span of $Slice_{sc-1}$, with $r_{max} = \frac{slicSpan}{2}$ and $\Delta r = \frac{r_{max}}{rc}$. Also, the wrong description of length is fixed, now the length of each radial path is correctly defined by its circumference $2\pi r$. The modified/corrected radial path is given by

$$radialPathMss(i) = \left\{ polarMap\left(\frac{2\pi}{a}, (i+1) \cdot \Delta r \right)_z \atop ; 1 \leq a \leq (i+1) \cdot \Delta r \cdot 2\pi, a \in \mathbb{N}_0 \right\},$$

and the global path

$$radialPathMss_{global} = \left\{ \bigcup_{i=0}^{n-1} radialPathMss(i) \right\}.$$

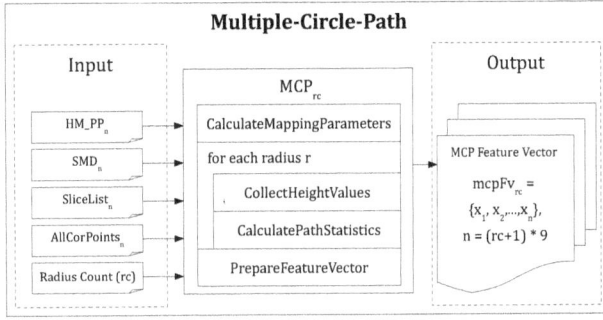

Figure 16. The proposed processing pipeline in detail: Multiple-Circle-Path feature

The modified MCP feature requires a preprocessed height matrix HM_{PP}, the scan metadata SMD, the set of slices $SliceList$, the corresponding points $AllCorPoints$, and the radius count rc as input. As shown in Table 1, nine statistics are calculated for each path: *min, max, span, incremental length, cumulative length, mean, variance, standard deviation,* and *rms*. The feature results in $rc + 1$ circular path lines with nine statistical values each. The result of the step is a feature vector $mcpFv_{rc} = (x_1, x_2, x_3, \ldots, x_n) \in X, with\ n = (rc + 1) \cdot 9$, as shown in Figure 16.

Table 1. Summary of calculated path statistics

	Path Statistics	
1	PathMin	$pathMin(path) = min(path)$
2	PathMax	$pathMax(path) = max(path)$
3	PathSpan	$pathSpan(path) = max(path) - min(path)$
4	PathLengthInc	$pathLengthInc(path) = \sum_{i=1}^{|path|-1} |path_{i+1} - path_i|$
5	PathLengthCum	$pathLengthCum(path) = \sum path$
6	PathMean	$pathMean(path) = \dfrac{1}{|path|} \sum path$
7	PathVariance	$pathVar(path) =$ $\dfrac{1}{|path|} \sum_{i=1}^{|path|} (path_i - pathMean(path))^2$
8	PathStd	$pathStd(path) = \sqrt{pathVar(path)}$
9	PathRms	$pathRms(path) = \sqrt{\dfrac{\sum_{i=1}^{|path|}(path_i - pathMean(path))^2}{|path|}}$

4. EXPERIMENTAL SETUP

We use a self acquired test set created within the scope of the project. The test set contains six individual 9mm firearms, each two of the same brand and model. The weapons (two instances each) are *Walther P99* (wa_a, wa_b), *Ceska 75B* (cz_a, cz_b) and *Beretta 92FS* (be_a, be_b). Regarding evaluation goal E_2, we define the following three class sets: $C_{WA} = \{wa_a, wa_b\}$, $C_{CZ} = \{cz_a, cz_b\}$, and $C_{BE} = \{be_a, be_b\}$. With respect to evaluation goal E_3, the complete set of classes is given by $C_{ALL} = \{wa_a, wa_b, cz_a, cz_b, be_a, be_b\}$.

Regarding E_1, the evaluated parameterizations are: for MSS $fs = 5$, $sc = 20$, $st = 1$, and $ac = \{8, 16, 32\}$. The used radius start and radius step for the corresponding circle window algorithm are $rStart = 5$ and $rStep = 1$. According to the MSS parameterization, we use the MAP feature with three angle counts $ac = \{8, 16, 32\}$. Regarding the MCP parameterization we evaluate the feature with three radius counts $rc = \{10, 15, 20\}$.

We use three different classifiers from the WEKA data mining toolbox [25] for the evaluation: a) a support vector (*SM*) classifier (*SMO*: sequential minimal optimization algorithm), b) a Bayesian Net (*BN*) classifier, and c) a NearestNeighbor (*NN*) classifier. We use a 10-fold stratified cross-validation for all parts of the experimental evaluation. The classification results are appraised with respect to the evaluation goals (E_1, E_2, and E_3) and the used parameterizations. We use the following performance measures: True positives TP, false positives FP, true positive rate $TPR = TP/(TP + FN)$, false positive rate $FPR = FP/(FP + TN)$, precision $P = TP/(TP + FP)$, and Cohens Kappa value (K).

5. EXPERIMENTAL RESULTS

The results for E_1: 'Determination of an initial parameterization for the MSS processing and the feature extraction steps' with regards to the used feature parameterization are shown along with the results for E_2 and E_3 in Table 2, Table 3, Table 4, and Table 5.

Table 2. E_2 results for MAP ($ac = \{8, 16, 32\}$) (10-fold stratified cross-validation)

ac	C	TPR			FPR			Precision			Kappa		
		SM	BN	NN	SM	BN	NN	SM	BN	NN	SM	BN	NN
8	WA	1	0.91	0.95	0	0.04	0.04	1	0.96	0.96	1	0.83	0.91
	CZ	0.96	0.75	0.91	0.04	0.08	0.08	0.96	0.92	0.92	0.91	0.57	0.83
	BE	0.67	0.41	0.71	0.33	0.58	0.29	0.67	0.40	0.72	0.33	-0.16	0.41
16	WA	1	0.91	0.95	0	0	0.04	1	1	0.96	1	0.84	0.91
	CZ	0.96	0.75	0.95	0.04	0.08	0.04	0.96	0.92	0.96	0.91	0.57	0.91
	BE	0.67	0.5	0.58	0.33	0.5	0.41	0.67	0.5	0.59	0.33	0	0.17
32	WA	1	0.91	0.95	0	0	0.04	1	1	0.96	1	0.84	0.91
	CZ	0.96	0.75	0.95	0.04	0.08	0.04	0.96	0.92	0.96	0.91	0.57	0.91
	BE	0.71	0.5	0.62	0.29	0.5	0.37	0.71	0.5	0.63	0.42	0	0.25

The experimental results regarding E2: 'Experimental determination of the accuracy of discrimination regarding two firearms of the same brand and model', are shown in Table 2 for the modified MAP feature and in Table 3 for the modified MCP feature related to the used feature parameterization, the applied classifiers, and the performance measures as introduced.

Table 3. E_2 results for MCP ($rc = \{10, 15, 20\}$) (10-fold stratified cross-validation)

rc	C	TPR			FPR			Precision			Kappa		
		SM	BN	NN	SM	BN	NN	SM	BN	NN	SM	BN	NN
10	WA	0.96	0.79	0.91	0.04	0.04	0.08	0.96	0.94	0.91	0.92	0.64	0.83
	CZ	0.92	0.83	0.91	0.08	0.08	0.08	0.91	0.92	0.92	0.83	0.7	0.83
	BE	1	0.88	1	0	0.08	0	1	0.91	1	1	0.76	1
15	WA	1	0.79	1	0	0.08	0	1	0.9	1	1	0.63	1
	CZ	0.96	0.83	0.92	0.04	0.08	0.08	0.96	0.93	0.92	0.92	0.7	0.83
	BE	1	0.86	1	0	0.42	0	1	0.96	1	1	0.77	1
20	WA	1	0.79	1	0	0	0	1	1	1	1	0.66	1
	CZ	1	0.83	0.92	0	0.08	0.08	1	0.93	0.92	1	0.7	0.83
	BE	1	0.96	1	0	0	0	1	1	1	1	0.92	1

The evaluation results regarding E_3: 'Experimental determination of the accuracy of discrimination regarding six firearms, each two of the same brand and model' are shown in Table 4 for the modified MAP feature, and in Table 5 for the modified MCP

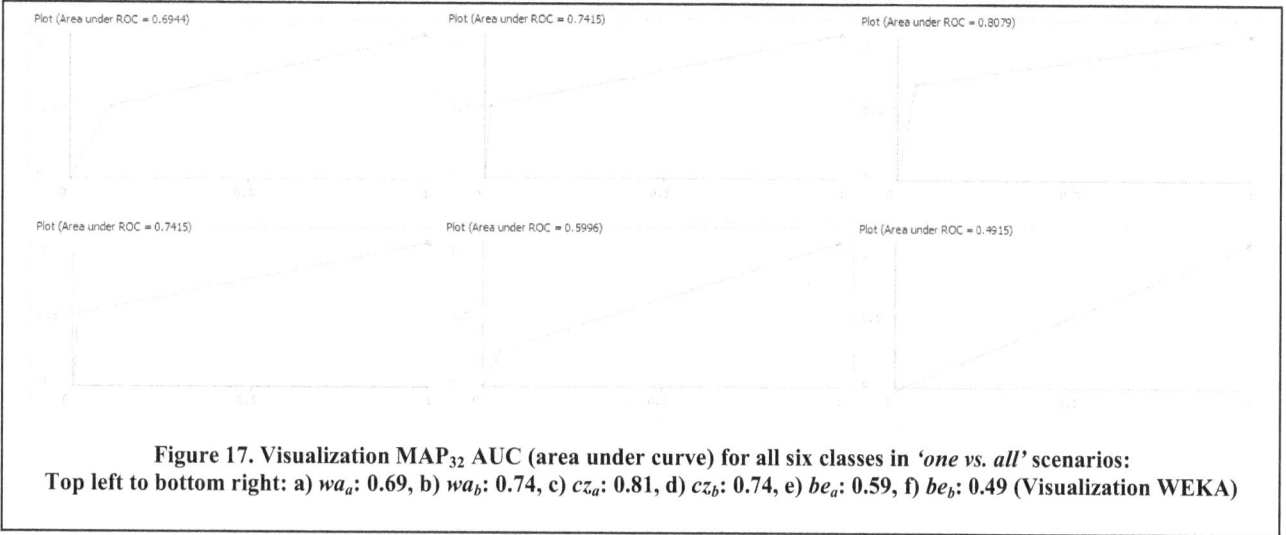

Figure 17. Visualization MAP$_{32}$ AUC (area under curve) for all six classes in *'one vs. all'* scenarios:
Top left to bottom right: a) wa_a: 0.69, b) wa_b: 0.74, c) cz_a: 0.81, d) cz_b: 0.74, e) be_a: 0.59, f) be_b: 0.49 (Visualization WEKA)

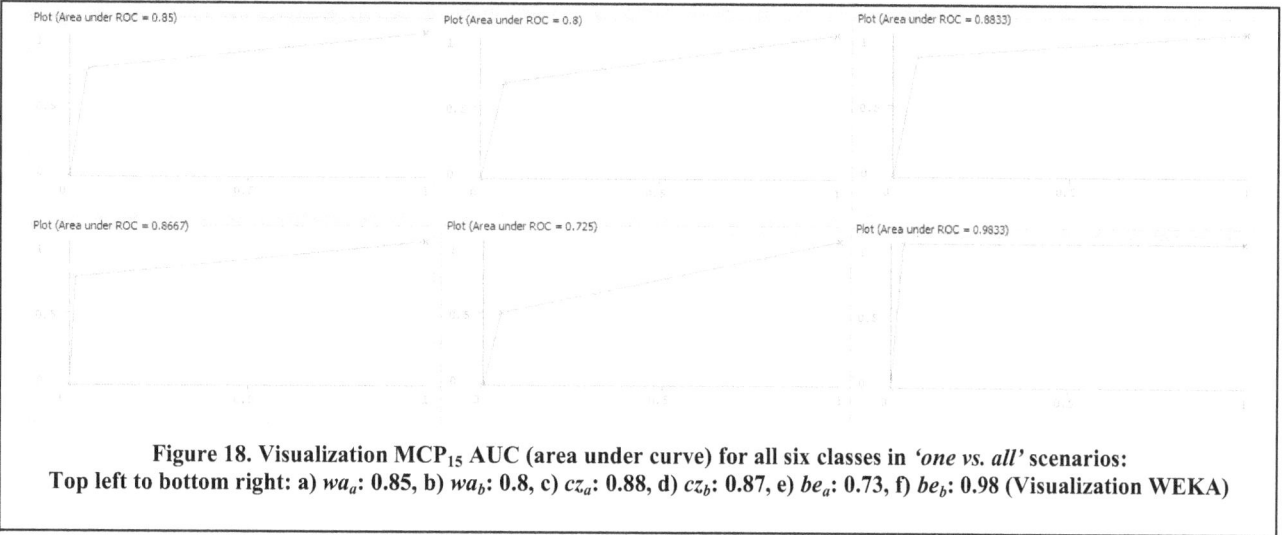

Figure 18. Visualization MCP$_{15}$ AUC (area under curve) for all six classes in *'one vs. all'* scenarios:
Top left to bottom right: a) wa_a: 0.85, b) wa_b: 0.8, c) cz_a: 0.88, d) cz_b: 0.87, e) be_a: 0.73, f) be_b: 0.98 (Visualization WEKA)

feature. The results are presented in the same manner as before, the only difference is the change of the class sets.

Table 4. E_3 results for MAP ($ac = \{8, 16, 32\}$)
(10-fold stratified cross-validation)

ac	C	TPR			FPR			Precision			Kappa		
		SM	BN	NN	SM	BN	NN	SM	BN	NN	SM	BN	NN
8	ALL	**0.61**	0.37	0.51	**0.08**	0.12	0.1	**0.65**	0.35	0.51	**0.53**	0.23	0.41
16	ALL	**0.65**	0.44	0.52	**0.07**	0.11	0.1	**0.66**	0.45	0.51	**0.58**	0.32	0.43
32	ALL	**0.73**	0.41	0.54	**0.05**	0.12	0.09	**0.74**	0.42	0.53	**0.68**	0.29	0.44

Table 5. E_3 results for MCP ($rc = \{10, 15, 20\}$)
(10-fold stratified cross-validation)

rc	C	TPR			FPR			Precision			Kappa		
		SM	BN	NN	SM	BN	NN	SM	BN	NN	SM	BN	NN
10	ALL	0.81	0.63	**0.83**	0.04	0.06	**0.03**	0.84	0.65	**0.84**	0.76	0.55	**0.8**
15	ALL	**0.92**	0.75	0.86	**0.02**	0.05	0.03	**0.93**	0.76	0.88	**0.9**	0.7	0.85
20	ALL	**0.91**	0.86	0.88	**0.02**	0.03	0.03	**0.91**	0.86	0.88	**0.88**	0.83	0.85

We select the two best performing features MAP$_{32}$ and MCP$_{15}$ from the evaluations E_2 and E_3 to provide a visualization of the AUC (area under curve) for both features. Each of the six classes is considered in a *'one vs. all'* scenario to calculate the curves for both features. Same as before, we use the WEKA data mining toolbox and a 10-fold stratified cross-validation in combination with the *SM* classifier to create the curves. The resulting curves along with the AUC values for the MAP$_{32}$ feature are shown in Figure 17 and the curves and result values for the MCP$_{15}$ feature are shown in Figure 18.

6. CONCLUSIONS AND FUTURE WORK
In this work, we proposed a pattern recognition approach for automated firearm identification based on topography representations of firing pin impressions. We introduced and preliminarily evaluated the novel Multiple-Slice-Shape (MSS) approach for a close coupling of preprocessing and feature extraction stages, solely based on topographic data. Additionally, we suggested an initial parameterization for all stages of the introduced digital processing pipeline. We presented our modifications for the Multiple-Angle-Path (MAP) feature and the Multiple-Circle-Path (MCP) feature, aiming at an optimal integration of the feature calculations into the MSS processing concept. In contrast to state of the art, the suggested modifications enable the calculation of the features without dependency on annotated data e.g. reference circles. Compared to state of the art

169

and despite the fact that the annotated reference circles are no longer necessary, the achieved classification accuracy of both features is in all cases improved or at least equal.

Regarding the evaluation goal E_2, the results for the experimental evaluation of the modified MAP feature, considering three different angle counts and classifiers are shown in Table 2. The best results are achieved by using the *SM* classifier and a parameterization of the MAP feature with 32 angles. Compared to prior work, all results are improved or at least equal. For example MAP_8 regarding *WA*, here the *TPR* is increased from 0.79 to 1, or MAP_{16} regarding *CZ*, here the *TPR* is increased from 0.92 to 1, and MAP_{32} regarding *CZ*, here the *TPR* is increased from 0.91 to 0.96. With respect to the evaluated parameterizations and the used classifiers, the evaluation results regarding E_2 and the modified MCP feature are shown in Table 3. The best results for the MCP feature are achieved by using a radius count $rc = 20$ and the *SM* classifier. Compared to the original versions, the results are improved. For example MCP_{10} regarding *WA*, here the *TPR* is increased from 0.79 to 0.96, or MCP_{15} regarding *CZ*, here the *TPR* is increased from 0.87 to 0.96, and MCP_{20} regarding *WA*, here the *TPR* is increased from 0.92 to 1.

Referring to evaluation goal E_3, the observed results for the MAP feature are summarized in Table 4. Again, the use of 32 angles and the support vector classifier leads to the best results. Compared to state of the art, the achieved *TPR* is increased in all cases. Regarding MAP_8, the *TPR* is increased from 0.51 to 0.61, regarding MAP_{16}, the *TPR* is increased from 0.54 to 0.65, and regarding MAP_{32}, the *TPR* is increased from 0.56 to 0.73. The results for E_2 and the MCP feature are shown in Table 5. The best results are achieved by using the MCP feature with 15 or 20 radii together with the *SM* classifier. Regarding MCP_{10}, the *TPR* remains unchanged at 0.83, regarding MCP_{15}, the *TPR* is increased from 0.82 to 0.92, and regarding MCP_{20}, the *TPR* is increased from 0.86 to 0.91. Overall, the results of the experimental evaluation clearly indicate a notable improvement of the classification accuracy for both features.

The Area under Curve results for one exemplary chosen MAP and one exemplary chosen MCP parameterization (Figure 17, 18) seem to back up the results of the classification accuracy evaluation (Table 2, 3, 4, 5). With one exception, all AUC results are higher than 0.5, which would represent flipping a coin. Regarding MAP_{32}, the best AUC result is 0.88 for the class cz_a and the worst result is 0.49 for be_b. Regarding MCP_{15}, the best AUC result is 0.98 for the class be_b and the worst result is 0.73 for be_a. The fact that the same class achieves the worst results for MAP and the best results for MCP is at least uncommon. One reason clearly is the center point determination. The MAP feature still uses the center point of $Slice_0$ and in some cases the shape of the Beretta firing pin leads to a $Slice_0$ that is completely out of center. This is an identified limitation and needs to be addressed in future work. In contrast to this, the MCP feature uses an averaged center point and benefits from the uncommon shape.

Future work also includes, but is not limited to: First, an extended evaluation of parameter values for the processing steps and the feature calculations, aiming at answering the question: whether the utilization of more slices, more angle groups, and more profile-lines may help to further improve the classification accuracy. Second, the results have to be validated on an extended test set containing more individual guns and ammunition types. Third, the design and implementation of more and extended local and global features should be addressed. Additionally, a feature selection is suggested to reduce the dimensionality of the feature vectors. It should also be evaluated if the MSS approach is generally applicable for a fully automated alignment and registration of samples.

7. ACKNOWLEDGMENTS

This work is supported by the German Federal Ministry of Education and Science (BMBF) through research program under contract number FKZ: 13N10816. The documents content is under sole responsibility of the authors. We would like to thank Jana Dittmann, Andrey Makrushin, Tobias Scheidat, and the AMSL research group Magdeburg for all the interesting discussions and valuable comments. We also want to thank the German federal-police and the state-police of Saxony-Anhalt for providing real world cartridge samples.

8. REFERENCES

[1] Uchiyama, T. 2008. Toolmark Reproducibility on Fired Bullets and Expended Cartridge Cases. *AFTE Journal.* 40(1), (2008), 3-46.

[2] Chu, A., McClorry, S., Geiss, R., Read, D., Howitt, D. and Hill, M. 2014. *Consecutive and Random Manufactured Semi-Automatic Pistol Breech Face and Fired Cartridge Case Evaluations.* Technical Report No. 244565. University of California.

[3] Fischer, R. and Vielhauer, C. 2015. Towards automated firearm identification based on high resolution 3D data: rotation-invariant features for multiple line-profile-measurement of firing pin-shapes. In *Proceedings of SPIE 9393, Three-Dimensional Image Processing, Measurement (3DIPM), and Applications 2015*, 93930Q-93930Q-10.

[4] Xin, L., Zhou J. 2000. A Cartridge Identification System for Firearm Authentication. In *Proceedings of the 5th Int. Conference on Signal Processing* (WCCC-ICSP 2000), 1405-1408.

[5] Geradts, Z., Bijhold, J., Hermsen, R. and Murtagh, F. 2001. Image matching algorithms for breech face marks and firing pins in a database of spent cartridge cases of firearms. *Forensic Science International*, 119, 1 (June 2001), 97-106.

[6] Li, D. 2006. A New Approach for Firearm Identification with Hierarchical Neural Networks Based on Cartridge Case Images. In *Proceedings of the 5th IEEE International Conference on Cognitive Informatics* (ICCI2006), 923-928.

[7] Thumwarin, P. 2008. An Automatic System for Firearm Identification. In *Proceedings of the International Symposium on Communications and Information Technologies* (ISCIT2008), 21-23.

[8] Thumwarin, P., Prasit, C. and Matsuura, T. 2008. Firearm identification based on rotation invariant feature of cartridge case. In *Proceedings of the SICE Annual Conference* (SICE2008), 45-49.

[9] Leng, J., Huang, Z., and Li, D. 2010. Feature extraction and classification of cartridge images for ballistics identification. *In Proceedings of the 23rd International Conference on Industrial Engineering* (Vol. Part III, IEA/AIE'10), 331-340.

[10] Ghani, N.A.M. et al. 2010. Analysis of geometric moments as features for firearm identification. *Forensic Science International*, 198, 1 (2010), 143-149.

[11] Kamaruddin, S.B.A., Ghani, N.A.M., Choong-Yeun L. and Jemain, AA. 2011. Firearm recognition based on whole firing

pin impression image via backpropagation neural network. In *Proceedings of the International Conference on Pattern Analysis and Intelligent Robotics* (ICPAIR2011), 177-182.

[12] Ghani, N.A.M., Kamaruddin, S.B.A., Choong-Yeun L. and Jemain, AA. 2012. Firearm identification using numerical features of centre firing pin impression image. In *Proceedings of the IEEE Symposium on Computer Applications and Ind. Electronics* (ISCAIE12), 293-296.

[13] Ghani, N.A.M., Kamaruddin, S.B.A., Choong-Yeun L. and Jemain, AA. 2013 Classification of pistol via numerical based features of firing pin impression image. In *Proceedings of the IEEE Symposium on Computers & Informatics* (ISCI2013), 165-169.

[14] Bolton-King, R., Evans, P., Smith, C.L., Painter, J., Allsop, D. and Cranton, W. 2012. What are the Prospects of 3D Profiling Systems Applied to Firearms and Toolmark Identification?. *AFTE Journal.* 42(1), (2010), 23-33.

[15] Smith, C.L., Robinson, M. and Evans, P. 2000. Line-scan imaging for the positive identification of ballistics specimens. In *Proceedings of the 34th Annual IEEE International Carnahan Conference on Security Technology*, (2000), 269-275.

[16] Bachrach, B. 2002. Development of a 3D-Based Automated Firearms Evidence Comparison System. *Journal of Forensic Sciences* 47(6), (2002), 1253-1264.

[17] Senin, N., Groppetti, R., Garofano, L., Fratini, P. and Pierni, M. 2006. Three-Dimensional Surface Topography Acquisition and Analysis for Firearm Identification. *Journal of Forensic Sciences* 51(2), (2006), 282–295.

[18] Sakarya, U., Murat, U. and Erol, L. 2008. Three-dimensional surface reconstruction for cartridge cases using photometric stereo. *Forensic Science Int.* 175(5), (2008), 209-217.

[19] Suapang, P., Yimmun, S. and Chumnan, N. 2011. Tool and Firearm Identification System Based on Image Processing. In *Proceedings of the 11th International Conference on Control Automation and Systems* (ICCAS2011), 178-182.

[20] Fischer, R. and Vielhauer C. 2014. Digital crime scene analysis: automatic matching of firing pin impressions on cartridge bottoms using 2d and 3d spatial features. In *Proceedings of the 2nd ACM workshop on Information hiding and multimedia security* (IH&MMSec '14), 77-82.

[21] Vielhauer C. 2006. *Biometric User Authentication for IT Security: From Fundamentals to Handwriting*. Springer New York, USA, 2006

[22] Keyence Corporation, http://www.keyence.com/, last check: 19.02.2015

[23] Gruen, A. and Akca, D. 2005. Least squares 3D surface and curve matching. *ISPRS Journal of Photogrammetry & Remote Sensing* 59 (2005), 151-174.

[24] Gonzales R., Woods R. and Eddins, S. 2004. *Digital Image Processing using MATLAB*. Pearson Education - Prentice Hall, 2004

[25] Hall, M., Frank, E., Holmes, G., et al. 2009. The WEKA data mining software: An update. SIGKDD Exp., vol.11, no.1, 2009, 10 –18.

Author Index

.